PEARSON   ALWAYS LEARNING

Jim Patterson • Tim Donahue

Enjoyment of Theatre

Custom Edition for East Carolina University

Taken from:
The Enjoyment of Theatre, Ninth Edition,
by Jim Patterson and Tim Donahue

ISBN 10: 1-323-14855-8
ISBN 13: 978-1-323-14855-6

The Enjoyment of Theatre's balanced coverage of performance and history provides a comprehensive and accessible introduction to theatre for both majors and nonmajors. This text establishes the aesthetic underpinnings of theatre art and then explores performance and production topics such as playwriting, acting, directing, design, and the theatre industry. *The Enjoyment of Theatre* also covers the full span of theatre's 2,500-year history.

SPECIAL FEATURES OF THE NINTH EDITION

This ninth edition builds on proven features from past editions. The emphasis throughout this comprehensive revision has been to make theatre even more accessible to undergraduate students. *The Enjoyment of Theatre* continues to offer an engaging, full-color design complemented by rich images and lively features. Also noteworthy is the fact that this edition of *The Enjoyment of Theatre* will sell for less than most competitive texts on the market today, making this edition accessible to all students through its content, coverage, design, and price. Special features include

- **An entirely new chapter** on musical theatre that describes the evolution of the United States' acknowledged and unique contribution to world theatre.
- **The chapter on theatre design** has been reconceived and rewritten in response to feedback from instructors using the text.
- **All chapters have been revised** to update and clarify the previous edition.
- Twenty-five **Spotlight** sidebars placed throughout the book in which key questions of theatre's art and history, as well as significant individuals are discussed in detail.
- **Many new illustrations and photographs** will help students to visualize important places and events. The photographs include productions at colleges and universities that we believe will give students an insight into the theatre produced by schools much like their own. There are also photographs from current Broadway plays and musicals as well as from important regional theatres throughout the country. The caption for each image clarifies and enriches the text.
- Clearly stated **Objectives** at the beginning of each chapter that will alert students to what is important for them to take away from their reading of each chapter.
- **Key Terms** at the conclusion of each chapter alert students to significant, and probably testable, concepts. These terms, listed with the page number on which the term appears, also serve as a brief review.
- **A Glossary of Key Terms** at the end of the text includes definitions of all key terms with notation of the page on which the term first appears.
- **A clearly written context** for each history chapter along with revealing maps places theatre in time and space.

ORGANIZATION

The Enjoyment of Theatre is organized in three parts: locating theatre, experiencing plays, today's theatre and its makers, and theatre of other times and places. Throughout, we examine theatre as an artifact of culture. Instructors may opt to use The Enjoyment of Theatre in its totality for a course organized as a survey of theatre past and present, or they may make selective use of any combination of sections, emphasizing certain aspects of theatre while omitting others.

ANCILLARY SUPPORT

The authors have written for the instructor's use a comprehensive Instructor's Manual and Test Bank (ISBN 0205929761) available electronically via Pearson's Instructor's Resource Center at www.pearsonhighered.com/irc. Powerpoints (ISBN 020592977X) are also available. (Instructors should contact their local Pearson representative for access to these downloadable resources.) The IM/TB resource provides a brief explanation of the text's content and organization, suggested course organizations for semester or quarter courses, photos, and approaches to teaching each chapter (chapter goal, key questions, important concepts, activities, and assessments).

For a complete listing of the instructor and student resources available with this text, please search for The Enjoyment of Theatre 9/e at http://www.pearsonhighered.com/.

ABOUT THE AUTHORS

The Enjoyment of Theatre continues with the coauthor of the seventh and eighth editions of this popular textbook, Jim Patterson. He is a member of the Stage Directors and Choreographers Society and has directed plays across the United States in summer festivals and at colleges and universities. For many years, he was director of undergraduate studies and, later, headed the MFA program in directing at the University of South Carolina. He served as artistic director of the USC Summer Repertory Theatre. His coauthor, Tim Donahue, is new to The Enjoyment of Theatre but not to theatre. Together, Donahue and Patterson have coauthored two trade theatre books: Stage Money and Theater Careers. They are also the authors of A Concise History of Theatre, a new textbook, published by Pearson.

ACKNOWLEDGMENTS

We would also like to thank the reviewers who helped us with the development of this project, including:

Jim Bartruff, Emporia State University
Christopher Flynn, Pearl River Community College
Kevin Kern, University of West Florida
Dawn Larsen, Francis Marion University
Hugh Murphy, Barry University
Melony Tisdale, Kentucky State University

PART

I

LOCATING THEATRE, EXPERIENCING PLAYS

Theory and Criticism

Part I focuses on ways of understanding theatre, ways usually called theory and criticism. Theory is an attempt to explain the nature of something and tries to answer such fundamental questions as what is it and how does it work? Criticism develops a considered judgment or discussion about the qualities of a specific play or performance. What does this particular play mean and how does it convey that meaning by its form and structure? How does this particular production present the play to this audience? Why were these particular choices about acting, directing, and design made? How does this production try to communicate its ideas to the audience? How well did it succeed? Part I ends by considering some of the people who use theory and criticism as they work with and in today's theatre.

Theatre

Performance and Art

Street dancers work the crowd in Madrid, Spain.

OBJECTIVES

When you have completed this chapter, you should be able to:

- Define *performance* and list traits shared by performances.

- Define *art* and list traits shared by arts.

- Discuss how theatre differs from other kinds of performance (e.g., lectures, games, parades, and rituals).

- Discuss how theatre differs from other kinds of arts (e.g., painting, sculpture, opera, and dance).

- Discuss, using specific examples, similarities and differences between art and life; performance and life; dramatic character and real person; dramatic character and actor; performing art and visual art; and performing art and sport.

- List and explain the traits that constitute theatre.

- Explain in what sense theatre is a system of relationships (rather than a thing).

- Explain how theatre resembles and yet differs from film and television.

WHY THEATRE?

People choose to go to the theatre for many reasons. Theatre's immediacy, relevance, and engagement appeal to people in many different ways simultaneously. Part of theatre's appeal is social: It's a good place to be part of a great event. Part of its appeal is sensuous because theatre pleases the senses through the talent of its actors, the spectacle of its visual display (i.e., scenery, costumes, and lighting), and the beauty of its language and music. It appeals, too, by engaging the imagination with its stories and characters, which offer us experiences we have never had—and may never have—but which we recognize as possible: exotic yet familiar, good and evil, funny and sad. And theatre appeals intellectually because it engages the audience with relevant issues. The immediacy of theatre is exciting because it is happening now right in front of us, not recorded and projected for us to view.

Theatre is both a performance and an art. Most of today's theoretical work sees theatre as a kind of performance; previous theories saw it as a kind of art. Both views are correct. By shifting between the two perspectives, we can understand more about the theatre than would be possible from either standpoint alone.

THEATRE AS PERFORMANCE

An activity in which some people do something while other people watch is a performance.

Many different kinds of performance exist on a continuum from humdrum and everyday to formal and special. People perform in everyday life—that is, they shift their actions, and sometimes even their appearance, depending on what they are doing and for whom. For example, they might dress and behave one way when applying for a loan but dress and behave differently when competing in a triathlon. They may perform many informal roles in life—student, parent, athlete, and consumer. These informal roles are constantly shifting because people change their behavior for other people in certain situations.

On the other hand, some performances in life are formal and clearly structured and may

FIGURE 1.1

Street Performance

Theatrical moments abound around the world. The leaning statue performs in Chicago; the mud couple performs in Madrid, Spain. No matter where the street performers work, they create a makeshift stage in hopes of earning money.

seem even more special because they do not happen every day. In performances such as religious services and weddings, there are usually agreed-on sequences of events and predetermined sets of words. In games and sports, there are rules that must be followed and time constraints that must be observed. More highly structured still are such performances as circuses and fairs, where people come together on special occasions as an audience to watch trained people do things for their enjoyment. Most formal of all are performances of the sort found in theatre, opera, and dance because in these instances, people gather to watch specially trained people perform in highly structured works of art—hence the name performing arts to describe this special group.

Traits Shared by Performances

All performances, both informal and formal, share certain traits. They have:

- Doers (performers, actors)
- Something done (a speech, ritual, or play)
- Watchers (spectators, audiences)
- Performance sites (a stadium, church, theatre, or street)
- Movement through time (beginnings and endings)

In a fight between spectators at a hockey game, the fighters are the doers (performers or actors); fighting is the something done; the crowd that turns its attention from the ice to watch the fight is the audience, the watchers, or spectators; the performance site is the stands where the fight is taking place. The fight begins and ends. The fighters are rarely self-aware that they are performing. In a theatrical performance, the actors do a play for an audience, usually in a theatre building, and the performance takes time.

IMMEDIATE AND EPHEMERAL   The relationship between the doers and the watchers leads to one of performance's greatest appeals—its immediacy. Because it happens in real time, with the performer and spectators brought together in the event, performance has a compelling sense of "now."

The same interaction that gives live performance this power of immediacy, however, also makes it ephemeral—fleeting, nonrecoverable. In performances, as in life, events happen and are gone, never to be recaptured. Although a storyteller (another kind of performer) may repeat a story for different audiences, the storyteller is a human being and not a machine. For this reason, each time a storyteller works, the performance is different. No matter how hard a performer might work to make each performance identical, the performer cannot succeed because audiences affect performance, and audiences change at every performance.

An exception to this generalization is when performances exist in such media as radio, film, television, and video. Recorded performances exist physically on film stock as images or as electronic impulses and can be recovered exactly as they were made and repeated unchanged many times. Live performances do not leave a record. Exact copies do not exist. They cannot be played again and again without change. When the moment in performance is gone, it is entirely gone. Thus, performance is ephemeral.

Traits Causing Differences among Performances

Different types of performances, although sharing some traits, do not share all; that is, performances are not identical. They differ according to their:

- Purposes (the reasons for which they are done)

    Church services are held so that people can worship; games, so that someone can win; auctions, so that people can exchange goods and money.

- Relationships between doers and watchers

    At spectator sports, the watchers (fans) interact often with one another—talking, buying drinks—but they seldom interact with the players, except indirectly, to scream at a player's mistake or to cheer for a score. At a parade, on the other hand, watchers interact often and directly—waving and smiling. Spectators may watch for a while or even leave to do other things, coming back only in time to catch the end of the parade. In a recorded performance (radio, film, TV), performers and spectators aren't even at the same site: They don't occupy the same time or place and so *cannot* interact.

- Organizing principles (the reasons performances begin and end and seem all to be part of the same event)

    Auctions are organized by the things to be bought and sold; they begin when the auctioneer holds up the first item for sale and end when the last item has been sold. Church services are organized neither by rules nor by items to be sold but by a schedule determined by custom, symbolism, and doctrine.

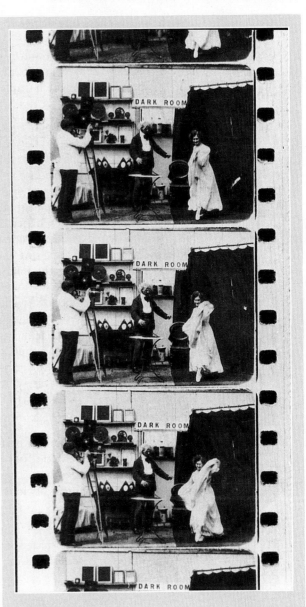

FIGURE 1.2

Film

Film, like theatre, often uses actors and scripts; unlike theatre, it gives its audiences projected images, not actual people. Film, unlike theatre, can be shown repeatedly without change. Technology and economics for many years meant that most people experienced film as a member of an audience, sitting in a darkened movie theatre. Now many people watch film in their own homes through electronic media.

■ Self-awareness (the degree to which the people involved know they are at a performance and why)

> In street fights, spectators do not come together purposefully; they encounter the fight by accident. But people come to a boxing match or circus specifically to watch trained people perform. Boxing matches and circuses, then, are self-aware in a way that street fights are not.

Obviously, none of these traits (i.e., purposes, relationships, organizing principles, and self-awareness) is better than another; each is simply different, and from different combinations of these differences come different types of performances. A final, extended example of one kind of performance—ritual—may clarify how traits can combine differently to produce a kind of performance.

Rituals share many elements across cultures. They often incorporate such elements as masks, costumes, dance, music, and some sort of text, although the texts may be improvised and transmitted orally rather than in writing. Rituals usually have as their purpose some sort of cultural outcome—to heal, to honor, to mourn. An identifying element is the community bonding of those present; that is, one of the results of a ritual is to bind members of a community together. Such bonding is probably enhanced because ritual lacks any clear separation between performers and audience—those attending participate regularly and directly in the activities. Some rituals accomplish things within the belief system of the celebrants. For example, in many Christian churches, the ritual of baptism is a prerequisite for the subject's soul to enter heaven after death. In addition, rituals sometimes lack a dedicated space and can take place over an extended period of time.

THEATRE AS ART

In addition to being a kind of performance, theatre is also a kind of art. Just as there are many different kinds of performances, there are many different kinds of art—poetry, novel, painting, sculpture, architecture, music, dance, and theatre, to mention only the most obvious.

Traits Shared by Arts

Just as all performances share some traits, all arts, however different they may be in some ways, share certain traits. For example, all art:

■ Is artificial

> That is, art is made rather than natural (existing in nature). This idea is at first difficult to grasp because we often prize art for how closely it resembles nature, thrilling to a portrait or a painting precisely because it so closely resembles the thing it copies. Still, an artist makes art; it does not just happen.

■ Stands alone

> Art may have but does not need any practical use in real life. An advertising jingle may be arresting and tuneful, but it is not normally considered a work of art, because its purpose is to sell something. For many, a piano sonata has no practical use in the world and may not even be hummable, but it is an example of musical art.

- Is self-aware

    Artists know in a general way what they are trying to do, and they possess a preparation and a discipline that allow them, within limits, to accomplish what they attempt.

- Produces a certain kind of response

    The response is aesthetic: An aesthetic response includes an appreciation of beauty and some understanding that goes beyond the merely intellectual or the merely entertaining.

Traits Causing Differences among Arts

Although all arts share certain traits, they also differ in certain ways, and it is these differences that allow us to distinguish among the kinds of art. Arts differ in:

- Their relationship with time and space

    Some arts unfold through time; for example, music or novels require time to move from their beginnings to their endings. Other arts exist in space. A building or a piece of sculpture occupies space and does not move from a beginning to an end over time; it is best seen when a person walks around it, looking at it from several sides.

- Their principles of organization

    Some arts are organized by stories; in them, lifelike characters seem to be thinking and talking and doing things that appear to be much the way people do them in real life. Other arts do not use stories but instead are organized by patterned sounds (music) or patterned colors (painting).

- Their idea of audience

    Novels and paintings, for example, assume they will be enjoyed by solitary individuals; opera and dance, on the other hand, assume that groups of people will assemble to enjoy them. The ways by which arts reach their audiences also differ.

- Their mode of presentation

    Some arts, such as novels, are transmitted by the printed page; others, like film, rely on mechanically produced images; still others, like opera, dance, and theatre, require live performers in the presence of a live audience.

Matt Orton

FIGURE 1.3

Comic Antics

The live actor performs before a live audience. Even this complicated comic routine, although specifically staged and carefully rehearsed, will change from performance to performance. Here, a moment from *Scapin* at Montevallo University.

In short, theatre is a kind of performance that shares some traits with other sorts of performances: It has doers and watchers, a place of performance, and movement through time; it is immediate and ephemeral. Although resembling other kinds of performances, it is not identical with any of them; it has its own purposes, relationships, principles, degree of self-awareness, and relation to time.

Theatre's Relationship with Other Arts

Theatre's relationship with other arts is complex. Sometimes it contains them, other times it merges with them, and often it transforms other arts for its own purposes (and vice versa). Scenery and costumes routinely use techniques of painting and sculpture, and plays so often include songs and dances that we have the expressions *theatre music* and *theatre dance*. Works such as *Porgy and Bess* or *Sweeney Todd* so completely merge opera with musical theatre that they are performed by both theatre companies and opera companies, and songs such as "The Impossible Dream" become famous simply as songs, having lost all association with the play in which they first appeared, in this case the 1965 musical *The Man of La Mancha*.

Sometimes, too, the same story rests at the center of several different arts. *Romeo and Juliet*, for example, has been staged as a play, a ballet, an opera, several films, and *West Side Story*, a Broadway musical. In each case, the artists made quite different choices, selecting from *Romeo and Juliet* those elements that could be best communicated through their own art. For opera, the composer selected those moments best communicated through music; for dance, the choreographer selected the moments best communicated through movement; and so on. Such choices focus the audience's attention in different ways.

Shakespeare's play leads us to watch and listen to the actor speak Shakespeare's poetic dialogue, but opera leads us to listen to the music, perhaps barely following the story, and dance may ask us to watch movement only, almost ignoring story and character. All three invite the eye.

Theatre, then, resembles other arts in being artificial and self-aware and in intending to evoke an aesthetic response rather than to produce an immediately useful item. It differs from other arts in its relation to time and space, its principles of organization, its anticipated audience, and its mode of presentation, and it has a complicated relationship with many other arts.

THEATRE AS PERFORMING ART

From what we have examined about theatre as a particular kind of performance and a special kind of art, we can now say more about the major characteristics of theatre.

■ Theatre uses a special kind of performer—the actor.
  An actor is a performer who impersonates, that is, who uses the pronoun *I* and means somebody other than himself or herself. Thus, actors differ from street fighters, for example, who neither intend to perform nor pretend to be someone other than themselves. Actors differ even from jugglers and music video stars, who do not say *I* and mean someone other than themselves.

Spotlight

Life/Art/Performance: *Frost/Nixon*

Are David Frost and Richard Nixon in *Frost/Nixon* the real Frost and Nixon?

President Richard Nixon resigned in disgrace in 1974 over the crime called "Watergate." In 1977, the British journalist David Frost interviewed Nixon on television about his presidency—many hours of tape were cut down to four 90-minute shows. In 2006, dramatist Peter Morgan turned the story of those interviews into a play, *Frost/Nixon*. In 2008, director Ron Howard turned the play into a film, using Morgan's script and the same two actors who had played Frost and Nixon in London and New York.

A chain of life, art, and performance was thus forged: Hours of interviews were shaped into four TV shows; the televised interviews and their backgrounds were turned into a play; and the play was turned into a movie. At the heart of the play was what National Public Radio critic Bob Mondello called "a David and Goliath mismatch" based on the idea that Frost was a TV lightweight; Nixon a power hitter: "It could almost have been called Froth-Nixon." It also, according to Ben Brantley of the *New York Times*, "blithely rejiggered and rearranged facts and chronology," including "the show's high point, a late-night phone call Frost receives from a drunken Nixon" (which was a "pure fabrication").

Howard's film used Morgan's script but was seen as different from the play. Manohla Dargis, also from the *New York Times*, found it "a talkathon embellished with camera movements." Mondello, however, cited Howard's "semi-documentary approach, [which] has the effect of giving Frost more heft on screen...." To Mondello, it was less the supposedly lightweight Frost who brought Nixon to near-tears and a near-admission of guilt than television itself—"that unblinking eye...." He pointed out that the play made the same point intellectually, but the film made it visually and in close-ups, "theater being a medium of words, and film a medium of images...."

There is no question that the original interviews, the play, and the film were effective. Quotes such as "theatrical smackdown," "briskly entertaining," and "the aura of a boxing bout" were used. Supposedly real events, therefore, were turned into successful art, both theatrical and cinematic, in which "larger-than-life seems truer-to-life than merely life-size ever could" (Brantley).

But were the televised interviews of 1977 "real" events, or were they, too, art? Surely the winnowing of thirty hours to six hours comprised manipulation, compression, pointing, and "dramatizing," hence making it art.

Were, then, the unedited thirty hours of taped interviews the "reality?" Were Frost and Nixon any less performers in them than the actors in the film and the play? Both Frost and Nixon were paid well for those hours; both had reputations at stake. When were they not performing? Were they ever in their adult lives not performing? Where in the chain of life, art, and performance was their "reality"?

- In theatre, live actors perform in the presence of a live audience.

   A live actor in the sense used here is not the opposite of a dead actor but rather an actor who is in the physical presence of the audience. Thus, theatre actors differ not only from other kinds of performers but also from other kinds of actors. Theatre actors differ from actors in film or television, for example, because in those media the picture or image of the actor (rather than the actual actor) is offered to the audience.

   Theatre actors must both impersonate and be physically present because it is these two traits—impersonation and presence—that separate them from various other performers, on the one hand, and from actors in other media, on the other.

- Theatre is both immediate and ephemeral. Because in theatre actors and audiences share both space and time, theatre is both an immediate and ephemeral art: that is, it has a strong sense of *now*, and it cannot be repeated exactly.

- Theatre depends on action (which for now we can think of as stories and characters) to organize and bind the theatrical event.

   We can think of stories as worlds created for artistic purposes, worlds that resemble (but are distinct from) the actual world in which we live: *virtual worlds*, an expression that recalls the invented worlds of the computer's virtual reality. Part of the reason that theatre's virtual worlds resemble our own real world so convincingly is that these virtual worlds are inhabited by characters. Characters might be thought of as virtual people because characters are artistic creations intended to resemble people. Well-created characters are often so compelling, so lifelike, that we feel as though we know them personally. We may even begin to talk of them as though they were real people. But characters are not real people; they are created by a playwright for the play, just as any virtual world is created.

- Theatre's virtual world is more intense and concentrated than the world in which we live.

   Because everything on stage has been selected and placed there by someone for a purpose, everything on stage is important—it has meaning for an audience. Therefore, everything on stage gains a significance that it may lack in real life. For example, it is not unusual for theatre audiences to be captivated by an onstage scene in which an actor cooks a meal or uses a washing machine. Obviously, cooking or using a washing machine is not very interesting in real life, but, on stage, these simple actions can provide insight because theatre transforms them from ordinary to meaningful activities.

■ The theatre uses a real performance space but usually with artificial (that is, made-for-the-purpose) settings.

Theatre uses a defined performance space that is physically in the presence of the audience and limited by existing architecture. It can give us representations—replicas—of actual places (e.g., a city street), but it can give them only on a scale appropriate to its own performing space and to the actors working in or in front of the scene. Film, on the other hand, can take us anywhere and show us images of actual places, even on a vast scale (the Grand Canyon, outer space). Because film shows images of places rather than real places, it can range far in its presentation of objects and spaces.

Many kinds of activities easily shown on film (horse races, car crashes) are difficult to present on stage. Film and television can show not only races and crashes but also selective close-ups that direct our attention and heighten the impact of the events: speeding hooves, snorting nostrils, exploding gas tanks, collapsing fenders. Theatre has no exact equivalent to film's close-up on stage, but theatre can heighten focus by the use of staging, lighting, and sound.

FIGURE 1.5

Choices

Artists make choices that sometimes seem unusual. Although realistic approaches are often seen on stage, this production of *Big Love* from Virginia Commonwealth University made abstract choices.

Theatre audiences love spectacle, like horse races presented on stage, even though they know they are seeing an obvious trick; they seem to appreciate the skill required to create the illusion. Indeed, it is one of theatre's paradoxes that the restrictions of theatre's real space seem to increase the audience's enjoyment of difficult scenes produced there.

■ Theatre proceeds at its own pace through time.

We can't play a performance again, play it backward, or fast-forward it to see how it will come out. We can't put a theatrical performance aside for

VanderVeen Photographers

FIGURE 1.6

A Heightened Vision

Theatre artists create worlds more intense and concentrated than the world in which we live our everyday lives. This moment from Tennessee Williams' *The Glass Menagerie* avoids the specific world suggested by the playwright. Instead, this production at Triad Stage in North Carolina incorporates video, an illuminated floor, and makes Tom, the narrator of the play, an onlooker.

a while and pick it up later. If we don't like a performance, we cannot jump to another station or change channels. If we don't understand a moment in the theatre, we cannot stop and go back to it, hoping to grasp its significance the second or third time through. In other words, as members of a theatre audience, we do not control the way the theatrical performance unfolds as we can control the pace at which we watch a DVD or read a poem or a book. For better or worse, the theatre performance proceeds at its own pace and must be followed at that pace. Some audience members find the lack of interruption or replay a significant part of theatre's attraction.

■ Theatre is not a thing (an object) but a process, a system of constantly altering relationships among actor, action, audience, time, and space.

Changing even one of these relationships changes the whole. We might be tempted to think, for example, that a play in the theatre and a play on film have only mechanical differences, but a filmed play has no live actor and can be stopped and replayed, and the camera "sees" for the audience. These changed performance-audience relationships change the whole process.

■ Theatre is lifelike, but it is not life.

Because theatre is an art, it is artificial—made by artists. Theatre's artificiality, however, is sometimes more difficult to see than the artificiality of other arts because theatre is also a performance. Theatre uses real human beings pretending to be other human beings engaged in actions that look much like those we see in life. So convincing is it that sometimes people have confused a theatre performance with real life. There are many apparently true stories about people attending their first play who have rushed on stage to save a character who is being threatened, like the man who tried to save Desdemona from Othello.

Theatre in fact sometimes seems so lifelike that it has often been used as a metaphor for life. The most famous example of the metaphor is probably Shakespeare's "All the world's a stage / and all the men and women merely players," but there are others, such as "This world is a comedy to those that think, a tragedy to those that feel." We need to remember, however, that a metaphor is a special kind of comparison, one that implies but does not use the words *like* or *as*. We know that the real sense of these quotations is that the world is like a comedy or like a tragedy. And, clearly, the metaphor comparing life and theatre cuts two ways, equating the stage with the real world and at the same time pointing out how individuals' qualities change over time, making one person seem like many people.

Life and theatre move forward through time. Just as life has a past, a present, and a future, plays have a beginning, middle, and end, and in plays, as in life, these stages are defined through time. Life and theatre exist in space; that is, like actors on a stage men and women in life take up space and move through space. Life and theatre have men and women doing and saying things: While some people act and speak, others listen and watch. Those who act and speak in life are *like* actors in the theatre, whereas those who listen and watch in life are *like* audiences in the theatre. And the lives of real people that we know often don't seem different from the actions or stories that we see when we go to a play.

Despite such similarities, however, life and theatre are different in many ways, only a few of which need be suggested. Most lives last for years; most theatre lasts a few hours. Life often seems diffuse, confused, and inexplicable; theatre appears concentrated, orderly, and meaningful. Life may be dangerous, but theatre is safe. Although theatre may bring us up close to a human activity (like a murder) that is terrifyingly *like* life in its immediacy, we as audience are separated from it and so can watch it in safety and experience it without physical danger.

KEY TERMS

Check your understanding against this list. Brief definitions are included in the Glossary; persons are page-referenced in the Index.

aesthetic response 7	criticism 1	performing arts 4
art 6	ephemeral art 10	presence 10
audience 4	impersonation 10	ritual 6
characters 10	performance 3	theory 1

2

Theatre
The Performing Audience:
Three Roles

In Barcelona, Spain, an audience gathers for a high school matinee of *Grease*.

OBJECTIVES

When you have completed this chapter, you should be able to:

- Describe ways in which theatre audiences are social.

- Explain how the size and arrangement of audiences affect their ability to be social units.

- Explain how permission and self-image promote the social quality of audiences.

- Explain how theatre audiences are interactive.

- Explain why theatre audiences can serve as an index to culture.

- Describe how business and theatre interact.

- Explain the fundamental tension between theatre as art and theatre as business.

- Describe funding patterns in today's theatre in the United States.

Theatre is not only a performance and an art, it is also an expression of the time and place that produce it—an expression of its culture. Often, too, theatre is a business, and, in our own time, big business. As keys to culture and engines of finance, audiences are central to understanding both how theatre works as an expression of its culture and how it works as a business.

THEATRE AS PERFORMING ART: THE ROLE OF THE AUDIENCE

Social Audiences

Most people enjoy the companionship of others—they are social beings who enjoy feeling they are members of a group. Every good theatre audience is a group in which the response of each audience member depends both on the performance and on the responses of other members of the group. If a theatre audience fails to coalesce as a group, the performance itself will be less successful. A sense of groupness in the audience, then, is critical to unleashing the full power of the theatre. Although there are no hard-and-fast rules about how to build an audience's sense of itself as a group, several factors are at work.

SIZE AND ARRANGEMENT   Both size and seating arrangement are important. One person in a theatre audience is not enough. To enhance a performance, a theatregoer's response needs to be amplified, joined by the responses of others. Forty thousand people in a theatre won't work either because so many people can't relate *intimately* with the stage. Although there's no magic number for a theatre audience, some numbers are clearly too small and others are too large. Probably the number is about right if the audience fits well within the space, and each person can easily hear and see the performance. The best audience space for a theatre is, therefore, one small enough to define an audience (to help it see itself as part of a group) but not so small as to confine it (to make it physically uncomfortable). A hundred people in a large theatre will feel uncomfortable, but the same number in a small space may easily enjoy the play. Also, the arrangement of seats interacts with the number of spectators and the size of space to affect the audience's sense of itself as a social unit.

FIGURE 2.1

Social Theatre

Going to the theatre can be an exciting shared experience. This sense of a special collective experience is critical to unleashing the full power of theatre.

FIGURE 2.2

Stage-to-Audience Relationship

Audience size and seating arrangement are important. An audience member's experience is amplified by the presence and responses of others in the audience. Audiences at small "studio" productions enjoy a special intimacy. Here the actress is surrounded by the audience, seated on four sides.

PERMISSION There is an unspoken agreement in theatre between actors and audiences that what the actors embody on stage is not real life and that it is permissible to respond to it in unusual ways (e.g., laughing out loud at a character who is crying or applauding when a sympathetic character shoots one who threatens). This agreement gives audiences permission to respond in safety to whatever transpires on the stage; that is, no audience member will be harmed by onstage threats or sanctioned for responding to onstage actions. This shared permission contributes to shaping the audience into a social unit. Permission is thus a social phenomenon that bolsters theatre-going as a social experience.

SELF-IMAGE Each theatre audience develops a self-image, which also enhances the audience's sense of itself as a group. An audience's self-image influences its behavior, including its dress. Part of the self-image comes from society's expectations. Members of a theatre audience do not wear pajamas, although they watch television in them comfortably. Part of the self-image comes from specific expectations set up by the particular theatre or production, often as a way to enhance the enjoyment of a performance. For a special celebration in the theatre or a special play, for example, the theatre might encourage audience members to dress formally, but for another kind of play at a different theatre, audience members might be encouraged to wear T-shirts and jeans. These two audiences would likely expect different experiences from their night out at the theatre, and they will behave accordingly.

Interactive Audiences

Audiences are not just social units; they are *interactive* social units, with individual audience members interacting both with the performers on stage and with one another. Obviously, no one can say for certain precisely how an audience will respond during a play or how any individual in an audience will respond at a given moment. Performances differ, audiences differ, and individuals in audiences differ.

When performances are successful, however, most members of the audience behave similarly much of the time. That an audience is a group rather than a collection of individuals or a mob suggests that audience members will respond to many of the same things in roughly the same ways—and indeed they do.

Audience Approval

- **Applause.** Audiences usually clap their hands at any point during the performance that warrants response and usually at the end of each scene or section.

- **Laughter.** When something is funny, audiences usually laugh, anything from a belly laugh to a snicker. Sometimes audiences will laugh because they're uncomfortable (nervous laughter). Depending on the intentions of the playwright, actors may dread hearing this kind of laughter because it shows the performance is not working.

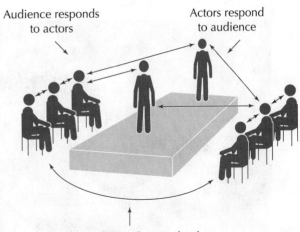

Audience responds to actors

Actors respond to audience

Audience responds to each other

FIGURE 2.3

Theatre's Interactive Nature

Audience members affect one another; actors affect and are affected by the audience.

- **Silence.** When something is sad, audiences may cry, although today's theatre audiences don't shed tears as easily as audiences once did or as easily as audiences now laugh. Although we associate applause, laughter, and tears with success, silence is often a sign of a successful performance: "You could hear a pin drop." Especially at the end of a well-performed serious play, silence is often the audience's response, as if applause were too frivolous for the moment.

- **Curtain Call.** At the end of a play, actors take a bow for as long as the applause continues (although to milk an audience—try to make the audience extend its applause—is considered bad form).

- **Standing Ovation.** To show exceptional approval, audiences may stand and applaud. In recent years, standing ovations often have become a commonplace response to most every performance, no longer reserved to show *exceptional* approval.

- **Encore.** In past times, audiences might clap so long that actors gave an encore—a repeated piece—just as many musicians do today.

Audience Disapproval

- **Withhold Applause.** To show disapproval, audiences may simply withhold the usual responses of approval.

- **Noise.** More likely, though, they will become noisy. Coughing, shuffling feet, whispering, and rattling programs are all signs of unease or boredom;

Ken Berne Images

FIGURE 2.4

Audience Response

Theatre, because of its immediacy, can have powerful effects on audiences. This moment from the La Jolla Playhouse revival of Lynn Nottage's *Ruined* seems boisterous and fun-loving, a contrast to the serious tone of other moments in this Pulitzer Prize-winning drama.

each person may think he or she is being quiet, but many people moving at once, however unconsciously, can become quite loud—and horribly revealing.

■ **Protest.** More aggressive signs of disapproval come when members of the audience boo or leave the theatre. In some ages, audiences were even more aggressive, yelling at the actors and even throwing things on stage.

An audience's disapproval most often signals a bad performance (about which we say more in Part II), but it may signal instead an audience that fails to enter into the created world prepared by the playwright and the actors. Occasionally such an audience just doesn't understand theatre well enough to enjoy it. More often, though, audience members refuse to enter the created world because they are alienated from the particular performance. Sometimes they are encountering a performance they did not expect from reading the play's title or the reviews of the performance. More likely, members of the audience are embarrassed, shocked, or angered to find a play with political, religious, or ethical views they deplore. They may be reacting to particular scenes whose language, violence, or nudity they find shocking.

THEATRE AS CULTURAL EXPRESSION: THE ROLE OF THE AUDIENCE

Culture

The idea of culture is a complex one. For our purposes, culture is that set of beliefs, values, and social behavior that a group shares. People have called the culture of the twenty-first century a consumer culture (one that values the acquisition of goods), a popular culture (one that prefers reality TV, hip-hop, and graphic novels to ballet, opera, and Jane Austen), a communication culture (one saturated with such means for sharing ideas as texting and blogging), and a mass culture (one produced by the media and intended for the greatest number of people). The point is that there are always several layers of culture—cultures within cultures. Still, it is possible to distinguish in a general way US culture from, say, Afghan culture or Ugandan culture. As we use the word *culture*, then, we are trying to suggest a complex web of traits that compete, merge, and exist alongside one another and that constitute a recognizable cluster—a worldview.

Culture and Audience

In preparing their art, theatre artists must make decisions that are meant to touch the audience's culture—to enhance its enjoyment by touching its central concerns. In deciding what play to produce, for example, producers will consider the needs of the likely audience; in deciding where to produce it, they will match the size of the likely audience with the configuration of available spaces. Playwrights must write plays that will bring real audiences with real cultures into the theatre and affect them once they get there. Designers and directors must figure out ways to guide the responses of audiences through visual cues, so that the play "means" for audiences what they want it to mean; that is, they must provide visual clues that give the play appropriate cultural resonances. Actors must imagine how audiences will respond to moments of performance and then perform in ways that prompt appropriate responses, based in part on shared cultural understandings of vocal and physical meaning ("body language"). When an audience has a shared culture with the performance, they have a shared context in which to experience and understand it.

Mirror of Culture

By studying both the choices of theatre artists and the responses of the audience, we can glimpse something about the world existing outside theatre—the culture. Through the choices made by theatre artists, we can begin to infer what they think their audiences—and therefore the larger culture—seem to want or need. It is in this way, and because of these linkages, that theatre, probably more than any other art, expresses and partakes of the culture of which it is a part. A poem, say, can appeal to an individual reader who may or may not be aligned with the culture of the time but theatre requires the response of an audience. For such reasons, theatre has been called, metaphorically, a "mirror of life." But for several reasons, we must be cautious in any conclusions that we draw.

First, theatre is at the *center* of some cultures but peripheral to others. Cultures in which theatre was central include those of Greece in the fifth century BCE and of Western Europe in the Middle Ages. These theatre performances were part of major civic and religious festivals that were held on important days. At these times, much of the community was involved, and most citizens attended; rich citizens in Greece and guilds in the Middle Ages, as we shall see, supported the festivals, including the theatrical performances embedded in them. By contrast, today most Americans don't attend theatre. Many can't afford it, many don't have access to it, and some don't like it. Were we to study theatre in an attempt to understand the culture of fifth-century BCE Greece or Western Europe during the Middle Ages, we could be fairly confident that the audience in the

FIGURE 2.5

Theatre and Culture

Audiences have embraced musical theatre. Big, spectacular musicals rule Broadway and then become staple fare across the country. Here, the hit musical, *The Full Monty*, revived by Ball State University Theatre.

theatre fairly represented most living in that same time and place (the culture). Studying theatre to grasp traits of our own culture, however, would require us to remember that theatre now appeals to only a limited group, and so its audience may represent only a small subset of today's larger culture. Still, by asking the question, "Who goes to the theatre and why?" we can glean something about a culture's values and interests.

Second, although theatre is a mirror of life, we must remember that a mirror can be distorting instead of accurate. A bathroom mirror shows a person his or her physical appearance, and some theatres do seem to show life more or less as it is lived at a particular time and place. A fun-house mirror, however, stretches, compresses, and otherwise distorts the image, and some theatres show the audience such a distorted image of itself, highlighting its horrors or poking fun at its foibles—interpreting and critiquing rather than merely presenting the culture. The point is that theatre can offer important insights into people and cultures so long as inferences are drawn carefully, cautiously, and tentatively.

Third, changes in audiences, theatres, and cultures are connected. When performances are free or inexpensive, people from all economic classes can attend, a circumstance that influences the choice of play, for example. When a single ticket costs several hundred dollars (as they sometimes do in today's professional theatres), affluent patrons will probably be overrepresented, again influencing the choice of plays. When men and women are equally free in a culture, both can be expected in theatre in roughly equal numbers, but in cultures in which women are thought to need protection (e.g., in the 1800s in the United States), gender differences within audiences may be striking. Race and ethnic heritage may also figure significantly, both because all cultures do not prize theatre equally and because some people may be segregated or denied access to theatre based on race or ethnicity. Then, too, theatre audiences expect different things from the performance, often because of their level of education. Audiences are to a degree self-selected—that is, some people will want musicals; others, comedies; still others, plays that are politically challenging or sexually free. All such factors must be weighed before generalizing about the relationship between a theatre's audience and its culture.

THEATRE AS BUSINESS: THE ROLE OF THE AUDIENCE

Just as audiences are important to theatre as art and cultural expression, so audiences are important to theatre as business. In a commercial theatre (i.e., one run as a business), the audience pays the bill. For much of theatre's early history, theatre was not a business—that is, it was not a commercial opportunity for people to make a living. Rather, theatre was a communal celebration in which volunteers did most of the work, and bills were paid by the community or church or wealthy citizens as their religious and civic duty.

Since the Renaissance (c. 1500s), however, many theatres in the West have been a business; subsidy has given way to pay-as-you-go, and audiences have provided the money that pays the bills. Some people argue that theatre thus places too much emphasis on making a profit and not enough on artistic expression. But someone has to pay, and it has yet to be demonstrated that

FIGURE 2.6

Mirror of Life

The playwright and director George C. Wolfe wrote *The Colored Museum* in 1986. This revue of eleven satirical sketches on African American culture launched Wolfe's career. Here, a production at Ball State University.

the effects of commercialism on theatre are worse than the effects of patronage (i.e., when a king or church subsidized performances). Other people argue that the business side of theatre should simply be ignored. But the business side of theatre cannot, in fact, be ignored. Actors, designers, and playwrights have to make a living, just like bankers and secretaries and autoworkers, so paying the bills is surely as important as other factors affecting theatrical art.

Balancing Business and Art

The role of audience in the business of theatre sets up tensions almost at once with its role in the art of theatre. As we have seen, for theatrical performance to work, a theatre audience must have a sense of itself as a social group. But a major force in theatre tugs against this idea of a coherent group, and that force is money. The economics of theatre demands that the audience be big enough to pay for the scenery and costumes, actors, support personnel, the rent on the

Sara Krulwich/New York Times/Redux Pictures

FIGURE 2.7

Spectacle Rules

The extravagant, flying musical, *Spider-Man: Turn Off the Dark*, cost more than $75 million dollars to produce. During poorly received previews, the production shuttered for revamping, then resumed preview performances. Only after 182 preview performances did the production open on June 14, 2011, and then to poor reviews. Still, audiences flocked to *Spider-Man*, often earning the production weekly grosses of more than one-and-a-half million dollars.

building, the author's royalties, and the maintenance of the space. A desire for profit—income over and above expenses—demands that audiences be bigger still: bigger audience, more profit. Therefore, although the art of the theatre may suggest that the best-sized audience for a particular play in a particular space is two hundred, the business of the theatre may demand an audience of two thousand, a size that will almost certainly degrade the audience as a social unit. Some tension between theatre as art and theatre as business is almost inevitable. Some compromise on both sides is inescapable. Such a compromise, however, must be a careful one.

Bringing Business to Art

The language of business dominates talk about wholly unrelated fields. It is not uncommon to hear students described as *consumers* at a university, and the graduates described as the university's *products*. We routinely speak of *spending* or *saving* or even *banking* something as elusive as time. We ask governments and doctors to be more *efficient*, and we expect agents for athletes to *negotiate* megasalaries and advertising contracts. The talk and decisions around theatres now, not surprisingly, are as much about profit, loss, bottom line, and labor relations as about the meaning of plays and the aesthetics of production.

Similarly, business executives now lead all sorts of organizations, including those not usually considered businesses, like charities or not-for-profit arts organizations. Such people bring with them the outlook and practices of corporations. Their skills in policymaking and management often allow them to transfer from one sort of enterprise to another: first CEO of a corporation, then governor of a state, and later president of a university or health maintenance organization.

University presidents, for example, are now seldom drawn from the world of scholarship, and managers of hospitals may or may not have training in medicine. Just so, Broadway theatres are run by a loosely tied group of executives drawn mostly from business and real estate, many of whom have little experience in theatre.

Businesses now take considerable interest in the arts for their contributions to the quality of life as well as possible commercial benefit. They, or the foundations growing out of them, give major support to the visual, musical, and performing arts. A luxury home builder, for example, underwrites weekly radio broadcasts of the Metropolitan Opera, and the Ford Foundation funds a program to support emerging playwrights. Businesses routinely support theatres in cities around the country, buying blocks of tickets and advertisements in the programs, awarding grants for specific projects, or even sponsoring selected productions. Not only are such ventures believed to be excellent advertisement for products, but they are also thought to be good ways of demonstrating that businesses are good corporate citizens. Event-related spending by audience members for such things as hotels, restaurants, parking, souvenirs, and refreshments makes a considerable impact on local businesses. As a bonus, businesses have come to believe that having a professional symphony, ballet, or theatre company in a city makes it easier to recruit managers and executives.

Changing Patterns in Business and Theatre

Just as audiences changed over time to embody a changing culture, so, too, has the business of theatre shifted to embody changes in business. For example, when businesses outside the theatre were small and often home based, theatre companies were centered on one or two families who put on plays and shared expenses, income, and work. Such sharing companies were among the earliest ways that theatre organized itself to do business.

SHAREHOLDER COMPANIES When cities grew large enough to house a theatre company more or less permanently, several unrelated people formed larger and more complex sharing companies, with the most contributing members of the company owning several shares and the least significant owning a share or a fraction of a share. Members of such companies tended to specialize, performing only certain kinds of roles or undertaking only certain tasks of production, such as playwriting or costuming. Such companies even hired other people, paying them a salary rather than allowing them to join the company. The theatre company in which Shakespeare worked was of this sort. He owned shares in the company as well as in the building in which the company performed, making him (like the other shareholders) both businessman and theatre artist. Business is not necessarily in opposition to art.

By the late 1800s, business outside of theatre had changed its ways of organizing, and so had theatre. In such countries as Germany, theatre had come to be thought of as a cost of government, and so all major German cities subsidized theatres, allowing tax dollars to join with ticket sales to pay expenses. In several countries, notably France and, later, England, government-supported theatres existed alongside commercial theatres.

Joan Marcus

FIGURE 2.8

Broadway Ticket Prices

Here, a scene from *The Book of Mormon* on Broadway where it won nine Tony Awards, including Best Musical in 2010. The top price for a regular orchestra seat is $175. However, premium seats, the best orchestra seats, can cost as much as $477. Yet, *Mormon* continues to sell out.

THE COMMERCIAL PRODUCER IN THE UNITED STATES   The United States set a different pattern. Here, private enterprise mostly ruled. The old sharing system gave way to a system of for-profit partnerships headed by entrepreneurs who saw theatre mostly as a way to make money. Business people (as distinct from theatre people) began to invest money, sometimes in a theatre company but more often in a single production, and they expected to recover their investment, with profit, from ticket sales. In New York City and on the road, these producers controlled theatre buildings and the productions playing in them. The commercial producer typically found investors, planned and ran the show, and paid the theatrical personnel (who then became employees). Ticket sales were needed not only to pay the bills but also to make a profit for the investors, who were no longer theatre artists themselves. Paid advertising and public relations became an important part of theatre's business, just as they had become important tools of other businesses.

CORPORATIONS   Recently, the costs of production have escalated so dramatically that ticket sales and paid advertisements alone no longer generate enough money, and so the sale of film, television, and video rights has become an increasingly important source of funding. Businesspeople and midlevel managers increasingly assumed responsibility for producing theatre, bringing with them the ideas and techniques of business and management. Too, these businesspeople, lacking experience in theatre, transferred much of the artistic power—once belonging to actor-sharers—to directors and designers. The once centralized power of the producer has dispersed among others: the director, the general manager, and other

Spotlight

Perseverance Theatre

Macbeth was set in the context of southeast Alaska's indigenous Tlingit culture and performed by an all–Alaskan native cast. This piece toured the state and, later, was remounted a third time for performances at the new Smithsonian National Museum of the American Indian in Washington, D.C. Here, Macbeth conspires with the "First Murderer."
Photo courtesy Perseverance Theatre.

Perseverance Theatre, Juneau, Alaska

When Molly Smith graduated from American University, she dragged fifty old theatre seats with her back to Juneau, Alaska, her hometown. She was determined to start a theatre. In 1979, she borrowed ten thousand dollars from her grandmother and Perseverance Theatre was born. Its mission has not changed: to tap the potential of Alaska through the passionate creation and presentation of theatre. The theatre is dedicated to "engaging community, pursuing excellence, embracing risk, and inspiring self-discovery." Perseverance creates theatre by and for Alaskans.

Perseverance has premiered more than fifty new plays by Alaskan and other American playwrights, among them *The Long Season*, a musical about the Filipino Alaskan experience, and *columbinus*, an exploration of adolescence and the phenomenon of school shootings. The 2007–08 season included two productions that reflected Alaska's culture—*Battles of Fire and Water*, based on the Russian and Tlingit wars over the land where Sitka now stands, and *8 Stars of Gold*, celebrating Alaska's fiftieth year of statehood. In 2011 it staged *The Blue Bear* based on Juneau author Lynn Schooler's memoir of the same name.

Perseverance Theatre is now the largest not-for-profit professional theatre in Alaska. It has a budget of about one million dollars, small when compared to other not-for-profit professional theatres in the United States. Beginning in the 2011-2012 season, Perseverance is traveling productions each season to Anchorage, Alaska's largest city holding forty percent of the state population.

Perseverance Theatre began, then, from the impulse to reflect Alaska's culture. Molly Smith is now the artistic director of the Arena Stage in Washington, D.C., but the theatre she founded in Juneau still prospers.

coinvestors, many of whom are now major entertainment corporations (like the Walt Disney Company) rather than, as previously, wealthy individuals.

NOT-FOR-PROFIT EXPERIMENTS   Starting about fifty years ago, severe pressures on the commercial theatre led to cautious experimentation in ways of producing theatre other than as a strictly profit-making enterprise. As a result, today the greatest number of productions in the US's professional theatre are now produced by not-for-profit organizations. The contrasts between these commercial for-profit and not for-profit professional theatres are significant:

■ A commercial theatre production is formed as a business partnership to produce only one production. Eventually the partnership ends. A not-for-profit theatre is organized as an ongoing enterprise. It produces a series of plays each season and intends to do so indefinitely.

■ Commercial productions are usually planned as open-ended runs to be performed as long as enough theatregoers buy tickets to make the run profitable. A not-for-profit theatre plans a slate of plays for a season with a fixed number of performances allotted to each production.

Almost all of the income for commercial productions is generated by ticket sales. Not-for-profit theatres, however, generate only about 40 to 60 percent of income from ticket sales; the remainder comes mostly from donations. The federal tax code is structured to give tax breaks to not-for-profit contributors. That same code generally views commercial productions as it does any business partnership, fully taxable.

Not-for-profit theatres throughout the country as well as the three not-for-profit theatre organizations that produce on Broadway give the US theatre new plays, revivals of important older plays, and musicals new and in revival. Clearly, the quality of their offerings is high, rivaling that of the for-profit productions. Since the 2000 season, more than 60 percent of "Best of..." Tony Awards went to not-for-profit productions or to productions originated in not-for-profit groups.

EDUCATIONAL THEATRE   Educational theatres are subsidized. Although the out-of-pocket costs of their productions must often be defrayed by the sale of tickets and program advertisements, the salaries of the faculty (who usually direct, design, manage, and mount the productions) are almost always paid by the university. Because the students who act and crew the productions are seldom paid, the majority of the labor costs associated with producing plays is charged to the college or university, not to the production. This substantial subsidy allows such theatres to be somewhat adventurous in their selection of plays and the ways in which they are presented. University audiences are also different from those of the commercial or not-for-profit professional theatre; this difference also encourages university theatres to make more adventurous play selections.

THE NATIONAL ENDOWMENT FOR THE ARTS   With an occasional exception, federal government funding for theatre in this country has been conspicuously absent. Therefore, one closely watched development was the establishment in 1965 of the National Endowment for the Arts (NEA), whose purpose was to encourage the development of all arts throughout the country. It did so in two major ways: by establishing state arts councils as coordinating and funding units and by subsidizing some existing performance groups. To receive grants, theatres had to be organized as not-for-profit theatres, a departure from the commercial Broadway model.

The NEA continues to be controversial. Not all citizens agree that government should fund art when urgent social problems remain unsolved and unfunded. Not all citizens agree that taxpayers should pay for art that some find offensive. The latter issue led to a threatened cutoff of the NEA's funding in 1990 and 1995. Both issues promise to be debated for some time to come.

The precedent set by the NEA may help account for a relatively new phenomenon: Cities and counties are supporting theatre as a form of recreation for citizens who seek an alternative to well-established programs in sports and crafts. By contributing both advice and money, local governments strive to improve the work of local community theatres, which they view as an important resource for the participants and their audiences. Community leaders increasingly see the arts, including theatre, as important to a community's quality of life and attractiveness to newcomers and new businesses, comparable to other amenities, such as parks, libraries, and schools.

KEY TERMS

Check your understanding against this list. Brief definitions are included in the Glossary; persons are page-referenced in the Index.

applause 17	for-profit 26	sharing companies 23
culture 18	milk an audience 17	standing ovation 17
educational theatres 26	not-for-profit 26	
encore 17	producers 24	

3

How to Read a Play

As You Like It in a Theatre South Carolina production where the "love-poem scene" has been reimagined to include hanging books.

OBJECTIVES

When you have completed this chapter, you should be able to:

- List and explain Aristotle's six parts of a play.
- Explain the interrelationships among the six parts.

- Describe different kinds of plot.
- Explain "wholeness of action."
- Explain some essential ways a play is different from life.

- Identify some common types of characters.
- List and explain some traditional theatre genres.

SEEING VERSUS READING

Seeing a play and reading a play are different experiences. They require different tools and different approaches. Seeing a play is the only complete theatrical experience. Reading a play sensitively means understanding what it is and how it works.

First, a play is not theatre; that is, reading a play from a book offers an incomplete experience. Because of the incompleteness of the written text, some theatre artists talk of the play's script as a "notation" for production, others as "a pretext rather than a text." To make an analogy with music: A written play is like musical notes on a page; the performed play is like the music heard when a musician turns the notes into music. The incompleteness of the written play makes reading a play different from reading a newspaper or a novel. The newspaper and novel are both complete in themselves; their language fills them out. A play, on the other hand, is only a part—although an important part—of a different kind of experience.

Second, reading a play means understanding that playwrights create plays by making choices. To be successful, the playwright must persuade an audience by convincing it of the essential truth of the play. A playwright's goal is not simply to tell a story but to tell it in a certain way. The playwright, using only words, must shape characters and actions that allow actors to perform and designers to design so as to produce certain effects in audiences. Playwrights, then, are always shaping, although indirectly, the meanings and pleasures that audiences glean from the play. Both of these traits have implications for how to read a play.

Filling in the Blanks

Because the play is intended for performance, its written text leaves large areas blank. The play reader must learn to fill in these blanks through clues embedded in the text (such clues are, in fact, clues to performance). For example, in a novel, many paragraphs may be devoted to describing the place where the novel takes place; in plays, such lengthy descriptions are absent because the place of the play will be shown visually, through scenery and lighting, in the theatre. A play reader must visualize the place from clues.

Because the playwright, through choices, is constantly shaping the perception of the audience, a reader's job is to discover how. That is, a reader must locate the choices made by the playwright and from these choices try to infer what the playwright wanted to do to audiences, using actors. The task is not always easy because the tendency of any reader is to "believe" the story, to see it as "the way things are." To guard against this tendency, a reader should remember that every play begins as a stack of blank paper and that any story can be told in several different ways, each having quite different results. It is the task of the reader to discover which way the playwright decided to tell the story and what the anticipated results of that decision are.

Thinking Critically

Reading a play means making the effort—and knowing how to make the effort—to understand the play, both how it will appear in the theatre and what choices the playwright made and why. These ideas are often hard to keep in mind because the written play can be read with pleasure *as if* it were self-contained, and it can be

FIGURE 3.1

Creating the World: Environment

A script may call for a specific location or merely suggest an environment. In Shakespeare's *Twelfth Night* the setting is a mythical country, Illyria. The reader must then envision what this imaginary setting might look like. Here, in a Barry University production, Illyria is presented as a timbered, two-story series of platforms with a forestage that suggests a pier.

so convincing that it is hard to imagine it being any other way. But it is important to remember that the written play is only one part of theatre (a play is not self-contained) and that the play results from choices made by a playwright specifically to affect audiences in certain ways.

Reading a play, then, requires techniques of critical thinking that can be learned. In this chapter, we examine the process of play reading in three stages: preliminary work, play analysis, and organizing a coherent response.

PRELIMINARY WORK

Before beginning to read the play, some preliminary work will more than repay the time. The idea here is to get ready to enter a new world: What does the world look like? Who are the "people" living in this world?

Title

Reading begins at the beginning—with the title, the first piece of information. The author believed that the title said something important about the play; therefore, it is a clue to at least one important part of the play. Titles like *Richard II* and *Cats* are straightforward; on the other hand, titles like *Half Off* and *Top Girls* are mysterious until well into the play.

Cast of Characters

This list provides vital information about the size and traits of the cast—their names, ages, gender, and relationships. Introductions are as important in reading a play as they are in entering a room at a party.

Opening Stage Directions

The description of the play's setting (i.e., the place where the play takes place) is usually given here, as are descriptions of the play's opening moments. In plays that have been produced, these stage directions often reflect the actual Broadway or London production; in other plays, they give the playwright's vision. Reading them, we may be able to visualize (and hear) the play's opening.

Time for Questions

The reader should think about the information so far and begin to ask questions. What kind of theatre is being used? What is the historical period of the play? What did buildings, furniture, clothing look like in this period? What is the opening mood—joyful or somber, tense or relaxed? How do characters get on and off the stage? Is the setting indoors or outdoors? Are there doors, and if so, where? Where do the characters enter from?

First Reading

Then, with the beginning as strongly visualized as possible, the reader begins to read the play, underlining and making notes on:

- What happens in the play
- Who makes things happen and who tries to stop things from happening; also, what is the relative importance of the characters
- What key words, images, and ideas run through the play (including the relevance of the title)

Ending

It is important to pause briefly over the ending to contemplate the outcomes of the story. Did the characters achieve their individual goals? Were the outcomes serious or playful? Who ended the play better or worse off than they began it?

After the first reading, the reader is familiar with the play and has a sense of what it is about and what happens in it, as well as who its characters are. The next stage aims at an orderly and informed analysis of the play. Such an analysis may finally result in a judgment about the play.

PLAY ANALYSIS USING THE PARTS OF THE PLAY

Plays can be analyzed from many different points of view. A historian, for example, might read a play to discover something about the period in which it was written; a linguist might read it to study ways in which language is used or ways in which the use of language has changed over time. Many critical methods are available to help with an analysis of plays, and several are discussed in Chapter 5.

Aristotle

A theatre person most often reads a play for information about how it will appear in the theatre. One useful method of extracting this sort of information was first offered by the ancient Greek, Aristotle, whose ideas are adapted here for modern use.

Aristotle identified the following six parts of a play:

1. Plot
2. Character
3. Idea
4. Language
5. Music
6. Spectacle

Two points need to be made here. One, the order of the parts is important because it suggests the precise nature of the relationship among them. Two, the six parts should not be thought of as boxes into which sections of the play are placed; rather, they are parts of a system, a network of interrelationships so connected that a change in any one can have important effects on all others. These relationships are exceedingly complex, but, in brief, reading down the list gives a sense of control (e.g., the nature of the plot controls the kind of characters that must appear in it; the kinds of characters control the kinds of ideas possible in the play, etc.). Reading up the list suggests source materials (e.g., music, in the sense of sounds, is the material out of which language is made; ideas are the material out of which characters are made, etc.)

Although old, this breakdown is still useful. We can go through almost any play and show how every aspect of the play—every speech, movement, and event—relates to these six parts.

Plot

Plot is the ordering of the incidents in a play. This means that plot is not only what happens in the play, but it is also the order in which things are made to happen and the reasons why things are put in that order by the playwright.

PARTS OF PLOT Plot is itself made up of many parts. Aristotle and later critics have offered names for the most common of these parts.

■ Exposition. The giving of information about past events. The greatest amount of exposition often comes at the beginning of the play, when audiences know least about events and characters. In some plays, however, important exposition is delayed

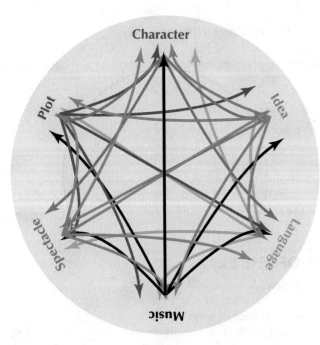

FIGURE 3.2

Parts of a Play

The six parts of a play constitute a system; a change in any one changes all the others. As the arrows show, the relationships are reciprocal: In other words, plot determines the kind of character needed; character is the stuff out of which plot is made.

until very late; in a murder mystery, for example, the most important facts about past events ("whodunit") come at the end.

- **Point of Attack.** The place in the *story* where the playwright begins the *plot*. Greek playwrights tended to begin their *plots* late in the story and so are said to have a late point of attack; Shakespeare tended to begin his plots toward the beginning of his stories and so is said to use an early point of attack (Fig. 3.3).

- **Action.** The central chain of events in the play, particularly because those events are the central character's attempt to achieve an important goal. Action and character are tightly bound and are understood through each other, so that an answer to the question "What is the play's action?" always requires the inclusion of character.

  Successful action in most plays has wholeness, that is, it has a beginning, middle, and end (in terms of logic, not time). The beginning of a play means that nothing necessary comes before it. A play's action usually begins when a character makes a discovery. When characters discover, they usually are led to decide (to act). Discovery therefore propels action and moves a play from its beginning to its middle, during which characters will make other discoveries, some of which will result in a reversal (a change in the direction of the action, usually occasioned by a discovery that is contrary to the character's expectation). The end of a play comes when no necessary action remains.

FIGURE 3.3

Plot and Story

Plot is the arrangement of the incidents, the way the story is told. When plot and story begin at about the same point, the play has an early point of attack. When the plot begins late in the story, the play has a late point of attack.

If the action is not a logical whole, the play will not be understandable to the audience as a work of art. Wholeness is fundamental. It is one of the most important aspects that distinguish art from life.

Unlike a play, a life is not perceivable as a whole, especially while it is being lived. Our lives are diverse and complicated; we carry on several "actions" of which we perceive only dimly (and often incorrectly) the beginnings; the endings are always over life's horizon.

In a play, on the other hand, wholeness is visible and allows the audience to understand, and so to learn. A dramatic character might be confused or out of control or in an identity crisis, but the audience sees the whole of the situation (beginning, middle, and ending) and so is not confused. It is important to remember that drama is able to reveal life to us because it is an invention and not real life.

■ Complication. The opposing or entangling of the action. Often at the beginning of the play the action seems simple: A character desires to accomplish something. Obstacles then complicate this desire, particularly the efforts of other characters to frustrate the action or even to destroy the central character. Complications are most often revealed as discoveries by characters and reversals in the course of the action.

A common kind of complication, one that is central to most (but not all) plays, is conflict. In situations in which one or more characters try to thwart the ideas and actions of another, conflict results. Conflict between characters may provide an easily understandable moral or philosophical opposition (e.g., good versus evil), but other conflicts are between a character and a force (e.g., society, fate, or gods, which may be personified).

Most plots have many complications. Each complication changes or threatens to change the course of the action because the character must deal with the complication before pursuing the original goal. Complications are either caused (by some agency like another character, a god, or a force) or accidental (the result of something like a storm, a flood, or a chance meeting of characters). Caused complications are usually thought to be better than accidental ones, especially in serious plays.

■ Rising Action. Action of increasing complication.

■ Crisis. Derived from the Greek word for decision, crisis means "decisive moment," a turning point in the action. Crisis usually results when the play's major discovery leads to the major reversal. We expect to find rising action from complication to crisis; after the crisis, we anticipate falling action.

■ Falling Action, Resolution, or Denouement. "The untying"—the unraveling of complication, the declining action as crisis is passed and complication is resolved.

KINDS OF PLOT   In one sense, there are as many kinds of plots as there are plays, but some basic patterns tend to repeat and so have been given names. Two in particular can be cited.

Causal Plot (also known as linear, climactic, or antecedent–consequence plot). The incidents of linear plot can be seen to lie along a line of causality from beginning to end. The word *climactic* is sometimes used because such plots build to a climax, the most exciting moment of the plot for the audience. (Note that the term differs from *crisis*; *climax* refers to an audience's response to plot and not to a part of the plot.)

Causal plots are of two major types: single line of development, with no subordinate lines (e.g., Sophocles's *Oedipus the King*), and multiple lines of development, consisting of a major line and several subordinate ones, often called "subplots" (e.g., Shakespeare's *Hamlet*).

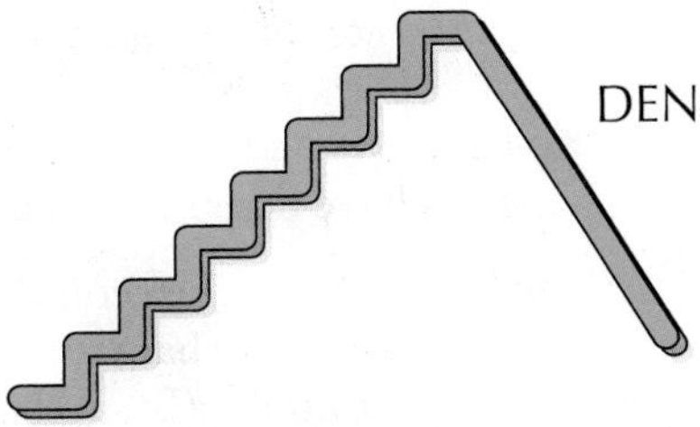

Episodic Plot (also known as contextual or thematic plot). The incidents (episodes) of episodic plot do not follow one another because of causality; rather, they are usually ordered by the exploration of an idea, with each scene exploring a new aspect of a problem or enlarging the study made to that point. Many contemporary plays often employ a nonlinear structure to link scenes by thematic or emotional associations.

Only the imagination of playwrights limits the way plots are organized. Nontraditional and experimental arrangements are constantly being tried, and old organizations, like plots of spectacle, language, or character, are occasionally still used.

Character

A dramatic character and a real human being are not the same thing. Dramatic characters are inventions of playwrights. The fact that dramatic characters pursue human goals, speak human words, and embody human responses means only that dramatic characters are part of an artistic creation that is *about* life, not life itself. Dramatic character is, at best, an imitation of selected aspects of humanity.

In addition to being imitations of people, dramatic characters are functions within a plot. That is, they were created by the playwright to perform certain tasks within the plot. Each character can be analyzed in every scene for its function, using the play's parts: for example, to further the plot, to reveal

CRISIS

DENOUEMENT

COMPLICATION

FIGURE 3.4

Complication, Crisis, and Denouement

Rising action typically comprises many smaller complications. The turning point (crisis) initiates the falling action (denouement).

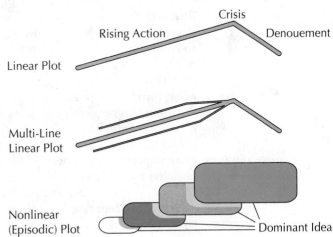

Crisis

Rising Action — Linear Plot — Denouement

Multi-Line Linear Plot

Nonlinear (Episodic) Plot — Dominant Idea

FIGURE 3.5

Kinds of Plot

Greek tragedy typically has a simple linear plot. Shakespearean tragedy has a multilinear plot. Many contemporary plays have episodic plots.

information about character, to express ideas, or to contribute to spectacle. To understand what function a character performs in the plot, it is often helpful to ask *what would not occur* in the story if the character were removed.

KINDS OF CHARACTERS   Some kinds of characters repeat often, and so critics and scholars have designated them as follows:

- Protagonist. The central figure in the main action.
- Confidant. A character in whom the protagonist or another important character confides. (Because this word comes from Latin, sometimes a female character in whom the protagonist confides will be spelled *confidante*, but pronounced the same.)
- Antagonist. In a play with conflict, the character who opposes the protagonist.
- *Raisonneur.* Or author's character—one who speaks for the author, directly giving the author's moral or philosophical ideas; usually not the protagonist.
- Foil. One who sets off another character by contrast: comic where the other is serious, stupid where intelligent, shrewd where naive.

In many plays, characters can be divided into sympathetic and unsympathetic, the former created to appeal to audiences, the latter to repel them. The fate of these groups at the end of plays usually embodies the major moral stance of the play and so should be noted.

CLUES TO CHARACTER   Because playwrights cannot describe characters to us directly, we must seek clues about their appearance, motivations, and behaviors. A reader must remain alert for such clues, especially noting places such as these:

- Stage directions, although some playwrights do not discuss characters in stage directions.
- What other characters say; however, we must understand these other characters to know how to interpret what they say.
- What the characters say about themselves, with the same problem of interpreting what they say.
- What the characters do—their acts.
- Relationships between characters; under increasing complications, the real nature of relationships—hate, love, friendship, dependence, forgiveness—shows more clearly.
- Most important, the plot itself—for example, decision reveals character; complication forces decision. Characters often change as the plot develops; leading characters often behave and think differently at the end of the play; they have "learned." Accounting for such changes helps one gain understanding of both character and play. Some critics even say that "the play is understood by its ending," a great oversimplification but often a useful notion.

Idea

No play is without meanings. A play does not have to be filled with intellectual speeches to offer meanings, and a careful reader learns how to find and understand them. Even the silliest comedy has meaning because it imitates human action and

FIGURE 3.6

Creating the World: Character

The play reader may have only a name and sex and age of the playwright's character but then must imagine the full character, including what is worn and how the character looks. In a theatrical production many artists collaborate to create fully realized characters: Pantalone from the 1600s, a gentleman from the 1800s, a white police officer in Africa, and two characters from contemporary plays produced by Theatre South Carolina.

because it expresses a time and a society. Not all playwrights set out to teach, but we can extract meaning from their plays nonetheless.

Plays seldom offer single, simple meanings. The best offer many meanings, and any attempt to reduce these to "the idea of the play" or "the theme of the play" greatly oversimplifies the work. Meanings fall into two major categories: idea—meanings contained entirely within the play; and extrinsic meaning—those meanings (perhaps wholly unintentional) in the society and the period of which the play is an expression. We are concerned here with idea.

The play's idea comes in part from its plot. We tend to generalize from example, and the playwright, by choosing and ordering events, has created an example (the play). We can then generalize from that example, seeing that (in this playwright's view) certain causes lead to certain (good or bad) events.

In plays organized by conflict, the victor in the conflict may embody the "good" way of behaving, whereas the loser embodies the "bad." They are rewarded or punished accordingly, through, for example, money, love, promotion, or pardon. Comedies often end with the formation of a new society; by discovering who is included and who is excluded from this society, a reader can often grasp the major idea of the play by asking questions: Why were these people included and those excluded? What were the traits of each group? The behaviors of each group?

The play's idea comes also from character. In an effective play, the major ideas are embodied in the character and action of the protagonist. If the character is positive (approved by the author, "good"), then the protagonist embodies a good. These "goods" and "bads"—the defining elements of the play's moral world—are best understood through the system of rewards and punishments in the play. Typically, the protagonist explains his or her own idea near the play's crisis; rewards and punishments usually appear in the play's denouement.

The play's language can also reveal idea. Important characters' speeches before and after crises are especially revealing, as are important characters' speeches when they are on stage alone or with a confidant. The speeches of raisonneurs, especially when close to the complications and crises, often reveal idea, as do many speeches during the denouement when the playwright (through the characters) is tying up questions and resolving issues raised by the play.

Language

As we have seen, language through the speeches of characters is an important carrier of meaning. But language as an act, separate from the meaning of the words, can also reveal idea, as, for example, whenever words or images repeat often in a play. The frequent appearance of the word *death* in a play about love would suggest that the play's idea is probably not "Love conquers all." Similarly, repeated images or metaphors carry meaning. One such image in *Hamlet* is of weeds, which support an idea about the protagonist as fighting against an evil, choking, destructive environment.

As an "act" separate from the meaning of the words, language is also one of the most revealing clues to character. The choice of words and the length of sentences can tell the reader something about the circumstances of a character—social class, level of education, complexity of thought, for example. As well, the rhythm of a character's speech may indicate something about mood or lifestyle.

Music

In musical plays, the importance of music to character, mood, and rhythm is clear. In nonmusical plays, the reader must understand that the language itself embodies music, because language in plays is intended to be spoken aloud. Spoken language inevitably has pitch and rhythm and itself is musical.

Like language, music reveals clues about plot, character, and idea. For example, regular, slow rhythms create different moods from sharp, staccato ones. Verse, especially rhymed verse, is usually more formal than prose; in serious plays, verse seems to add weight to the action, whereas in comedy it often enhances the wit of a line by accentuating a word or nuance.

Spotlight

Stanley and Blanche in this *Streetcar* at
Triad Stage in North Carolina

Reading a Play and Organizing a Response

A Streetcar Named Desire may be the US's
most often-produced play. Written by Tennessee
Williams (1911–1983) and first produced on
Broadway in 1947, *Streetcar* has remained popular with both critics and audiences. The play has
been variously interpreted—as the collapse of the
Old South and the rise of the New, as a struggle
between civilization and savagery, and as a clash
between the sexes. Its most famous scene is the
rape of Blanche DuBois by Stanley Kowalski (the
husband of Blanche's sister, Stella). The critical
excerpt that follows focuses on that scene:

> Because [Blanche] refused to become the
> woman in the traveling salesman joke, the
> stereotype of the nymphomaniacal upper-
> class girl, [Stanley] rapes her. His famous
> line rationalizing the rape, "We've had this
> date with each other from the beginning,"
> summarizes both the struggle for mastery in
> which he and Blanche have engaged, lead-
> ing to the crucial combat, and his ultimate
> reduction of her to the whore of his his-
> tory, who provokes and enjoys yet another
> encounter.... If it ended with the rape, the

play might justifiably be regarded as representing post-war life in the South, where the
most provocative problem was the shift from
the aristocratically dominated tenor of social
intercourse to the first-generation, lower-
middle-class urban mores brought to the fore
by the returning soldiers. But the troubling
focus of *A Streetcar Named Desire* is not that a
drunken man, left alone in a two-room flat of
the French Quarter with his drunken sister-in-
law, subdues and violates her, but that the act
becomes public and the woman is punished.
She is taken away under the consenting gaze
of all the characters on stage.... She had been
victimized by Stanley's—and implicitly patriarchy's—historical discourse.

from "Southern Bellehood (De)Constructed:
A Case Study of Blanche DuBois"
by Biljana Oklopčić

This short excerpt illustrates how an analysis of
a scene can be organized into a written response.
The subject (the rape scene) is introduced by
explaining why Stanley rapes Blanche (she won't
demean herself by becoming a joke or a stereo-
type). Stanley's line of dialogue is used as evidence
to bolster the claim that Stanley and Blanche have
been engaged in a struggle for dominance and
that Stanley plans to win through violence. That
the play does not end with the rape is used as
evidence to conclude that the play is not about
a changing South, another common interpretation of the play. A final bit of evidence—the play's
punishment of the raped woman rather than the
rapist—is used to argue a sociopolitical point: that
this play, by showing a woman overcome by male
violence, can be generalized to a world outside the
play where women are victimized by patriarchy.

The issue is not whether you agree with
this reading of the scene. The issue is that this
evidence supports this reading. Another reader
could have a different response to the scene and
organize another essay.

Craig Schwartz

FIGURE 3.7
Spectacle
The imagined spectacle of the reader will probably prove quite different from the actual spectacle of performance. Here, a production of *Palestine, New Mexico* at Center Theatre Group, Los Angeles. A setting of a dimensional stonelike wall surrounds the stage. Two fires on the ground and the projection of a building behind the stone outcropping complete the sense of spectacle.

Spectacle

In reading, it is especially important to try to visualize the action so that the contribution of spectacle to the performance can be imagined. To be sure, much of the spectacle in today's theatre is the work of designers, whose individual genius cannot be predicted from the page. The cues for their work are there, however, in the same text the reader uses. The imagination must work to keep spectacle in the mind's eye while reading.

Spectacle, like language, can embody idea, clarify character, and forward plot. A burning cross on stage captures a racial situation that needs no words to describe; two female characters, one dressed in red and the other in pink, predispose us to think of them as differing in their degree of "feminine propriety"; a pistol drawn from a purse may be enough to cause the antagonist to retreat in defeat and the protagonist to prevail, without any words being spoken, because in this instance what is seen (the spectacle) is enough to communicate the idea.

Spectacle—which on stage is always working on the sense of sight—is the hardest of the six parts to understand from the text. It is necessary to imagine it as fully as possible, but the imagined spectacle of the reader will probably prove quite different from the actual spectacle of performance, although both should probably suggest the same meanings.

ORGANIZING A RESPONSE

The result of a play analysis should be an organized response to the text. An organized response should be *informed* (based on a knowledge of drama and theatre), *orderly* (consistent and well reasoned), and *defensible* (based on the evidence offered by the text and capable of explanation to somebody else).

Response Based on the Parts of a Play

Analysis should reveal how the parts work together in the play. A response probably should not simply begin with plot and then move to each part in turn, but any response will want to be based on answers to questions about the parts, questions like:

- Is the plot internally consistent? How is the plot organized? What is its point of attack? Its crisis? Its major complications?
- Is each character active, interesting, and consistent? Does each have a function throughout? What would or would not happen if the character were removed from the play?
- Are the play's ideas important, and are they embedded in character and plot?
- Is the language interesting and expressive?
- Does the play's music (including its spoken language) support and enrich character and idea?
- Is the spectacle interesting and appropriate? Does it support rather than overwhelm the other parts of the play? What opportunities for spectacle are suggested?

Response Based on Genres

The word genre means simply a kind or type. In general literature, the word customarily refers to such types as novel, poetry, and drama. Within drama, the word is used to distinguish recurring types (specifically recurring forms) of drama—tragedy, comedy, and so on.

Generic criticism is a major branch of dramatic criticism, so much so that whole books have been written about, for example, the nature of tragedy. Our understanding of genres often changes under historical pressure, so that within any one category we can have several kinds—neoclassical tragedy, Romantic tragedy, heroic tragedy, and so on. Here it is possible to give only the broadest useful definitions of five major genres:

1. **Tragedy.** A work of the highest seriousness, with a serious protagonist in a serious action with serious consequences. Human decision is central to tragic action.
2. **Comedy.** A work whose issues are usually social and mundane (rather than spiritual or moral), with a protagonist involved in an action without deeply serious consequences. Usually, as well, human decision is limited, comic characters being comic because they are locked into types or into intense self-interest.
3. **Tragicomedy.** A work that mixes elements of tragedy and comedy, often by giving otherwise serious plays a happy ending, or vice versa, but often by conferring a degree of seriousness on characters and subjects usually not so treated.
4. **Melodrama.** A work of apparent seriousness with issues cast in terms of extremes (good and evil), the actual issues being less profound than the language suggests. Endings often show good rewarded and evil punished, in keeping with characters who are aligned according to morality; good (hero, heroine) and evil (villain).

5. **Farce.** A comic work whose aim is laughter, from a non-English word meaning "to stuff," indicating that farce is stuffed with laughter-producing elements. The typical protagonist in farce pursues a mundane, often trivial action, and characters often lack decision. Both the characters and the plots of farce have been called mechanical, and it is in the working out of its machinery that farce often provokes its best laughter.

To organize an informed, orderly, and defensible response, either in speech or in writing, a reader uses an analysis based on the parts of a play and its genre. Such a response should go beyond personal response to the play (although personal response is important). It should demonstrate an understanding of the play and how it might work in the theatre; it should not be merely a gut reaction. Certainly, part of the enjoyment of theatre depends on gut reaction—but only part.

KEY TERMS

Check your understanding against this list. Brief definitions are included in the Glossary; persons are page-referenced in the Index.

action 33	crisis 34	idea 37
antagonist 36	denouement 34	plot 32
causal plot 34	discovery 33	point of attack 33
character 35	episodic plot 35	protagonist 36
climax 35	exposition 32	*raisonneur* 36
complication 34	foil 36	reversal 33
confidant 36	generic criticism 41	rising action 34
conflict 34	genre 41	spectacle 40

4

How to See a Play

Do these dancers in a scene from *Pride and Prejudice* seem to be in the period of Jane Austin's 1813 novel? Do the lighting and setting seem strange?

OBJECTIVES

When you have completed this chapter, you should be able to:

- Describe major differences between reading and seeing a play.

- Explain how an experienced audience member can both participate in and observe a performance.

- Explain differences between actor and character and between real person and dramatic character.

- Explain differences between plot and story.

- Explain differences between dramatic and theatrical styles and discuss how they may be related.

EXPERIENCING THE PERFORMANCE

Reading a play and watching a performance are different sorts of activities. The play text comes to us only as words on a page. The performance that we see results from putting together several arts—the written text, the actors, the scenery, costumes, and lighting. Text is repeatable, but performance is not—we watch it moment by moment, responding to many stimuli (e.g., sensual, emotional, and intellectual) and unconsciously fusing them into a whole. The written text appeals to our intellect and emotions; performance in the theatre appeals most immediately to our senses and only through them to our intellect and emotions.

Taking It In

Studying a play is, therefore, different from studying a performance. In studying a play text, we analyze—we take a play apart to see how it *might* work on stage. In studying a performance, we "take it in" through our senses (mostly sight and hearing) and see and hear how it *does* work on stage. In analyzing a play, we can stop to think or return to a difficult passage to reconsider it. In studying a performance, we watch and hear a moment go by—in real time; later we can only *recall* (not retrieve) that moment.

For such reasons, criticism of performance requires an approach somewhat different from that of play analysis.

Performance criticism can use, cautiously, Aristotle's six parts of a play text, but with the understanding that the nature of theatre radically alters the relationships between these parts. For example, spectacle takes on more importance because theatre is visual. Modern theatre especially has endowed spectacle with great meaning—in the ability of light to focus attention and create mood, in the ability of setting and costume to give information about time and place, and so on.

In the analysis of a play text, plot, character, idea, and language dominate. But in the analysis of a performance, these four parts (residing mostly in the play) are submerged within and expressed through music and spectacle, through being spoken by actors and appearing physically on stage (Fig. 4.1).

An example can clarify this point: Character in a play text is revealed only through written words. Character in performance, however, is revealed through the work of the actor, for whom the written text (and its six parts) is the basis of the artistic creation *but is not the artistic creation itself.* Character in performance depends not only on what the words of the play *say* but also on what the actor *does*—with voice, body, costume, and makeup. To discover character in performance (to understand what the actor is doing with and to the text) means to ask not only the questions asked during play analysis but

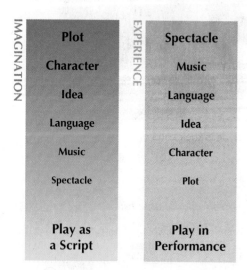

FIGURE 4.1

Parts of Performance

In reading a play, plot, character, and idea claim first attention; in watching a play, spectacle, music, and language seem to dominate.

another set as well, including such questions as these: How does the actor say the words? How does the actor react to the words and actions of others? How does he or she stand? move? wear costumes? create rhythms? create images?

New Questions

Performance criticism thus introduces a whole new set of questions to textual analysis: What are the arts of the actor, the scenic designer, the costume designer, and the lighting designer? And how are these arts fused with the written play?

- Play analysis examines only the art of the playwright; performance criticism, however, examines the arts of the other theatre makers as well. For this reason, Aristotelian analysis remains a good starting point for thinking about performance, but it is only a starting point; it must be supplemented.
- Performance criticism means looking in two directions at once—at the play and at the audience because performance binds the written play to a particular audience. Play analysis and performance analysis are thus inevitably linked, but they are different.

Lenny Cohen

FIGURE 4.2

Point of View

The script is the foundation for a production, but the director's approach can startle an audience. This production at Triad Stage of Ibsen's *Hedda Gabler* upends many of the conventions associated with the original 1891 production.

In analyzing play texts, we saw that playwrights made decisions aimed at shaping the perceptions of the reader. In analyzing productions, we see that each theatre artist is also making such decisions. That is, actors build their performances through a series of decisions, each aimed at promoting a certain understanding and eliciting a specific response from the audience. Designers envision and then build their costumes and settings, their stage lighting and sound tracks, so as to communicate certain ideas to their audiences and to evoke certain kinds of responses from them. Whereas playwrights have only a general audience in mind, theatre artists must prepare their productions for specific audiences that will be physically present in the theatre. Just as play analysis requires an effort to remember that a playwright is trying to persuade the reader to a certain point of view about a series of events, a performance analysis requires us to remember that theatre artists have made decisions to create *this* performance as it is.

Any play carries within it possibilities for many different productions, some similar, others wildly different. One production might try to reproduce the play more or less as the playwright created it; another production might try to modernize the play, bringing its appearance and approach more in line with contemporary values; still another might use the elements of production to comment on or even critique the world of the play (the world created by the playwright) exposing its ideas as unworthy or unjust. Just as play analysis requires an effort to discover and understand the choices of the playwright, performance analysis means trying to see and understand the choices made by theatre artists, who want us to accept the performance as they have envisioned it.

Just as play analysis requires us to think critically about what we read, performance analysis requires us to think critically as we watch the performance unfold in the theatre. We can consider the techniques of performance criticism in three parts: preliminary work, performance analysis, and organizing a response.

PRELIMINARY WORK

The preliminary work of performance criticism begins before the audience member arrives at the theatre and continues to the opening of the curtain. The preliminary work includes considering:

- The art of theatre itself
- The nature of the work itself
- The program distributed to the audience
- The clues offered by the theatre's physical surroundings

The Art of Theatre

Analyzing a performance means in part knowing enough about theatre to do so. Knowing the role of each theatre artist, for example, enhances the ability to understand a performance. Understanding the role of the theatre audience in performance—that it can affect performance and so has some responsibility to "work" with actors in creating the event—suggests a need to consider responses as a part of the critique of performance.

Thus, knowledge of the art of theatre supports a critique of any single performance. Attending theatrical performances, taking courses in theatre arts, and reading books about theatre provide this general knowledge. In a lifetime of attending plays and reading about theatre, a person becomes a knowledgeable member of an audience and so is better equipped to engage in performance criticism.

The Work Itself

An audience member should take the time to learn something about the material to be performed before arriving at the theatre. Some people like to read a play before seeing it; others prefer simply to learn something about it through reviews and advertisements. From whatever source, audience members should arrive at the theatre with a general idea of what they are going to see because expectations will affect the way a performance is perceived. Just because *Cat on a Hot Tin Roof* has a funny-sounding title does not make this play a comedy, and anyone arriving at the theatre expecting a comedy might be angered or confused by the performance. Taking children to see *Who's Afraid of Virginia Woolf?* because it sounds like a children's story will probably result in an unhappy shock.

The Program

An audience member should read the program before the play begins. It almost always indicates the place or places where the action will unfold and introduces the characters who will appear on stage, giving their names and sometimes major

FIGURE 4.3

What to Expect

The title of the production and signs advertising it suggest what an audience might expect. *We Will Rock You* seems to promise raucous music and romance, according to this sign outside a Madrid theatre.

relationships. Programs may include a synopsis of the play's major action, high-lighting the most important moments and thereby suggesting where the audience's attention should focus. Sometimes in the program there will be notes written by the director, designer, or dramaturg. Such notes may be especially helpful because they sometimes point to the major issues with which the production grapples or explain the director's special point of view in staging this play. The program may also indicate where intermissions occur and for how long. (Programs also often offer helpful, if inessential, information, such as what good restaurants are close to the theatre and what attractions are coming next to that theatre.)

The Physical Surroundings

An audience member will be repaid for spending a few minutes looking around the theatre and listening to sounds because theatre artists will often try to establish a proper mood for a play even before it begins. Country-and-western music in the background probably reveals something important about the production and sets a mood quite different from that established by a Bach concerto or a rap song. Lighting may be used to establish mood, and scenery (where visible) may suggest things like time, place, and social class.

Sometimes oddities (e.g., small platforms with scenery or lighting stands) appear in an area normally reserved for audience seating. Such spaces alert an audience member that the performance may spill over from the stage and into the auditorium, a signal that the production may be unusual in other ways as well.

The purpose of the preliminary work is to become prepared for the moment when the performance itself begins. The more prepared for the performance, the better able the audience is to follow the performance as it moves at its own rate through time.

PERFORMANCE ANALYSIS

The goal of performance analysis is to help the audience member reach greater enjoyment through understanding—not merely a statement like "I really liked that," or "I was bored." Rather, the audience member needs to be able to explain the reasons behind such responses. These reasons usually have to do with the selection of the play, the appropriateness and skill of the actors, the suitability of the visual elements, and so on. Much of the rest of this book deals with ways of understanding and evaluating the several arts involved in performance. The purpose of this section, however, is to offer a way of looking at the contributions of these arts and to serve as an introduction to issues involved in the complex problem of performance analysis.

Watching while Participating

To analyze a performance, an audience member must do two things at once: participate in the performance (i.e., entering into the action, empathizing with the characters, and so on) and watch the performance (i.e., "standing back" from the story and characters to observe how the effects are being achieved). This dual

Spotlight

Uta Hagen as Desdemona in Shakespeare's *Othello*.

Seeing a Play: Performing Character

Blanche DuBois in *A Streetcar Named Desire* is one of the great roles in the US's theatrical repertory. The first two women to perform it were Jessica Tandy and Uta Hagen; both received rave reviews on Broadway. Because they appeared within months of one another, people compared them. What the comparisons revealed was that two different Blanches could come from the same script. One critic described their differences:

In Miss Tandy's acting Blanche's mental collapse was closer to the surface throughout the play and the agony of the last act [which includes the rape scene] was implicit in the preliminary scenes. Blanche had slipped into the limbo of the psychopathic world before the time of the play....Although [Miss Hagen's] Blanche is overwrought from the beginning, the evil furies attack her at specific moments in the narrative and she slips over the borderline in the course of the play.

This is a point of view that leaves the first act with less significance than it had in Miss Tandy's performance. But it fills the last act with terrifying wildness. Hagen is a decisive actress of great strength and power who has constructed the part with lucid deliberation, artfully underscoring the meaning of individual scenes. When the malevolence of the world tortures Blanche beyond the point of endurance, Miss Hagen reaps the reward of her method and vividly describes the agony, fright and loneliness of a woman who has been pushed out of human society into the pitiless seclusion of madness.

> Quoted in "Alternative Visions of Blance DuBois: Uta Hagen and Jessica Tandy in *A Streetcar Named Desire*" by Susan Spector

Some of these differences came from the techniques of the actresses themselves, but some too came from quite different views of the play. Elia Kazan, who directed Tandy, wrote that, from Stanley Kowalski's point of view, Blanche was a destructive and dangerous woman who, if left alone, could wreck his home. (Kazan adopted Stanley's point of view, even confessing that he hated Blanche.) When Hagen took over the role, she disagreed with this interpretation and requested a different director (who, incidentally, never got credit). Together they found a Blanche who "was the victim of a destructive society rather than a madwoman disrupting a healthy world." The result was that "Hagen's Blanche...left audiences feeling they had watched a delicate woman driven insane by a brutish environment epitomized by Stanley Kowalski. Tandy's Blanche...left audiences feeling that a madwoman had entered an alien world and after shaking that world had been successfully exorcised."

Clearly, drama and performance differ. In *Streetcar*, both actresses spoke the same words, wore identical costumes, and moved within the same stage settings, but their characters were different because their interpretations of the play were different. Neither actress's interpretation is right or wrong. One script can contain many performances. Analysis of drama and of performance also differs. In dramatic analysis, scripts can be consulted repeatedly for evidence, but in performance analysis, evidence exists in seeing the performance or relying on accounts of others who saw the performance.

view of performance is as rewarding as it is difficult to achieve, but with practice any audience member can learn to participate and observe simultaneously. (This is not to say that audience members *must* analyze a performance to serve the audience's role in the theatre; most audience members are content with just the experience.) Again, if carefully used, Aristotle's ideas can help us think through this dual view, and the vocabulary in Chapter 3 can, with adaptation, serve us here as well. The play's central values in performance are its story, characters, and ideas, reached through language, music, and spectacle as expressed in acting, scenery, costumes, lighting, and sound.

Values Inherent in the Play

Drama as imitation of human action allows audience members to generalize from particular stories, characters, and ideas to more general human truths. Because the stories, characters, and ideas are invented and concentrated for the play, they seem even more important than similar events (unselected and unfocused) seem in real life. Thus, the concentration of theatre art accounts for much of its power, but that same concentration complicates the task of performance analysis.

STORY   Plays as imitations of human actions are compelling because they tell stories. Story is similar to, but not identical with, Aristotle's plot. While experiencing theatre, we cannot analyze plot—we cannot perceive the ordering of the incidents and the reasons for that ordering—we can only follow and respond to the story of the play, to the tale of "what happened."

Stories are made up of incidents that have coherence; that is, the incidents are related to one another for a reason. Stories are not only compelling in themselves (we are interested in what happens), but they are also compelling because they serve as the framework within which the characters, words, ideas, and values of the play unfold. In a sense, then, we understand the characters, ideas, and values of a performed play through the story that it tells. It follows that if a production fails to "tell the story," little else the production does much matters.

FIGURE 4.4

Altering the Given Circumstances

Pericles, one of Shakespeare's lesser plays, was presented in 2010 by the Utah Shakespeare Festival under the title *The Adventures of Pericles*. The narrator in *Pericles*, re-imagined as a modern high tech archeologist seen at the right, selects the scenes from Pericles adventures over 15 years for the audience to experience.

Suspense.   Suspense is the unfolding of events in such a way that audiences want to know what happens next. "And then what happens?" they ask. Suspense requires preparation—curiosity must be created. And suspense must be satisfied—the audience must learn what happens, and what happens must be understandable in terms of what the audience expected might happen. Suspense, then, requires preparation, connectedness, and resolution.

Surprise.   A happening that is unexpected at the time but quite logical when viewed in retrospect is called surprise. Therefore, surprises, to work, must be prepared for within the world of the performance; that is, surprises are not the same as mistakes or accidents. For example, if during a love scene on stage a bed collapses, it is a surprise if the bed was supposed to collapse (perhaps for purposes of comedy); if the scenery simply broke down, it is not a surprise but an accident.

CHARACTERS   In performance, characters and story are interrelated, as characters and plot are in a play. We understand each through the other. But characters in performance, unlike characters in a play, are created by the actors' choices of vocal and physical traits as well as by the words printed on the pages of the play text and the decisions and actions in that text. Characters in performance are therefore complex creations that are based on the characters in the play but are nonetheless different from them.

Audiences respond to characters for different reasons. Often characters are appealing because audiences can identify with them. "I recognize myself in that character" or "I can identify with her" are strong sources of pleasure or suffering in the theatre. We like to see the mirror held up so that we can watch those like ourselves. Audience members recognize others they know in characters, too. "Isn't that something Uncle Albert would do!" This human response may be the essential appeal of stories, whether novels, plays, or other literary forms. Some characters are said to have universal appeal (or to be a universal character); the appeal of such characters is that they are recognizably like human beings of many different times and places.

Some characters appeal to feelings deep within us. Such characters, we say, appeal to us at a subconscious level, through some subconscious reference. For example, the Greek tragedy *Oedipus Rex* has survived for two thousand years. One critic said it causes us to "think the unthinkable"—a man who has children by his mother after unwittingly murdering his father. All these things are in the play text. But in performance they are given a terrible immediacy that gives them life, size, and horror—*this* man and woman, *this* bloodshed, *this* scream.

Still other characters appeal because we recognize others in them, a trait especially clear in the case of historical characters. Seeing an actor portray a character we think we know offers a special treat for audiences, who will often flock to see an actor portray former luminaries in works such as *Abe Lincoln in Illinois* or *Picasso at the Lapin Agile*. Here the delight is not only in enjoying the character in the performed play but also in watching to see how closely the actor meets our preconceptions of the real person. To take advantage of this associative response, the performance must depict people with whom the audience has strong ties and must present them in convincing—and perhaps visually recognizable—ways.

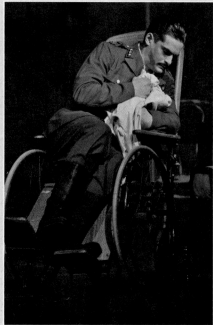

Pete Smith

FIGURE 4.5

Character

Audiences are attracted to some characters because they seem recognizable, whereas other characters are inviting because they represent something exotic. Here, scenes from *The Shape of Things* at Purdue University Theatre (*left*) and of *Macbeth* at the University of Michigan. Are these characters recognizable or exotic? The woman in *Shape* may be triumphant or dominating. Her hair, costume, and the video camera says she is in the recent time. *Macbeth,* from the costuming and wheelchair, is late nineteenth or early twentieth century. The soldier is removed, probably sad. Does his sadness make him "like us" or does the one hundred or so year gap from him to us make him exotic?

IDEA   Often the ideas that are revealed through a performance are given the least thought while we sit in the theatre and watch, but they are what we talk about most once we leave the theatre. There is a good reason for this phenomenon. Performance is transitory; theatre is "the home of the Now." When we leave the theatre, the vividness of the acting—the onstage images and sounds—fades. We seldom remember sensory stimuli clearly; afterward we can only describe them. We are therefore left with the intellectual content of the play in performance, which is verbally expressible and so may remain fresh and sharp in our minds.

In fact, the ideas within the performance may become more important with the passing of time. If experiencing the immediacy of the performance has moved us, it has become part of our lives, and now we want to know what it means to us.

Ideas are embedded in all play texts and performances. Some ideas are more interesting and more important than others, to be sure, but ideas exist in all. Whereas the ideas of play texts come mostly through the plot and dialogue, ideas in performance come most immediately through the specific choices made by the actors and designers (of scenery, costumes, lighting, and properties). For example, images in performance can communicate ideas vividly, even without words (although words, of course, deepen and extend the ideas). For example, an actor with a shaved head, wearing paramilitary garb, quite clearly communicates an ideology even before he speaks. A set that positions a computer so that it looms menacingly above the actors makes a clear (although nonverbal) statement of a power relationship, a statement that the actors' words and performance enhance and modify. It is through such means that specific performances of Shakespeare's *Julius Caesar* have offered ideas about Nazi Germany and South American dictatorships, even though the play's ideas were about the nature of rule in Republican Rome and, perhaps, Elizabethan England.

Ideas that are not well integrated into the performance are distracting and theatrically unsatisfying. Indeed, to update an old theatrical adage, "If you want to send a message, use Twitter." The saying means that ideas are not the end-all or be-all of performance. Ideas are only one important element in judging the importance of a play in performance, even though they tend to dominate later discussions of performance, lingering after the immediate, sensory elements of performance have faded from memory.

Idea in performance succeeds only if other, theatrical values of the play succeed because ideas come to audiences through the other elements of specific performance.

Aspects of the Specific Performance

Story, character, and idea reside mostly in play text; music (what we hear) and spectacle (what we see) reside in performance. Indeed, the word *theatre* literally means "seeing place," and auditorium "hearing place"; the spectator is one who watches, the audience those who listen. Therefore, audience members will also want to ask questions about the elements of performance that may be distinct from the play text itself. Three such elements are central to understanding most performances: the given circumstances of the performance, its theatrical conventions, and its style.

GIVEN CIRCUMSTANCES   We may define the given circumstances of a performance as those basic traits that determine the world of the stage: the age, sex, social class, and physical health of the characters; the time and place of the action; the mood established on the stage; and so on.

Usually, the written play determines the given circumstances, but not always. For example, the play *Everyman* comes from the English Middle Ages, and so the performance usually proceeds as if it were unfolding then and there. But a director may wish to emphasize the timelessness of this action and so perform it as if it were taking place in England of the 1990s or in the US West during the gold rush. In producing a French comedy of the 1660s, a director might want to do it "authentically," making it as close as possible to what the original production might have looked like. Or the director might decide that the fun within the play is more important than the circumstances of its original production and so select materials based on their brightness and color, even using techniques of cartoons or caricatures as guiding principles. Clearly all such decisions will necessarily affect not only the visual aspects of the production but also the sounds selected as background and the techniques used by the actors.

MAKING IT CLEAR   Whatever the decision about given circumstances, the circumstances for every production must be made clear to the audience through the visual aspects of production (i.e., scenery, costumes, lighting, and properties), the sounds and music of the production, and the work of the actors. An audience member engaged in performance criticism must determine what the given circumstances of production are and then examine how those circumstances were communicated through the arts of production. Only then can some evaluation of this aspect of production be made through answering questions like these:

- What seem to be the source and purpose of the production's given circumstances?
- Are the circumstances clear?
- Are they consistent throughout the production?

CONVENTIONS   A convention can be thought of as a contract between theatre artists and audiences, an agreement to do things a certain way for the good of all. It is a shortcut between what is meant and what is done. Each of the arts within theatre has conventions. Several examples can clarify.

In today's theatre, it is a convention that months or years can pass between the acts of a play, even though common sense tells us that, in fact, only a few minutes have passed.

A convention in scenic design is the agreement between actors and audience that when a setting depicts a room of a house, a door in that room leads to another room of the house or to the outdoors. Common sense tells us that the door actually leads to an area backstage. Another sort of scenic convention allows a yellow circle hung aloft to represent the sun.

An acting convention from the eighteenth century was that a hand raised to the forehead, palm out and the eyes cast upward, indicated suffering.

In musicals, characters sing their emotions. This use of music is a convention because common sense tells us that music neither accompanies our lives nor changes as we shift activities and moods.

Such agreements between artists and audiences enhance performance and so work for the good of both. Audience members trying to understand and evaluate a performance need to watch for the conventions operating in a production:

- Are the conventions clear?
- Are the conventions similar to other, familiar theatrical conventions? To conventions on television? Or are they in some way distinctive?
- Do the conventions seem aimed at promoting the view that the onstage world is quite like real life, or do they aim rather to call attention to the differences of the stage from life?

FIGURE 4.6

Abstraction

This setting has been significantly abstracted by the water that runs through the plank-board floor of the setting in a rather formal manner. Note the musicians for this production of *Brother Wolf* at Triad Stage, North Carolina.

G. Allen Aycock

STYLE   The word *style* is one of the most useful and yet one of the most confusing that is applied to any art. Part of the confusion comes from the word being used in so many ways in daily life: Clothes are "stylish"; there is "New Orleans–style" jazz, different from "Chicago style"; there are kosher-style dill pickles; many performers are said to have their own personal "style."

In art, including theatre art, the word *style* is used to describe a recurring cluster of traits that seem to set one type off from another type of the same art—two styles of painting, for example, or two styles of music. Dramas (written texts) have style, and so do performances. It is therefore possible to speak both of dramatic style and theatrical style.

Generally, a play written in a particular style will also be performed in that style; that is, the dramatic and theatrical styles are the same. But in some instances (for reasons we return to later), theatre artists may decide that the performance should be in a style different from that of the written play.

Styles tend to change over time. For example, some seventeenth-century plays and productions displayed something we now call a neoclassical style, whereas early nineteenth-century plays and productions generally showed what we call a romantic style. Contemporary theatre is marked by its tendency to use many different styles among its productions, but, for a single production, there is usually a single style.

Abstraction.   Expressing reality through formal qualities rather than observable realistic detail is called abstraction. An artist can choose any point along a continuum from quite abstract to wholly lifelike. For example, a painting that is simply a splash of red interrupted by dots of black is quite abstract, whereas a near-photographic portrait of Marilyn Monroe is quite lifelike.

Similarly, a theatre artist can either:

- Reproduce observable reality
- Render parts of reality as generalized but understandable shapes
- Abandon reality almost entirely

For example, scenic designers might choose to reconstruct a room on stage, making it as much like a real room as possible; they might make all walls transparent and use furniture specially made of steel; or they might choose to show only an open space with platforms and geometric shapes. Lighting designers might, through color and angle, suggest real sunlight, or they might choose to flood the acting area with blue light. Costume designers might use real clothes taken from a thrift shop, or they might construct a covering of metal and cardboard in such a way as to disguise the shape of the human body.

Decisions about the level of abstraction are choices about style and are themselves often closely related to the selection and use of detail.

Detail. At issue here are both the *amount* and the *kind* of detail. Again, an artist can choose anything along a continuum from no detail to overwhelming detail, and along various continua of kinds of detail: natural/artificial, expensive/cheap, urban/rural, and so on. For example, the abstract painting could be a splash of solid red with a single black dot, or it could be highly textured layers of many shades of red with numerous black dots of varying textures. The portrait of Marilyn Monroe might show her dressed in a solid fabric or in a highly patterned one, wearing no jewelry or bedecked in brooches and rings.

Similarly, theatre artists can make choices about amounts and kinds of detail. An actor, for example, can move often, crossing the stage, sitting and standing, gesturing nervously (much detail); or she might remain quite still, using no gestures, and speak in a monotone (little detail). A scenic designer may fill a room with furniture and bric-a-brac (much detail) or leave the same room utterly unadorned except for a single chair stage center (little detail). The costume designer might choose a rich silk dress covered with dollar signs sewn in sequins (much detail) or a plain black leotard (little detail).

Again, all such decisions are matters of style, and they often interact with the materials selected for rendering the details.

FIGURE 4.7

Style: Detail

Here, a scene from *Angels in America: Millennium Approaches* is set in an imagined Antarctica. The unrealistic background and the pinpoints of light are details that suggest the scene is a dream. Here, a production at Wake Forest University.

Material.   Choosing material means making decisions about such things as mass, line, color, and texture. Different materials produce different effects. An oil painting differs from a charcoal sketch; a building in stone differs from one in wood.

In theatre, too, certain kinds of materials predispose audiences in certain ways. For example, a setting built entirely of aluminum tubing calls on an audience's association with science or industry, perhaps, and invites a sense of detachment, coldness, cleanness. Such a setting is different from an otherwise identical setting made of bare wood, which an audience might associate with a previous time and so derive a sense of tradition, comfort, and warmth. Similarly, costumes made of burlap will "say" something to an audience quite different from otherwise identical costumes made of satin or wool or cotton, each of which encourages its own set of associations.

Line and Texture.   In examining visual elements in production, performance critics must therefore ask such questions as:

- Are the colors pastel or saturated?
- Are the textures smooth and shiny or rough and pocked?
- Are lines curved or jagged?
- Are masses large and unbroken or broken up?

Actors   Although more difficult, similar questions about actors can lead to an understanding of their style:

- Do the actors seem to be real people involved (unknowingly) in a real situation, or are they clearly aware of themselves as performers (perhaps they address the audience directly from time to time)?
- Are the actors using many small details of voice and movement, or are they relatively still, both vocally and physically?
- What materials of voice and body have the actors selected for the performance (soft or loud voices, erect or slouching posture, and so on)?

ORGANIZING A RESPONSE

The result of critiquing a performance should be an organized response to the performance itself. Because most performances are based on plays, a piece of performance criticism will most often need to address two related questions:

- What are the major values of the play?
- How are these values revealed or transformed through performance?

As with play text analysis, performance criticism should be *informed* (based on knowledge of theatre), *orderly* (consistent and well reasoned), and *defensible* (based on evidence offered by the performance itself and capable of explanation to someone else).

Good performance criticism often synthesizes the values of play and performance; that is, the critic does *not* usually begin with a discussion of story, characters, and idea and then move to a discussion of given circumstances, convention, and style. Rather, the critic tries to communicate how the performance (i.e., the work of the actors, director, and designers) reveals the story, characters, ideas, and values of the play. In the course of the discussion, many of the questions given in this chapter will be answered for the particular production.

Some other guiding questions might be the following:

- Are the given circumstances of the production clear? How do they relate to the given circumstances of the play itself? How are these given circumstances made clear?
- What are the conventions of the production? Do they seem to work with those of the play? How or how not?
- What is the style of the production, and how is that style achieved? Is it the same style of the written play (if that question is answerable)? Are the various theatrical arts in the same style?
- Is the story clear? How do the several elements of production enhance its suspense and surprises?
- Are all characters clear? Are they interesting? How has each actor made the character clear? Interesting? How have the several elements of design contributed to these goals?
- Are the ideas clear? Compelling? What elements of production have worked to further these goals?
- Did the audience seem attentive and appreciative, and how did the audience responses fit with my own?

KEY TERMS

Check your understanding against this list. Brief definitions are included in the Glossary; persons are page-referenced in the Index.

abstraction 55	story 50
auditorium 53	style 55
convention 54	surprise 51
given circumstances 53	suspense 51

5

Mediating the Art and Business of Theatre

The revival of *South Pacific* at Lincoln Center Theatre was a good business move as well as an artistic success.

OBJECTIVES

When you have completed this chapter, you should be able to:

- Distinguish between those who influence the art of the theatre and those who influence the business of theatre.

- Explain what constitutes a good theory.

- Discuss the kinds of questions that theorists ask.

- Distinguish between a critic and a reviewer.

- Discuss what a dramaturg does.

- Describe what experts in marketing, public relations, and advertising do.

- Compare modernism and postmodernism.

- Describe the roles of agents and casting directors.

Mediators indirectly shape audiences and performances. They "mediate" because they stand between entities: art and business, performance and audience, and so on. They influence which plays and performances are available and how plays are read and performances are seen. Mediators may not work directly with artists or performances in the theatre, but they nevertheless help mold the perceptions of audience members and sometimes those of theatre artists as well. Mediators, then, are intermediaries who link an audience to a performance or an artist to a production.

Mediators both produce and use theory and criticism, sometimes only to explore intellectual possibilities, sometimes to sell tickets. They sometimes act as consumer advocates, suggesting which plays are worth seeing.

Theorists, critics, reviewers, and dramaturgs mediate the art of the theatre. Agents, casting directors, and marketing people—public relations experts, advertising agencies—mediate the business of the theatre.

MEDIATORS OF THEATRE ART

Theorists

A theory is an intellectual construct that seeks to explain a phenomenon. In theatre, there are two kinds of theories: dramatic theory, which deals with plays (e.g., Aristotle's theory of tragedy) and performance theory, which deals with live performance and has no single example comparable to Aristotle.

Theorists seek to answer such questions as: What is theatre? What is drama? They may seek to answer questions about genre as well: What is tragedy? What is comedy? They may seek to answer social or political questions: What role has theatre played in the maintenance of the status quo? How is drama implicated in racism?

An ideal theory meets several requirements. It should be:

- Systematic, meaning that it is reasoned and orderly
- Internally consistent, meaning that no one part of it contradicts any other part
- Sufficient, meaning that it gives all the information necessary to understand the phenomenon
- Congruent, meaning that it accounts for all available evidence and contradicts none

Theories are thought better still when they offer their dense explanations both briefly and clearly.

THEATRICAL THEORIES TODAY   There are no ideal theories. One can examine, for example, a play through any number of theories.

Theories of drama and theatre have multiplied in the postmodern period— that is, the period since just after World War II, when many previous assumptions about the nature of truth as "scientifically verifiable" and "objective" have come under serious attack. Most postmodern theories rest on new assumptions about

G. Allen Aycock

Courtesy NyghtFalcon

FIGURE 5.1

Modernism and Postmodernism

Productions of *Tobacco Road* and *The Diary of Anne Frank* at Triad Stage in North Carolina illustrate the sharp contrasts of modern and postmodern staging. With a run-down trailer as a background, *Tobacco Road*'s setting is crammed with realistic detail, clearly a modern approach. The steeply slanted overhead nonrealistic structure and a random array of nonperiod furniture for *The Diary of Anne Frank* signal a postmodern approach.

the world and people's place in it, which the following comparisons between modernism and postmodernism may help clarify:

Modernism rests on:	Postmodernism rests on:
The industrial age	The information age
Reason, science	Nihilism, meaninglessness
Causality	Randomness and probability
Hierarchy and authority	Participation, dialogue
Autonomous individuals	Socially shaped people
History as progressive	History as nonlinear, discontinuous
Dualities, opposites	Differences rather than opposites

The multiplication of theories of drama and theatre is itself an expression of postmodernism, which prizes difference and chance.

Among the most important current theories are the following:

- Feminist Theory. An amalgam of film theory and a branch of psychoanalytic theory, with various goals: for example, to study a historically male theatre vis-à-vis women, to examine gender in performance, and to define a feminist aesthetic.
- Marxist Theory. An attempt, influenced by the philosophy of Karl Marx, to explain links between art and economics by asking some version of questions such as these: Who profits by the current arrangements for publishing and producing plays? Why do audiences approve of plays and productions that seem to endorse an oppressive status quo? How can audiences be persuaded to see and act on their own economic oppressions?
- Semiotics. The study of signs, an attempt to understand how audiences make meanings from the auditory and visual clues given in a performance; a potentially powerful theory for explaining theatre and its effects because semiotics endorses the essence of theatre as a "seeing and hearing" place.

THE IMPORTANCE OF THEORIES   Theories and theorists of theatre are important because they influence the practice of theatre. Theories shape artists and the audience's expectations and responses. At the extreme, theories affect what is and is not acceptable. Granted, it is not easy to say which comes first—the theory or the practice. It is unclear whether theory leads practice by urging theatre artists in one direction or another, whether theory follows practice by codifying after the fact what audiences find satisfying in plays and production practices, or whether theory and practice simply change along parallel paths, both influenced by each other or by some larger force. At various times in history, probably any of these causal relationships have occurred.

When a once-accepted theory begins to fall into disfavor, competing theories and practices jostle around until some new theory gains widespread acceptance, after which patterns of plays and productions again begin to coalesce. Until a new theory gains dominance, however, both plays and productions are remarkable for their blends of styles. We are living in such an age, when there is no dominant theory of theatre, or, for that matter, any other art form.

The creation of theory, then, is an activity of major importance, one now located mostly in universities, where whole courses are sometimes devoted to the work of a single theorist—"Aristotle on Tragedy," for example. From universities, theories filter into the general consciousness through the work of other mediators and artists.

Critics

Criticism is a considered examination of a play or group of plays, usually by applying theory. The line between criticism and theory is not always clear, however, because many theorists are also critics, and many critics make theoretical statements. Like theory, criticism has two branches: dramatic criticism (the study of plays) and performance criticism (the study of performances).

FIGURE 5.2

Marketing

This quotation from a newspaper review makes a promise to the theatregoer, one of fun and escape. Producers often feature quotes outside the theatre to attract ticket buyers.

Probably because theories of drama are more fully developed than theories of performance, dramatic criticism continues to be the more widely practiced. Today, different dramatic critics focus on quite different subjects—a play's form and structure, its images and metaphors, its politics and sexuality, and so on; their focus usually depends on what theories guide the critic's inquiries. Critics and their criticisms are often labeled by the issues they address: formal critics and formal criticism, Marxist critics and Marxist criticism, feminist critics and feminist criticism. Most performance critics, absent well-developed theatrical theories, often seek to describe and explain the complex impacts of discrete moments of performance.

Criticism today, both dramatic and performance, unfolds mostly in university classrooms and academic publications. Like theory, criticism is a serious intellectual undertaking, needing reflection that militates against deadlines and other pressures. For this reason, most of the best modern critics have academic connections; only a few of today's best critics are also theatre artists.

Because of its academic home, criticism might be expected to affect mostly scholars and students. But criticism reaches a larger public—theatre audiences—because theatre artists (especially directors and dramaturgs) routinely read criticisms of past productions to help them think about the play they are preparing. Through such research, criticism affects the work of theatre artists directly and, through them, audiences. Because today's audience members seldom read criticism, however, its influence on them is indirect, filtered through theatre directors and dramaturgs. Like theorists, then, critics are important because they influence theatrical practice and so, indirectly, audiences, both in how to see plays and what plays to see.

Reviewers

Reviewers see plays and then write about them for publication in magazines, newspapers, television, radio, and the Web. Their orientation is toward consumer protection; that is, presenting themselves at best as an "ideal audience," they recommend or warn against performances on the basis of a taste shared with their readership.

Reviewers may popularly be called critics, but the two words are not synonymous. Reviewers are seldom critics. They do not rely consistently on theory; they rarely pretend to objectivity. They lack the time to process and reflect on what they have seen, their work usually appearing in a daily or weekly medium. Sometimes a review must be written in hours, depending on the deadline. Often, the format is so limited (one minute on radio or television) that little can be said at all. Reviewers evaluate both the play and its performance. They do not attempt to tell readers or listeners what performance is or how it works, however, but they do tell them whether the performance is likable within certain limits.

Some reviewers have theatrical backgrounds or education. Some do not. Experienced reviewers have trained themselves to recognize their own responses and to turn them into interesting, often witty prose, one of the functions of reviewing being to entertain.

Some reviewers develop power within their communities. The New York reviewers were once said to have life-or-death power over Broadway productions; recent research shows, however, that reviewers influence only about 10 percent of Broadway ticket purchases. Positive reviews are believed to be essential for Broadway nonmusical plays but less than crucial for the financial success of Broadway musicals. Reviewers' mediation extends beyond the review itself, nonetheless, whenever quotations from the reviews are included in theatrical advertising. Because of this practice, some reviewers may try to write quotable reviews, eager, perhaps, to see their names on theatre marquees with those of the actors. They have then crossed the line between mediation and participation.

Dramaturgs

A dramaturg is a specialist in dramatic literature and dramatic and theatrical history who works with theatrical production. Dramaturgs need strong grounding in theory and criticism because they are regularly called on to explain plays and justify decisions made about their productions. Although long active in European theatres, dramaturgs became common in the not-for-profit theatres in the United States only after World War II. They now work on the staffs of many resident theatre companies. Dramaturgs are almost unheard of in the commercial theatre. Most gain their training in universities, some of which now offer graduate degrees in dramaturgy.

The tasks of dramaturgs differ from theatre to theatre. Most perform some combination of the following functions:

- Assisting in the selection of plays
- Reading and evaluating new plays
- Providing historical and literary background to directors, designers, and actors
- Assisting directors, sometimes by advising on the production

- Working on plays—adapting, restructuring, translating
- Writing notes for theatre programs
- Preparing materials for use in advertising, public relations, and education
- Devising educational materials for schools

Clearly, dramaturgs influence both productions and audiences directly: productions, by participating in decisions about what plays are produced and how they are produced; audiences, by writing program notes and educational and public relations materials aimed at preparing audiences to appreciate the production. By shaping plays and productions, dramaturgs influence audiences indirectly as well as directly.

MEDIATORS OF THEATRE BUSINESS

Marketing

Marketing is a business discipline that oversees public relations and advertising. The chief precept of marketing is that a business should be focused outward to its various markets. For a theatre, marketers may break down the audience into various niches—by age, educational level, racial, and gender makeup—and target them accordingly. A knowledgeable producer may realize that the theatre has, as well, smaller but important market groups—reviewers, donors, investors, local government officials, even artists the producer wishes someday to hire.

Developing customer subgroups within a general audience population may require changes in dates and times of performances, ticket prices, special amenities for special donors, public relations, and advertising. Some theatres, for example, have designated certain performances as "singles' nights" to appeal to one such subgroup. Some theatres have changed traditional days of performances: Theatres did not used to perform on Sundays, until marketing surveys revealed that Sunday matinees were attractive to many customers. Some productions, especially musicals, now perform twice on Sundays. Other marketing research has suggested that advertising copy can be adapted to other niche audiences: Teacher guides, for example, are used to attract school groups; discounted day-of-performance ("student rush") tickets can appeal to a subset with more time than money; a play with African American or Hispanic or gay and lesbian content can use special public relations and advertising approaches.

PUBLIC RELATIONS AND ADVERTISING   A specialist in public relations strives to position a theatre organization vis-à-vis its several publics—town, neighborhood, business

FIGURE 5.3

Selling the Brand
The Disney Corporation has made the logo of *The Lion King* a worldwide brand.

Spotlight

Can these shows actually live up the expectation of the punchy quotes pulled from reviews?

The Impact of Theatre Reviewers

Producers try and create excitement by quoting excerpts from theatre critics. Many theatregoers believe that reviews are important to box office success, particularly those published in the *New York Times*.

Evidence suggests the impact of reviews is overestimated. Marketing surveys conducted by the Broadway League, the trade association of Broadway theatre owners and producers, report that the most influential source of information leading to ticket purchases is word of mouth, meaning recommendations from friends and co-workers. The Broadway League discovered in year-after-year surveys that newspaper reviews influence less than 20 percent of ticket sales. Another finding, also hard to believe, is that advertising has little reported effect on ticket sales despite its great expense. What your friends and neighbors think and say is more important than advertising and reviews.

The facts show that musicals can succeed despite receiving negative reviews. Long-running hit *Jersey Boys* originally got mostly positive but some very negative reviews from major newspapers, including those from the *Village Voice* ("We've seen it all before.") and the *Wall Street Journal* ("...move the whole thing to New Jersey."). Money-making powerhouse, *Mamma Mia!* originally got mixed-to-negative reviews from New York reviewers, calling it "forgettable," "improbable and lackluster," and "bland, hokey, corny, stilted, and self-conscious." Clearly, these shows have prospered without reviewers' endorsements.

Reviewers are mediators of theatre, but in truth, their impact on box office is often overrated. For the artists involved, a negative review may be emotionally devastating. But the financial results, the only results that matter on Broadway and in Broadway-inspired touring, may matter very little.

community. Advertising does the same thing. The difference is that public relations seek free media coverage, whereas advertising pays for its placement in media. As a result, advertising will always say what the theatre wants said about the production when the theatre wants it said; public relations cannot be so controlled. A schedule for advertising can be precise; usually, public relations cannot dictate when, or even if, media will cover a theatre's offerings.

The tools of public relations include press releases, artist interviews, photos and video clips, and the staging of public events that attract free media coverage. "Broadway Barks," for example, is an event to promote pet adoption and support animal shelters by having stars from current Broadway shows meet the public. The media coverage it draws calls attention to the productions in which the actors appear.

Advertising consists of posters, direct mailings, billboards, flyers, television and radio spots, and advertisements in newspapers, magazines, and even other theatres' programs.

Theatres differ radically in the funds they can devote to public relations and advertising. A student director may well handle all advertising personally, probably by photocopying posters and flyers made on a home computer. New York producers customarily contract with an advertising firm to promote their productions, and stars often have their own press representatives. University theatres often have somebody to coordinate marketing, including publicity; when money is available, advertising may include some combination of radio and television spots, newspaper ads, posters, and flyers.

THE HOOK   At whatever level, publicity campaigns try to capture the attention of potential audiences and lure them to the production. For each production, publicity people search for an angle, a "hook," that will set this production apart: the actor who goes on with a broken ankle, the actor whose mother played the same role in the original Broadway production. With the director and, if such a person exists, the producer, the person in charge of advertising will create an image—a logo—or phrase for the production. This image or phrase will grow out of the interpretation governing the production and will inform the graphics and text used in advertising it. (For a play about love, will we emphasize the rose or its thorns? A pink rose or a black one? Will we use the word *love* or the word *passion*?)

A well-conceived advertising campaign will not aim to bring everybody to the theatre but to bring those people likely to enjoy and understand the production. In fact, one responsibility of public relations and advertising is to alert people to productions that might be unsuitable for certain groups (e.g., parents with young children). Thus, with the concept of markets firmly in mind, a sophisticated theatre will create different advertising campaigns for different potential audiences.

Agents and Casting Directors

Agents are mediators between artists and the professional theatre. Casting directors work for the producing entity and sift through an acting pool to find the most suitable actors for a production (most of whom are represented by agents). Agents and casting directors serve both for-profit and not-for-profit theatres.

Agents link professional theatre artists (not only actors, but also playwrights, directors, and designers) with the businesspeople who hire them. Theatre artists pay a part of their income, usually 10 to 15 percent, to the agent who successfully connects them to the job. In addition, the agent negotiates favorable terms for contracts, helps sort out disputes, and collects and distributes money.

An unspoken assumption, whether true or not, is that actors or playwrights who don't have agents lack the skill to succeed. Often, they are merely beginners with no track record. Inescapably, agents usually guard the gate of the professional theatre; getting in without one is hard.

Play Readers

Play readers mediate between playwrights and producing entities. They read unproduced plays, both unsolicited scripts and those submitted by agents, to discover possible plays for the producing organization. Major New York not-for-profits may receive as many as a thousand scripts a year for a four- to six-play season. Artistic staff members can't read this many scripts and practice their craft. The work, therefore, is assigned to readers, who winnow the list, leaving the most promising scripts for the artistic staff to choose from. The play reader needs at least the skill to reject the absolute duds and not to throw away the rare masterpiece.

FIGURE 5.4

Advertising

It can cost from $5 to $25 million to open a musical on Broadway. Extensive and expensive advertising helps to protect this investment. Here the signage near the Times Square TKTS booth.

KEY TERMS

Check your understanding against this list. Brief definitions are included in the Glossary; persons are page-referenced in the Index.

PART

II

TODAY'S THEATRE AND ITS MAKERS
Theatre Practice

After briefly introducing the many kinds of theatres that exist today, Part II explores theatre artists—playwrights, actors, directors, designers, and technicians—as they train and as they work. It tries to to answer questions such as: What is the nature of the artist's work? What skills do the artists need to practice their craft? Where do they gain such skills? In what venues can they practice their craft? How are they rewarded?

All the artists of the theatre have differing skills, acquired through differing means. Together they must collaborate if the production is to be a success. As in a sports team, one great athlete without teamwork from the rest of the players will rarely win a game; it's the same in the theater: All the artists must share a collaborative strategy to lead the show to success.

6

Making Theatre Today
The Context

The Civil War staged at Virginia Commonwealth University.

OBJECTIVES

When you have completed this chapter, you should be able to:

- Identify the principal theatre configurations and stage shapes.
- Differentiate among the main producing structures in the United States, with an understanding of the strengths of each.
- Explain several types of theatre funding.

Before studying the people who make theatre happen, we need to examine the contexts in the United States in which they work. In what kinds of spaces can they make their plays? Are some arrangements of actors and audiences better than others for certain sorts of plays? What kinds of producing arrangements are available, and what are their strengths and weaknesses? Finally, how can theatre productions be financed, and what are some implications of the different funding sources?

THEATRE SPACES

Given the diversity of theatres around the country, it should not be surprising that theatre artists choose different sorts of physical spaces in which to work. With various elaborations, three basic theatre spaces now dominate: proscenium, thrust, and arena stages. In addition to these three, a few less common arrangements are also used.

Proscenium Stages

Since the seventeenth century the most popular theatre shape in western Europe and the United States is the proscenium theatre; proscenium theatres are marked by a proscenium arch or frame that separates the stage and the auditorium.

Alley Stage

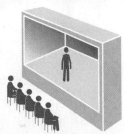

Proscenium Stage

The stage behind the proscenium arch is typically equipped with a rigging system, which allows scenic pieces to "fly" (be lifted out of sight above the stage floor), and a trap system, which allows objects and people to sink below the stage floor or to rise from it. Some are equipped with wagons or "slip stages" that allow scenery to be moved into place from the wings, which are the spaces on each side of the stage usually hidden from the audience's view. In most proscenium theatres, there is an area that extends a few feet in front of the arch, called the apron or forestage.

The area on the audience side of the proscenium—the auditorium, or front of house—is arranged so that almost all seats face the stage. Ground-level seats are orchestra seats. Balconies (also called galleries or mezzanines), which may curve around at least part of the side wall, are above the ground-level seats. Older proscenium

Thrust Stage

Arena Stage
(Theatre in the Round)

FIGURE 6.1

Basic Theatre Spaces

Actor–audience relationships in four configurations; alley (audience on two sides of the actor); proscenium (audience on one side); thrust (audience on three sides); and arena (audience surrounding actor).

houses have small, separate balconies, called boxes, usually on the side walls of the theatre near the stage. These boxes were at one time the most prized seats in the theatre, but they are now usually avoided because of their bad angle for viewing the stage (i.e., bad sight lines) and are often used as lighting positions instead.

Thrust Stages

Some plays, especially those of Shakespeare and his contemporaries, were not written for production in a proscenium theatre. For this reason, several theatre companies, especially those whose repertory stresses plays from the past, have sought a variation of the theatre used in Shakespeare's day. Such groups have built theatres with thrust stages (also called Elizabethan, Shakespearean, or three-quarter-round stages).

In such theatres, there is no arch separating the actors from the audience. Instead, audience members are placed on three sides of the action, usually on a raked (slanted) floor to improve sight lines, and in balconies. Actors enter the playing area from the back or through vomitories (tunnels that run through and under the audience and open near the stage itself—also called Voms). Because in this theatre elaborate stage machinery cannot be concealed behind a proscenium arch, and because, too, of the close physical relationship between the actors and the audiences, thrust stages tend to rely on acting, costumes, and properties rather than complex scenic effects. Indeed, in such theatres, without a front curtain and proscenium arch to mask them, all scene changes and all actors' entrances must be made in full view of the audience. Of the many thrust theatres, perhaps the best known are those at the Festival Theatre in Stratford, Ontario, Canada, and at the Guthrie Theatre in Minneapolis, Minnesota, both of whose repertories stress revivals of masterpieces from the past.

FIGURE 6.2

Utah Shakespeare Festival

The popularity of the thrust stage has spread in North America. Many not-for-profit theatres, including the Guthrie Theatre in Minneapolis and the Stratford Shakespeare Festival in Canada, feature stages in which audiences surround the playing area on three sides. Here, the Adams Shakespearian Stage in Utah.

Arena Stages

The audience in a theatre with an arena stage surrounds the playing area, hence its other name: theatre in the round. Many people prize the closeness of actors and audiences in arena staging, an intimacy especially well suited to many plays in the modern repertory.

With neither a proscenium arch nor a back wall to mask movements, all property and scenic shifts and all actors' entrances must be done either in blackout or in full view of the audience. Perhaps for this reason, arena stages tend to avoid elaborate scenic effects in favor of close attention to the details of costumes, properties, and acting.

Although less common than either proscenium or thrust stages, arena stages exist throughout the country, most notably at the Arena Stage, Washington, D.C., and the original Alley Theatre, Houston, Texas.

FIGURE 6.3

Arena Theatre

For staging in the round, both actors and scenery need to be visible to all audience members no matter their seating location. This arena stage has four vomitories (actor tunnels used for entrances and exits). Only three are visible here.

Other Configurations

Sometimes from choice and sometimes from necessity, acting companies take their performances to audiences instead of having audiences come to them. For such performances, a wide assortment of spatial arrangements must be found or created.

BOOTH STAGE The booth stage has long been a popular solution. Here, actors erect a curtain before which they play, either on a raised platform or in a cleared area. The result is much like the thrust stage, with the curtain serving both as a place from which to make entrances and as a background against which to perform. Because it meets the basic needs of performance and can be quickly erected and dismantled, the booth stage was a favorite of traveling companies.

ALLEY STAGE Alley stages place the audience on two sides, with the actors performing between them, and often with scenic units at each end. In some countries, such arrangements are found in regular theatres; in the United States, however, they are used mostly by actors who find it necessary to perform in school gymnasiums.

FIGURE 6.4

Alley Theatre

Audience members use the stage area to find their seats on either side of the central acting alley. Here, the stage is set with scenery at either end for a production of *Black Watch* at St. Ann's Warehouse in Brooklyn, New York.

Finally, only the imagination limits the space in which actors perform for audiences. In the United States, we have records of theatre taking place in streets, parks, factories, and even elevators—again, an index of the great diversity of our theatre.

THEATRICAL VENUES IN THE UNITED STATES

Theatre now touches most cities throughout the country. Although its diversity makes classification difficult, we can divide US theatre first into professional and amateur groups (each with several subcategories). But because some theatres do not easily fit into these categories, a third group, theatres for special audiences, is also used.

PROFESSIONAL THEATRE

The definition of professional theatre is complex, but the bottom line is that people who work in professional theatre get paid adequately (not a token amount). Professional theatre artists often belong to unions that specify when and how they can work and for how much. No matter where union theatre artists work, their professionalism is often governed and guarded by a union contract. They can practice their craft at professional for-profit or not-for-profit regional theatres across the United States.

Broadway

Broadway is the term used to describe a small area in New York City where theatres with at least five hundred seats each are the remainder of what was once the center of glamour, glitz, and theatrical legend in the United States. Of the forty Broadway theatres, five are owned or managed by not-for-profit professional theatre companies; the other thirty-five are commercial venues for license. Only productions in Broadway theatres are eligible for prestigious Tony Awards.

Broadway connotes professional theatre at its best, whether for profit or not: elaborate settings, rich costumes, distinguished stars, polished performances, and sophisticated musicals and plays. A testament to Broadway's authority in theatrical matters is that many other theatres, both amateur and professional, strive to imitate it, and in marketing, use the Broadway brand name whether warranted or not. From across the country (and much of the world), people flock to New York City theatres to experience Broadway. They expect theatre written by the best-known playwrights, music by the leading US composers, performances by the best actors, and productions designed by the best artists available, for which they are willing to pay—in 2013—as much as $175 for the established price of an orchestra seat for a musical. "Premium Seats," marketed as the best seats in the house, can cost as much as $477 or whatever the buyers are willing to pay.

Although New Yorkers also attend the commercial Broadway theatre in large numbers, tourists make up a sizable part of its audiences. Broadway audiences comprise mostly affluent US citizens, a social group that tends to be middle-class or above, white, mature, and somewhat conservative in taste and politics. Commercial Broadway producers reported that in the 2010–2011 season, the average family income of Broadway theatregoers was $244,100. (The median income for all US families from 2006 through 2010 was $51,911.)

FIGURE 6.5

Big and Splashy

Broadway theatres make a impression with marquees, bright lights, and signage. Here, the exterior of the 1,400-seat Lunt-Fontaine theatre promises important theatre stars and a name-brand musical.

BROADWAY'S COSTS   Much of Broadway's appeal, and many of its problems, stem from money. The cost of producing a show climbs each year as does the average price of theatre tickets, increasing faster than the general rate of inflation. The 2008 stage musical *Billy Elliot*, for example, based on a popular movie, was budgeted at about $18 million from start-up to opening night. Costs have continued to climb for several reasons: As real estate prices in Manhattan soar, so do the costs of licensing theatre space. Personnel costs rise with the demands of the unions. Costs of the goods and services needed to open a show—lumber and metal for scenery, fabrics for costumes, and advertising in newspapers and on television—have increased at an alarming rate. Money is also needed to keep a show running once it has opened. Costs are now so high that even a fairly modest show must run months (rather than weeks) to recapture its original investment.

FIGURE 6.6

Discount Tickets

Discount ticket outlets are in many major cities in the United States and in much of western Europe. Shown here, the newly remodeled TKTS discount outlet in Times Square is a major tourist attraction.

Huge costs have encouraged a "hit-or-flop" syndrome—a commercial Broadway with no place for the modest success. A hit can make big money; a flop can lose millions overnight. Not-for-profit professional theatres off and on Broadway, by comparison, can thrive as modest successes because their costs are significantly lower and some money, typically 40 to 60 percent of budget, comes from grants and donations.

DISCOUNTING BROADWAY TICKET

COSTS Broadway theatres, both for-profit and not-for-profit, have tried to ease the costs of tickets. For example, three low-priced ticket sources—TKTS booths in Times Square, South Street Seaport in lower Manhattan, and downtown Brooklyn—all sell tickets for Broadway and Off-Broadway shows not sold to capacity, mostly at half price, on the day of performance. In mid-2012, for example, 85 percent of Broadway productions were available for some seats at some performances at significant discount through the three TKTS outlets. TKTS sold about 14 percent of Broadway tickets.

Other sources for discounted Broadway tickets include such Internet sites as Playbill.com and BroadwayBox.com. Tickets for many productions that are not sellouts can be bought online in advance from these sites at a discount of about 35 percent. With a Playbill.com printout coupon, for example, a theatregoer can buy discount tickets in advance at the box office at no additional cost; if a ticket service were used, service fees would be added to the price of the ticket.

The Road

Many communities regularly import recent Broadway hits by booking the touring theatrical companies (**road shows**) that each year crisscross the country. These commercial tours seldom use the original Broadway cast, but they do use professionals and can even recoup the losses of a Broadway flop. Because road companies travel with complete sets and costumes, they are usually able to offer polished performances of recent hits to audiences who would otherwise be unable to see them. Business is best for big-name musicals, good for plays with well-known stars, and risky for everything else, although certain kinds of shows that may never see Broadway (e.g., family-friendly productions) have found a niche on **the road**. Many road shows are produced by the Broadway League, the trade organization of Broadway producers, and thus are unionized. Other shows are sometimes nonunion.

Off Broadway

The name Off-Broadway derived from the location of its theatres, which were once away from the Broadway theatre district; they are now all over Manhattan. Off-Broadway houses are now contractually defined by their limited capacity (100 to no more than 499 seats) and by their lower-than-Broadway salaries.

The goals of Off-Broadway differ from those of Broadway. Off-Broadway often seeks to serve as a showcase for new talents: Untried artists can work; established artists can experiment with new techniques; and new playwrights can find production.

Although Off-Broadway continues to offer employment to actors, directors, and playwrights (producing three or more shows for every one of Broadway's), its production costs have risen and, with them, its need to succeed at the box office. As risk has become less practical, Off-Broadway has become a less expensive version of Broadway, for which it sometimes serves as a tryout space. Productions that succeed Off-Broadway may move to Broadway, often with the same casts, directors, and designers, but with larger budgets. A very small number of Off-Broadway productions transfer to Broadway, about two or three a season. Like Broadway, Off-Broadway has a mix of commercial and not-for-profit producers, with the largest share of productions being not-for-profit.

Lower ticket prices Off-Broadway attract a more diverse audience and therefore allow a somewhat more varied repertory. In addition to small musicals and comedies, Off-Broadway produces some serious works and is now home to most new serious plays. For about half what it costs to see Broadway shows, Off-Broadway fare includes revivals from the classical repertory of plays, small musicals, and original plays.

Off-Off-Broadway

As Off-Broadway moved closer to Broadway—in practice, if not in location—some artists felt the need for an alternative theatre where authors, directors, and actors could work closely together to produce plays in an artistic, rather than a commercial, environment. Thus, Off-Off-Broadway appeared in the late 1950s as a place dedicated to the process of creating art and exploring the possibilities of the theatre. It did not want to become a tryout space for Broadway or to succumb to Broadway's or Off-Broadway's commercialism.

Productions feature imaginative but seldom elaborate sets and costumes. Although the casts and designers in such spaces are not necessarily union members and are seldom paid even their expenses, they continue to work, exploring the limits of a vision that is often socially, politically, or artistically alien to current US values. Ticket prices even lower than Off-Broadway's encourage attendance, and the excitement caused by unknown plays and artists draws adventurous patrons to coffeehouses, lofts, cellars, churches, and small theatres tucked away all over Manhattan and even some of the other New York City boroughs.

Although sometimes amateurish and often controversial, the offerings of Off-Off-Broadway in venues that seat ninety-nine patrons or fewer provide a

Spotlight

Richard Pilbrow's design for The Steppenwolf Theatre Company's Upstairs Theatre (*right*), the mid-sized of the three Steppenwolf theatres, is quite spare and steeply raked. His design for Chicago Shakespeare Theatre's Courtyard Theatre is ornate, with horseshoe-shaped seating that surrounds a thrust playing area.

Theatre Building Design

There are many designers for a stage production, but their work is ephemeral, lasting only as long as the show runs. There are even more designers and technicians working together to erect a new theatre building. They expect their work to last beyond their own lifetimes, sometimes even for centuries. The specialists include architects, engineers, building code experts, acousticians, and interior designers. Theatre specialists, another group of designers, then collaborate to devise the actor–audience relationship, suggest the necessary backstage and off-stage areas including fly space and rigging, wing space, space under stage, dressing rooms, orchestra pit, lighting and sound systems, hydraulics, and the like. These theatre consultants make the building a theatre.

Richard Pilbrow: A Theatre Consultant

Richard Pilbrow, one of the world's leading theatre consultants, is a leader in the movement to reestablish intimacy in large performance spaces. Starting as a stage manager in the 1950s, he became a pioneer of modern stage lighting in Britain; his designs have been seen in major cities worldwide.

Founder of the successful firm, Theatre Projects Consultants, Pilbrow has worked on some of the most significant theatre projects in the world. He served as theatre consultant on the Walt Disney Concert Hall in Los Angeles designed by architect Frank Gehry. Opened in 2003, the Walt Disney Concert Hall seats 2,265, but, with Pilbrow's close wraparound seating design, the theatre is recognized for its excellent acoustics and intimacy. His company contributed to the design of the Royal National Theatre of Great Britain in London and the restoration of the New Amsterdam Theatre in New York City, controlled by the Disney Corporation. Meanwhile Pilbrow produces shows in London and still designs lighting and projections for productions all over the world.

Pilbrow theatres reflect the style and needs of the theatre owners. Two projects in Chicago can demonstrate his range. Chicago Shakespeare Theatre, the 500-seat Courtyard Theatre, which opened in 2000, is a golden-colored auditorium, holding a long thrust stage, with seating on risers for the three sides, and two horseshow-shaped balconies. The thrust stage emulates the staging conventions of Shakespeare's Globe and Rose theatres. The Steppenwolf Theatre Company's Upstairs Theatre from 1993 is the middle-size of the three Steppenwolf theatres, seating 299, in a proscenium relationship. The Upstairs Theatre is quite spare, with grey walls and purple, steeply raked seating, a space intended for more experimental works. Together, they are two successful theatre spaces, constructed within a few years in the same city for two not-for-profit groups but strikingly and appropriately different in appearance and impact.

FIGURE 6.7

Not-for-Profit Regional Theatre

One of the oldest not-for-profit theatres in the United States, the Guthrie Theatre was founded in Minneapolis. It recently opened its new three-theatre complex built at a cost of more than $125 million. This distinctive new structure features a "bridge to nowhere."

Amanda Ortland/Guthrie Theatre

genuine alternative to the commercialism of both Broadway and Off-Broadway. Off-Off-Broadway remains a focus of experimental and political theatre in New York.

Regional Not-for-Profit Theatres

The vitality of regional professional theatres is one of the most heartening developments in the US theatre. In cities throughout the United States and Canada, professional theatres bring art to their audiences. Unlike the Broadway theatre, these groups are almost always organized as not-for-profit enterprises and so in theory can be more adventurous with play selection, production style, and personnel decisions. They contribute to theatre throughout the United States by diversifying and enriching its repertory, developing new audiences, training and revitalizing theatrical artists, and providing employment opportunities. Perhaps for these reasons, regional theatres have been called "the conscience of the American theatre."

Regional theatres vary in size and ambition. The best of them offer five major benefits:

- They provide a forum in which new plays and classics can coexist and provide an alternative to the comedies and musicals that are now the mainstays of Broadway. Some, like the Arena Stage of Washington, D.C., have earned reputations through the excellence of their classical revivals. Others, like the Actors Theatre of Louisville, have been especially successful in sponsoring new plays. Such theatres have reversed the tradition of having plays begin in New York and then trickle down slowly to the rest of the country. Much new drama now appears first around the country. The best of it moves beyond its local area and throughout the country, often ending in New York.
- They develop new audiences for live theatre. The art of theatre suffers without knowledgeable audiences because theatre artists become complacent, accepting the ordinary or the mediocre rather than demanding the excellent. With the growth of regional not-for-profit professional companies, audiences

across the country have come to appreciate live theatre as an art form and a cultural resource.

- They are a training ground and an energizing center for theatrical artists. Colleges and universities begin the training of many young artists; the professional regional companies introduce young artists to the profession, allowing them to work intensively with experienced artists. Today, many of the best talents in acting, directing, and designing begin their careers at one of these regional companies—and some elect to stay there throughout their careers.

- They are an important opportunity for the seasoned professional. Commercial theatre can dull an artist's creativity and vitality because its repertory is restricted and because its productions, when successful, can run for years, a numbing experience for an artist. Moreover, the commercial theatre seldom offers those roles from the classical repertory that stretch the actor's craft. For these reasons, the best actors are often anxious to spend time with a resident theatre, where they can play a wide variety of roles from many of history's best plays. The exchanges between the regional and the New York theatres seem to be raising the standards of the entire profession.

- They provide more jobs. In New York City, job opportunities are dismal. There are many more professionals than there are jobs. Regional theatres offer an alternative to New York. For several years, more professional actors have been working outside than inside New York; designers, few of whom get more than one show per season in New York, are now shuttling back and forth across the country, providing scenery, lighting, and costumes for professional productions.

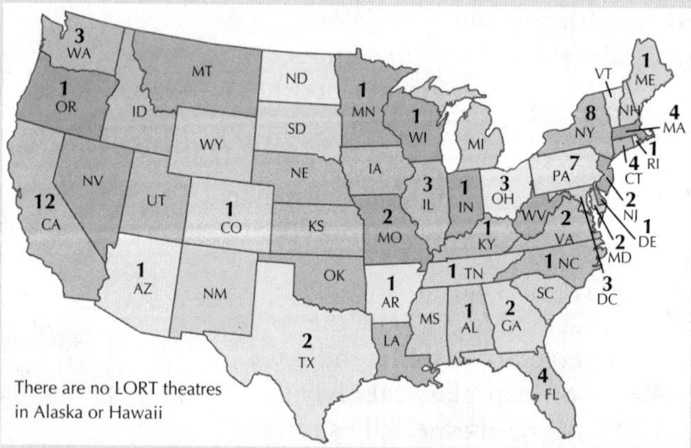

There are no LORT theatres in Alaska or Hawaii

FIGURE 6.8

League of Resident Theatres (LORT)

This select group of seventy-two not-for-profit professional theatres is among the largest and most prestigious in the United States. As shown, most are on the east and west coasts, but so is most of the population. There are many more not-for-profit professional theatres that are not represented by LORT.

Dinner Theatres

Throughout the United States, dinner theatres offer Broadway shows from past seasons, usually musicals, as the mainstay of their repertories. The quality of such companies varies widely. Some use union personnel, and their quality tends to be higher than those that rely on nonprofessionals. The number of dinner theatres is small compared to their heyday in the 1970s. The National Dinner Theatre Association has fewer than twenty-five members, but nonmember dinner theatres probably exist as well.

Restrictions of space and budget cause almost all dinner theatres to simplify the scenery and costumes of the originals in favor of smaller casts, smaller orchestras, and fewer sets, but, like Broadway, most seek to entertain rather than to elevate or instruct their audiences. In addition to the play itself, they add the sociability of drinks and dinner, so that an evening in the theatre is an occasion, not unlike going out for dinner before seeing a show on Broadway.

AMATEUR THEATRE

Amateur theatre is, technically, theatre performed and produced by people who are not paid. The two major kinds of amateur theatres in the United States are educational theatres and community theatres.

Educational Theatres

Theatre has a long history in US colleges and universities. Theatre and drama were at first extracurricular, performed at special events (e.g., commencements). They were later included within the curriculum of such departments as classics or English. Drama and theatre became college subjects in their own right only early in the twentieth century, when George Pierce Baker instituted classes in playwriting (and later play production) at Radcliffe College (1903), Harvard (1913), and Yale (1925). By 1914, Carnegie Institute of Technology was offering the first theatre degree. Shortly after World War II, many colleges and universities organized departments of drama and offered, in addition to course work, first undergraduate and, later, graduate degrees.

Although differing in principal emphases, the functions of some educational theatres, especially at the graduate level, now parallel those of many regional professional companies: training future artists, developing new audiences, expanding the theatrical repertory, and providing jobs. Other theatre programs, however, especially at the undergraduate level, have kept their emphasis on broad, general undergraduate education, referred to as liberal arts.

A major goal of academic programs is the education of students in theatre's literature, history, and theory, as well as at least introductory training in acting, directing, playwriting, design, and technical production. Although each program is unique, the general pattern of instruction involves some combination of formal classroom work and public performances of selected plays.

More than two thousand theatre programs exist today. In small cities without resident professional companies, theatre productions at a college or university may be the best or even the only ones for miles around. College and university theatres thus introduce thousands of students to drama and to a variety of staged plays. For many students, these productions are their first brush with live theatre.

Educational theatres usually display a commitment to a wide range of plays and production styles. Alongside standard musicals, comedies, and domestic dramas, collegiate seasons are likely to include significant works from the past as well as experimental works. Consequently, audiences for university theatre productions often enjoy more variety than those for community or dinner theatres.

FIGURE 6.9

Educational Theatre

Presenting a diverse repertory of plays is part of the educational mission of college and university theatre. Heavily subsidized, and thus not as concerned with box-office success, educational theatres present newer plays along with classics from many eras. Here, a production of *The Underpants* by Steve Martin at Purdue University Theatre.

Too, the number of people required to maintain theatre in an academic setting has given the employment potential of the profession a healthy boost. At the college and university level alone, more than ten thousand productions are mounted each year and more than four thousand teachers are employed. When the growing numbers of high school drama classes, elementary programs in creative drama, and producing groups devoted to children's theatre are considered, it becomes clear that the academic complex is a major source of jobs. Indeed, educational theatre, considered at all levels, is probably the largest employer of theatre artists and scholars in the United States.

Community Theatres

Community theatres exist throughout the country and are almost always organized as not-for-profit entities. Cities with one or two regional professional companies may have a dozen community theatres. In towns with neither professional nor educational theatre (except, perhaps, the annual high school play), a community group may produce plays in a school, a church, or a civic auditorium, providing entertainment and recreation for both participants and audiences.

Community theatres vary enormously. Some pay none of their participants, drawing directors, actors, and office personnel from volunteers in the community; others pay a skeleton staff—a technical director, box office manager, and artistic director—who work for a governing board of community volunteers. Almost no community theatres pay their actors or stage crew.

In cities and towns without professional companies, community theatres fill the important roles of introducing new audiences to the theatre and of keeping live theatre a part of cultural life. Where professional companies do exist, community theatres serve important recreational needs of people for whom participation in theatre is a greater pleasure than sitting in an audience. In their constant search for volunteers to help with production, such theatres regularly introduce many new people—especially young people—to the world of the theatre. Community theatres are, in fact, the first theatre experience for many people who later enter the profession. Finally, the relatively modest ticket prices of most community theatres bring into their theatres many who might not pay the price of a regional professional company. Some of these newcomers will become lifelong supporters, not only of their local community theatre but also of the regional professional companies and, when in New York, of its commercial theatres.

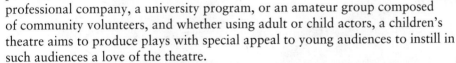

FIGURE 6.10
Not-For-Profit Theatre
Regional theatres often do innovative retellings of classic tales. Here, Tuta Theatre in Chicago with a surprising version of *Alice in Wonderland* by Lewis Caroll, called simply *Alice*.

CHILDREN'S THEATRE

Children's theatres have both professional and amateur companies. Whether an established professional company, a university program, or an amateur group composed of community volunteers, and whether using adult or child actors, a children's theatre aims to produce plays with special appeal to young audiences to instill in such audiences a love of the theatre.

The repertory usually consists of plays specially written for kids, using stories and issues of interest to that age group. Their range varies greatly—from imaginative retellings of popular fairy stories, myths, and legends to treatments of contemporary social problems like drugs and divorce. With relatively modest ticket prices and an unusually high commitment to their audiences, children's theatres introduce many young people to the art of the theatre and, from this large group, recruit some as lifelong supporters of all kinds of theatre.

KEY TERMS

Check your understanding against this list. Brief definitions are included in the Glossary; persons are page-referenced in the Index.

alley stage 73
amateur theatre 81
apron 71
arena stage 72
balconies 71
booth stage 73
boxes 72
Broadway 74
community theatre 82

educational theatre 81
forestage 71
front of house 71
galleries 71
Off-Broadway 77
Off-Off-Broadway 77
orchestra 71
professional
    theatre 74

proscenium arch 71
proscenium
    theatre 71
road show 76
sight lines 72
the road 76
thrust stage 72
vomitories 72
wings 71

7

Playwrights

Ma Rainey dominates the stage in August Wilson's play, *Ma Rainey's Black Bottom,* at Philadelphia Theatre Company.

OBJECTIVES

When you have completed this chapter, you should be able to:

- Understand the implications of the words playwright and playwriting.

- Differentiate dramatic dialogue from ordinary language.

- Discuss the playwright and the playwright's cultural position.

- Explain the playwright's relationships with dramatic

and theatrical conventions, with audiences, and with the rehearsal process.

THE NATURE OF PLAYWRIGHTS AND PLAYWRITING

We must not misunderstand the nature of the playwright's craft. Playwrights create replicas of human action—not records of it or responses to it. The complexity of playwriting is suggested by the language that we use to describe it—*playwright* and *playwriting*. Plays are both *made* and *written*.

Playwright

Wright means "maker." Just as a wheelwright is a maker of wheels and a cartwright is a maker of carts, a playwright is a maker of plays. Playwrights create and organize actions, using human-like beings (characters) to do so; they craft replicas of human actions and then set forth these replicas in language (writing). It is partly accident that what a playwright does looks like what a novelist or poet does—setting down words on paper. If playwrights had a different set of symbols to work with (like a musician's notes or a choreographer's notations), the differences between playwrights and other writers would be clearer.

Playwriting

Although we refer to a play*wright*, we also talk of *playwriting* and so acknowledge the importance of writing to what a playwright does. Playwrights set forth their replicas of human action in large part by inventing "language" for dramatic "characters" to speak to one another; that is, playwrights write dialogue that actors (pretending to be characters) will speak to one another. Dramatic dialogue, however, is not like ordinary language; it must forward plot, reveal character, and express ideas, all in a compressed form. The fact that playwrights write words for actors to say and for audiences to hear means that their language must be more active, more intense, and more selective than either everyday speech or

FIGURE 7.1

Not-for-Profit then Broadway

The 25th Annual Putnam County Spelling Bee made its appearance at Second Stage in New York, a widely respected not-for-profit theatre. Earning enthusiastic reviews, the musical was transferred to a small Broadway theatre where it prospered. With its brand name established, it has been seen across the United States. Here, a production at Kutztown University in Pennsylvania.

other kinds of fictional speech (novels). Playwrights also "write" nonwords: silences, gestures, rhythms, and visual images.

Drama and Literature

This dual nature of playwright and playwriting gives a clue to a quality of drama and dramatists that is sometimes misunderstood. Drama is not primarily literature, and dramatists are not primarily literary artists, although both can be studied as if they were. There is a dimension of literary art in drama, of course, but there are other essential dimensions as well. Many highly respected novelists and poets are quite incapable of writing for the stage, though many have tried. Conversely, the language of many highly regarded playwrights, when analyzed as literature, can seem alternately feeble or overblown (e.g., Eugene O'Neill), but when actors speak the lines in the theatre, the effect is powerful and lasting; such playwrights are fine theatrical artists, but they are not good literary artists. Only the rare person is both literary artist and theatre artist in equal measure, Shakespeare being the premiere example.

SOURCES OF PLAYS AND PLAYWRIGHTS

Plays

An idea, an overheard conversation, a need to cry out against an injustice, an urge to break out of self have all given rise to plays. This germ may sit in a mind for years before something else urges it into life, or it may bloom at once and become a play written in the heat of the moment. Plays have been written in seven days and plays have been written in seven years. Plays have been partially written and then put away, often forever.

Plays have most often been written by individuals—playwrights. However, they have also been written by two-person teams, the most famous in the United States probably having been George S. Kaufman and Moss Hart (*You Can't Take It with You*). They have also been written by collectives, groups of people either dominated by one individual (who, as in the case of Bertolt Brecht, took most or all of the credit) or functioning as a unit, with individual egos submerged in it. Collectives work best when a shared idea unites the individuals: Collective playwriting has been, for example, practiced by a number of feminist theatres in which the collective is an externalization of an ideal of sisterhood.

Here, we are concerned mostly with individuals. Generally, they write in isolation for this public art of theatrical performance. Increasingly, however, playwrights may work with actors, both to try new ideas and new scenes and to improvise around ideas, the improvisations then forming the core of the playwright's next step. Or playwrights may work with a director or a producer, not quite in a collaboration, but certainly in a creative relationship.

Musicals also have playwrights for the nonmusical script, called "book-writers" or "librettists"—the irony of calling any kind of playwright a book-writer not seeming to matter. (The script is "the book"; actors who haven't yet learned lines are "on book," so such playwrights are not really thought of as writing books but writing *the* book.)

The librettist is in a different position from the playwright and is far more likely to be working on somebody else's idea than an original one of his or her own. It is not story or character, after all, that drives the musical; it is music. As a result, the book must serve the music's needs, creating cues, setting up situations for kinds of music, and driving to climaxes that will be musically expressed.

Playwrights

FROM THE THEATRE   Playwrights frequently come from within the theatre; they are "people of the theatre" who are "theatre-wise." For example, the Roman actor Plautus was a playwright who wrote plays for himself and his actors, and the French actor Molière was a playwright who created vehicles for himself and his troupe. Shakespeare, only a minor actor, wrote many of his most famous roles for other actors in his company, actors whose special strengths and weaknesses he understood and exploited. Such people of the theatre most often work within the dominant theatrical styles of their day, and they probably dominate the theatrical mainstreams.

FIGURE 7.2

A Man of the Theatre

The seventeenth-century theatrical genius Jean-Baptiste Poquelin, known by his stage name Molière, was a company manager, playwright, and a gifted actor, playing many of the roles he created. Here, as *Sganarelle* in his commedia dell'arte inspired farce.

FROM OTHER FIELDS   Playwrights may start out as something else—not as actors or directors, but as something from outside the theatre altogether. These are not people of the theatre; they are not theatre-wise. Indeed, these newcomers, uninitiated in the current conventions of the theatre, may write in new and refreshing ways and so exert a strong appeal for those bored with current practices. Margaret Edson, for example, was a kindergarten teacher in Atlanta when her prize-winning play *Wit* was first produced in 1995 at the South Coast Repertory Theatre in California. When *Wit* was revived on Broadway in 2012, Edson was still teaching in public school and said she had no other ideas that compelled her to make a second play.

New plays can benefit from the newcomer's gift of ignorance; that is, newcomers may not follow the plays of the mainstream theatre in form, style, length, subject matter, or language.

THE INSIDER PLAYWRIGHT   Social insiders can make successful playwrights but usually they write about a limited or minority culture instead of the mainstream. Black, gay, and feminist playwrights, for example, have written from a position (perhaps constructed) as insiders in the black, gay, and feminist cultures and outsiders in the social mainstream. This kind of insider playwright became more common in the United States in the 1960s. Since then, many such playwrights have worked in political theatre—what we call "identity theatre"— the tendency being for the minority-culture playwright to dramatize the problems of that minority in opposition to the mainstream, and thus to make it visible to the mainstream.

FIGURE 7.3

Angels in America: A Gay Fantasia on National Themes

Tony Kushner's Pulitzer Prize-winning play is actually two plays under a collective title. The first play is titled *Millennium Approaches*; the second is called *Perestroika*. Here, a production by Ball State University.

A CASE IN POINT   Tony Kushner's *Angels in America* opened on Broadway in the early 1990s after earlier productions in Los Angeles. One of the outstanding dramas of the late twentieth century, it was a controversial play that located itself in the heart of the culture. Its principal subjects included homosexual life, only recently real to most Americans; AIDS, an epidemic little more than a decade old when the play was written; love and personal loyalty; and, through the real historical figure Roy Cohn, political and moral corruption. The character of Cohn, a homosexual homophobe and an assistant to the notorious Senator Joseph McCarthy, opened the play to resonances far beyond what it would otherwise have achieved; so, too, did the brilliant concept of the angels of the title. They, and their lair in heaven, gave the play a metaphysical dimension and a level of spectacle that lifted it far above most dramas of the nineties. Written in a contemporary idiom, the play was the resonant, meaningful work of a playwright who "wrote what he knew" but metamorphosed his experiences into a penetrating look at the United States at the end of the twentieth century and at the situation of some ordinary Americans at the turn of the twenty-first century—powerless, alienated from government and God alike, comforted by personal relationships, getting along on grit, humor, and luck. It was funny and unsettling and startling and visually splendid, and it put the theatre itself back at the center of the culture, at least for a while.

THE PLAYWRIGHT'S CAREER

Once a playwright gets started and has some productions, however, the way forward isn't necessarily either clear or easy, as some real-life careers show:

- Edward Albee had his first plays produced in Europe and then in the United States when he was twenty. By twenty-four, his short plays dominated Off Broadway; when he was twenty-six, *Who's Afraid of Virginia Woolf?* had a Broadway production and was an immediate success. In the years since, he has been on or Off Broadway many times and has been awarded three Pulitzer Prizes, a Kennedy Center Lifetime Achievement Award, and a National Medal of Arts, but he has also had periods of relative neglect. In his eighties, he is still writing and still seeing new plays produced.
- Charles Gordone was a professional actor who had worked on his play *No Place to Be Somebody* for years before it was finally produced Off Broadway when he was forty-four. It won the first Pulitzer Prize ever awarded an African American playwright and made Gordone instantly—but temporarily—famous. The critic Walter Kerr called him "the most

FIGURE 7.4

Edward Albee's *At Home at the Zoo*

The playwright expanded his one-act play, *Zoo Story* (first produced in Germany in 1959) to include a prequel to *Zoo Story* (*right*), called *Homelife* (*left*). First performed in 2009, Albee has stipulated that *Zoo Story* alone may only be performed by nonprofessional and educational theatres.

Mark Garvin

astonishing new American playwright to come along since Edward Albee." In the more than two decades that remained of his life, he had other careers as actor, teacher, and cowboy poet, but he never again had a new play produced in a major venue.

■ Megan Terry's first plays were performed in a small theatre in Seattle in her early twenties, but at about age thirty she began a long-term association with the Open Theatre in New York. *Viet Rock* was both famous and notorious in the 1960s, a rock musical that came from the Open Theatre's collaborative and transformational style. Terry was hailed as an early feminist playwright for *Calm Down Mother* and *Approaching Simone,* the latter winning an Obie. When she was forty-three, Terry left New York (the Open Theatre had disbanded) and joined the Omaha Magic Theatre as resident playwright. She has written and cowritten many plays produced there. With more than forty plays published and produced around the world and a recipient of many important awards, Terry remains a productive playwright in her sixties and chooses to work outside the commercial theatre.

All three of these playwrights were "successful" but in different ways and at different ages. None had a straight-line career from first effort to major achievement or a straight-line career of hits thereafter. All displayed great talent. All received both extravagant praise and harsh rejection. Taken together, they pose a question: What is a successful playwrighting career?

TRAINING PLAYWRIGHTS

Unlike actors, directors, and designers, playwrights do not, as a rule, go through structured periods of formal training. To be sure, there are playwriting programs in US universities, but their record of producing playwrights who write plays of recognized quality is poor. Courses in playwriting often familiarize theatre students with the problems of the playwright and give an enriching new slant on other areas of theatre work; advanced degrees in playwriting are frequently combined with scholarly work in such a way that playwriting becomes an adjunct of critical study. Playwriting as an academic discipline, however, suffers from the same problems as creative writing in general, and when it seems to produce results it is because the same factors are at work: teachers who are themselves artists and who teach as much by example as by precept; constant encouragement of creativity itself, so that the student is surrounded by other writers and playwrights; and strong professional links with agents, producers, and publishers, so that entry into the mainstream is helped.

Many rules have been laid down for playwrights. They have seldom proved to be permanent—or to be rules. Rather, playwrights are well advised to follow some old maxims:

■ Write what you know.
■ Write for your own time.

- Write action, not speeches.
- Write for actors, not readers.
- Be passionate, not timid; truthful, not nice.

It often helps, too, to be selfish and ruthless. Writers work in solitude and with many obstacles; personal relationships sometimes suffer.

If, on the other hand, the playwright is in it only for the money, all bets are off, and he or she is wise to play it safe, aim for the middle, listen to marketing research, and imitate whatever made money most recently. Many playwrights make their income writing for television and film or teaching in colleges and universities.

FIGURE 7.5

Genesis of a Play

Plays come from all sorts of beginnings—personal experience, memory, an overheard conversation, or a famous event. *The Civil War*, performed here at Virginia Commonwealth University, was rooted in US history.

FROM PAGE TO STAGE: PROFESSIONAL ISSUES

Writing the Play

Plays begin as a great variety of things: a story overheard, a chance remark, or a note jotted down on a slip of paper. Plays may set out to retell a legend or myth; they may treat a bit of history or a slice of daily life; they may be adapted from a novel or a ballad; or they may be an imagined, onstage symbol or gesture. Moving forward from that genesis is part of the playwright's talent, and it is one of the elements that separates playwrights from wannabees.

Lots of people have *ideas* for plays. The problem is turning them into *scripts*. For many, the thought of writing a full-length play is a stopper, as formidable as the idea of writing a four-hundred-page book. And true, full-length plays rarely get written quickly or easily; they demand the commitment of months, at least.

How do you leap from the genesis to the play—to character, dialogue, action—to all those pages? In part, the answer lies in the concepts of dramatic theory, not because most playwrights deliberately apply dramatic theory but because they must work in terms of certain dramatic elements, whether or not they call them by the same names: above all, character, language (dialogue), and action. Idea, too, may be the genesis of a play and may dominate conscious thinking during much of the creative process, but "How do I dramatize the idea?" is an unproductive first question for a playwright to ask because plays are about human action, not ideas.

AFTER THE GENESIS   What happens, then, after the genesis—after the inspiring observation or accident or thought? The playwright tries to move forward. The urge to make a play is there; it is conscious. It drives the imagination—both conscious and unconscious thought. Certain paths are opened for such thought by the nature of the genesis:

■ If the genesis is a story that will also be the play's story, the next step is character: What kind of people are doing these things?
■ If the genesis is a person or the playwright's self (character), then the next step may be language (a burst of statements of character) or action, but, inevitably, action has to come early because dramatic character is character in action.

Richard Anderson Photography

FIGURE 7.6

A Ten-Play Cycle

August Wilson devoted much of his life to a ten-play cycle, each installment devoted to a particular decade of African American life in the twentieth century. Here, *Ma Rainey's Black Bottom*, set in the 1920s, in a production at Center Stage, Baltimore. The "Black Bottom" was a dance craze in the 1920s. In the play, a small group of African American musicians joke and argue, as they wait on the famous singer Ma Rainey to make some recordings. The play's climax is shown here, a fight between two of the musicians ending in murder.

■ If the genesis is an idea—outrage at an injustice, satirical amusement at a subject, a thought (e.g., "Revenge is easy to talk about but hard to do")—then the next step is probably character but may be story, a chain of incidents that embody and illustrate the idea.
■ If the genesis is language—an overheard remark, a single great line—then the next step is probably character: Who says it and why?
■ If the genesis is a situation ("Two guys and a girl are trapped in a stalled elevator, see..."), then the next step might be some dialogue but has to be an action: What do they do, not what do they say?
■ If the genesis is history and a real person, then the playwright is already bound by some incidents, probably some meaning, and perhaps even some language (e.g., famous quotations, letters, and so on); the next step is probably story—trying to make a fictional beginning, middle, and end of a real life.

THE DEVELOPMENT   Playwriting is an act of the imagination. It is neither entirely rational nor entirely conscious, but certain things will take shape:

- Situation—rough ideas of setting, social level, relationships, and important aspects of the play's world: politics, religion, and conditions of threat
- Tone—comic or serious or satirical or mixed
- Plot—not merely the story but the ordering of the incidents as they relate to character, action, and idea
- Form—whether the play is to be long or short, in quick scenes or long acts, or in a single piece or three or five

Other matters include rhythm, pace, rising and falling action, and crisis, as well as, in certain kinds of drama, "big moments," and surefire act endings. The seasoned playwright, who has worked a lot with actors and may have certain actors already in mind, may also write consciously to give actable depth to character and dialogue for those actors.

DIALOGUE   Much of this work will be externalized as dialogue. Playwrights must try to become masters of spoken language, both by hearing it and by creating it. The language of a play carries a huge burden: not only the meaning of the words but also character and tempo and the externalization of much of the action. As well, each character should have unique speech patterns and vocabulary; ideally, each character could be recognized by language alone.

Dialogue can take on a life of its own and lead away from what the playwright sets out to do in a scene. Character may lead this digression, but so can idea, or the interplay of characters-in-action may simply be too tempting. Playwrights can welcome a certain amount of such digression, but they have to cut it off if it threatens the progression of the play itself. Other theatrical concepts are useful here, whether or not the playwright uses the same terms: through line, motivation, objective. Working with actors on such a scene will help: Seasoned actors show unease or confusion when motivations go off on a tangent. This can be particularly true when the playwright has let dialogue, especially dialogue about idea, go off on its own.

FINISHING A DRAFT   As plays take shape, playwrights may show them to other people—lovers, acquaintances, or theatre professionals. When a draft is finished, some playwrights set to work again with a director or a producer or with actors. However it goes, the play is not finished until it is on a stage in front of an audience.

PRACTICALITIES   Playwrights always have to strike a balance between their own imaginations and the realities of the theatres in which they work. Plays must, among other things, provide a framework for other theatrical arts, especially acting and design, and so plays are circumscribed by both theatrical and dramatic conventions. These matters, and the technical means of accomplishing them, are

Spotlight

Ken Berne Images

Ruined, based on a civil war in the Congo, was commissioned by the Goodman Theater in Chicago where it was first performed. It moved to the Manhattan Theatre Club where it was extended nine times. It won the Pulitzer Prize for drama in 2009 and has been seen around the country in not-for-profit regional theatres.

Lynn Nottage: A Good Playwright

Born in Brooklyn, Lynn Nottage wrote her first play at the age of six. She knows that her urge to be a playwright came from stories heard in childhood. "I think a lot about the question of why I write," she said. "I think for me the journey begins downstairs at the kitchen table of my house.... To come home from school, and my grandmother would be sitting at the table, and my mother would be sitting at the table. The woman from across the street would be sitting at the table. And they all had stories to tell. They were nurses, teachers; they were activists; they were artists. And I think that is where I got all of my inspiration as a writer."

Nottage's plays center on the history of powerlessness of African American women.

"I think the African-American woman's voice is important because it is part of the American voice," Nottage said. "But you would not know that by looking at TV or films.... [M]y mission as a writer is to say, 'I do exist. My mother existed, and my grandmother existed, and my great-grandmother existed, and they had stories that are rich, complicated, funny, that are beautiful and essential.'"

Nottage earned a BA from Brown University and an MFA from the Yale School of Drama. She spent four years as national press officer with Amnesty International "writing press releases, op-eds, and speeches" before devoting her efforts to the theatre.

Nottage's first produced play, a ten-minute one-act, won the Heideman Prize at the Humana Festival of Louisville's Actors Theatre. Nottage went on to receive a Guggenheim Fellowship and a MacArthur Fellows Grant, commonly called the "genius" grant. Her plays have been produced by most of the leading not-for-profit theatres in the United States and other countries. Her 2008 play *Ruined* received the Pulitzer Prize in drama and a handful of other important prizes.

Loosely inspired by Bertolt Brecht's *Mother Courage and her Children*, *Ruined* takes place in a brothel in today's war-torn Democratic Republic of the Congo. Mama Nadi makes her living selling liquor and pimping her girls to soldiers from all sides. Her cardinal rule is not to take sides in an African civil war. "Survival is the only art I recognize," she says. Mama Nadi embodies the relationship of Western governments to Africa's destruction: She accepts profit if she can find it, but she does nothing to stop the ruin of people and societies.

"A play exists as a literary form," Nottage believes, "until the first moment you sit down in a rehearsal room and allow a group of actors to read it. Then it becomes a dramatic form. During the rehearsal process, you make discoveries because there are things that work beautifully on a page as literature but have no dramatic life."

things that playwriting courses can teach or the playwright can learn in the theatre itself as apprentice or actor.

AUDIENCES "The drama's laws / The drama's patrons give," wrote Samuel Johnson in the eighteenth century. He meant, of course, that audiences, by their attendance and their responses, decide what traits plays ought to have and which plays are good or bad. Audiences, rather than critics or theorists, establish the "laws" of drama.

Getting the Play Produced

In recent years, the number of theatres in which new plays can be produced in the United States and Canada has increased—notably, the not-for-profit theatres. In addition, such organizations as the National Playwright's Conference of the O'Neill Theatre Center give first productions to a wide spectrum of scripts, many of which are later produced elsewhere. New York, however, remains the goal of most playwrights. There are two reasons: money and status. Broadway royalties are far higher than anywhere else, and Broadway production is subject to the best reviewing and is the most prestigious.

Plays are not produced at any of these theatres by accident. Nor are many new plays that attract widespread attention scripts that come out of nowhere. Most are submitted to regional theatres or Broadway or Off-Broadway producers by agents, important mediators in the business and art of theatre. Far less often, a play may reach a producer by way of an actor or a director. In any case, the playwright's first high hurdle is finding that first production, whatever the medium used to reach a producing organization.

Working with the Play in Rehearsal

Producers have readers who read scripts and make comments. When a script is accepted for production, it already has an accompanying list of such comments as well as the producer's own views, added to these will be the ideas of the director when one is chosen. Each principal actor will add ideas, and each of these people—producer, director, actors—may have still other ideas that have come from friends, spouses, lovers, and relatives.

Changes in a script, however, are rarely simple; a Broadway playwright said some years ago that altering a play is like taking bricks out of a wall: For every one that is taken out, half a dozen others have to be put back. At times, the playwright wonders what it was about the play that ever caused people to want to do it because they have asked for so many changes that nothing seems to be left of the original.

Paying the Playwright

Standard Broadway contracts give the playwright a percentage of the theatre's weekly gross, a percentage that climbs as the gross climbs past certain plateaus. On a hit, these figures can be impressive—thousands of dollars a week; on a modest success, they can be a thousand a week or less; and on a flop, nothing. There is, of course, the significant additional income of film and television sales—and, perhaps most important, there is the secondary income of amateur and stock production.

FIGURE 7.7

Paying the Playwright

Marsha Norman's 1983 play *'night, Mother*, a Pulitzer Prize winner, has been revived continuously in the United States and Europe, earning her a steady stream of royalties. This 2007 production was in Madrid.

Amateur rights are handled mostly by two organizations, the Dramatists Play Service and Samuel French, Incorporated. They collect royalties on productions by amateurs (i.e., community, school, and university theatres) for the life of the play's copyright—since the Copyright Law of 1977, the author's life plus fifty years. Although the royalty on a single performance of a play is small, the collective royalty per year on a play that is popular with the nation's several thousand community and college theatres can be large, and even plays that fail on Broadway can become staples of amateur theatre and go on providing income for decades.

In short, playwriting is a difficult craft that requires special talent, and it is made far more difficult by the conditions under which plays must find production. A recent study of produced playwrights found that on average they made only 15 percent of their income from play royalties. Many potential playwrights now move to television and film, and there is some question whether—despite grants, theatres, and organizations that encourage new plays—playwrights will continue to decline in number until the theatre itself recovers its vigor. Relatively few people make a living as playwrights. The same can be said, however, of actors, directors, and designers.

WHAT IS GOOD PLAYWRITING?

Good playwriting is playwriting that produces good theatre. Exactly what makes a play good is the subject of continuing dispute, even among theatre scholars, but some of the traits of such plays have already been suggested in Chapters 3 and 4. The questions at the ends of these chapters can offer a beginning glimpse of what makes for good playwriting.

The great German theorist and playwright Johann Wolfgang von Goethe (1749–1832) suggested another set of questions to help assess the worth of a play and playwright: (1) What did the author set out to do? (2) Did he or she do it? (3) Was it worth doing? These questions are useful inasmuch as they remind us that playwrights might exhibit great technical skill (they set out to do something and did it well) yet still produce an inconsequential play (it wasn't worth doing). Great plays, finally, must do more than entertain, although they must do that at a minimum.

KEY TERMS

Check your understanding against this list. Brief definitions are included in the Glossary; persons are page-referenced in the Index.

copyright   96
dialogue   93
royalties   96
wright   85

8

Actors

Shakespeare's *Richard III* at Virginia Commonwealth University.

OBJECTIVES

When you have completed this chapter, you should be able to:

- Explain the paradox of the actor.

- Explain the relationship between actor and character and between character and real person.

- Explain the goals of rehearsal.

- Understand the actor's vocabulary.

- Explain how an actor creates a role.

- Discuss the possibilities of acting as a profession.

THE NATURE OF ACTING

Actors stand at the center of the theatre. Without them there is nothing—an empty building, a hollow space. Directors cannot direct or designers design without actors; the playwright can create only works to be read like novels. The actor alone can make theatre without the help of other artists.

The accomplished actor is also a good performer; a superior performer, however, may not be a very good actor. Some kinds of theatre put a higher premium on performing than on acting; circus high-wire work, for example, requires great performers and has no use for actors. Musical comedy, on the other hand, requires both acting and performing, for the ability to "sell" a song requires performing of a high level. In short, the performer plays to the audience; the actor plays the character for the audience.

Accomplished and experienced actors respect the etiquette of their profession, an etiquette that includes being:

- Prompt: They arrive for rehearsals on time, alert, and ready to work.
- Prepared: They bring to rehearsals whatever homework on the play has been requested.
- Constructive, not destructive: They do not make comments about other actors, do not break out of character while another actor is working, and do not indicate in any way that another actor's experiment with a character is dumb.
- Respectful: They talk to the director about problems, not to other actors, the costume designer, or the playwright.
- Aware: They know the theatre's past and its literature.

Artistically flexible actors know that only through remarkable efforts of concentration is progress made.

Being and Pretending: A Paradox of the Theatre and the Actor

To reach emotional truth, it has been said, the actor must be the character; on the contrary, another point of view insists that the actor must always stand aloof from the character and pretend. If an actor were really to be the character, how would he or she control onstage behavior? What would keep the actor from becoming inaudible at times? What would keep the actor playing Othello from actually killing the actor who plays Desdemona? What would cause the actor to modulate the voice, control the tempo of a performance, or listen to other actors? And, contrarily, if the actor always pretends, what will he or she be but a lifeless imitation of humanity? How will the actor keep the

FIGURE 8.1

The Heart of the Theatre

Only the actor can make theatre without other support. Here, Lily Tomlin does her classic characters in a one-person show without aid of costumes or props.

speeches from sounding like empty nonsense? How will gestures be anything but graceful hand waving?

Because the actor is at the center of the theatre, this paradox is the paradox of the theatre itself: To be convincing, one must lie. The actor both is and pretends, exploiting both technique and inspiration. It is never enough for the actor to be satisfied that a sigh or a smile is perfectly truthful; the sigh or smile must also have the carrying power and the communicative value to be perfectly truthful to the audience.

This concept of theatrical truth was first described by the French theorist Denis Diderot (1713–1784). He used the expression "the paradox of the actor" as the title for an essay on acting in which he tried to capture what seems to be an essential contradiction in the actor's art: To appear natural, the actor must be artificial. Or, said another way, successful acting is making the audience believe that the falseness onstage is true.

Two Approaches to Acting: Inspiration versus Technique

Our own age is one whose theatrical heritage is primarily a "natural" one, at least in the realistic theatre. The actor's ability to create a sense of emotional truth is much prized. There are at least two ways of reaching this goal: relying on inspiration and developing technique.

Modern US actors sometimes speak disparagingly of an actor who is "technical," meaning one who builds character out of careful, conscious use of body and voice (e.g., rehearsed inflections and carefully chosen poses and gestures). Their belief is that "technical" actors work mechanically and so fail to bring

FIGURE 8.2

The Paradox of the Actor

Every age has its own idea of what seems "natural" or "real," including these Romantic illustrations that look decidedly unreal to us. Yet actors using these gestures were, just like modern actors, experiencing the paradox of the actor—to find images of the natural and the real through a process that is unnatural and unreal.

imagination and life to their work. The technical actor is seen as "full of tricks."

At the other extreme is the "inspirational" actor's approach to emotional truth. Although carefully rehearsed, the inspirational actor's characterization is not assembled from external behaviors but is created through application of mental and emotional techniques that supposedly work to reach the actor's emotional and mental center and then somehow push outward into onstage movement and vocalization. In theory, the character created by the inspirational actor will be more "natural" because it rises from inner sources that also give us music and poetry. To the inspirational actor, her approach is fresh and her creation original.

Must actors choose how they will work? Must it be one approach or the other? Actually, there is a continuum that links these extremes. Most actors probably use a combination of the technical and the inspirational approaches.

The Actor and the Character

In the literary sense, character is a dramatic construct that represents human personality and that expresses itself through action. The effectiveness of a character depends on how well it fits into and affects plot. This idea, derived from Aristotle, has an important implication for the actor: Character is defined on the basis of its function within the artistic whole, the play, and not merely on the basis of how well it imitates a human being. Therefore, a character in a specific play may be a convincing imitation of a human being in its superficial attributes—the character may talk like a human being and may have preferences in clothes and food and entertainment like a human being—and yet it may be a "bad" or "ineffective" character in that it makes no important contribution to the action of the play. An actor who concentrates on mannerisms of the character and fails to grasp and act on the character's function as contributor to the action will fail.

For the actor, character means something like "the imitation of a human being as it expresses itself through the words and the decisions created by the author, in relation to the other characters in the play and their decisions and words." The actor's character exists on the stage (only) and has no life off the stage; the actor's character exists in an artificial time scheme that is quite different from the time scheme of real life.

In short, the actor is a person; the character is a construct. For the character to seem to be a person during the two or three hours of performance, actors must use their consciousness, their instruments meaning their bodies and voices, and their imaginations.

FIGURE 8.3

Inspiration and Technique

Seeing only the finished performance by gifted actors, it is usually impossible to tell whether inspiration or technique was employed to hone the character for performance. Here, a production of *The Miracle Worker* at Barry University. Is there a way to discern how these actors arrived at their characterizations?

Training Actors

Although there are supposedly actors who are "born," and although there have been young children without training who were deeply talented actors, it is a fact of theatrical life that all actors must train long and hard and must refresh that training throughout their careers. There was a time when would-be actors "came up through the ranks" as apprentices, moving from small roles in minor companies to larger roles and more important theatres, gaining experience along the way. They learned by observing, taking hints and techniques from experienced actors. Nowadays, the apprentice system of actor training has been mostly superseded by formal training, either in a college or in one or more private studios.

Actor training does not refer to one specific kind of study or to a set period of time. There are a number of effective actor-training systems. The most influential in the United States and Canada are those based on the ideas of Konstantin Stanislavski. Other systems have very different foundations, such as the psychological theory of transactional analysis or the theory of games and improvisations. Different as these are, they are helpful in varying degrees to different actors. No one system is best for everybody. The important thing about these systems is that they organize the work of the actor's consciousness, instrument (body and voice), and imagination. Without a workable system, the would-be actor makes progress only randomly, repeating mistakes and often making bad habits worse.

No matter what the system, actor training almost always involves at least these three characteristics:

- Analyzing the script
- Training the actor's instrument
- Training the actor's imagination

Analyzing the Script

The dramatic script is the foundation of the actor's work. Imagination and instrument are the means through which the script is embodied. Training in script analysis has three principal goals: understanding the entire drama, understanding the place of the character in the whole drama, and understanding the details that comprise the character.

UNDERSTANDING THE ENTIRE DRAMA   On the first reading, the actor will be making judgments and sorting out impressions. The actor will read the script as

FIGURE 8.4

Training the Actor's Body

Actors must focus their mind and body on the here and now, absorbing character, given circumstances, through line, and an understanding of the entire drama. A trained, relaxed, and supple body helps the actor accomplish these goals. Here, a movement class for actors at Southern Illinois University.

a "notation" for a performance: The potential for production will be grasped, at least in general. An awareness of the play's totality will take shape. Of particular importance to the actor on first reading will be the style of the play, its main impact on its audience, and its overall shape. Under style, the actor will understand the degree of abstraction of the script; the kind of language, whether poetic or mundane; and the historical period. The impact will be comic or serious and will be expressed most importantly through language or action, idea or spectacle. The shape will describe the play's gross structure and its overall rhythms, whether it builds slowly or quickly to crises, whether it relaxes gradually from them or drops abruptly. This first contact with the totality of the play will also indicate what demands it will put on its actors—the special requirements of their instruments and the relative degree of intensity of the emotions to be embodied, among others.

UNDERSTANDING THE PLACE OF THE CHARACTER IN THE WHOLE DRAMA   The actor is trained to ask, How does my character contribute to the whole?

Dramatic action means change; when a character is offstage, changes are taking place, and when the character returns, those changes must be noted and accommodated. The actor balances two lines of development: the character's and the play's.

UNDERSTANDING THE DETAILS THAT COMPRISE THE CHARACTER   A deeper understanding of the play and the character's part in it emerges from repeated readings, as does a detailed sense of just what the character is. The actor may keep a notebook about the character, including those things discussed under the character section in Chapter 3, especially action and decision, with character traits as they appear in the stage directions, the character's own speeches, and the speeches of others. All must be evaluated in terms of the production and should be discussed with the director and the other actors. For example, one character says to another that she shows "facial contortions" and her voice goes up "two octaves." The actor playing the character described must know whether these things are true (that is, whether the other character's description is accurate) and then work out when and where to use these traits.

It is essential for actors, as for all theatre makers, to look at the play in terms of its theatricality (see Chapters 3 and 4). Such a breakdown gives them a grasp of the play's entirety and of its potential to be effective in performance. It should not, however, dictate character. Grasping a play's idea, for example, must never suggest to the actor the reason for the character's existence, nor should the actor worry about how to "play the idea," or worse yet, how to be the idea. The actor who says something like "In this play, I represent goodness" simply has not done the proper homework. Except in pure allegory, characters do not represent ideas; they represent persons (who may embody or apply certain ideas).

In the same way, script analysis should help the actor to avoid moral value judgments. Characters in a play are not "good" or "bad" to themselves. Few real persons say, "I am a villain." The actor does not, then, play a villain; the actor plays the representation of a person whose actions may be judged by others, after the fact, as villainous.

Spotlight

Meryl Streep has been honored more than any other living actress.

Meryl Streep: A Good Actor

Meryl Streep embodies the best qualities of good acting and the good actor. Streep's versatility is obvious: In the last few years she has played leading roles in *Mamma Mia!* and *Doubt* (both acclaimed film performances) and *Mother Courage and Her Children* on the stage. In 2010 she received an Academy Award for her film portrayal of the first female British PM Margaret Thatcher in *The Iron Lady*. Such a variety of roles on stage and screen demonstrate that she is not merely hiding behind a series of well-written parts.

She has earned a shelfful of acting awards for her work onstage and in movies and television. She has been nominated for an Oscar seventeen times, winning three times for best actress. She has also received two Emmy awards for work on television and two Screen Actors Guild awards, among many others.

Meryl Streep was well trained. As a youngster, she studied opera. At Vassar College, she studied acting as a drama major. In 1975, she graduated with an MFA degree in acting from Yale University's School of Drama, whose actor training was firmly based on the ideas of Stanislavski as interpreted in the United States. Sense memory, imagination exercises, vocal production, and improvisation were also part of the Yale curriculum.

Known for her meticulous and painstaking preparation for each role, Streep is regarded by her fellow actors as a perfectionist in her craft. In preparation for John Patrick Shanley's *Doubt*, Streep visited the author's first-grade teacher (then seventy years old) to observe her speech patterns because Shanley had told her that this teacher was the model for Sister Aloysius, the character Streep played. Streep joked that she wanted to sound like someone from Shanley's neighborhood. In *Music of the Heart*, another film, she learned to play the violin by practicing six hours a day for eight weeks.

Clearly, Streep has the creativity, imagination, discipline, and stamina that mark any fine actor.

Put most simply, training in script analysis is training to read. It is training to understand what is on the page—not what might have been put on the page but was not and not what the actor might prefer to find on the page. Script analysis deals with a limited amount of information and tries to squeeze every drop from it; it neither invents nor guesses. Most of all, it requires that the actor read every word and understand it in clear detail; from that clarity and that detail will come an understanding of the script that can be returned to again and again when acting problems arise.

Training the Instrument

"Stage movement" and "voice production for the stage" sound like (and may be) titles of academic courses. They suggest that the subject matter can be learned and that then, like familiarity with Shakespeare's plays or a knowledge of calculus, they can be forgotten or assimilated. In actuality, the training of the instrument—the actor's body and voice—is a lifelong process.

THE BODY   The actor's body need not be heavily muscled, but it should be flexible, strong, and responsive. The actor does not train as an athlete does (one set of muscles would be developed at the expense of others); instead, the goal is resistance to fatigue, quick responsiveness, and adaptive ability (that is, the ability to imitate other kinds of posture and movement or to adapt movement to, for example, aged posture and movement or the posture and movement of a body much heavier).

Many people who want to learn to act are so tense that they are quite literally unable to act, to "do." Physical tension causes sudden, random, or pathological movement (shaking, trembling) and dangerous misuse of the vocal mechanism. Tense actors may think of themselves as intense and not tense; they see themselves as "really into" a role, when the teacher or the audience sees nervous, confusing, and uncontrolled movement. These actors are busy expressing their own feelings, leaving little room to communicate the character's feelings to an audience.

Relaxation exercises cover a broad range from disciplines as different as modern dance and yoga. All are intended to cause the consciousness to let go of the body, to return it to its natural state of receptiveness and awareness, and to make the body itself supple and loose.

Centering.   Many disciplines, among them Eastern meditative religions and some schools of modern dance, emphasize exercises that focus on a bodily center—that is, a core of balance and physical alignment, a place from which all movement and energy seem to spring. This idea of a center concerns both the body (i.e., balance, weight, and placement) and the voice (i.e., breathing and sound making). In yoga, the abdomen below the diaphragm is such a center; in some modern dance, the center is slightly above the pelvis.

Centering leads the beginning actor away from the mistaken idea that the physical self is located in the head and the face, that the voice is located in the

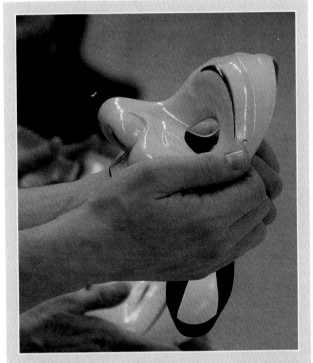

FIGURE 8.5

Mask Work

Transformation of physical identity is often taught with mask training. The masks have a "character," but the actor can't use his face to express the moment, so it must be expressed through the body. Here, an acting class at Wayne State University.

mouth and the throat, and that the physical relationship to the rest of the world is located, through gravity, in the feet; rather, the actor finds the center somewhere near the crossing point of an X of arms and legs—a center of gravity, a center of balance, and a center of diaphragmatic breathing.

Body Language and Nonverbal Communication.   We all express our emotional states and our basic psychic orientations through body language. The actor learns to move the physical center to match that of the character. The actor also learns how all of us communicate without words, through such simple gestures as the waving of a hand ("hello" or "come here" or "no thank you") to complex statements of posture and gesture that say things completely different from the words that pass our lips. Such training takes two forms: study of the subject (much of it still in the fields of psychology and anthropology) and application to the actor's body.

- *Rhythmic movement,* including ballroom dancing, simple modern dance, disco dancing, and the like to help the actor to move to an external rhythm.
- *Period movement and use of properties,* including historically accurate and theatrically effective use of fans, canes, swords, and shawls; the list is long.
- *Movement in costume,* including theatrically effective movement and gesture in wigs, capes, hoopskirts, and boots; again, the list is long.
- *Movement onstage,* including adjustments to the stage space and audience sight lines. Traditional interior settings do not have walls that meet at the same angles as rooms, so stage furniture in such settings is rarely angled as real furniture is. As a result, "crosses" (movements from one point onstage to another) take unreal routes. On thrust and arena stages, the actor learns to play to all of the audience, to adapt posture and movement so that each section of the audience is treated fairly. Too, the actor must learn ways of bending, sitting, and standing that are appropriate to the stage in that they are not awkward or unintentionally comical.

THE VOICE   The human voice is a product of controlled muscular work and chamber resonance (i.e., head and chest). Its shaping and control are not simple. Nonetheless, we make sounds and shape them all the time—only to find that our everyday sounds are inadequate for the theatre because they cannot be heard, they cannot be understood, or they are unpleasant. Unlearning and relearning are necessary for most actors.

The actor trains the vocal mechanism for maximum control of every word that is uttered, as well as for the production of sounds that are not words. He or she also seeks training and does exercises in breath control, relaxation of the vocal apparatus, dexterity, resonance, and such technical matters as dialects and accents.

Training the Imagination

Actors go through a process in a training atmosphere and are encouraged to discover their imaginations. Whether the imagination itself can be trained remains open to question. Most certainly, actors can try to encourage the nonrational brain to speak up and make itself heard.

PLAY Dramas are "plays"; actors are "players." Yet beginners are often anything but playful. A terrible seriousness rules the work. To counter this tendency, they learn how to play, both to play games and to approach the creative act joyously. Many theatre games are versions of children's games or of adult "parlor" games that are noncompetitive fun.

CREATIVE EXERCISES In the belief that all people have imaginations and are creative, teachers devise exercises to free actors from both embarrassment and inhibition.

Image Exercises. The creative mind probably works, at least a good deal of the time, in images rather than in words (although many words are themselves images). Image exercises encourage the actor to grasp the mental pictures the brain offers. For example, simple character creation around pictures, objects, or sounds can be beneficial. An actor is given an object and told to perform a related character for the group: A knife is set out; the actor bends forward, walks with difficulty, the body held to protect its center greedily. From "knife," the actor went to "sharp," sharp in business, a miser, then added the element of "a cutting wind."

Craig Schwartz

FIGURE 8.6

Training the Imagination

While these two actors are actually on a metal skeletal setting, they must imagine they are in a real place, perhaps a bedroom. Here a production of *Next to Normal* at Center Theater Group, Los Angeles.

Visualization. Group exercises build a scene, each member contributing details and working to see the scene. Such an exercise is useful in touching the actor's sense of creativity, in sharpening concentration and sense of detail, and in preparing for those times in rehearsal and performance when the actor must "see" for the audience.

Sense Memory. Like group storytelling, individual recounting of the picture around a memory encourages a sense of detail and of sense memory. As many senses as possible are incorporated. Such sense memories (awareness) need not come from childhood; they can come from the day before, even moments before. The purpose is to cause actors to capture a sensory moment in all its fullness and, through both remembering it and recounting it, to cause them to be able to create such sensory reality around moments that come not from memory but from the theatre.

Improvisation. No single word and no single tool has been more used and misused in the last several decades than improvisation. Improvisation—the creation of quasi-theatrical characters or scenes or plays without the givens of drama—has been used to create theatre (without a playwright), to enlighten an actor about a character, to structure theatre games, and to teach aspects of acting. In a sense, it is the basis of some of the other techniques; having an actor create a character around an image is such a use of improvisation. It can be used to apply the imagination, to stimulate it, or to supply raw materials not within the actor's experience. For example, an improvisation focused on a frightening event might help the actor who has never experienced true fear.

THE QUESTION OF TALENT   Well-trained actors can achieve impressive levels of success. They use their flexible voice and agile body, their intellectual skills, and their developed imagination to embody their roles. Beyond that, is there such a thing as talent? Clearly, actors and other theatre artists differ in their abilities to respond to playscript and character in ways that are artistically satisfying for an audience. They differ too in what sorts of stories they are best in presenting; some are best at comedy, some at drama, some at supporting roles, and some as leads. Some have proposed that talent might be best defined as the ability to gain, to improve, to expand through training and experience. Allied to talent, but subtlety different, is persistence and drive, the willingness to work repeatedly to advance as a theatre artist.

One might look at classical singers and dancers for an analogy of the importance of talent. Clearly classical singers and dancers must have innate capabilities in their bodies to succeed. Just as clearly these performers also need training to succeed. It may be that music and dance teachers are better than teachers of acting at recognizing the talent of their prospective students. Yet many more erstwhile singers and dancers enter training than ever make careers as singers and dancers. Maybe the identification of talent is problematic for all artists.

FIGURE 8.7

Concentration

The ability to concentrate on the given circumstances the playwright has provided is an important skill the actor must master. Here, in a moment from *The Civil War* at Virginia Commonwealth University, these actors seem to have no room to consider anything but each other.

Acting Systems

Ideas originated or articulated by Stanislavski, modified by the American Method and subsequent theories, continue to dominate the work of most US actors.

THE AMERICAN STANISLAVSKI SYSTEM   In this approach, the actor is trained to analyze character to discover:

- Given Circumstances. These are the undeniable givens that the actor must accept: age, sex, state of health, social status, educational level, and so on. Often given circumstances are contained within the script, either in stage directions or in dialogue; sometimes they must be deduced or even invented. (How old is Hamlet? Was he a good scholar at the university? Is he physically strong or weak?)

- Motivation. Realistic theatre believes in a world of connectedness and cause. All human actions in such a world are caused or motivated. To play a character in such a world, the actor looks for the motivation behind each action. Some teachers have their students make notebooks for each character with a column in which a motivation can be noted after each line or gesture. It is important that the student actor understand that, in this system, all behavior is motivated—every word, every movement, and every inflection. All action results from choice.

- Objective. Like motivation, the objective is part of a system of causality. It is the goal toward which an action strives. Motivation leads to action; action tries to lead to objective.

- Superobjective. "Life goal" might be a synonym of superobjective if a dramatic character were a real person. The superobjective includes all objectives pursued by a character and excludes all improperly defined objectives. For example, we might say that Hamlet's superobjective is "to set the world right again"; his objective in the first scene with his father's ghost might be "to listen to this creature from Hell and put it to rest" (thus setting the world right by quieting the ghosts in it). In this case, the objective and the superobjective agree. If, however, the superobjective was defined as "to take my father's place in the world," and the objective in the ghost scene was defined as "to listen to the ghost out of love for my father," the two would have to be brought into sympathy. By defining the superobjective, the actor is able to check on the validity of all the character's objectives. When all the objectives fit under the character's superobjective, the character is more whole and understandable.

Both the objective and the superobjective must be active. We have expressed them here as infinitives—"to set," "to listen"—but the actor does better to express them in active terms beginning with "I want," so that their strength and vitality are clearly visible. This "I want" is sometimes called the through line of the role. It isn't enough for the actor to know these things about a character. The actor must move and speak so the audience may learn about the character through what the actor knows. Developing objectives and superobjectives is a creative act. There may be superficially correct objectives and superobjectives for a character that are not especially effective for the play or for an audience. The actor must find and act on revealing and arresting objectives and superobjectives.

In developing his system of acting, Stanislavski was interested both in actor training and in the problems of performance. His work cannot be viewed as

FIGURE 8.8

Movement

Period costumes or costumes of other lands present a challenge to actors. They must wear them with ease and move in such a way that the garments seem to be clothes rather than costumes. Here, a moment from *M Butterfly* at Philadelphia Theatre Company.

merely a study of how the actor prepares; rather, it is also a prescription for the continuing refreshment of the performing actor. His system allows the actor to create what has been called the "illusion of the first time" again and again. Put most simply, this means that the actor is able to capture the freshness and immediacy of the "first time" (for both the character and the audience) by going back each time to the mental and emotional roots of the truthfulness of the performance. This process is possible only if performance is grounded in truth discovered during rehearsal—or, in some cases, during performance itself.

Continued performance for the trained actor, then, is not merely a matter of repeating rehearsed sounds and gestures night after night; it is a matter of returning to or discovering internally satisfying truths (motivations and objectives) and satisfyingly effective externalizations of them. Such an approach may not be perfect, but it is far better than the repeated performance that grows tired with repetition and that leaves the actor disliking both the performance and the audience because of boredom.

Audience response to performance sometimes suggests at what points a performance is effective or poor, and the actor works at correcting errors as the performance period continues. Thus, the creation of a character must seem completed by opening night, and yet it is never truly finished.

BEYOND STANISLAVSKI: ACTING IN A POSTMODERN THEATRE   Although Stanislavski's ideas still dominate actor training in the United States, they may be under challenge, especially outside the commercial theatre. Plays different from those associated with modern realism often require quite different approaches by the actor. Today's new plays and new views of theatre—especially those that are highly experimental—may lead to a different sort of training for the actor.

Many recent plays are not organized by cause and effect; they do not assume a world of causality or connectedness, achieving their unity instead through ideas, perhaps, or mood or visual images. Actors in such plays might, therefore, be expected to place less emphasis on issues like motivation, superobjective, and through line and more, perhaps, on matters of vocal and physical flexibility, symbolism, and aesthetics.

Many recent plays present multiple levels of reality, with irony and parody often important. Actors preparing for such plays may be asked not only to play the role but also to comment on the role at the same time. Such a request seems to mean that actors must engage the audience in the role while, at the same time, requiring the audience always to recollect that they are watching a role being acted and not a life being lived—the double audience response described in Chapter 2.

One technique for accomplishing this dual process has been costume manipulation and cross-gender casting: The audience may watch a female actor, cast in a male role, put on and take off her costume (and so her role); in this way, the actor

FIGURE 8.9

Working with the Director

Here, actors receive feedback from the director after a rehearsal of *Macbeth* at the University of Michigan. Actors, along with other creative and technical support people, are part of a team dedicated to make the play come alive for an audience.

can both play and comment on the role and at the same time reveal the social construction of gender within the play and a society.

Separating the voice and the body of the actor is another such technique: The audience hears an actor's prerecorded voice over loudspeakers while seeing the actor moving and, perhaps, hearing him speak.

Many new plays deny the actor a single role or a stable character, the point of these plays often being that human beings themselves lack stable identities. In such plays, actors play multiple roles (including those of animals or inanimate objects) or many characters, and they do so without the changes in costume or makeup that have historically suggested such changes. Called transformations, such rapidly shifting roles would seem to place a greater premium on vocal and physical dexterity and imagination than on truthful inner work or a strong through line.

AUDITION, REHEARSAL, AND PERFORMANCE

Actor training goes on long after actors get on the stage. Most actors continue to work on their instruments throughout their careers, and many return to professional workshops to refresh and sharpen their inner work. After the initial period of actor training, however—college, sometimes graduate school, or an independent studio or teacher—the actor begins to look for roles and, having found one, begins the work of building and performing a character. Each step in the process has its special conditions, and for professional actors these steps will be repeated again and again throughout their lives.

Audition

Most actors get roles through auditions ("tryouts"). Stars are the exception; sometimes productions are built around them instead.

Most auditions are done for the director. Usually, the stage manager is there as well, along with someone representing the producer, if there is one. Somebody is there, as well, to read with the actor if a scene with another character is being read. (Usually, the stage manager does this.) At many auditions, actors are expected to bring prepared monologues.

The most important things an actor can show in an audition are basic abilities and the capacity to work creatively with the director and other actors. One of the director's problems in auditions is to try to sort out the creative actors from the "radio actors"—those who have the knack of reading well on sight but who lack the ability to create. Therefore, actors are often asked to improvise as part of auditions and to work with other people. Cleverness in a first reading is not necessarily an advantage. What may count more is the capacity to work creatively and interpersonally.

Rehearsal

Once cast, the actor will undoubtedly arrive at the first rehearsal with many questions. One of the functions of rehearsal is to answer those questions and to turn the answers into performance.

Actors often work slowly in rehearsal. An outsider coming into a rehearsal after, let us say, two weeks of work might well be dismayed by the apparent lack of progress. Actors may still be reading some lines in flat voices, and, except for bursts of excitement, the play may seem dull and lifeless. This situation is, in part, intentional. Many actors "hold back" until they are sure things are right. They do not want to waste energy on a temporary solution to a character problem. Temporary solutions have a way of becoming permanent: Other actors become accustomed to hearing certain lines delivered in certain ways and to seeing certain movements and gestures; they begin to adapt their own characters to them. Instead, many find it productive to withhold commitment for a good part of the rehearsal period.

EXPERIMENTING   The actor experiments. Some of this experimenting is done away from rehearsals; homework takes up a lot of the actor's time. Much of it takes place in rehearsals. Again and again, an actor will say, "May I try something?" Or the director will say, "Try it my way." *Try* is the important word—*experiment, test.* The good actor has to be willing to try things that may seem wrong, absurd, or embarrassing.

Most important, the rehearsal period is a time for building with other actors. Actors use the word *give* a lot: "You're not giving me enough to react to," or "Will it help you if I give you more to play against?" Such giving (and taking) symbolizes the group creation of most performance.

At some point during rehearsals, the creative and lucky actor may have a "breakthrough." This is the moment when the character snaps into focus.

Motivations and actions that have been talked about and worked on for weeks suddenly become clear and coherent. The breakthrough may be partly a psychological trick, but its reality for the actor is important: The creative imagination has made the necessary connections and has given usable instructions to the instrument. The character is formed.

CREATIVE PROBLEM SOLVING   The rehearsal period, then, is not merely a time of learning lines and repeating movement. It is a time of creative problem solving, one in which the solving of one problem often results in the discovery of a new one. It is a time that requires give and take, patience, physical stamina, and determination. It frays nerves and wearies bodies. The intensity of the work may cause personal problems. Nonetheless, many professional actors love rehearsal more than performance because of its creativity.

Performance

Performance causes emotional and physical changes associated with stress. Some change, of course, is helpful; it gets the actor "up" so that energy is at a peak, ready for the concentrated expenditure that rehearsal has made possible. Too much stress, however, cripples the actor. Stage fright and psychosomatic voice loss are very real problems for some. Ideally, good training and effective rehearsal will have turned the actor away from the root cause of stress (dependence on outside approval of the performance); when this does not happen, the actor may have to return to relaxation work or find therapeutic help.

Craig Schwartz

FIGURE 8.10

Illusion of the First Time

These actors repeat their performances dozens of times, yet they must be fresh and immediate at each performance. This eye contact, for example, must continue throughout the performances. Here, a moment from the musical *Parade* at Center Theatre Group in Los Angeles.

Opening nights raise energy levels because of stress and excitement. As a result, second nights are often dispirited and dull. The wise actor expects this pattern. Again, preparation is a help—complete understanding of the role and of the total performance, creative rehearsal work, and open lines between consciousness and imagination. Before the second and subsequent performances, the prepared actor reviews all character work, goes over notes, reaffirms motivations and objectives. The good actor does not say, "Well, we got through the opening; the rest will take care of itself."

Once in performance in an extended run, actors continue to be aware of a three-pronged responsibility: to themselves, to the other actors, and to the audience. Those responsibilities cannot end with the reading of the reviews.

WHAT IS GOOD ACTING?

Understanding the art of the actor depends, first, on the ability to separate the actor from the role. An attractive or well-written role can obscure the actor's lack of imagination; a poorly written role can hide the actor's excellence; an unsympathetic role can make the actor seem unsympathetic. By learning to read and see plays, we learn to distinguish the character from the actor, and then to see what kind of material the actor had to cope with. For example:

■ Good acting has detail and "texture" (variety and human truth), but it is not merely a collection of details; it has what one artist calls a "center" and another a "through line"—a common bond tying all details together and making the whole greater than the sum of its parts.
■ Good acting has the capacity to surprise. Its truth is recognizable, but it goes beyond imitation to revelation.

Good acting, then, has technical proficiency, truth, a through line, and creativity; bad acting calls attention to itself, lacks technical control, dissolves into mere details because of its lack of a through line, and never surprises with its creation. A good actor possesses creativity, concentration, determination, stamina, access to the imagination, playfulness, the ability to cope with rejection, nonrational thinking, and detailed emotional memory.

KEY TERMS

Check your understanding against this list. Brief definitions are included in the Glossary; persons are page-referenced in the Index.

9

Directors

A Midsummer Night's Dream at Frostburg University with a unique "Springboard."

OBJECTIVES

When you have completed this chapter, you should be able to:

- Describe the major tasks of a director, noting which are mostly artistic and which mostly managerial.

- Differentiate the worshipful from the heretical director and discuss strengths and weaknesses of both approaches.

- Describe the purpose and process of production meetings.

- Describe the director's work with actors.

- Explain the director's use of space.

- Define the art of the director.

There have always been theatre people who exercised a strong, central influence on productions, but directing, in the sense that the word is now used, is a phenomenon of the late nineteenth century and has continued into the twenty-first. Despite the relatively late appearance of directors, they are now the dominant figures in theatrical production.

THE NATURE OF DIRECTING

When directors came into being, the responsibility for many tasks formerly done by several people, or not done at all, was vested in one person: the director. Directors came into being to unify and to bind all elements of a performance together into a cohesive whole—of both interpretation and presentation. *Interpretation* here means that the actors and designers all understand the play in the same way and agree on the nature of the intended audience. *Presentation* here means all the elements that the audience will see and hear—text, actors, scenery, properties, costumes, lighting, and sound. All must fit together, be of one piece, and be appropriate for the intended audience.

To be sure, the degree to which directors unify, make pictures and illusion, and organize and manage depends in part on their situation. For example, in commercial theatres like Broadway's, overall artistic vision and production control may rest with a producer rather than a director, and many routine details of rehearsal and performance may devolve to a stage manager instead of remaining with the director. On the other hand, in high schools and small community theatres, these tasks often fall to the director, so that he or she must personally supervise (or even execute) almost every aspect of a production. No matter the producing circumstance, however, the director is the undisputed head of the team.

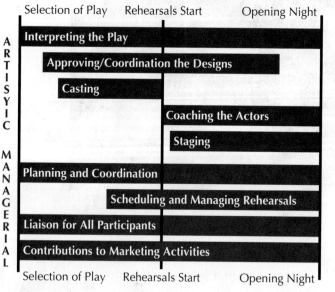

Director's Responsibilities

Selection of Play   Rehearsals Start   Opening Night

A R T I S Y I C — Interpreting the Play

Approving/Coordination the Designs

Casting

Coaching the Actors

Staging

M A N A G E R I A L — Planning and Coordination

Scheduling and Managing Rehearsals

Liaison for All Participants

Contributions to Marketing Activities

Selection of Play   Rehearsals Start   Opening Night

FIGURE 9.1

The Director's Responsibilities

The modern director is both artist and executive. The work begins at play selection and ends after (sometimes long after) the first performance. Many tasks go forward simultaneously, ending and beginning at different times.

A Director's Responsibilities

The director's acknowledged responsibilities are spread over at least seven major areas.

- Selecting or approving the play (including work with a playwright on an original script)
- Interpreting the play (analyzing and researching the playscript)
- Coordinating and communicating the production (scenery, costumes, lighting, sound)
- Developing a ground plan
- Casting and coaching actors

- Staging (including blocking, orchestrating voices, and setting tempos)
- Planning, coordinating, rehearsing, and polishing the production

This list suggests that a director's responsibilities are not only artistic but also managerial. However, these responsibilities are not discrete and separable.

A Director's Traits

This wide range of responsibilities requires a person of many abilities. Effective directors must master these traits:

- Directors need skills in organization to plan, coordinate, and schedule. Such skills include an ability to put ideas in order and to combine them with the ideas of other people, as well as the ability to order rehearsals, schedules, and budgets.
- Directors need abilities in making decisions, including the clearheadedness to define problems and see the conditions under which they must be solved (including limitations of time, budget, and available talent).
- Directors need sensitive interpersonal skills to coax performances from actors and to work effectively with all other members of the production team, inspiring each whenever possible, working creatively with them on group solutions to complicated problems, and imposing solutions only when absolutely necessary.
- Directors must have artistic vision and talent, which, although hard to define, are absolutely essential for successful productions.
- Directors need both stamina and concentration if they are to exercise their talent and carry out their many responsibilities.

Directors have to be both artists and managers in almost all of their work, and they are unique among theatre professionals precisely because of this unusual combination of traits. Within the same person, then, the artist proposes and the manager disposes, sometimes at widely different times and sometimes simultaneously.

A Director's View of Text

What is the director's responsibility to the dramatic text? Is it the director's job to put the play on

Craig Schwartz

FIGURE 9.2

Text-Centered Directing

The "worshipful director" respects the playwright's text. Here, a 2010 production of Frank Gilroy's 1964 *The Subject Was Roses* follows the author's suggested realistic setting, period, and costumes. This kitchen setting has running water, a working refrigerator, and stove—all the features of a 1940s kitchen.

the stage with utmost fidelity, or is it the director's job to create a theatrical event to which the script is merely a contributing part? Can the director cut lines or scenes, transpose scenes, or alter characters? Can the director "improve" the play, or must it be treated as a sacred object? Directors vary widely in the way they answer such questions. Their views range from veneration of the text by the Worshipful Director to near indifference by the Heretical Director; the play is seen as a holy object on the one hand and as a merely useful artifact on the other.

THE WORSHIPFUL DIRECTOR'S APPROACH   This directorial approach is playwright-centered. The worshipful director believes that nothing should stand in the way of the script as the playwright wrote it.

The Worshipful Director Argues:

The play is the only permanent art object in performance; it is a work of art in its own right, to be treated with respect and love. By examining it, we can know its creator's intentions—what meanings the playwright meant to convey, what experiences the audience was meant to have, what theatrical values were being celebrated. The playwright is a literary artist and a thinker, and the playwright's work is the foundation of theatrical art. It is the director's job to mount the playwright's work as faithfully and correctly as humanly possible.

Quirky modern interpretations are suspect, however: To show Hamlet as a homosexual in love with Rosencrantz or Guildenstern would be absurd and wrong because we know that such a relationship would never have been included in the tragic view that Shakespeare held.

The director's job is not primarily to create theatre; it is to cause the play to create theatre. The difference is crucial. The director says quite properly, 'I must allow the play to speak for itself and not get in the way.' To do otherwise is to betray the play, and I will not do it even if the 'betrayal' is great theatre.

The text-centered director, then, will often stage a production without cuts, with male roles played by males, and with no attention given to ethnic diversity in casting. The playwright's given circumstances will be scrupulously followed: sets, costumes, and props will reflect the author's dictates. By choice, the hand of the text-centered director is seldom discernible.

For plays under copyright, this is the contractually mandated approach to directing. Licenses for play scripts include a clause that the production present the play "as written." Court precedent has established, for example, that roles must be cast in the gender as specified by the playwright.

THE HERETICAL DIRECTOR'S APPROACH   This approach is director-centered rather than text-centered; it puts the director on a par with the playwright.

FIGURE 9.3

Director-Centered Directing
Here, in a theatre in Barcelona, Spain, a run-through of Ibsen's *Hedda Gabler*. Note the strikingly modern set—leather sectional seating, chrome verticals, and glass partitions. This director obviously ignored Ibsen's 1890 stage directions and changed the play's given circumstances.

The Heretical Director Argues:

Interpreting the text means making a theatrical entity of it for an audience—not 'finding its meaning' or 'doing it correctly.' There is no single interpretation of a play that is correct. There are only interpretations that are right for a given set of performers under a given set of conditions for a given audience.

How, then, can a director judge the rightness of the production? The director does not, any more than a painter judges the rightness of a painting. The director's final criterion is the satisfaction of an overall goal: Is it good theatre? Fidelity to some 'authorized' or time-honored view of the play is not, simply in and of itself, a good thing. It is foolish to say that the director did the play wrong unless what the director did was to make bad or dull theatre. The director has to be faithful to a vision, not to tradition or academic scholarship or propriety; only when that vision fails can the director be said to be wrong.

Does this mean, then, that the director has no responsibility to the 'meaning' of the play? Yes, in the sense that the director's responsibility is to the meaning of the performance, of which the play is only a part. Are we, then, to have gay Hamlets? Yes, if such interpretations are necessary to make the plays into effective theatre and if they are entirely consistent within their productions. It is impossible to know what somebody else's intentions were; an intention that was dynamite in 1600 may be as dull as dishwater in the early twenty-first century.

The heretical director believes, then, that the author's script is only the starting point for a new theatre experience. The playwright's words are among the least important features of the director-centered production. There may be textual interpolations from other sources; the playwright's text may be cut and rearranged; there may be cross-gender or color-blind casting; there may be striking visual images that seem to have little to do with the text. In short, the director-centered approach sees the director as a cocreator of the production. This approach to directing aligns with postmodernism.

The extremes of the heretical director's views can lead to results that many people find offensive or meaningless; on the other hand, those views can also lead to innovative and exciting productions.

A CONTINUUM   Both sorts of directors take a risk: The heretical director takes the chance of being ridiculous, the worshipful director of being banal. At their best, however, both can create productions that thrill audiences: the one with revelations of familiar material and the other with a brilliant rendition of the strong points of the classic.

The heretical and worshipful directors seem to be at the extremes of a continuum. The vast majority of directors in this century tend to approach productions somewhere between these two extremes. That is, they unobtrusively blend elements of both directorial approaches. Ours is an eclectic, postmodern era.

THE DIRECTOR AT WORK

The following seven steps are those that all directors take whether or not they are aware that they are taking them. Not all directors will necessarily approach each step in the same order, but the process presented here is an orderly one that can lead to a successful production.

Selecting the Play

Directors in community, school, and university theatres most often select the plays they direct; in professional theatre, directors at least approve the scripts (if they are staff directors at a regional theatre, say) or find themselves matched to a play by a commercial producer. Directors choose to do plays because the plays excite them; idea and spectacle are probably the most common elements to prompt directorial interest. Experienced directors also have acquired the ability to study the script in depth before accepting an assignment. Once the play has been selected or approved, the task of interpretation begins.

Interpreting the Play

The work of interpretation is an open-ended process that is based on analysis and research, some of which was described in Chapters 3 and 4.

ASSESSING POTENTIALS AND CHALLENGES   In early readings, the director usually has both positive and negative thoughts about the play and its audience impact. Two lists could be made, one of potentials (strengths) and one of challenges (weaknesses). These two lists taken together would show how the director's ideas were forming. Just as artists in any form are inspired by obstacles, so the director is inspired by a script's problems. Let us suppose that the director is considering Ibsen's *A Doll's House,* a realistic nineteenth-century play. The play is a classic of its kind and so has established merit; on the other hand, it is also old enough to seem dated to a modern audience in language and some plot devices. Therefore, after early readings, the director could list some strengths and weaknesses:

FIGURE 9.4
Mood
Scenery, color, lighting, costume, and fog set a satanic mood for the University of Montevallo production of *Macbeth.*

Matt Orton

Potentials	Challenges
Strong subject matter	Creaky structure—melodramatic
Excellent central character	Dated language (unless a new translation)
Great third-act climax	Some "serious" stuff now "funny"
Good potential for probing Victorian attitudes	Soliloquies, set speeches hard to make convincing today

ANALYZING THE TEXT   No matter what the orientation toward the text, the director must now work to analyze it: take it apart, reduce it to its smallest components, and "understand" it. Here, to *understand* means to allow the director to stage it. (Sometimes the director will be aided in this task by a dramaturg.) This job of analysis has many aspects, which are often explored simultaneously, both before and during rehearsals.

As a beginning, the director will want to ask and answer the kinds of questions suggested in Chapters 3 and 4. But the director's analysis will be much more detailed. Each decision about the play must be measured against an idea of how the anticipated audience will react. In thinking about audience, the director will explore many of the issues raised in Chapter 2, but again in considerably more detail. To see the differences between a director's analysis and the more general analyses offered elsewhere, we can look briefly at five representative areas.

Tone, Mood, and Key.   Funny/serious, cheerful/sad, light/heavy—the possibilities are many and must be identified for each act, each scene, and each line, as well as for the entire play. Neither laughter nor powerful emotion belongs unchangeably to every line of a script. Even when the proper tone is found for the play, the lines alone will not deliver that tone to an audience. For example, laugh lines must be carefully set up and "pointed," with both business (small activities performed by actors) and timing; moments that have potential for powerful emotion must be mined by the director, working with the actors.

Of particular interest in this aspect of interpretation is mood, the emotional "feel" that determines tempo and pictorial composition, and key (as in "high key" and "low key"), the degree to which effects are played against one another or against a norm for contrast. High-key scenes may even go to chiaroscuro ("light/dark") effects that use the darkest darks and the lightest lights, as in dramatic painting.

The Six Parts.   The director must study the play, perhaps using Aristotle's six parts (see Chapter 3), to find which parts are most important and which can be used most creatively to serve the play. Spectacle (including lighting, costume, the pictures created by the actors' movement, and scenery) and sound (including music, sound effects, and language) are often parts the director can manipulate and can bring to the play as "extras" that the playwright has not included. Character, idea, and story, on the other hand, are usually integral to the script itself, although subject to considerable interpretation and "bending" by director and actors. Many directors annotate their scripts in great detail for these three parts, some marking every line of dialogue for its contribution to character, idea, or story. Such annotations give the director both an overall sense of the play's thrust and specific instances of that thrust at work.

An analysis of these elements of the play is critical. A part misunderstood at this stage can mean that a moment or even an important thread through the entire play is lost in performance. To miss a major emphasis can mean a failed production. For example, a play that depends heavily on the beauty and intricacy of its language spoken in performance (sound) will usually suffer if directed to emphasize story or character, with the language overlooked or ignored (a frequent problem in productions of Shakespeare's plays). A play of character, if directed for its story, often has incomprehensible spots and long stretches during which nothing seems to happen. Therefore, the director must not only pick the part or parts that she can give theatrical life but must also pick the part or parts that the script gives theatrical life. Such choices mean knowing which part(s) is most important, where in the play each has its heights and depths, and how the director will give theatrical excitement to each.

Action and Progression. Performance is active and most plays have progressive actions; that is, they occur through time (audience time and their own time), and they must seem to increase in intensity as time passes—that is, as the audience is led from playwright's preparation through complication to crisis and resolution. When an audience enjoys a performance, whether a period comedy or a serious contemporary play, its responses might be compared to a parabola: They start at a low point, rise higher and higher as time passes, and usually fall off after the climax. The director wisely structures the performance to serve this perceptual structure (or another equally satisfying one). In short, the director cannot allow a performance to become static.

FIGURE 9.5

Environment

The bright colors in the costumes and set, coupled with the ramp into the audience that is studded with lights lets the audience know that fun is in store. Here, *A Funny Thing Happened on the Way to the Forum* at Southern Illinois University

It is not enough, then, to find the important elements and to know where the script emphasizes them. The director must now discover how each element grows in interest as the performance progresses. The word *progression* must be used again and again: What is this character's progression? What is the progression of the story? Is there progression in the spectacle?

If the progression is missed, the audience will become confused or bored.

Environment. As the actor determines given circumstances, the director determines environment: place, time of day, historical period.

Questions of tone, mood, and key also influence the director's thinking about environment. There are excellent reasons for putting a murder mystery in a country house on a stormy night, just as there are excellent reasons for putting a brittle comedy in a bright, handsome city apartment. The director thinks not only of the rightness of the environment for the characters (e.g., if they are rich they should have a rich environment, if Russians they should have something Russian, and so on) but also of the rightness for the indefinable subtleties of mood: the laziness of a warm day, the tension of an electrical storm, the depressing gloom of an ancient palace.

COMMUNICATING DECISIONS   The director holds production meetings with designers and technicians to consider budget, designs, shifting of scenery, time for costume changes, location of offstage storage space, and many other matters. As decisions are made, each designer provides the director with a detailed plan in the most appropriate form: color renderings and fabric swatches for costumes; ground plans, scale drawings, renderings, and models for sets; light plots with gel colors for lights. The sound designer (when one exists) may work with an annotated script and lists of sounds (music, sound effects). These renderings, plans, and other materials represent the culmination of the designers' work with the director: detailed, readable plans for a total production, all in harmony with one another and with the director's interpretation of the text.

Creating the Production

Through early attempts at assessment and analysis, the director develops strong ideas about the production of the play. These ideas will probably be modified and deepened as the director works with the play, but the director's interpretation is the springboard that will shape the whole, guiding the rehearsals and the work of both designers and actors.

FINDING A SPRINGBOARD   The director needs a springboard, a taking-off place from which to make a creative leap. The terms *concept* and *directorial image* are also used, but concept implies rational thought, and image implies picture making, and the director's process at this stage may be neither rational nor pictorial. Perhaps a directorial springboard can be seen as a combination of concept and image.

Certainly, few directors begin their creative work with a reasoned, easily stated idea. On the contrary, many directors begin with a seemingly random, sometimes conflicting medley of ideas, impressions, and half-formed thoughts whose connections may still be hidden. It is then the director's task—and the exercise of a special talent—to sort all these out and to find their connections and to see which can be given theatrical life and which cannot. Therefore, much of the director's preliminary work is a sorting out of raw materials from a whirlwind of impressions.

AGREEING ON INTERPRETATION AND PRESENTATION   Directors are rarely designers, but they know the practical needs and the aesthetic values of both play and production. When feasible, meetings between the director and the designers begin months before rehearsals; practicality may dictate, however, that they come only weeks or even days before casting.

At early production meetings among director and designers, matters of budgets, schedules, and working methods are discussed. Then, once the director has set out the interpretation and approach, the director and the designers work together to translate that interpretation into the presentation—the stuff of theatre.

Spotlight

Phyllida Lloyd's production of *Mamma Mia!* on Broadway.
Joan Marcus Photography.

Phyllida Lloyd: A Good Director

Phyllida Lloyd is a British director whose successful career certifies that she is expert at analyzing scripts and solving the problems they present. Her productions are consistently characterized by superb acting and technical polish. In Britain, she has directed classics and revivals of modern classics, new plays, and opera. In the United States, she is best known for two financially and aesthetically successful productions that could hardly be more different: *Mamma Mia!* and *Mary Stuart*.

The most widely known is the musical *Mamma Mia!* based on the hit songs of the Swedish group ABBA. More than thirty million people have seen the stage show. Lloyd also directed the 2008 movie, her second film. Starring Meryl Streep and Pierce Brosnan, the movie matched the stage musical's huge financial success.

"A great deal of the success of *Mamma Mia!* has been due to the audience recognizing themselves on stage or screen," said Lloyd in the *New York Times*. "It also seemed normal to us that you could be thoroughly silly one moment and deadly serious the next...."

Lloyd's production of Friedrich Schiller's 1800 play *Mary Stuart* in a new translation played the small Donmar Warehouse, transferred to a commercial run in London in 2005, and played Broadway in 2009. The play presents the final days of Mary Queen of Scots as she battles with Queen Elizabeth I for England's throne. Mary is imprisoned as Elizabeth ponders whether and how to execute Mary. Schiller imagined the two rival queens' meeting, staged by Lloyd in a rainstorm. Lloyd capitalized on the play's sense of history and language, sober in tone and theme.

Lloyd said, "Aside from the gender issue, the play deals with the ethics of government—what price homeland security, how to take a potentially unpopular decision and still remain in favour with your electorate. It also portrays two women being 'managed' by a group of seemingly eternal bureaucrats....[The two women are not] able to live their lives like the men around them without jeopardy or reproach.

"I have been very lucky and I think it all goes back to state subsidy for the arts. I gained my training and confidence and credentials in the not-for-profit world and in England that does not mean on the fringe of things. It means right at the centre. It is that experience of handling big projects, big groups of people if you like that led to a commercial musical and then to Hollywood. In the UK there are however—just as in the States—less women directing huge budget musicals, running big institutions and obviously directing anything but lower budget movies—which says something about how when the economic stakes get high girls are seen as a greater risk." For Lloyd, film directing is open to at least one woman. In 2011, she directed *The Iron Lady*, a film about the first woman English prime minister, Margaret Thatcher, that starred Meryl Streep in the title role.

 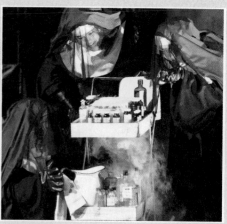

FIGURE 9.6

Springboard

Two quite different productions of *Macbeth* communicate the director's springboard into the visual elements of each production. The three witches in the left image suggest the Virginia Commonwealth University production's Kabuki influence, whereas the witches in the University of Michigan production seem to be nurses in a hospital setting. Both productions have elements of the Heretical Director's springboard.

They come to share a vision of mood and decide how best to express it through the visual potency of lighting, set, and costume; they know that inconsistency of mood leads to a severe weakening of the performance. They work to ensure that all elements of the production fit together. The director also works with the designers to achieve progression in the designs to support the progression in the play.

Developing a Ground Plan

The ground plan is a "map" of the playing area for a scene, with doors, furniture, walls, and other details indicated to scale (often one-quarter inch to a foot). In a realistic interior, the director can almost design the acting space by simply setting down several directorial needs in detail:

- The number and location of entrances and exits
- The number and location of seating elements
- The number and location of objects that will motivate behavior and movement (for example, stoves and refrigerators, fireplaces, closets, and bookcases)
- Visibility (Can actors be seen in important moments?)
- Special requirements of the script (For instance, is a trap door needed?)

These requirements may be determined by directors before they meet with their designers. Some directors even give their set designer a ground plan, complete except for small matters of dimension. Others might remain open until the designer has created a ground plan around a more general statement of needs.

In the nonrealistic play, or sometimes in the realistic play with exterior scenes, directors may have less rigorous requirements. Still, for variety, mood, and emphasis, the director will probably specify:

- Differences in level (e.g., platforms, staircases, balconies)
- Separation of playing areas
- The location of seating elements (e.g., benches, low walls, swings, and so on).

Other design elements may be suggested or required by the director as well; for example, the size and shape of the space where a crowd is used, where a sense of the isolation of a single figure is wanted, or where a feeling of cramped oppression is sought. Special effects may require special space.

Once ground plans are established, they become the basis for all staging. Drawn to scale, they can be used with scale cutouts of furniture and actors to plan staging. They are also the basis for the three-dimensional model that the designer usually provides.

Casting and Coaching Actors

The producer or director puts out a casting call and schedules auditions or tryouts. In New York, a great deal of casting is done through agents, casting directors, and private contacts. In university and community theatres, almost the opposite situation holds true, because maximum participation is wanted and thus closed or private auditions are educationally suspect. In repertory theatres, of course, in which the company members are under contract, the director must work rather differently to make the contracted company and the plays mesh, and casting and play selection influence each other.

CASTING   Casting is of enormous importance in the success of a production as it depends on finding the right actors for the right roles, always a balancing act between the real and the ideal. Although several actors in a cast—whether in professional, educational, or community

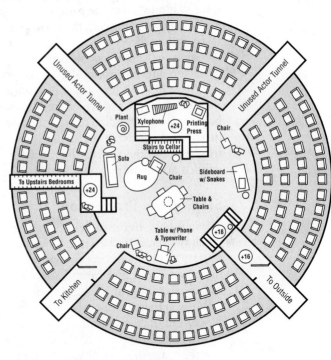

―――― Existing Arena Theatre Plan

―――― Platforms, doors for this show

―――― Furniture

FIGURE 9.7

The Ground Plan

This map of the playing space shows all of the major scenic elements. Ground plans become the basis for staging the entire production. Here, the ground plan for an arena production of *You Can't Take It With You.*

productions—may be ideal for their parts, other casting decisions may well be a compromise. Even in the plushest professional situations, actor availability, salary requirements, or billing demands can thwart the best intentions.

One twentieth-century director maintained that casting is 80 percent of a play's interpretation—the right actor will enhance the director's interpretation of the play and production, but the wrong actor will undermine the decisions made by the director and designers.

COACHING   When the actor and director work in a productive collaboration, the director functions as a coach who advises, inspires, and encourages the actor. The director becomes the sounding board and the artistic conscience of the actor—mentor and interpreter, bringing to the actor's work another dimension, another voice, another view of the whole play with all its characters. Most directors and actors work quite well together. Credit for much of this goes to the director's social skills, although some of it must go to the patience and determination of the actor. The most potent factor may be, in the end, the knowledge that both are engaged in a creative enterprise whose success benefits both. The more precise and sure the director can be, the better. Precision and sureness come from preparation, and so the basis of the most productive actor–director relationships is the director's own work in advance of rehearsals.

Most modern directors involve themselves closely in their actors' creation of their roles. The influence of Stanislavski, in particular, has led to collaboration between actor and director that has developed, in some cases, into a great dependency on the director. Particularly in educational and community theatres, great trust is put in the director by the actors, and many interpretations are virtually handed down entire from director to actor.

Staging the Production

Staging is one of the director's most important responsibilities. No matter how much the actors and even the director are devoted to inner truth and to characterization, the time comes when the director must shape the actors' moves and timing and must give careful attention to movement, picture making, and rhythm. This process of putting the play on its feet is also called blocking.

It is in the nature of theatre that the visual details of the stage have significance, and the director must make that significance jibe with interpretation. Significance is the crux of the matter. We live in a world in which movement and visual arrangement signify: They mean something.

Modern staging pays meticulous attention to picturization and composition as a way of signaling to the audience important aspects of the play and its production. These silent aspects of staging were probably not seen before the mid-nineteenth century, except in special cases. Much of what is taught about directing today is devoted to these matters.

PICTURIZATION   Picturization is the storytelling aspect of staging. It's about revealing character, emotion, and motive through movement, body language, and the actor's small activities (e.g., drying dishes).

Jason Ayer

FIGURE 9.8

Picturization

The director places these two characters quite far apart in Theatre South Carolina's *The Violet Hour*. Perhaps the inspiration was "there is a gulf that neither can bridge." Later, as this second moment suggests, they have crossed the "bridge."

Movement.   As actors are aware of and exploit "body language," so the director is aware of and uses "movement language." Stage movement is often more abundant than real-life movement. In a real situation, people often sit for a long time to talk, for example, whereas on a stage characters in the same situation will be seen to stand, walk, change chairs, and move a good deal. Partly, this abundance of movement results from the physical distance of the audience—small movements of eyes and facial muscles do not carry the length of a theatre. Partly, it results from the director's need for variety, for punctuation of action and lines, for the symbolic values of movement itself, and for the changing symbolic values of picturization.

Stage movement is based partly on the received wisdom of the movement implied by such statements as "Face up to it," "She turned her back on it," and "He rose to the occasion." Too, it serves to get characters into positions with which we have similar associations: "at the center of things," "way off in the blue," and "out in left field." The director is concerned with direction, speed, and amount of movement. Direction reveals both motivation and human interaction; speed shows strength of desire or strength of involvement (impassioned haste, for example, or ambling indifference); amount is perhaps most useful for contrast (a character making a long movement after several short ones or in contrast with the small moves of several other characters).

Movement patterns have a symbolic value much like that of individual movements and can be derived from the same figures of speech: "twisting him around her finger," "winding her in," "going in circles," "following like sheep," "on patrol," and many others suggest patterns for characters or groups. They are used, of course, to underscore a pattern already perceived in the play or the scene.

Visual Symbolism.   The exploitation of the stage's potential for displaying pictures is not entirely limited to the proscenium theatre but has its greatest use there. With thrust and arena stages, this framing is impossible. Because audiences are located on three or all four sides of the stage, each segment of the audience sees a different picture. Thus, only certain aspects of picture making have universal application, and of these the most important by far is visual symbolism.

Stage Relationships.   Puns and traditional sayings give us a clue to how another kind of visual symbolism works and also suggest to us how the mind of the director works as it creates visual images of the sort that communicate to us in dreams. "Caught in the middle," "one up on him," and "odd man out" all suggest arrangements of actors. The additional use of symbolic properties or set pieces—a fireplace, associated with the idea of home ("hearth and family"), for example—gives still greater force to the picture. Thus, a character who "moves in" on the hearth of a setting while also moving physically between a husband and wife ("coming between them") and sitting in the husband's armchair ("taking his place") has told the audience a complicated story without saying a word.

COMPOSITION   Composition is the technical aspect of blocking that leads the audience to see clearly what the director believes is important.

Visual Aesthetics.   Most stage pictures are well composed, or good to look at, but directors are often careful to study the production with an eye to improving the

FIGURE 9.9

Movement

This jarring, violent moment in *A Lie of The Mind*, combined with the actress's expression, cements an important step in the play's progression. Here, a production by Rep Stage, Maryland.

Stan Barouh

aesthetic quality of the scenes. They try to eliminate obvious visual flaws: straight lines, lines parallel to the stage front, evenly spaced figures like bottles on a supermarket shelf. They look for **balance**, so that the stage does not seem heavy with actors on one side and light on the other—unless that is the director's point. Composition is, finally, an irrational matter and a highly subjective one; directors who concern themselves with it in depth learn much from the other visual arts, especially traditional painting.

Focus. A stage is a visually busy place, with many things to look at; therefore, the audience's eyes must be directed through composition to the important point at each moment. A number of devices achieve **focus**:

- *Framing*: in a doorway, between other actors, and so on
- *Isolating*: one character against a crowd, one character on a higher or lower level
- *Elevating*: standing while others sit, or the reverse, or getting on a higher level
- *Enlarging*: with costume, properties, or the mass of a piece of furniture
- *Illuminating*: in a pool of light or with a brighter costume
- *Pointing*: putting the focal character at the intersection of "pointers"—pointing arms, swords, eyes, and so on

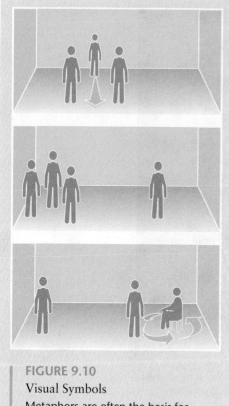

FIGURE 9.10

Visual Symbols

Metaphors are often the basis for movement. Here, for example, "He came between them" (above); "Odd man out" (middle); "She ran circles around him" (below).

Focus is largely a mechanical matter, but it is an important one that affects both movement and picture making.

Mood. Mood is established most readily with lighting and sound and with the behavior of the characters. However, certain visual effects of character arrangement contribute, as well: horizontals, perhaps, for a quiet, resigned scene or looming verticals and skewed lines for a suspense melodrama.

Mood values are subjective and irrational, however, and hard to describe. In reality, what the director remains watchful for are clashes of mood, when movement and visual symbols conflict with other mood establishers.

RHYTHM   Rhythm is the result of repetition at regular intervals. The elements of **rhythm** in the theatre are those things that regularly mark the passage of time: scenes, movements, speeches, and words. For the director, rhythm includes tempo and timing, both aspects of progression. The director is concerned, then, not only with the interpretation of character and the visual signals of interpretation but also with the rate(s) at which things happen.

We have seen that speed of movement is important to movement's meaning. Now we can say that it is also important to intensity and rhythm. We associate quickness with urgency, slowness with relaxation; change in speed is most important of all. We might compare this phenomenon with the beating of a heart: Once the normal heartbeat (base rhythm) is established, any change becomes significant. The director establishes the base rhythm with the opening scenes of the play and then creates variations on it, and the shortening of the time between moves, between lines, and between entrances and exits becomes a rhythmic acceleration that gives the audience the same feeling of increased intensity as would a quickening of the pulse.

Pace is the professional's term for "tempo," but it is not a matter of mechanical tempo. Much of what is meant by pace is, in fact, emotional intensity and energy. Tempo must grow naturally out of understanding and rehearsal of a scene, not out of a directorial decision to force things along.

Timing is complicated and difficult, something felt rather than thought out. Comic timing is the delivery of the laugh-getter—a line or a piece of business—after exactly the right preparation and at just that moment when it will most satisfy the tension created by a pause before it; it also describes the actor's awareness of the timing that has produced previous laughs and of how each builds on those before. The timing of serious plays is rather different and depends far more on the setting of (usually) slow rhythms from which either a quickening tempo will increase tension or a slowing will enhance a feeling of doom.

FIGURE 9.11

Focus

The lower diagrammed photo makes evident the composition of a moment from *Look Homeward, Angel* at Theatre South Carolina.

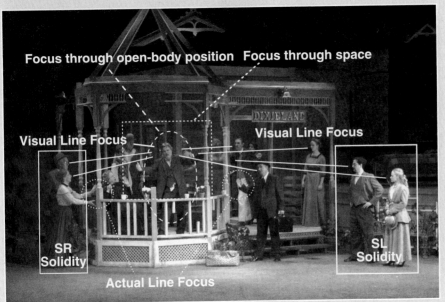

Planning, Coordinating, Rehearsing, and Polishing

In a commercial Broadway production, many managerial functions are performed by the producer or the producer's office. In community and school theatres, the director performs most or all of them: Scheduling, budgeting, personnel selection, research, and some aspects of public relations all fall to the director's lot.

Scheduling includes the overall flow of production work from inception to performance, including production meetings, rehearsals, and the coordination of design and technical schedules, at least for purposes of information (including costume fittings for actors, clearing of the stage for construction work, and so on). These schedules are kept by the director or the stage manager on such an easily read form as an oversized calendar.

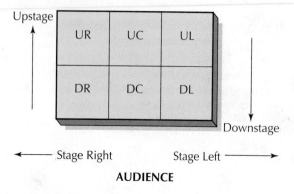

Upstage

UR	UC	UL
DR	DC	DL

Downstage

Stage Right ← — — → Stage Left

AUDIENCE

FIGURE 9.12

Proscenium Stage Areas

"Up" and "Down" are away from or toward the front of the stage, dating from the era when the stage sloped from back to front; "Left" and "Right" are from the actor's point of view when facing the audience.

THE DIRECTOR AS LIAISON   Throughout the work of the production, the director is the person who ensures that all members of the production team are pulling in the same direction, working together to ensure a successful production. He or she makes sure that the actors know what the designers are doing, and vice versa, that actors go promptly for costume fittings, that the designers provide needed drawings to the technical staff, and on and on. He or she mediates disagreements and serves as final arbiter of differences. In short, the director is that crucial person who is most responsible for realizing the potential of theatre.

REHEARSING AND POLISHING   Every director has a rehearsal pattern, and every pattern has to be adaptable to the special needs of each cast and each play. In general, however, a structure like the following is used.

First Rehearsal: The Read-Through.   The cast gathers, many strangers to one another. The director plays the role of host, making introductions, breaking the ice, and moving these individuals toward cohesion. The play will probably be discussed at some length, the director explaining general ideas and the overall direction; the designers may be asked to show and discuss models and sketches. Certain practical matters are got out of the way by the director or the stage manager (the signing of necessary forms, the resolving of individual schedule conflicts, and so on).

Then the play is read, either by the entire cast or by the director or the playwright. Some directors interrupt this first reading often, even on every line, to explain and define; others like to proceed without interruption so that the actors can hear one another. Either way, once the books are open and the lines are read, the rehearsal period is truly under way. Because the cast is not yet up and "on their feet" during the read-throughs, this period is often called table work.

Rehearsal by Units.   Rehearsing entire acts is often not the way to do detailed work, and so the acts are further broken down into French scenes (between the entrance and the exit of a major character) or scenes (between curtains or blackouts), and then further into beats or units (between the initiation and the end of an objective). These short elements are numbered in such a way that, for example, all the appearances of a major character can be called by listing a series of numbers, for example, 12, 13, 15, 17, meaning scenes 2, 3, 5, and 7 of the first act. By scheduling detailed rehearsals this way, the director often avoids keeping actors waiting. This same number system can be used to call scenes that need extra rehearsal.

As a general pattern, it can be said that many directors move from the general rehearsal of early readings into increasingly detailed rehearsals of smaller and smaller units, and then into rehearsals of much longer sections when the units are put back together.

Run-Throughs. A run-through is a rehearsal of an entire act or an entire play; it gives the director (and the actors) insight into the large movements and progressions of the play. After run-throughs, the director will probably return to rehearsal of certain small units to polish them, but, as performance nears, more and more run-throughs are held.

Technical and Dress Rehearsals. Technical rehearsals, the integration of lights, costumes, sound, and scenery into the performance, are devoted to any or all of

FIGURE 9.13

Composition and Balance

This composition looks realistically uncontrived but is balanced. While crowded with actors, note how the director of *Parade* uses placement of actors (who point) and lighting to create focus on the central couple. Here a production at Center Theatre Group in Los Angeles.

Craig Schwartz

these elements. The stage manager usually takes over the management of the script and the cues in preparation for running the show during performance. The director makes decisions affecting the look and sounds of the production and conveys them to the designers, often through the stage manager. These rehearsals are devoted almost exclusively to polishing, making the production look and sound its best.

Dress rehearsals incorporate costumes into the other technical elements, and final dress rehearsals are virtually performances. Nothing is now left to chance: Actors must be in place for every entrance well in advance of their cues; properties must be in place, with no rehearsal substitutes tolerated; costumes must seem as natural to the actors as their own clothes (achieved by giving them, weeks previously, rehearsal costumes that approximate the actual costume); every scene shift and light cue must be smooth, timed as the director wants it.

Opening. Once the show is open, for the director the journey is over. To be sure, polishing rehearsals may be called even after opening night or full rehearsals if the play is a new one that has gone into previews (full performances with audiences but in advance of the official opening) and needs fixing. As a rule, though, when the play officially opens, it belongs to the actors and the stage manager, and the director is a vestige of another era in its life.

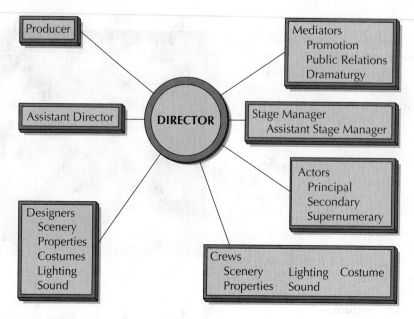

FIGURE 9.14

The Director as Liaison

The director is at the center of a network of people working for the success of the production.

TRAINING DIRECTORS

There is no one pathway that leads to becoming a director. Many of today's directors began as actors, choreographers, stage managers, or even designers. Some of today's directors have come from fields entirely outside theatre; others have pursued graduate work in theatre, specifically as directors.

Probably today's directors in the professional and commercial theatres have somewhat more varied backgrounds than do those within the educational theatre, most of whom have a graduate degree in theatre. Many professional directors (but not most academic directors) belong to the Stage Directors and Choreographers Society, a national union.

Directors of whatever background and training, however, are expected to have a body of knowledge and skills. For this reason, theatre accrediting programs generally do not recognize undergraduate majors or degrees in directing, only graduate ones. For people who want to pursue graduate work in directing, there are two usual pathways: a master of fine arts (MFA) degree in directing or, less often, a PhD in theatre history, criticism, or literature, with supervised opportunities in directing.

Because of the complexity of the director's responsibilities, it is difficult to know exactly how to train someone to be a director. Directing, like any artistic practice, has changed since its beginnings. Directing will doubtless change again in the future, but we cannot say with certainty how; for now, the director's training must remain wide-ranging and flexible.

FIGURE 9.15

Focus

This moment from Ball State University's production of *My Fair Lady* uses basic staging techniques to throw focus to the person with his back to the audience who is about to turn and face the audience. Although the people behind the central figure are basically in a semicircle, note the variety of postures.

Given the complexity of their task and the training needed, directors might be thought to be in short supply. In fact, however, the market for directors, in both educational and professional venues, is glutted. Unemployment rates are at least as high for directors as for actors. Perhaps this situation is less surprising when we remember that the director is at the center of a network of people working for the success of the production. For every one director there are many actors, designers, and technicians required: It takes a large pyramid of people to support the one figure at its top.

WHAT IS GOOD DIRECTING?

To understand directing, we must be able to assess what the director has brought to the play and what the play offered the director as strengths and weaknesses. Our evaluation of the direction, then, will depend on answers to such questions as:

- How well did the director analyze and interpret the script?
- How well did the director solve the problems presented?

It is important to separate the production being studied from the play being studied. The production is not necessarily bad because it fails to stage the "playwright's intentions," nor is it necessarily good because it either stages the playwright's intentions precisely or turns them upside down. As we have seen, different kinds of directors take different approaches; we must try to understand the approach and then evaluate it for what it is.

- Good directing is seen in an internally consistent, exciting production. It deals with the play's problems and exploits the play's strengths in terms of the director's approach.
- Good directing shows most of all in the work of the actors. If the actors are good and are working in a theatrically compelling whole, the director has laid a good foundation. If the actors have not been unified, if they seem to hang in space when not speaking, if they perform mechanically, if they lack motivation at any point, if they do not perform with one another, they have been poorly directed.
- Good directing has technical polish—smooth cues, precise timing, and a perfect blending of all elements—that radiates "authority," the artists' confidence in their work.
- Good directing creates compelling pictures and movement, but only when they expand the work of actors and playwright, never when they contradict—and never when they exist for their own sake.
- Good directing sets the performance tempo without giving it mechanical speed; there is no sense of too fast or too slow, but rather the organic tempo of a living entity.
- Good directing combines all elements into a whole; there is no sense of good ideas left over or of things unfinished. Everything belongs; everything is carried to its proper full development; nothing is overdone.

The good director, then, understands the play and takes a consistent approach to it, bringing the actors to life in a complete production. The bad director does not fully understand the play, often failing to ask detailed questions; does not coach the actors or coaches them only incompletely, or directs them mechanically in postures, positions, and movements dictated by a mechanical notion of visual symbolism and visual beauty; achieves not tempo but clockwork timing; and leaves ideas undeveloped and elements unassimilated.

KEY TERMS

Check your understanding against this list. Brief definitions are included in the Glossary; persons are page-referenced in the Index.

balance   131
beats (unit)   134
blocking   128
casting   127
composition   128
dress rehearsals   135
environment
   (of the play)   123

focus   131
French scenes   134
ground plan   126
pace   132
picturization   128
rhythm   132
run-through   135
springboard   124

staging   128
table work   134
technical
   rehearsals   135
timing   132

Designers and Technicians

Self Destruction Opera, a new play by David Jacobi, was produced at Clemson University.

OBJECTIVES

When you have completed this chapter, you should be able to:

- Explain how mood, abstraction, historical period, and socioeconomic circumstances affect design.

- Enumerate the major responsibilities of each

designer—scenery, lights, sound, costumes—and of the technical director.

- Discuss some of the important issues that face

scenery, costume, and lighting designers.

- List and discuss some major components of design.

FIGURE 10.1

Before Designers

This French theatre engraving from the 1600s shows a stage with a stock setting of houses in forced perspective. Carpenters and painters were undoubtedly used; however, that the setting was designed is questionable. Productions in the Greek and Roman eras also did not have especially designed settings.

Sitting in the modern theatre, we sometimes take scenery so much for granted that it is easy to forget that theatre does not have its roots in either spectacular effects or localized settings. We have become accustomed to the presence of physical environments that so closely suit the mood, meanings, and given circumstances of each play that we may lose sight of the fact that the theatre for a long period used little more than the theatre space itself as environment, and that for centuries after that it was satisfied with stock settings that could be used for many plays: a room in a palace, a garden, a forest. We live in a period of magnificent settings and superb designers; however, stage design has not always been considered fundamental to theatre or its performance. (The staging spaces and conventions of theatre through time are covered in Chapters 11 through 20.)

Much the same thing is true of costume designers, although it seems likely that their art, extended to include the making of masks, is an old one. Clearly, the sound designer is a recent innovation. Creators of lighting effects may be said to go back to the Renaissance, but the art of stage lighting came into its own when a controllable means of illumination was invented: gaslight from about 1830. Projection designers are a twenty-first century job classification.

ELEMENTS OF DESIGN

Designers manipulate several basic elements to produce a production that serves the play or musical. Some elements of design are more likely to be used by scene designers, others by costume designers, and still others by lighting designers. Yet to some extent, each of these six elements is used by all designers to create mood, atmosphere, and focus.

- Color: There are an uncountable number of colors and combinations of colors that designers use to create a specific world onstage.
- Line: The defining edge of a shape is called line. The outline or silhouette of a shape can convey meaning.
- Mass: Mass is the bulk or weight of objects on stage or their apparent bulk or weight.

- Composition: The overall arrangement and balance of items on stage. Costume, scenic, video, and lighting designers all contribute to the "look" found on stage.
- Texture: Like color, there are innumerable textures that contribute to the "feel" of a stage composition. Costume designers recognize the contribution of texture, for example, when fabrics are selected. So do lighting and scene artists.
- Light: The darkness or brightness of a stage picture, including those in the set, lights, and costumes help to convey the sense of a specific time and place. Lighting designers are especially concerned with the intensity, direction, and color of light.

Tony Penna

FIGURE 10.2

Elements of Design

This moment from a Clemson University production of *As You Like It* illustrates many of the elements of design in striking ways. The color is low-key, largely black. Line is solid on the floor and lacy, complex, almost organic above. Similarly the mass is heavy below and light above. Texture is everywhere, except for the flat black backdrop. Warm light comes largely from behind the figures; transmitted through the translucent fabric above, it brings the focus again to the center of the composition.

AREAS OF DESIGN

There are different disciplines of theatre design. Some of these disciplines are quite new, such as projection design, but others are traditional, such as, scene design, costume design, lighting design, and sound design. Sometimes and for some productions, a single designer will handle multiple parts of the design. Scenery and costume design will come from the same person or scenery and lighting design or lighting and sound design.

Scene Designer

Scene designers are responsible for the settings, transitions from one setting to another, masking if any, furniture, set dressing, and properties (or props). It is a scene designer's job to create a physical environment for the play's action. This created theatrical space normally may have the added function of supplying the audience with clues about the play's locale. Masking consists of curtains or other materials that hide the wings and fly areas from audience view when desired. Set dressing is the decorative items that complete the stage picture, such as books, lamps, vases, table cloths, and such.

Some important issues for the scene designer include:

- Number of settings: Can the entire play be played in one set, must different sets be designed and changed for each scene, or can some sort of unit set serve for all scenes?
- Shape and size of the stage: Will the audience surround it or look at it through a proscenium arch? If the stage is small, how can it be kept from seeming cramped? Will the actors play within the setting or in front of it?
- Sight lines of the theatre: What peculiarities of the theatre's architecture demand that the settings be built in special shapes so that every member of the audience can see?
- Means of shifting the scenery: Is there overhead rigging so that scenery can be "flown"—raised out of sight or lowered into sight—or is there an elevator stage or a turntable stage for bringing new settings in mechanically?
- Materials from which the scenery will be built: Is it better to use traditional flats of wood and canvas, will built-up details of wood or plastic be better, or will such special materials as poured polyurethane foam or corrugated cardboard or metal pipe better fit the requirements?
- Effects that make special scenic demands: Are there vast outdoor scenes in a proscenium theatre that require large painted drops and matching masking, will such unusual events in the play as earthquakes or explosions require special solutions, or does the floor need a trap door for sudden appearances or disappearances?
- Decision to imitate historical scenery that creates special requirements: For example, if a seventeenth-century play is to be done with Italianate scenery, that style decision will have a sweeping impact on scenic design and construction.

Some of these duties might fall to experts under the scene designer's direction, such as, experts in flying by wire or experts in magical effects.

In addition, the scene designer is normally in charge of the design or selection of all properties, the things used by the actors that are not part of the scenery, such as swords, cigarette cases, guns, and letters. When such things must be designed, as in a period play, the designer devises them and the technical staff builds them. When properties are acquired from outside sources, the designer haunts stores and antique shops and pores over catalogs of all sorts. In plays done with minimal scenery, as in arena staging, the properties can take on added importance.

Costume Designer

A costume designer is responsible for clothing, millinery (hats), hair styling, and shoes. The costume designer dresses both the character and the actor, creating clothing in which the character is expressed and the actor is both physically comfortable and artistically pleased. In some theatres, the costume designer may be responsible for properties that are worn by the actors, such as, swords or fans. Some of these specialized duties may fall to other experts under the costume designer's direction, such as, millinery specialists, wig designers, armor fabricators, and so on.

FIGURE 10.3

Little Shop of Horrors

The setting for this musical must make way for the plant, Audrey II, to grow as it is fed blood. In addition, the plant is a series of puppets that must be especially designed and manipulated; constructing them is a technical challenge. Here, a production at Ball State University Theatre.

Some important issues for a costume design include:

- Silhouette: The **silhouette** is the mass and outline of the costume as worn.
- The costume in motion: Does it have potential to swirl, billow, drape, or curve as it moves? Does it change with movement? Will it encourage, even inspire, the actor to move more dynamically? What aspects of it—fringe, a scarf, coattails, a cape, a shawl—can be added or augmented to enhance motion?
- Fabric texture and draping: Does the play suggest that costumes should have the roughness of burlap and canvas or the smoothness of silk? What is wanted—fabrics that will drape in beautiful folds, such as velour, silk, or jersey, or fabrics that will hang straight and heavily?
- Fabric pattern: Does the costume call for small, repeated patterns, very large designs on the fabric, or none at all?
- Enhancement or suppression of body lines: Does the production call for the pelvic V of the Elizabethan waist, the pushed-up bosom of the French Empire period, the pronounced sexuality of the medieval male codpiece, or the body-disguising toga? For the individual actor, are there characteristics like narrow shoulders, skinny calves, or long necks that must be diminished or disguised?
- Special effects: Some productions will require quick changes or animal, bird, fantasy creatures.

FIGURE 10.4

Making the Costume

This unnamed character, a "Fop" in *Cyrano de Bergerac*, is not only clearly drawn but the designer has given the costume shop a number of notes as well a quick sketch of the rear view of the design. Lace is to be gilded and much of the costume is to be made of a fabric with a metallic appearance, Lurex. The Fop will literally "glitter." Desmond Heeley designed *Cyrano* costumes for the Stratford Shakespeare Festival in Canada.

Especially for plays placed in the contemporary era, clothes may be purchased in stores. This can be more time consuming for the designer although often cheaper than having clothes built since there are so many choices to hunt down and consider. Some large theatres have shoppers to do this chore.

In addition, the costumer must consult with both scene and lighting designers to make sure that the costumes will look as they are designed to look under stage light and against settings.

Lighting Designer

A lighting designer is responsible for illuminating the actors and scenery; using light expressively to communicate time, place, or mood; and for lighting transitions. The possible uses of theatre light are countless. Through manipulation of intensity and direction, for example, a designer can change the apparent shape of an object. Through manipulation of intensity and color, the lighting designer can influence the audience's perception of mood. Also through manipulation of direction and color, the designer can create a world utterly unlike the one in which the audience lives, with light coming from fantastic angles and falling in colors never seen in nature. The lighting designer is usually responsible for projected shadows, clouds, and similar effects. Lighting changes can be subtle or bold, and may augment the pace of a play, scene, dance, or song. Among the lighting designer's special considerations are:

- Visibility/invisibility: The lighting designer has the special responsibility of making everyone else's work visible to the audience. Light is selective, and it can show the audience precisely what is to be seen. Sometimes that means making parts of the stage invisible or nearly so.
- Dimensionality: Light creates depth, for one example, and it can make an actor's eyes seem to sink into deep sockets or vanish in a bland, flat mask.
- Color/lack of color: Light gives or takes color, and it can make costume colors glow with vibrancy or fade into dirty gray.

Modern equipment has made theatre lighting highly flexible. Small, easily aimed lighting instruments and complex electronic controls, with computerized

FIGURE 10.5

Lighting and Scenery

Scene designers know that lighting will enhance their settings. Here, two images from the musical *Urinetown*, produced by The University of North Carolina–Charlotte. The left picture shows the set under "work lights" before the audience enters the theatre; the right image is the setting under lights designed to give dimension, color, and visibility to the set.

memories, have made possible a subtlety in stage lighting that was unknown even thirty years ago.

The lighting designer works with three fundamentals:

- color of light
- direction of light
- intensity of light.

As recently as fifteen years ago, the color of light was solely changed physically by the placement of a transparent colored medium affixed to the front of the instrument, usually called a gel, in the beam of light. Direction is a function of the location of the lighting instruments, of which hundreds may be used in a contemporary production. Current practice also often includes the use of scrolling color changers, devices that can automatically change the color on any standard lighting fixture by electronic control. Each instrument is plugged into an electric circuit either individually or with a few others to illuminate the same scene. The location of instruments is rarely changed during performance, and so designers are limited by the number of instruments and the number of electrical circuits available to them. Light intensity is controlled by changes in the electrical current supplied to the instrument; this process is called dimming and is done by computer control.

The lighting designer's plan is called a light plot (see Figure 10.6). It shows the location and direction of each instrument, as well as what kind of instrument is to be set at each location—usually either a soft-edged and wide-beamed floodlight or a hard-edged and narrow-beamed spotlight. The locations chosen

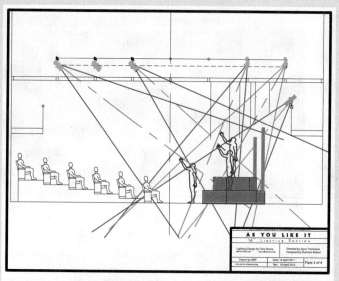

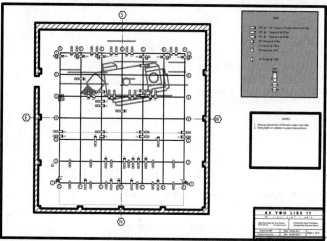

FIGURE 10.6

The Light Plot

Here, two printouts of a computer-aided lighting design for a production of *As You Like It* at Clemson University by Tony Penna. For clarity, the scenery and actors have been colored brown; the light from the fixtures blue. The top illustration is the stage and audience in profile. The bottom image is the theatre from above. It includes a key, here shaded light violet, that identifies the lighting instruments by type and shape. Where the instruments appear in the illustration, they specify the gel color, channel number, and dimmer number for each.

for the instruments are over and around the playing area, so that light falls on the actors for visibility, sculpting, mood, or time of day. First used in music concerts, automated lighting fixtures allow a computer to remotely control the size, shape, color, and focus of the light and to swivel the fixture to change the direction the light is aimed towards. Once expensive, these special-effect fixtures now seem affordable for more and more theatres. In addition, such subsidiary instruments as rows of simple lights without lenses called striplights, rows of lights at floor level along the front of many proscenium stages called footlights, and spotlights that an operator can swivel so that their bright beam can constantly illuminate a moving performer called follow spots are sometimes used.

Sound Designer

Sound designers are responsible for amplification of the actors' voice when used; recorded sound effects; selecting music; and sometimes writing or commissioning new music when used. In many cases, sound designers design the layout of speakers on stage and in the auditorium to clearly transmit the sound.

Projection Designer

A projection designer, if a production engages one, is responsible for locating, editing, or creating still or moving images projected on scenery or instead of scenery; designing the movement and transitions of projected elements; and selecting equipment for the projection and control of the projection equipment. More and more productions, especially those in the professional theatre, are incorporating projected images into design. Although projection designers may not actually execute every aspect of the design, they are charged with conceiving the effect. For example, if animation is needed the projection designer may hire an animator.

As a result a new, rapidly advancing design specialty has evolved during the last decade or so. The designation "Projection Designer" may not be uniformly used as the field is so new that a widely accepted title has not emerged. Some job titles seen in recent Broadway Playbills for this function include "video design" and "media design." Projection designers incorporate the skills set of scenic and lighting designers. In fact, before this design specialty evolved, scenic or lighting designers provided projections when used.

FIGURE 10.7

Projection Design

This setting for the musical *Next to Normal*, performed at the Ahmanson Theatre in Los Angeles, is backed by an LED screen that allows the projection designer to create varied images.

Craig Schwartz

THE PROCESS OF DESIGN

Designers create an environment on the stage, whether imitations of the real world or an abstract one. They go about their tasks differently in creating a particular world, but they all share a common goal: to create an environment within which the actors can create convincing life. This goal means that the designers must work as a team and that they must work in concert with the director so that a compatible and unified world is created.

Each production follows an improvised progression to the final design. At times, various players on the team will take the lead and the others follow. Directors may come to the first planning meeting with a clear vision of what the stage environment should be to support their approach to the playscript. Probably more often, the steps to derive the look of a production will be less direct, more metaphorical, more organic. The dramaturg may have a say about the play's structure, historical background, and specified or implied images. The designers might identify particularly constraining requirements of the script, such as a script made up of short scenes or one actor to play multiple roles.

Pete Smith

FIGURE 10.8

The Setting in Miniature

For a production of *Macbeth* at the University of Michigan, the set designer presented to the director and design team a model of the set, complete with suggested lighting. Every detail seems to be included in this meticulously crafted model.

The result of this phase will be the development of a shared concept or central metaphor for the production, sometimes called a springboard. A springboard is not the playscript's theme or larger meaning. Instead it is concerned with feeling, mood, atmosphere, sounds, and visual impressions. Production springboards, then, can be hard to articulate in straightforward language. A good concept/central metaphor is evocative, provocative, illuminating, and integrating. Sometimes the concept or central metaphor will be written out; sometimes not. In any case, the springboard will guide director and designers in creating a production with a unified result.

Design discussions must eventually move to visual products. Words for color, mass, and texture can be easily misunderstood. For example, what is blue? Is your blue the same one the person next to you imagines as blue? Designers will produce rough sketches at first. They may collect pictures from books, magazines, and the Internet to be inspirations or models for the design. Historic paintings can serve as models of color, form, costuming, or lighting. As the group agrees on an approach to visualize the production, the work products of the designers become more specific. Sketches will be replaced by polished, colored renderings. Ground plans will include measurements. Fabrics will be shopped and sample swatches shared. Scale models of the scenery may be built starting with so-called white models, which are unpainted cardboard, and advancing to fully-realized small painted models of the finished scenery. Technical drawings will be made that detail how the scenery will be built and from what materials. For some costumes, a muslin version may be cut, sewn, and fitted to the actor and then taken apart to serve as the pattern for the real costume, especially if the cloth used for the final costume is expensive. Costumes will be altered to resolve problems in fit and movement. Because the lighting designer's work affects and is affected by the color and reflectivity of the scenery and costumes, the lighting designer's work has a schedule different than the other designers. The lighting designer must plan ahead—typically lighting instruments are hung and cabled before scenery is fully installed—but cannot finalize the lighting design until scenery and costumes are complete.

FIGURE 10.9

Abstraction

This design for *M. Butterfly* at Philadelphia Theatre Company relies heavily on abstraction. It is not a literal representation of any known space. The repeated circular motif and the vibrant color contribute to the sense of "strangeness."

Mark Garvin

Design, then, is a process, requiring collaboration and communication, leading to a product by opening night. Design starts with the playscript, its concrete and abstract requirements, and moves forward in roughly defined steps that grow ever more specific until it is opening night and the design is complete.

Although many decisions are reached at production meetings, the designers do most of their work in solitude or with the technicians who execute their designs—the scene designer with the technical director and builders and painters, the costume designer with cutters and sewers, and so on. At some phase, each specializes and proceeds separately.

PLAYSCRIPT INTERPRETATION AND DESIGN

Some major components of design include tone and mood, the level of abstraction, historical period, geographical location, characters' socioeconomic standing, and the progression of the play to its end.

Tone and Mood

Designers pay close attention to the tone and mood of a playscript. The two extremes are comic and serious, but these two categories are simply not enough. Most plays have a range of tones that sometimes grow in a sequence and sometimes contrast, scene-to-scene or moment-to-moment.

Level of Abstraction

A theatre design may appear real, or to varying degrees fantastic, or almost purely abstract. At one extreme, the decision might be made to create a literal replica of a house in New England from about 1880 down to the last detail of

Craig Schwartz

FIGURE 10.10

A "Real" Space

Here, a fully equipped kitchen with a working stove and
sink complete with running water underscores this realistic drama. Frank Gilroy's prize-winning family drama, *The
Subject Was Roses*, was revived by the Center Theatre Group
at the Mark Taper Forum in Los Angeles.

the patterns in the wallpaper. At the
other extreme might be a setting of
stairs, ramps, and levels; lighting will
complete the abstract stage scene,
providing mood and scene changes.
The costume may represent a historical period. At the other extreme, the
costumer may design never-before-
seen silhouettes, ones that use elastic
fabric, extensions of limbs, and various kinds of padding to change the
outline of the human body.

In part, the decision about how
abstract the production will be
comes from the designers' and director's interpretation of the script. In
part, it comes from a decision about
how much the abstraction or literal-
ism of the play itself will be emphasized. In a realistic play, for example,
the decision to create literal settings
and costumes is not an inevitable
one. With equal justification, the
designers might decide to create a
mere suggestion of a real setting with
costumes that suggest the period but are not complete and realistic copies. In the
same way, the designers of a play of Shakespeare's, for example, may decide that
an abstract setting is inappropriate and may go to quite literal, realistic settings.

Historical Period and Geographical Place

Many playscripts are specific about where and when the play is set. The design
approach may be to meet those details with realistic specificity or to offer somewhat simplified or abstracted impressions of time and place. In other cases, the
director and designers may decide to shift the time and place specified in the
playscript, for reasons of theme, esthetics, or novelty.

Even the lighting design may be affected by historical period, when, for example, ideas about the direction and quantity of light and the quality of shadow
come from paintings and engravings of another period. Sound, too, can be affected if period music is used or if certain kinds of sounds are called for—a trum-
pet flourish or the sound of *Hamlet*'s "peal of ordnance."

When designs are meant to express a time period in a realistic way, they must
not only look like the period but also be what the audience *thinks* the period
looked like. What we know of the 1920s, for example, is conditioned by what
we have seen in cartoons, old movies, and magazines—but did all women really bob their hair, and did all men really wear knickers and high collars? In the

Elizabethan period, did all houses have plaster-and-timber fronts, and did all men wear puffed-out breeches and tight stockings? Did warriors in the tenth century wear plate armor?

Designers may modify historical detail for reason of esthetics and audience expectations. Some places and times have costuming silhouettes or hairstyles that are unattractive to present day audiences. A designer may knowingly step out of period on some details of design to better communicate with the audience.

Socioeconomic Circumstances

Wealth and social class influence clothes, furniture, and environment. The more realistic the play, the more important these considerations become. Socioeconomic considerations change with the specific era of the play but are usually shown through styles, color, fabric, fit, and cleanliness.

Progression

Does the design support the progression of the playscript, beginning, middle, and end? Sometimes design shows almost literally story shorthand or metaphors, such as "things are growing dark," or "everything is falling apart," or "now I see."

PRACTICAL CONSIDERATIONS

Designers must consider practicality. A workable door must be opened and closed without the wall rattling. A chair may be sat in. Costumes must be worn by actors, moved in, sometimes danced in, sometimes changed quickly, and they must be able to be laundered. Lighting must illuminate the actors and must not cast light on anything unintended. Some major practical considerations include at least four areas: budget and schedules, technology, the theatrical place, and the technical director.

Budget and Schedules

Demands of budget and schedule probably influence a designer before any designs are made. Some design solutions may be impossible if the budget is small. Should the director want to do a restoration play in strict period, there must be a significant budget for wigs, period undergarments, and shoes. Perhaps a simpler concept for the design will better accommodate the budget. Can a three-set comedy be performed on two sets, saving time and money, without lessening the production's impact? In addition, once designs seem finalized, contingencies may arise in construction and installation where budget and schedules require a designer to alter the design.

Technology

Technology affects what can be shown on stage, in what construction schedule, and for how much money. For example, large-scale molding formed from Styrofoam, originally designed for use on commercial buildings where they are

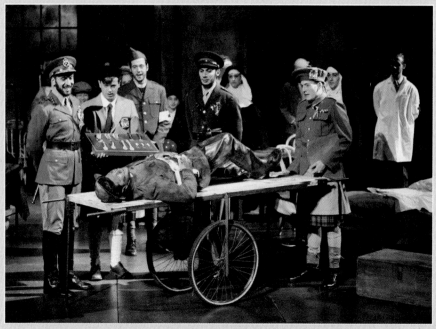

Pete Smith

FIGURE 10.12

A Change of Time and Place

The costumes tell the audience that Shakespeare's *Macbeth* has been moved to the period of World War I in this production at the University of Michigan. The set model can be found in a previous photo in this chapter.

covered in stucco, can be a cheap and featherweight source for architectural detailing on a theatre set. The technology for moving, focusing, and coloring stage lighting instruments is advancing rapidly, changing the way lighting designers work.

The computer has changed the ways in which many designers work, replacing pencil and paper with a mouse and a screen. Everything from sketching to coloring is possible with new, powerful programs that cut through such time-consuming jobs as labeling the designs.

Computer-assisted design (CAD), as this process is known, has familiar applications for building design. Simplified versions of CAD software are intended for homeowners' use in planning rooms, gardens, or small buildings. Architectural CAD programs used in theatre work in the same way; with such a program networked by an entire design staff; the savings in time and work more than make up for the expense of buying software and hardware and training staff in their use. Lighting designers also use such theatre-specific programs as Lightwright™ and Vectorworks Spotlight™.

CAD has made older drafting tools—compasses, T-squares, triangles—almost obsolete. It allows the designer to sketch in a simulation of pencil,

Spotlight

An actress in the costume of Queen Elizabeth I in *The Lost Colony,* North Carolina.

William Ivey Long, A Good Costume Designer

William Ivey Long exemplifies the training and talent required to become a nationally successful designer. Between 1977 and 2012, Long designed the costumes for sixty-three Broadway and forty-two Off-Broadway shows, an average of more than three productions a year. He has received five Drama Desk Awards in eighteen nominations and five Tony Awards in twelve nominations. At the same time, he designed four television and four theatrical movies. After a 2007 fire destroyed the costumes for the historic outdoor drama, *The Lost Colony,* in Manteo, North Carolina, Long designed a thousand costumes worn by 120 performers. He has designed for opera, ballet, a 1989 Rolling Stones tour, the Siegfried and Roy animal and magic show in Las Vegas, and sometimes designs for private clients, such as the film actress Halle Berry.

Long's special traits as a designer are a tireless attention to detail and, at the same time, a strong sense of the theatrical impact of costume designs, on actors and audiences. One producer called Long, "brilliant and fastidious." Long described his design objectives this way, "Everything I do is creating character and supporting the story through differences."

The famous example of Long's tenacity is the design of the central "yellow dress" from the dance musical, *Contact* (1999). The dancer wearing the yellow dress was supposed to be a goddess suddenly appearing in a bar. She was to be sexy, dance athletically and gracefully, and when done her dress was to fall right into place without her brushing the skirt down. In sum, the dress was to be magical without drawing attention away from the dancer. Long did nine versions of the dress. Later Long said, "I'm telling you, a lot of work goes into simple. Simple is hard." The dancer was a blond so getting a shade of yellow that didn't wash out her coloring was hard. The color also had to work under theatre lighting. One version of the dress was too scratchy for the male dancers who partnered the goddess. Then the dancer's underwear line could be seen through the dress. Over several versions, the length of the skirt got longer until the dancer said at a fitting, "This is the great length.... I feel like a woman. This gives me more power."

In retrospect, it seems inevitable that Long would be involved in theatre. Long's father was a theatre professor at Winthrop University in South Carolina. His mother was an actress and playwright. His two siblings work in theatre. Long grew up with theatre people and theatrical paraphernalia all about him. He made his first costume at the age of six, an Elizabethan ruff for his dog's neck. But as an undergraduate at the College of William and Mary in Virginia, he majored in history and then spent three years at the University of North Carolina at Chapel Hill on a PhD in Renaissance art history. But theatre called to him and he went on to earn an MFA in set design from Yale, in the years when students included actors Meryl Streep and Sigourney Weaver and playwrights Christopher Durang, Paul Rudnick, and Wendy Wasserstein. Yale connections eventually led to Long's first design gigs. With only one course in costume design and an unpaid internship with the couturier, Charles James, Long became a costume designer. Long said of his early choices, "If you're a very lucky person, you start questioning everything. School doesn't make you satisfied—it makes you hungry."

FIGURE 10.11

Teatro La Fenice

Audiences often expect that a production housed in a particular space will reflect the architecture of the theatre. Here, the Teatro La Fenice in Venice, Italy, that might lead the audience to expect a rather lavish production. A bare-bones physical production of an experimental theatre piece may not jibe with audience expectation at the Fenice (although theatre can be staged anywhere).

if that's what is wanted, and then to turn that sketch into an elevation or a three-dimensional picture. Directors can be "walked through" computer mock-ups of several design ideas. Set designers can then use the computer to take the agreed-upon idea to a rendering in any of several styles, from simulated watercolor to bright photorealism, and from there to scale elevations, detailed plans with dimensions, and final renderings from which a full-size scenic painting can be made. CAD is a great saver of time and tedium but no replacement for creativity.

The Theatrical Place

The nature of the theatre architecture itself greatly affects the design of a production. Theatres come in all sizes and shapes. Some spaces are enormous, seating from three to five thousand spectators. Other spaces may be mid-size, like many Broadway theatres that usually seat between one and two thousand spectators. Yet other theatres may be intimate, with audiences of fewer than one hundred. Designers must also take into consideration the formality of the theatre space: Is the theatre a gigantic, formal space with gilt plaster and crystal chandeliers such as the Palais Garnier in Paris? Or is the theatre quite modest in its aspect such as the Laura Pels theatre in New York located in a basement. The theatre size and decor then, may greatly influence the approach of production design. Each actor–audience relationship requires the designers to work within its parameters.

THE TECHNICAL DIRECTOR

Broadway productions have large technical staffs, and they contract out such jobs as scene construction and painting. Small community theatres may have only a single technician to do almost everything. In almost all kinds of theatres, however, a person exists to oversee the execution of designs and to organize and manage the technical production and its relationship with the theatre. In commercial productions, a company may be credited with this task, under the rubric of "Technical Supervision" or "Technical Supervisor." When the job is done by one person, the job title is usually technical director.

The technical director is responsible for the theatre building around the playing area and behind whatever barrier separates audience from backstage. The job is a tangle of details and responsibilities. In many small professional, community, and educational theatres, the technical director

- knows the theatre building thoroughly and coordinates its maintenance with the building's owner.
- sees that an ample stock of cables, nails, paint, and a thousand other things are kept on hand.
- sees to the upkeep of tools, from pencils to table saws.
- has oversight of backstage scheduling.
- knows what scenery and properties are in storage and maintains their inventories.

In short, the technical director has a huge responsibility and a day-to-day schedule that can be crushing without the most careful planning (and an even temper).

In university theatres, technical directors usually attend meetings at which plays are first selected; even at this earliest stage, their advice will be needed to determine whether a potential play is too demanding for the theatre's physical capabilities. Later, the technical director takes part in all production meetings, advising director and designer on the practicability of ideas and the likelihood of deadlines. Throughout, the technical director is responsible for setting and meeting scenic and property schedules. (Lighting may fall within his or her responsibility, as well; costumes generally do not.) In addition, in educational theatre, the technical director does a great deal of the actual work of construction and painting, as well as instructing students working on the production.

Courtesy David Popinski

FIGURE 10.13

Technical Workers

A backstage crew at Northeastern Illinois University Theatre prepares a production under the technical director's supervision. Note in the bottom photo the use of distressed Styrofoam to suggest heavier, more expensive materials.

TRAINING DESIGNERS

Because theatre designers create environments and use materials of the real world to make their art, they must be trained not only as artists but also as artisans. They study, therefore, at least two different subjects: the artistic and the technical. Some designers also need another sort of information, the historical, to prepare for their role as theatre designers.

Although some theatre designers, especially in eastern Europe, customarily design all aspects of a production, most in the United States specialize in one area: scenery, properties, costumes, lighting, or sound. All need certain kinds of basic information. For example, all need proficiency in dramatic analysis. Most need to learn about color, line, mass, composition, balance, and other basic elements of design, and most need to master basic techniques of drawing and rendering and use of CAD programs. They require some understanding of visual communication (that is, how people are likely to interpret certain colors, shapes, lines, and proportions). Finally, because every play presents a unique problem in design, all designers need skills in basic research methods that will allow them to pursue the design of any play independently.

Beyond such basic, shared areas of study are others specific to each area because the technical skills needed by each designer vary considerably. For example, scene designers and technical directors often study basic construction and (occasionally) carpentry; scene designers will usually take courses in scene painting as well. With the arrival of new metals and plastics in use for set construction came a need for training in welding and plastic form making. These designers will also often study engineering to discover how the aesthetic requirements of a design can be safely built and safely used. Costume designers usually study basic sewing techniques, pattern making, drafting, and draping, as well as some specialized areas like millinery. Lighting and sound designers may take courses in electricity, electronics, and instrumentation.

Because plays from the past are often performed, training in scenery, property, and costume design usually includes quite a bit of history. Scene designers, for example, need to know at least the history of architecture and furniture. Costume designers need to know the history of fashion, textiles, and accessories (e.g., jewelry and wigs). The history of visual painting often suggests not only the techniques of painters in each age that designers might want to use to capture the "look" of the age but also the telling details of design—fabrics, jewelry, upholstery, and so on. Sound designers, especially, often study the history of music.

In other periods, training in design came primarily through an apprentice system, in which a beginner worked with a more experienced artist until attaining an acceptable level of craft. Now proficiency in design and technical theatre usually comes from pursuing a graduate degree, especially the master of fine arts in theatre, at a university. The job market in design and technical theatre remains strong (unlike that in acting, playwriting, or directing), in part because the need for such people far exceeds the number well trained in these fields; university training often leads to steady work in either the professional or educational theatre.

FIGURE 10.14

A Sense of Place

Here, a setting for William Inge's *Picnic* at Ball State University. Note the silhouetted trees that form a frame for the set. The detail in the house on the left as well as the picket fence forms a stark contrast to the house on the right. These details with the silhouetted elements establish a sense of place.

WHAT IS GOOD DESIGN?

Good design is good art. But it is created in terms of the production, and it is created within the context of other artists' decisions. Knowing what is the product of a designer and what of a director can often be difficult, however, and, especially in our director-dominated theatre, assessing each designer's work is sometimes challenging.

Good design, above all, serves the actor—giving the actor good spaces in which to act, clothing the actor, and illuminating the actor.

Good design serves the production. It does not necessarily serve the "playwright's intentions"; interpretation may have greatly changed this production from those intentions. Obvious changes may have been made—in historical period, geographical location, social class—along with less obvious ones (e.g., genre, mood, style); the play may even have become the framework, in this production, for an idea the opposite of the original intention. In serving the production, good design meshes with other elements and does not call attention to itself.

Good design, when possible, is dynamic, not static: It has the capacity to change as the performance progresses. Such change is clearest in costumes and lighting.

Good design is not redundant. It does not merely "state the theme." It has its own complexity.

Good design has detail and texture, variety within the whole. Light is not merely a bland wash of light; a costume is not merely a wide stretch of draped and sewn fabric; and a setting is not merely a painted surface.

Good design has technical finish. Designers must design within the technical limitations of their theatres so that everything the audience sees is technically well done. Often, designers oversee the technical work or approve it; nothing second-rate should pass their eyes.

Good design is daring: It tries new technologies, avoids old solutions, and chances failure.

KEY TERMS

Check your understanding against this list. Brief definitions are included in the Glossary; persons are page-referenced in the Index.

computer-assisted design (CAD)   152
costume designer   142
dimming   145
elements of design   140
floodlight   145
follow spots   146
footlights   146

gel   145
light plot   145
lighting designer   144
mood   149
projection designer   146
properties (props)   142
renderings   148
scene designer   141

scrolling color changers   145
silhouette   143
spotlight   145
striplights   146
technical director   155
tone   149

THEATRE OF OTHER TIMES AND PLACES

Theatre History

THEATRE: PRESENT AND PAST

We study theatre's past in part to understand how theatre relates to the larger culture—how forces for change work in theatre and beyond it. We also study theatre's history to discover how we differ from and how we resemble the peoples and practices of other times and places. Finally, we study theatre's history to enhance our experiences of today's theatre, both as audience members and as theatre practitioners.

Theatre history, however, is no freer of fads, hidden agendas, and unstated assumptions than any other kind of history. In the United States, it has been heavily tilted toward US subjects, and secondarily toward British and European ones; it has remained fairly indifferent to those of Asia and Africa.

The growing globalization at the beginning of the twenty-first century, however, argues for widening our vision to include other cultures. This book continues to emphasize Western traditions because they have dominated North American culture, but we have treated major theatres and dramas of Africa and the East as well, pointing to interconnections when they exist and explaining conventions that differ from those with which we are most familiar.

As you read what follows, then, you should notice where emphases have been put and where omissions have occurred. You

should ask yourself why these are as they are, remembering that in history of all sorts, a lack of evidence in one area and an oversupply in another greatly affects how much appears on the page. Time is a quirky editor—through accident, war, intentional erasure, and neglect, it loses masses of information that would be thought vital if we could have them. The modern period, for example—especially since the invention of photography and cheap printing—has so much information available that we have a hard time limiting it. Remember, too, the old adage of historians: It is the winners who write history. And remember, finally, that until quite recently, most people went unrepresented in history, including theatre history, which took as its subject people like the ones who wrote the history: educated, male, close to the center of power, white, and often affluent.

It has been said that art validates the center of power. No more important understanding can come from the study of theatre's past than to learn how theatre art and sociopolitical power come together and drift apart, validating and sometimes reforming each other and at other times, becoming invisible to each other. To understand that relationship is to understand how theatre history is history.

THE SWEEP OF THEATRE HISTORY

Our history is concerned mostly with Western Europe and the United States, the cultures most directly relevant to us. We do from time to time, however, illuminate major theatrical traditions unfolding elsewhere, showing that other sophisticated traditions existed—and still exist—alongside our own. Within the Western tradition, three major shapes can be seen, and we have organized our history around them (see Figure III.1).

Part IIIA Facade Stages: The First Thousand Years (534 BCE–c. 550 CE)

The earliest confirmed records of theatre are those of Athens, Greece, in the fifth century (400s) before the Common Era (BCE). Greece was then at the western edge of several highly developed civilizations, most notably those in China, Persia, and Egypt. (Some scholars argued that ancient Egypt had theatre before Athens, but scholarship of the last thirty years or so has refuted the evidence.) Athens created a rich theatrical tradition with two kinds of formal drama: tragedy and comedy; actors playing in front of neutral backgrounds in outdoor spaces with audiences curved in front of them; a performance style that included music, dancing, and masks; and the world's first and still-important

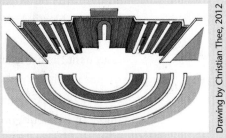

Drawing by Christian Thee, 2012

FIGURE III.1

Facade Stage

The Roman theatre at Bosra, Syria, built around 200 CE, where actors played on a facade stage such as is typified in the sketch, above.

work of dramatic theory, Aristotle's *Poetics*. When Alexander the Great unified the Greek-speaking people and took his armies eastward in the 330s BCE, he carried this theatre as far as modern Afghanistan and northern India. Although no direct connection can be proven, India developed its own Sanskrit drama and dramatic theory soon thereafter.

After Alexander, both political and cultural power in the Mediterranean moved westward from Greece to Rome. The Romans built unified theatre

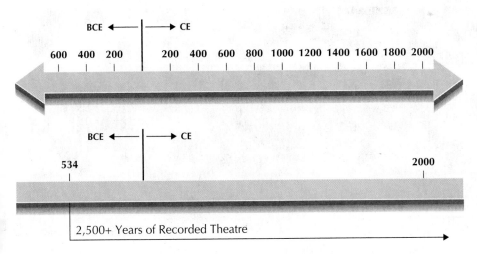

FIGURE III.2

Timelines

The timeline shows that theatre has a history of more than 2,500 years, compared with film's 110, and television's 60.

structures as far north as Britain and around most of the Mediterranean fringe, including North Africa. Rome had an important written comedy and a less important tragedy, both based on Greek models. But after the first century BCE its dominant form was mime, which left no dramatic theory or scripts of any quality but was hugely popular. When the Roman Empire split in two in the fourth century of the Common Era (CE), the eastern part, centered in Constantinople (modern Istanbul), flourished; the western empire declined and after the sixth century CE existed only in name. Theatre continued in the east, with mime a popular form throughout the vast eastern empire, stretching even to southern Russia. Theatre seems to have almost disappeared in the West. The first part of our history ends here.

Part IIIB Emblem, Environment, and Simultaneity: The Next 700 Years (c. 950–c. 1650)

Theatre—or at least records of theatre—did not surface again in Western Europe until the late tenth century CE. Then, "Latin music drama," a sung drama performed in Benedictine monastic churches as a part of the liturgy, appeared in England; a Christianized version of Roman comedies, perhaps staged, perhaps not, appeared in Germany. These two kinds of drama were soon joined by other

FIGURE III.3

Found Spaces

A single day's performance in a patio captures an audience of people passing by during Suzan-Lori Parks's *365 Days / 365 Plays* project. Found spaces are anywhere that actors and audiences can gather to witness a performance.

religious and secular theatres throughout Europe. In whatever venue, the medieval plays shared a staging that put the performance in existing spaces, found spaces, with symbolic distance, acting, and costumes. By the fourteenth century, secular plays and professional actors began to appear; and by the sixteenth, they had overwhelmed the previous religious dramas. In Japan starting in the fourteenth century, an entirely unrelated form, *Noh*, was appearing; based in Zen Buddhism, it was mystical, symbolic, and austere.

In the late sixteenth century, a professional, secular theatre replaced the religious theatre. In England and Spain, medieval theatrical conventions (i.e., generalized playing area and symbolic structures) persisted, but they now appeared in freestanding theatres rather than found spaces. Spanish and English public theatres, including Shakespeare's Globe, were partly open overhead, and both featured an elevated stage that thrust into the audience and, through doors at its back, opened to a part of the structure that housed dressing rooms and stage machinery. Theatres of great spectacle rose in the East about the same time—in Japan, *Kabuki*, which used the world's first rotating stage and in China, early precursors of Beijing opera. Both used stunning costumes, makeup, masks, and movement. With the end of England and Spain's Golden Ages, the second part ends.

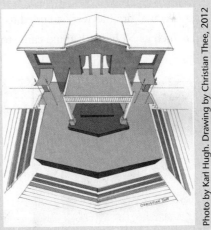

Photo by Karl Hugh. Drawing by Christian Thee, 2012

FIGURE III.4

Thrust Stage

The outdoor Adams Theatre at the Utah Shakespearean Festival has a stage with the audience seated on three sides.

Part IIIC Illusionism: From c. 1550 to c. 1950

Indoor theatres with a stage at one end became more common, and as did new staging conventions developed in Italy, theatre moved away from emblem and toward illusion. In Europe, an age of great scenic display and great scenic designers and inventors began in the middle of the seventeenth century albeit earlier in Italy. It was matched by great, sometimes pyrotechnic, acting. Theatres got bigger as cities grew, and performances attracted new audiences drawn by the spectacle.

With the coming of railroads in the mid-1800s, entire productions could travel, multiplying the potential audience and making theatre the most popular entertainment in European and US cultures. Until the twentieth century, theatre had few competitors for audiences.

After 1850, forward-looking artists moved the style of acting, scenery, and plays toward realism, the mirroring of surface reality. Such plays demanded, and audiences seemed to want, smaller theatres again, with both acting and scenic area entirely behind a proscenium, an architectural frame, through which the audience looked at the performance. Realism spawned immediate reactions in a variety of styles, all of which changed but failed to replace realism as the dominant form.

The increasing westernization of the world had profound effects on world theatre. As European colonialism swept through Africa and Asia, Western drama and theatre came along with it, with major effects: Realistic dramas and illusionistic staging began to be produced in European colonies; the dramatic and theatrical conventions of their own traditional dramas were adapted to fit a Western aesthetic more closely; and dramas such as Noh and Kabuki came to be viewed and treated as museum pieces.

FIGURE III.5

Proscenium Theatre

The Odeon in Paris has a large proscenium with a painted curtain.

Drawing by Christian Thee, 2012

PART

IIIA

FACADE STAGES
(534 BCE–c. 550 CE)

The first phase of theatrical and dramatic history for which we have records began in the sixth century BCE and ended around 550 CE, a period of about one thousand years. These thousand years are studied together because they share certain major conventions of performance:

- A *facade stage*, where actors performed in front of a neutral (nonrepresentational) background.
- A *relationship with religion*, in which plays were presented as a part of larger, religious celebrations.
- A *sense of occasion*, because performances were offered only on special occasions and never often enough to be taken for granted.
- A *noncommercial environment*, in which wealthy citizens or the state itself bore the costs as part of the obligations of citizenship.
- A *male-only theatre*, in which women participated only as audience.

This theatre appeared first in Greece and later, in modified form, in Rome. Roughly contemporary with Roman theatre was a theatre and drama in India, which may or may not have been related to those of the West.

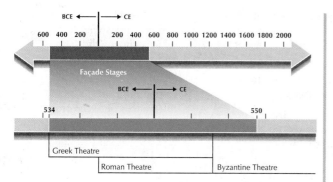

FIGURE IIIA.1

Timeline

Facade stages dominated theatre for its first thousand years. Drama and theatre, first recorded in Athens, Greece, in 534 BCE, appeared in Rome three hundred years later.

11

The Theatre of Greece

Originally built in the fourth century (BCE) the theatre at Delphi, like many Greek theatres, was altered several times.

OBJECTIVES

When you have completed this chapter, you should be able to:

- Explain why there are different theories of the origins of theatre and what some of those theories are.

- Discuss the relationship between theatre and religion in Greece.

- Discuss the role of competition in Greek theatre festivals.

- Trace the development of the Greek physical theatres and their plays and playwrights.

- Identify the major periods of Greek theatres with approximate dates.

- Explain how a Greek performance would have looked in the principal periods—what masks and costumes were used, what a chorus did, and what acting space was used.

- Explain important differences between tragic and comic performances and occasions.

CONTEXT

The first records of drama and theatre come from Athens, Greece, and date from the sixth century BCE. Within a hundred years, Athenian drama had reached a peak of excellence seldom equaled since. The result is that when people speak of Greek theatre today, they are almost certainly referring to the plays and productions of the fifth century BCE in Athens.

Why drama and theatre should have arisen there and not in other civilizations of the time remains a mystery, but the position of Athens in the ancient world offered some advantages.

A peninsula about half the size of New York state with numerous bays, harbors, inlets, and adjacent islands, the Greek peninsula has one of the longest coastlines in the world. Its geography made it, during the sixth century BCE, the leading merchant of the Mediterranean, a role it took over from the Phoenicians. Exporting pottery, olive oil, wine, and slaves, Greece brought in a variety of items from North Africa and the East, where advanced civilizations were already flourishing in Egypt, China, India, and Persia (today's Iran). In fact, Greece formed the western edge of the then-civilized world and served as a crossroads for trade.

To speak of "Greece," however, is misleading because there was no unified nation. Rather, on the peninsula were organized individual city-states, each called a polis (pl. poleis) and each consisting of a town and its surrounding countryside. Each polis issued its own coinage, raised its own armies, and so on. Although several were important (e.g., Corinth, Sparta, Thebes), by the fifth century BCE, Athens had emerged as both cultural leader and trading giant, with its own outposts in Italy, Sicily, France, and Spain. As the word *outposts* suggests, Western Europe was at the time a cultural backwater. And Athens itself was a small city by modern standards—100,000 people, about the population size of South Bend, Indiana.

By the fifth century BCE, the golden age of Athenian theatre and drama, Athens had already established the world's first democracy, providing a model for the participation of citizens in the decisions and policies of government. The polis had become so central in their lives that a later philosopher defined *man* as "a political animal" (i.e., as one who lives in a polis). Part of being political was being social—people who could, lived in the town, even though they might have a farm in outlying lands. Under Pericles, its great ruler in fifth-century BCE, Athens created statues, buildings, arts, and philosophies whose excellence made them important in European culture for more than two thousand years. By then as well, Athens had developed an alphabet that included both vowels and consonants, becoming the first in history to represent speech both systematically and consistently.

Athenians took great pride in their civic accomplishments. To celebrate its culture, facilitate the exchange of goods, and pay tribute to various gods, Athens sponsored a number of public festivals each year. At three of these festivals, each devoted to the god Dionysus, the earliest recorded theatre and drama appeared. Why did this new art arise? Why did it take the form it did?

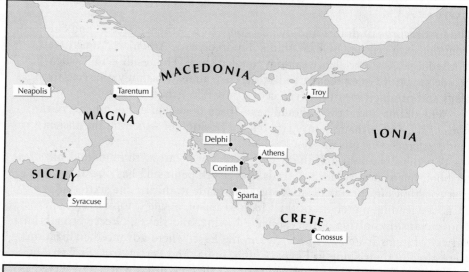

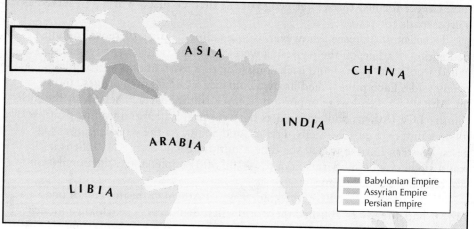

FIGURE 11.1

The Civilized World

By the fifth century BCE (400s), Greek city-states (top) influenced much of the Mediterranean, including some outposts on the Italian peninsula. But Greece was at the far western reaches of the civilized world, with older cultures well established in China, India, and much of today's Middle East (bottom).

Why was Athens, rather than Egypt, Persia, China, or India, the birthplace of drama?

THEORIES OF THE ORIGINS OF THEATRE

There is almost no written evidence from which to draw information about the origins of Greek drama. The exception is Aristotle's *Poetics*. There are, however, several theories about how theatre began.

Aristotle and the *Poetics*

The earliest account is Aristotle's *Poetics*, written about two hundred years after the fact. He claimed that "tragedy was produced by the authors of the dithyrambs, and comedy from [the authors] of the phallic songs." Dithyrambs were choral odes (poems performed by a chorus). Phallic songs were rites celebrating male sexual potency, but their precise nature is unknown. Because Aristotle was writing about two hundred years after the first recorded theatre performance, we have no idea where he got his information. In the absence of certainty, several theories have arisen to explain how and why drama came into being. These theories have relied on evidence drawn from anthropology and linguistics and from contemporaneous artworks, especially vase paintings.

The Ritual Theory

Probably the most fashionable, but not necessarily the most correct, view of the origin of theatre is the ritual theory, which proposes that Greek drama evolved from early religious rituals devoted to the god Dionysus.

The Great Man Theory

Some scholars propose that the appearance of tragedy and comedy arose as creative acts of human genius. Arguing that art neither evolves like a biological organism nor happens by chance, such scholars search for the birth of drama in a revolutionary invention of a gifted human being. According to this view, an artist purposefully synthesized elements that already existed in Athenian society into a new form, the drama.

The Storytelling Theory

Some scholars propose that Greek drama developed from storytelling. The idea here is that storytellers would naturally tend to elaborate parts of the telling by impersonating the various characters, using appropriate voice and movement. From here, it seems a short step to having several people become involved in telling the story; from this telling, it is thought, drama and theatre arose.

The Dance Theory

Other theorists suggest that movement rather than speech was at the core of drama. The idea here is that dancers first imitated the physical behavior of animals and humans. When dancers costumed themselves in appropriate skins and garments, they came to impersonate the animals and humans. When several dancers joined together in impersonation and then embroidered this performance with sounds and words, drama was born (the argument goes).

In fact, no one knows the origin of Greek drama. The argument over origins is often an argument over the nature of theatre itself. To anthropologists, who look on theatre as a kind of performance closely related to impersonations as different as the Mandan Buffalo Dance, the Iroquois False Face Society, and the Egyptian "Passion Play," the essence of theatre is ritual, and so they tend to favor the ritual theory. To artists who look at world theatre and see a form

Courtesy Guthrie Theatre

FIGURE 11.2

Aeschylus's *The Agamemnon*

The Guthrie Theatre produced a condensed Oresteia trilogy as *The House of Atreus* in 1968. The masks, designed by Tanya Moiseiwitch, left the mouth uncovered so the actor's articulation would not be muffled. The production, directed by Tyrone Guthrie, toured Los Angeles and New York, among other cities. This production was highly admired but it is important to remember that it was not a historical recreation of theatre staging in ancient Greece.

rich in human meaning and almost indescribable in complexity, only an artist's creation can explain its beginnings, and so they favor the great man theory. For those who believe drama began with the actor, the storyteller theory works best; for those who find the essence of Greek drama in its chorus, the dance theory seems most persuasive.

TRAITS OF GREEK THEATRE

During the preceding discussion, we have encountered three important traits of Greek theatre, traits that may seem odd when compared to current theatrical conventions.

- *Greek Theatre Was Closely Associated with Greek Religion.* A form of polytheism ("many gods"), Greek religion was both private (a part of daily life and centered in the home) and public (expressing itself at a number of major festivals, each devoted to a specific god). It was not a commercial activity.
- *Greek Theatre Was Performed Only on Special Occasions*—the Festivals. During its golden age, drama appeared only in Athens and at only three festivals of Dionysus: the City (or Great) Dionysia, the Rural Dionysia, and the Lenaia. An altar was a permanent fixture of the performance space.
- *Greek Theatre Was Choral.* In addition to actors, the performance of Greek drama required a chorus, a group of men who dressed alike, who were masked alike, and who moved, sang, and spoke together most of the time. The chorus affected Greek drama in important ways. Its costumes, songs, and dances added much spectacle to the performance. Because the chorus danced as it spoke, chanted, and sang, its rhythms indicated, both visually and orally, the changing moods within the play. Perhaps most important of all, the chorus—like the actors—participated directly in the action, providing information, making discoveries, deciding, and doing.

The chorus also influenced a number of theatrical practices. Because the chorus usually came into the performing space soon after the play opened and remained there until the end, its presence had to be considered in both the physical layout of the theatre and the action of the drama. It required a space large enough to move about in. Its presence had to be justified and its loyalties made clear whenever characters shared secrets. Because the vocal and visual power of the chorus was great, the actors undoubtedly adjusted their style of performance so as not to be overwhelmed by the impact of the chorus.

FIGURE 11.3

A Chorus

This chorus for a modern production of *The Agamemnon* at the University of South Carolina wore similar costumes and masks presenting the chorus as if it were a single entity in the production.

To these three traits, we need to add two others, which also differ markedly from modern practice:

- *Greek Theatre Was Competitive.* Dramatists competed for awards in writing, and actors competed for awards in performing. To ensure fairness in the competition, rules governed who competed, who judged, and who won.

  Plays were produced by the city-state in cooperation with selected wealthy citizens. (Women were not considered citizens.) At the Great Dionysia, three tragic writers (always male) competed each year for the prize. To compete, each submitted three tragedies and one satyr play (a short comic piece that followed the tragedies and occasionally burlesqued them). One day was set aside for the work of each tragic author; therefore, each year nine tragedies and three satyr plays were presented at the Great Dionysia. At the Lenaia, only four tragedies competed each year, each by a different playwright. At both festivals, five comic playwrights (always male) competed for a prize, and a single day was set aside for this competition.

- *Greek Theatre Was Subsidized.* How the competitors were selected is unknown, but, once chosen, each author was matched with a wealthy citizen-sponsor, who was then responsible for meeting the costs incurred by the chorus. These citizen-sponsors could have a major effect on the outcome of the contests. Legends tell us that *Oedipus Rex* lost its competition because of a sponsor too stingy to fund a suitable production, but that Aeschylus's *Eumenides* had costumes and masks so spectacular and frightening that pregnant women miscarried when they first saw the chorus—legend, remember—, the result of the lavish support of its sponsor.

PLAYS AND PLAYWRIGHTS

Of the thousands of plays written for the Greek theatre, only forty-six survive complete, although many fragments have also survived. Most plays came from fifth century BCE Athens and from four authors: Aeschylus (seven), Sophocles (seven), Euripides (eighteen), and Aristophanes (eleven). From these four authors came some of the world's greatest plays—plays that are still performed for their powerful effects on audiences; plays that have provided other playwrights (from William Shakespeare and Jean Racine to Eugene O'Neill and Wole Soyinka) with stories; and plays that have given their names to underlying patterns of human behavior ("Oedipus complex," "Promethean struggle"). A fifth name—Thespis—is important, although such a person may never have even existed.

Thespis

The semilegendary Thespis supposedly wrote tragedies using only one actor and a chorus. Although none of Thespis's works survived, they probably were based on the intensification of a single event rather than the development of a story because stories require that changes occur. With only one actor and a chorus, the opportunity to introduce new information into a scene (and thus introduce change into a situation) was severely limited. The continual disappearance of either the actor or the chorus to fetch new information would obviously have been awkward.

Aeschylus

Aeschylus probably introduced a second actor, thereby permitting change to occur within the play. Although a second actor would also allow conflict between two characters, Aeschylus still tended to depict a solitary hero, one isolated and facing a cosmic horror brought about by forces beyond his control. With such a grand tragic conception, Aeschylus required great scope, and so he often wrote trilogies, three plays on a single subject that were intended for performance on the same day. One of his trilogies, the *Oresteia* (458 BCE)—comprising the *Agamemnon*, the *Choëphoroe*, and the *Eumenides*—has survived intact along with several single plays. All display characteristics for which Aeschylus is admired: heroic and austere characters, simple but powerful plots, and lofty diction. His general tone is well summarized by an ancient commentator: "While one finds many different types of artistic treatment in Aeschylus, one looks in vain for those sentiments that draw tears."

Sophocles

Sophocles was credited with adding the third actor and with changing practices in scenic painting and costuming. Less interested than Aeschylus in portraying solitary heroes confronting the universal order, Sophocles wrote plays that explored the place of humans within that order. The tragedy of Sophocles's heroes typically erupts from decisions made and actions taken based on imperfect knowledge or

Spotlight

Sophocles's *Oedipus the King*, 427 BCE

Characters in classical Greek tragedies were always masked. Here an actor's mask from a Greek vase painting.

Part of a group of three plays often referred to as the "Theban plays," *Oedipus the King* is considered one of the greatest dramas ever written. *Oedipus* was much admired by Aristotle, who used examples from this play to illustrate his description of Greek tragedy. The other two plays in this Theban cycle are *Antigone* and *Oedipus at Colonus*. (The three were not written as a trilogy.) Sophocles is believed to have written more than one hundred plays, but only seven have survived.

The Story of the Play

Oedipus, king of Thebes, is appealed to by the people (the chorus) to save them from the plague that grips the city. Oedipus has already sent his brother-in-law, Creon, to the oracle at Delphi for a solution; Creon returns and announces that the oracle says that the city must banish the murderer of the former king, Laius. Oedipus vows to "reveal the truth" and save the city.

He calls the blind seer Tiresias to him and asks his advice. Tiresias is evasive and then, pressured, says, "It is you." Angered, Oedipus turns on Tiresias, saying that he and Creon are plotting against him. The old seer warns Oedipus of one who is "his children's brother and father, his wife's son, his mother's husband."

Oedipus rages again against Creon. His wife, Jocasta, widow of the former king, Laius, tells him of another old prophecy: Laius would be murdered by his own child. When she describes Laius, Oedipus is shaken and demands to see the one survivor of the killing of Laius. Oedipus speaks of his own long-ago visit to Delphi and a prophecy that he would kill his father and sleep with his mother, which caused him to flee Corinth, his childhood home. He recounts the later killing of a stranger at a crossroads.

A messenger from Corinth comes with news that Polybus, the king of Corinth and Oedipus's supposed father, is dead. Oedipus is not to grieve, however—Polybus was not, the messenger says, Oedipus's real father; rather, the messenger as a young man got the infant Oedipus from a shepherd; the baby's ankles were pierced—hence the name Oedipus, "swollenfoot."

Jocasta, suddenly frightened, begs Oedipus to give up his quest for the truth. An old man, the survivor of the attack on Laius, is dragged in. He was the shepherd who gave the infant Oedipus to the messenger; now, hounded by Oedipus, he says that the infant was to have been abandoned in the wild because he was the child of Laius and Jocasta, and there was a prophecy that he would kill his own father, but the shepherd gave him to the messenger to take away, instead.

Oedipus sees the truth: He is the source of the plague, the murderer of his father, later the husband of his mother. Jocasta kills herself.

Oedipus blinds himself with the pins in Jocasta's jewels. He begs to be driven from the city.

conflicting claims. Various aspects of the hero's character combine with unusual circumstances to bring about a disaster caused not by wickedness or foolishness but merely by humanness. For Sophocles, to be human was to be potentially a hero of tragedy.

The role of the chorus in Sophocles's plays remained important but not as central as in Aeschylus's. Conversely, the individual characters in Sophocles tended to be more complex, to display more individual traits, and to make more decisions. The result is that in Sophoclean tragedy, the actors, not the chorus, control the rhythm of the plays. Unlike Aeschylus, Sophocles did not need a trilogy to contain his tragedies; his plays stood alone. Of the more than one hundred attributed to him, seven have survived. Of these, *Oedipus Rex* (c. 427 BCE) is recognized by most critics as among the finest tragedies ever written.

Euripides

Euripides was never popular during his lifetime but came to be highly regarded after his death. Growing up at a time when Athens was embarking on policies of imperialism and expansionism, Euripides became a pacifist and a political gadfly. Although the populace viewed him with considerable distrust, the intellectual elite apparently admired him. It is reported, for example, that Socrates, one of the wisest men of the age, came to the theatre only to see the tragedies of Euripides and that Sophocles dressed his chorus in black on learning of the death of Euripides.

In comparison with the plays of Aeschylus and Sophocles, those of Euripides are less exalted and more realistic. His characters seem less grand and more human; their problems are less cosmic and more mundane. Euripides tended to examine human relationships and to question the wisdom of social actions: the purpose of war, the status of women, and the reasons for human cruelty.

In keeping with Euripides's iconoclastic outlook came changes in dramatic technique. Replacing the philosophical probings common in the plays of Aeschylus and Sophocles, Euripides substituted rapid reversals, intrigues, chase scenes, and romantic and sentimental incidents of the sort later associated with plays called *melodramas*. (Euripides is said by some to be the father of melodrama.) He further

Matt Orton

FIGURE 11.4

The Bacchae

This tragedy by Euripides premiered in 405 BCE at the Theatre of Dionysus, winning first prize. *The Bacchae* is a mythological account of a king who is punished by the god Dionysus for refusing to worship him. Here, a production at Montevallo University.

reduced the role of the chorus, until sometimes it was little more than an interruption of the play's action. As the role of the chorus declined and the subjects became more personal, the language became less poetic and more conversational. Many of the changes that Euripides introduced into Greek tragedy, although denounced in his own time, became standard dramatic practice during the following Hellenistic period.

Aristophanes and Old Comedy

Comedy was introduced into the Great Dionysia in 486 BCE, fifty years after tragedy. It seems never to have been comfortable there, perhaps because the festival was an international showcase for Athenian culture and thus often visited by foreign dignitaries. The real home of comedy was the winter festival, the Lenaia, where a contest for comedy was established in 442 BCE. At both festivals, an entire day was set aside for competition among the comic playwrights, five of whom competed.

Of the twelve extant Greek comedies, all but one are by Aristophanes; therefore, information about comedy during the classical period necessarily comes from these plays. It is possible, of course, that Aristophanes was atypical, and so the conclusions drawn from his works may be incorrect.

Although no two plays are exactly alike, surviving examples suggest a set structure for old comedy (the political comedy of the classical period):

- Division into two parts separated by a direct address by the chorus or choral leader to the audience, breaking the dramatic illusion.
- A first part consisting of a prologue, during which an outrageous idea is introduced, and then a debate as to whether the idea should be adopted, ending with a decision to put this "happy idea" into action (in Aristophanes's *The Birds* [414 BCE], for example, the happy idea is to build a city in the sky).
- A second part made up of funny episodes and choral songs showing the happy idea at work.

The happy idea is the heart of old comedy: It is outrageous and usually fantastic, and it contains social or political satire. In *The Birds*, building the city in the sky is an attempt to get away from the mess on earth. The happy idea also enables the spectacular costuming and behavior of the chorus, which often gives the play its name (the birds found in the sky).

THEATRE BUILDINGS AND PRACTICES

Although almost all extant Greek plays date from the fifth century BCE, most of the extant Greek theatre buildings date from later periods—sometimes much later periods. The result is unsettling: For the time when we know about theatre buildings and production practices, we know almost nothing about plays; conversely, for the time when we know the plays, we know almost nothing about the theatre buildings.

In Greek, *theatre* meant "seeing-place" or "spectacle-place." Athens' first theatre was apparently in the market, but it soon moved to the outskirts of town. There, the Theatre of Dionysus, Athens' first important theatre, was situated on a hillside, where the audience sat, with a circular playing area (the orchestra) at its base; a path or road separated audience and playing area and provided entrances (*parodoi*). This arrangement—hillside, orchestra, *parodoi*—was fundamental to all Greek theatres (see Figure 11.5). In many theatres of the time, however, the orchestra was rectangular rather than circular, an arrangement that would make sense inasmuch as tragic choruses (unlike the dithyrambic chorus) displayed themselves in ranks and files rather than in circles.

By the middle of the fifth century, a scene house (*skene*, "tent" or "booth") had been added at the edge of the orchestra opposite the audience. Its original layout is unknown, but it probably had two or three openings and was first needed as a changing room for the actors, only later becoming a kind of setting. It may first have been cloth (a tent) but was certainly wood in short order, becoming stone only centuries later. Whether wood or stone, it provided background and acoustical support and allows us to call the Athenian theatre a facade stage—a conventional form in which actors perform in front of a non-representational, often architectural, facade, with the audience arcing to three or fewer sides.

Because the fifth-century theatre was wood (rather than stone), it was impermanent, and so architectural examples of this theatre have not come down to us. The stone theatres whose pictures appear in many books are from later years, the periods for which we have no plays.

Audience

The outdoor theatre put the audience at the mercy of the weather; certainly, individuals must have used cushions, sunshades, umbrellas, and so forth. The Athenian hillside, with its wooden benches, could hold about fourteen thousand, and the audience was as visible as the actors in the sunlight. Theatre was apparently open to all, including women and slaves, but the exact social makeup of the audience is unknown. Records suggest that it could be unruly.

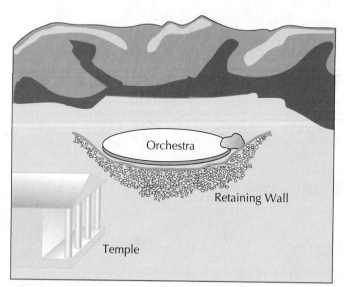

FIGURE 11.5

Theatre of the 400s BCE

A conjectural reconstruction of the early Theatre of Dionysus, showing orchestra, rock outcropping, and temple.

Acting

The first victor in the Athenian tragic contest is supposed to have been Thespis, who also acted in his play (c. 534

BCE)—hence, *thespian* for actor. Acting, like playwriting, remained a competitive activity during the classical period, and rules governed its practice. For example, all actors were male. Apparently no more than three *speaking* actors were allowed in the tragedies and five in the comedies, although any number of extras might be used. Because the leading actor, or protagonist, was the only one competing for the prize, he was assigned to the playwright by lot, so that chance rather than politics decided who got the best roles. The second and third actors were probably chosen by the playwright and the protagonist in consultation. With only three actors, doubling of roles was required because the plays themselves often had eight or more characters. If the protagonist had an exceedingly demanding role, like the title role in *Oedipus Rex*, he might play only one character, but the second and third actors were expected to play two or more secondary roles. Doubling, the use of masks, and the use of only male actors suggest that the style of Greek acting was more formal than realistic; that is, although the acting was true and believable *on its own terms*, its resemblance to real life was of considerably less importance than its fidelity to the dramatic action. Given the size of the audience, the physical arrangement of the theatre, and the style of acting, it should be no surprise that vocal power and agility were the actor's most prized assets. Actors, like sponsors and chorus members, performed as part of their civic duties. They were not paid professionals.

Settings and Machinery

The skene was the essential setting. We do not know whether its appearance was changed to suggest different locations; that is, we don't know whether there was scenery in our sense of that word. We do know that some sort of flat (two-dimensional surface for painting) existed, but we do not know how it was used, or where.

We do know that two machines provided special effects:

- The eccyclema was a movable platform capable of being rolled or rotated out of the skene to reveal the result of an offstage action. In Aeschylus's *Agamemnon*, for example, the body of the murdered Agamemnon is "revealed" (rolled out?), and in the *Eumenides*, the Furies (avenging goddesses) seem to have entered first while asleep (rolled into view?).
- The mechane was some sort of crane that allowed people and things to "fly" in and out. In Aristophanes's *The Clouds*, the character Socrates hangs over the performing space during some of his dialogue, and in Euripides's *Medea*, Medea flies away to escape her pursuers. In fact, Euripides so often has gods fly down to sort out the characters' problems at the end of his tragedies that a too-obviously contrived ending of a play came much later to be called (in Latin) a *deus ex machina* ("god from the machine").

Properties were numerous, and we read of altars, tombs, biers, chariots, staffs, and swords being used in tragedy. Comedies often required furniture, food, clubs, and so on.

John Buford

FIGURE 11.6

Outdoor Theatre

Outdoor theatres are not limited to the Greek era. *The Lost Colony*, an outdoor drama in North Carolina with a theatre space not unlike an ancient theatre, has been drawing summer audiences for more than seventy years.

Costumes and Masks

Because in Greek theatre one actor played several roles, costumes and masks were exceedingly important—they enabled audiences to identify quickly and certainly which character in the play the actor was impersonating. The mask and the costume, in a sense, were the signs of character. A different principle governed the chorus, whose goal was to make its individual members appear to be a group, and so choral costumes and masks were similar. Although historians once argued for "a tragic costume" for tragic characters, most now agree that some version of normal Athenian dress seems likelier. In tragedy, such dress was perhaps more elegant than normal, and in comedy it was certainly altered to make it laughable—ill-fitting, exaggerated, and so on—but the basic look was recognizable.

From references in plays, we know that a costume's appearance allowed audience members to know a character's traits:

- *ethnicity* (references are made to some dressed as Greeks and to others dressed as foreigners).
- *gender* (males and females are identified as such at a distance).
- *social role* (military heroes, servants, shepherds, and so on were visually identifiable).

In the case of comedy, the costume for certain male characters featured a stuffed, oversized penis (phallus). The color of costumes was also a sign: Reference is made to black for characters in mourning and yellow for an especially effeminate male character, to cite only two examples.

All performers, both actors and chorus members, wore masks. They were full-face masks, and they carried their own hairstyle and, of course, their own set facial expression. During the fifth century BCE, the masks looked natural in tragedy, but in comedy, they could distort features to provoke laughter. Again, masks for actors aimed for individuality and quick recognition of character, whereas choral masks stressed resemblance, membership in a group. Occasionally, comic masks resembled the faces of living people, a fact we glean from an account of Socrates, who, from his seat in the audience, stood up and turned so that others could see that the mask worn by the actor in a comedy mimicked his own face.

THE END OF ATHENS' GOLDEN AGE

At the end of the fifth century BCE, Athens lost its premiere position among the Greek poleis. First it was defeated by Sparta, a militaristic state with few aspirations to high culture. With Spartan influence came some sort of censorship, which had the immediate effect of toning down the political satire of Greek old comedies and substituting comedy with a less biting tone (called middle comedy). Then, near the end of the fourth century BCE (300s), Alexander the Great overran all the Greek poleis and folded them into a single, centralized government. He then conquered many of the advanced civilizations that abutted Greece, lands south through Egypt and east as far as India and modern Afghanistan and Pakistan. Founding Alexandria (Egypt) as his capital, he ruled one of the world's great empires in a brief age now called the Hellenistic period. As Alexander and his armies conquered lands, they exported Greek culture to them.

The culture of Hellenistic Greece, however, differed from that of Athens. The individuality of the various poleis declined, replaced by a cosmopolitan culture centered in Egypt. Gone were Athenian democracy, its great drama, and the centrality of its gods. The trend was toward a common government, common civilization, and common religion. The empire's center of gravity shifted away from the Greek peninsula, which now rested on the westernmost edge of Alexander's holdings, and toward the East, where different religious and philosophical systems were already highly developed. Towns and then cities grew up, as trade competed with agriculture for attention. Within a hundred years, the Hellenistic

FIGURE 11.7

The Theatre at Epidaurus

By the middle of the fifth century BCE, the Athenian theatre had a wooden stage house (skene) with roof and doors (number uncertain). By the beginning of the fourth century, the seating area was connected to the skene by two arches, seen here. Some scholars believe that the audience entered through these archways, as did the chorus at the plays' beginning. A well-preserved example of these Greek theatres is Epidaurus, seen here with a setting for a modern production of Aristophanes's *The Knights*.

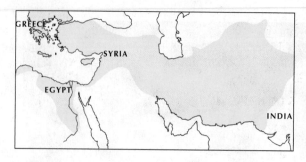

FIGURE 11.8

Hellenistic Greece

The conquests of Alexander the Great in the 300s BCE extended Greek influence but led to a shift of power away from Athens. Theatres began to be built throughout Greek lands and acting became professionalized.

world had more than four hundred cities with populations of more than 200,000, that is, twice the size of Athens during its golden age (fifth century BCE).

Greek drama changed. Plays began to be performed throughout Greek lands, not merely at Athens, and they were now performed on special military and civic occasions as well as during Dionysian festivals. Satyr plays disappeared. Tragedy declined in popularity; the tragedies that were written apparently modeled themselves on Euripides's plays, with a reduced emphasis on the chorus and an increased emphasis on sensation, realism, and melodrama. (Only fragments of such tragedies exist today.) Tragedies from the fifth century BCE continued to be revived, however, attesting to their power to move audiences. Comedy remained popular, but it abandoned both its political bite and its formal structure. New comedy, as Hellenistic comedy is now called, told domestic tales of middle-class life structured as a series of episodes interrupted by incidental choral songs. New comedies took as their subjects such things as love, money, and family, often including intrigues involving long-lost children and happy reunitings. Although there are many fragments, only one complete new comedy remains, *Dyskolos* by Menander, rendered in English as *The Grouch* or *The Grumbler*.

Although actors remained exclusively male, they became professionalized, organizing themselves into a performing guild called the Artists of Dionysus. From changes in the plays (and also in theatre buildings, costuming conventions, and masks), we can infer that acting style changed, becoming grander, showier, and more formal in tragedy, and probably less boisterous, more restrained, and more representational in comedy.

Aristotle and the *Poetics*

Of far greater consequence than the drama itself during these years was Aristotle's theory of drama, the *Poetics*, written early in the Hellenistic period. Providing a theoretical definition of the form tragedy (his theory treated neither comedy nor mixed forms), Aristotle set the boundaries for dramatic theory, with the following major points about tragedy:

- Imitates "action that is serious, complete, and of a certain magnitude."
- Takes "the form of action, not narrative".
- Produces "pity and fear and the catharsis of such emotions."

The meaning of Aristotle's definition has been endlessly debated, especially the phrase about catharsis, which some scholars believe refers to the response of audiences (though elsewhere Aristotle said he did not intend to talk about audiences) and other scholars think refers to emotions embedded within the episodes of the play itself.

Aristotle then defined and discussed the six parts of a play (see Chapter 3). The following are just a few of his many comments on drama, especially tragedy:

- *Plot.* Of the six parts, plot was the most important to Aristotle. He therefore discussed it in the most detail, considering its *wholeness* (having a beginning, a middle, and an end, connected by causality); its *unity* (so that if any part is removed, the whole is disturbed); its *materials* (suffering, discovery, and reversal); and its *form* (complication and denouement).
- *Character.* He argued that the best tragic protagonist is one who causes his own downfall through some great tragic error (*hamartia*).
- *Language.* The play's language should be both clear and interesting.
- *Spectacle.* Spectacle is the business of the stage machinist rather than the poet.

Because the *Poetics* is so packed with ideas and its translation is so difficult, its meaning has been debated for two thousand years. Certainly, it remains the base from which most discussions of dramatic theory must proceed, through either acceptance or rejection of its primary tenets.

FIGURE 11.9

Menander Mosaic

This second-century or early first-century (CE) mosaic from Pompeii is now housed in the Naples Museum. It illustrates a scene from Menander's *Ladies at Lunch*, of which only a few lines survive.

The Hellenistic Period and Its Theatres

Theatre buildings also changed. Great stone theatres sprang up both on the Greek peninsula and on conquered lands (especially modern Turkey), and they tended to share common features:

- A two-storied skene
- A long, narrow, high stage attached to the skene, usually with steps or ramps at the ends but sometimes with entrances and exits only through the skene. Its use is unclear.
- An orchestra, as before, but now of uncertain use.

FIGURE 11.10

Hellenistic Theatre Buildings

Stone remains of several Hellenistic theatres have led scholars to speculate that a typical Hellenistic theatre looked something like the reconstruction shown here.

Unfortunately, we do not know how plays were staged in Hellenistic theatres. Were actors on stage? in the orchestra? some combination of the two? Where was the chorus?

Costumes and masks also changed, and they changed in similar directions. Those in tragedy tended toward greater size and grandeur. Unlike masks of the golden age, the masks of tragedy during the Hellenistic period are the familiar masks of clichè, having a high headdress (*onkos*) as well as exaggerated, often distorted, eyes and mouths. Footwear for tragedy may have featured a high platform boot, called a *cothurnus*, rather than the soft slipper of former days. Such changes enlarged the physical appearance of the actor and brought him greater focus, suggesting an altered acting style. Comic masks ranged from somewhat lifelike to quite outrageous, matching the types of characters that began to repeat in comedies of the period.

Truth be told, drama and theatre from the Hellenistic period would not be important except for three things:

- The promulgation of Aristotelian theory.
- The mistaken assumption in relatively recent times that these buildings and practices of the Hellenistic era represented the buildings and practices of fifth-century BCE Athens.
- The strong influences of these plays, buildings, and practices on Roman theatre and possibly on Indian theatre as well.

Before leaving Greece, we should note that there existed alongside these state-supported festival theatres another kind of performance, the mime. Little is known about it except that it seems to have been popular and perhaps slightly disreputable. Its troupes included women; its actors apparently often played barefoot; and mime troupes were not allowed to perform as part of the festivals. This may in part explain why so little evidence about them has come down to us.

After Alexander died, his Hellenistic empire soon collapsed, with various pieces of it drifting into other rising centers of power. By a hundred years before the Common Era, Greece had fallen within the sphere of a spreading Roman influence as the center of civilization shifted west. From this time,

FIGURE 11.11

Greek Mime Characters

These terra cotta figures of comic characters—not individuals but stereotyped characters—were found together with others in a burial in the area about Athens. They date from the late fifth to early fourth century BCE. Originally they were brightly painted. These are the earliest known images of standardized comic characters and masks.

Hellenistic theatrical trends continued but were altered to bring them more in line with Roman practice. Not only were Roman theatres built on Greek lands, but Hellenistic theatres also began to be remodeled to make them look more like Roman theatres, producing hybrids that we now call Graeco-Roman theatres (the age itself is sometimes referred to as the Graeco-Roman period). Although records show that theatre performances persisted in Greece, the center of influence—and with it the theatre—had clearly shifted west, to Rome itself.

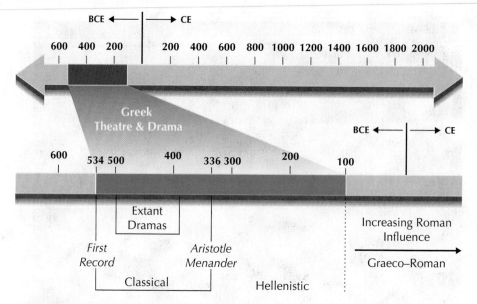

FIGURE 11.12

Timeline

Although Greek theatre's first records date from the sixth century BCE, its golden age was the fifth century (400s) BCE. The later Hellenistic period (300s to 200s) saw the building of stone theatres and the theorizing of Aristotle. After c. 100 BCE, influence shifted increasingly from Greece to Rome.

KEY TERMS

Check your understanding against this list. Brief definitions are included in the Glossary; persons are page-referenced in the Index.

chorus   170
cothurnus   182
eccyclema
   [eh-KIH-kleh-ma]   177
facade stage   176
flat   177
Graeco-Roman

period   183
Great Dionysia   171
Hellenistic period   179
mechane
   [MEH-kah-neh]   177
middle comedy   179
mime   182

new comedy   180
old comedy   175
onkos [AHN-kohs]   182
orchestra   176
protagonist   177
satyr play   171
skene [SKEE-nee]   176

12

The Theatre of Rome

Built in about 16 CE, this Roman theatre with much of the facade intact is in Merida, Spain.

OBJECTIVES

When you have completed this chapter, you should be able to:

- Discuss the relationship between theatre and religion in Rome.

- Trace the development of Roman physical theatres and their plays and playwrights.

- Identify the major periods of Roman theatres with approximate dates.

- Explain how a Roman performance would have looked in the principal periods—what masks and costumes were used and what acting space was used.

- Explain the important differences between the plays

of Plautus and Terence and those of Seneca.

- Explain the importance of Vitruvius and Horace.

FIGURE 12.1

Map

During Athens' golden age (400s BCE), Rome was simply one small city among many on Italy's peninsula, less important than the Etruscans to the north and the Greek colonies to the south. During Greece's Hellenistic period, however, a distinctly Roman culture emerged in Italy; it overtook the Greek culture by the start of the Common Era.

CONTEXT

Greek culture had penetrated parts of the Italian peninsula even before the golden age of Athenian drama, when Rome was only one small town among many. The native people of the Italian peninsula were mostly self-sufficient herders and farmers, who early established a republican form of government. Having relatively little interest in arts, literature, and philosophy, they excelled instead in practical activities, becoming superb agriculturalists, soldiers, engineers, builders, and rhetoricians. Their religion was polytheistic, with most Roman gods having clear Greek equivalents. (Bacchus corresponded to Dionysus, for example.) They also had a gift for adapting useful ideas from other cultures, whose practices they modified to suit Roman tastes and needs.

While Alexander the Great was building his Greek empire, a distinctly Roman culture began to coalesce. First, Rome unified much of the Italian peninsula and then, having built a navy, began to expand to other lands around the Mediterranean Sea, which was soon thought of as the "Roman Lake." By the third century BCE, Rome was a leading Mediterranean power. When Alexander's Hellenistic empire began to break apart, Rome moved to fill the void left in the West.

It was in this republican Rome that theatre and drama appeared in 240 BCE. Regrettably, the same major problem haunts the study of Roman theatre as that of Greek: For the periods when we know most about plays (BCE), we know least about theatres because they were built of wood and have not lasted; conversely, when we know most about theatres (CE), we know almost nothing about plays.

ROMAN FESTIVALS AND THEATRE OF THE REPUBLIC

Roman dramatic and theatrical practices mostly reproduced those of Hellenistic Greece but were modified by earlier Italian traditions of performance. Roman festivals, called *ludi*, differed from Greek festivals mostly by having activities such as acrobatics and rope dancing compete directly with plays for public attention. At first, there was a single play, but the number of plays grew steadily over time.

Drama

No Roman tragedy that was meant to be performed survives. Fragments suggest, however, that they resembled Hellenistic tragedy. Some presented upper-class Greeks (in which actors wore Greek costume); others told of upper-class Romans (in Roman attire). Seneca wrote nine tragedies that survive, but scholars believe they were not intended for performance. Tragedy was never popular in Rome, perhaps because as a people the Romans lacked deep interest in philosophy and ethics, the usual emphasis in Athenian tragedy.

Comedy was far more popular and, like tragedy, divided into two types: that written about Greeks (this time middle or lower class, and so costumed) and that about Romans (ditto). In addition to many titles and fragments, twenty-seven complete comedies survive, all by two authors: Plautus and Terence, both of whom wrote during the second century (100s) BCE and about the Athenian middle class. Both drew heavily from Greek new comedy for their stories and approach. *Neither used a chorus.* Despite these strong similarities, the two authors are different in other ways and so suggest quite a range within Roman comedy.

Plautus, the older of the two authors, was an actor as well as a playwright. Of the more than one hundred works credited to Plautus, twenty-one have survived, perhaps a tribute to his popularity or, just as probable, a historical accident. Probably his experiences as an actor accounted for the theatrical (as opposed to literary) qualities of his comedies. Plautine comedies are noted for:

- Loosely linked episodes.
- Many visual gags and much verbal wordplay.
- Characters who are ludicrous in appearance as well as behavior.
- Direct address to the audience, breaking dramatic illusion.

Among his many plays, *The Braggart Warrior*, *The Menaechmi*, *Pot of Gold*, and *Amphitryon* have been used by Shakespeare, Molière, and others.

The more refined comedies were written by Terence. His plays were more elegant than Plautus's but also less robust and free. They were more thoughtful but less fun. Terence's comedies had:

- Plots that often combined two or more of the Greek comedies into a single, highly complicated dramatic action.
- Prologues that were unusual because Terence argued matters of dramatic theory, encouraged audiences to behave politely, and defended himself from the attacks of critics.
- Carefully contrived actions that seemed to proceed by cause and effect, thus avoiding the episodic quality of Plautus's comedies.
- Characters that appeared more normal and human than Plautus's and thus more sympathetic.

It may help to distinguish Terence from Plautus to know that, although Plautus is occasionally performed even today, Terence almost never is. And

 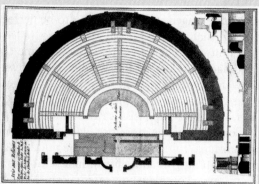

FIGURE 12.2

Theatre of Marcellus

This engraving (left) from the 1700s shows the exterior of one of the first permanent (stone) theatres built in Rome (c. 17 BCE). The site still exists and is a popular tourist attraction. The second engraving shows the stage of a Roman theatre, perhaps one that the Theatre of Marcellus might have resembled.

Terence, not Plautus, was used in schools during the Middle Ages as a way to teach the Latin language and proper Latin usage.

Although comedy had always been more popular than tragedy in Rome, its popularity waned within fifty years of Terence's death. Therefore, by the time the first stone theatre was built (55 BCE), the great period of Roman tragedy and comedy was over.

Theatre Buildings, Scenery, Costumes, and Masks

Roman theatres, like Greek theatres, were facade stages. As far as we can tell, their basic arrangement remained scene house, aisle ways, and orchestra. Assuming that Rome's early wooden theatres resembled its later stone ones, Roman theatres differed from Hellenistic theatres in several ways:

- They stood on level ground (rather than hillsides), with built-up, stadium-style seating.
- Their orchestras were half-circles, rather than full circles or rectangles.
- Their long, deep stages were closed at both ends by the building itself, which jutted out.
- They used a front curtain, the first to do so.

As in Greece, the facade of Roman theatres served as background. In tragedy, the doors of the facade represented separate entrances to a palace or other public building, with the stage floor representing the ground in front of the building. In comedy, the doors were entrances to separate houses, with the stage representing a street running in front of them. There were *periaktoi*, machines that could be rotated to reveal painted scenes. Records tell of two periaktoi, one near each end

Spotlight

At least seven of Plautus's plays were incorporated into the musical *A Funny Thing Happened on the Way to the Forum*, including the play *Miles Gloriosus* or "The Braggart Soldier." Here the character in a Virginia Commonwealth University production.

Plautus's *The Menaechmi*

Written by Plautus (c. 254–c. 184 BCE), *The Menaechmi* sometimes titled in English *The Twins*, is probably the most often revived Roman comedy. It has also served as a source for other works, most notably Shakespeare's *Comedy of Errors* and two US musicals, *The Boys from Syracuse* and *A Funny Thing Happened on the Way to the Forum* (which drew material from other Plautine comedies as well). The play's appeal probably comes from its farcical story, strong visual gags, and such familiar comic characters as the wily servant who outsmarts his master; the parasite, a hanger-on who sponges off a wealthy citizen; the courtesan, a cross between a high-class call girl and a mistress; and the nagging wife.

The Story of the Play

A businessman from Syracuse takes Menaechmus, one of his identical twin sons, on a business trip, where the youngster disappears in a crowd. After a fruitless search, the father returns home alone, where, griefstricken, he dies, and the grandfather renames the remaining twin Menaechmus in honor of the lost brother. When this second Meneachmus grows up, he leaves with a servant to search for his long-lost twin. This information is revealed in a prologue before the action begins.

After years of searching, Menaechmus 2 arrrives in the city of Epidamnus, where unknown to Menaechmus 2, Menaechmus 1 has been living with a wealthy but quarrelsome wife. Following yet another argument with his wife, Menaechmus 1 storms out of the house, stealing a dress to give to his mistress, Erotium. Menaechmus 1 gives his present, orders a feast, and then leaves with his parasite to attend to business. Thus is the stage set for dual confusions.

Erotium, seeing Menaechmus 2, insists that he sit down and eat a feast that she has prepared (for Menaechmus 1); when Menaechmus 2 has eaten, she asks him to take a bracelet (an earlier gift from Menaechmus 1) to a jeweler. He's happy to oblige. Meanwhile, the parasite, having become separated from Menaechmus 1, returns and sees Menaechmus 2 leaving the feast with the bracelet. Angry at Menaechmus for eating without him, he tells the wife about the gifts to Erotium, so that when Menaechmus 1 returns, he finds that his wife is in a tizzy and his mistress has locked him out of her house. He leaves just as Menaechmus 2 returns, carrying the dress and bracelet. He encounters the angry wife, who first attacks him and then decides he's crazy, ties him up, and carts him off to a doctor. Menaechmus 2, of course, has no idea what's going on: He's had a splendid free meal and tried to do a favor in return, only to be assaulted and called crazy.

The mistaken identities are finally sorted out by Menaechmus 2's servant, who thus earns his freedom. Menaechmus 1 announces that he will sell everything he owns (including his wife) and return with his brother to Syracuse.

of the stage. Because they could not possibly have hidden the whole facade, they must have served simply to inform the audience of location, not to portray any place in a realistic way. Although these early wooden theatres were temporary, they could be quite spectacular, according to ancient accounts.

As in Greece, all actors of comedy and tragedy wore masks, and the masks resembled those of Hellenistic Greece, with high onkos and distorted eyes and mouth for tragedy, and a range from somewhat realistic to comically distorted for comedy. The conventions of costuming were also rooted in Hellenistic conventions, with actors wearing a version of either Greek or Roman dress (depending on the kind of tragedy or comedy).

Audiences

Theatres of the ludi were free and open to all, and probably somewhere between ten and fifteen thousand people attended. Great care was taken to ensure the comfort of audiences, with wide and numerous aisles allowing for ease of entering and exiting the space.

THE EMPIRE AND THE END OF ROMAN DRAMA

About a hundred years before the beginning of the Common Era, Rome's republican government gave way to an imperial one, and soon thereafter it confronted the growing challenge of a new religion, Christianity, that had arisen in one of its own territories. Whereas Rome was perfectly happy to accommodate this new god (it had routinely adopted the gods of any culture with which it came into contact), Christians refused to allow their god to be assimilated into the Roman pantheon. Indeed, they insisted that their god alone should be worshipped, a rigidity unwelcome in a culture whose religion depended more on traditions than passions. Jews also irked the Romans for their unwillingness to be assimilated into Roman pantheism.

Within three hundred years, the Roman Empire

FIGURE 12.3

Roman Comedy

Although a few comedies by Plautus are still produced, Roman comedy is most popular today in adaptation by Molière, Shakespeare, and US musical theatre. Here, *A Funny Thing Happened on the Way to the Forum*, a 1963 Broadway musical based on several Plautus plays, revived by Fairmont State University.

had spread as far north as England, through parts of Africa and the Middle East, and as far east as Syria. Christianity had spread with it. This expanding empire traded widely, importing luxury items from the East and exporting mass-produced, useful articles. The sprawling empire encouraged more roads, better water management, a strong civil service, and a permanent military class. Travel, encouraged by both war and trade, promoted a kind of cosmopolitanism. Despite their growth, Romans still did not define themselves through their art, literature, or philosophy. Instead, they concentrated on increasing personal comforts (through elegant homes, public baths, and entertainments) and continued to demonstrate their superiority in practical matters.

Three Important Texts

Two how-to manuals, both written near the turn into the Common Era, are of special importance to theatre and drama because, when they were rediscovered during the Renaissance (c. 1400s), their advice on how to build theatres and write plays was put into practice.

VITRUVIUS   The Roman architect Vitruvius wrote a ten-volume work, *De Architectura*, on how to lay out a city. As a part of this larger work, he set down guidelines for building both theatres and the scenery to go in them. Without illustrations and with often ambiguous descriptions, the books were easily—and badly—misinterpreted by Renaissance designers, but their influence was enormous.

HORACE   The Roman poet Horace described how to write good plays in his *Ars Poetica*, a work that was to exert even more influence during the Renaissance than did Aristotle's *Poetics*, which it superficially resembles. Unlike Aristotle's work, a philosophical inquiry into the nature of the form of tragedy, Horace's is a practical guidebook aimed at people who want to write plays. As such, it is considerably more prescriptive than Aristotle's work, suggesting such things as:

- The importance of keeping comedy and tragedy separate.
- The need to have a unity of time and of place as a way of achieving unity of action.
- The need for drama to teach as well as please.

Ars Poetica had no immediate influence on Roman practice. Its importance, like Vitruvius's, comes from its powerful influence much later on Renaissance theory and drama.

SENECA   The third important text is really a set of texts. Although Roman tragedy and comedy were not played in public theatres by the 100s, dramatic readings were apparently given at banquets in private homes. Ten such literary tragedies have come down to us, nine by Seneca, who wrote them just after the turn of the Common Era. The importance of Seneca's tragedies rests neither on their literary excellence nor on their position among contemporary Roman audiences, but on their monumental effect on later writers, who discovered, translated, and copied them, probably because they were at the time both linguistically and physically more accessible than the previous Greek tragedies.

Seneca's plays display five characteristics also assumed to be typical of Greek Hellenistic tragedy:

- A chorus that is not well integrated into the action, and so the (usually four) choral odes (songs) serve to divide the plays into five parts.
- Protagonists that are often driven by a single dominant passion that causes their downfall.
- Minor characters that include messengers, confidants, and ghosts.
- Language that emphasizes rhetorical and stylistic figures, including extended descriptive and declamatory passages, pithy statements about the human condition (*sententiae*), and elaborately balanced exchanges of dialogue.
- Spectacular scenes of violence and gore.

Although Seneca's plays are now rarely performed, they are important, like the writings of Vitruvius and Horace, because of their influence on Renaissance writers, who rediscovered tragedy through Seneca and tried to follow what he did in writing their own tragedies.

Marjorie F. Hill

FIGURE 12.4

The Theatre of Herod Atticus

This Roman theatre, built into the slope of the Acropolis in Athens in 161 CE originally featured the traditional highly decorated facade of columns; time, however, has taken its toll. Note that the stage is connected and thus unified with the seating area that accommodates about five thousand. The seats have been renovated in modern times for the theatre is still used, mostly for concerts.

Theatre Buildings

Despite these three important written sources, theatre buildings rather than texts dominated the empire. In the Common Era, Rome built great stone theatres, first on the Italian peninsula and then throughout its empire (remains are still visible in Libya and Turkey, for example). Although the basic pattern of scene house, aisle ways, and orchestra remained, stone theatres were probably more ornate than earlier wooden ones. Now used by audiences rather than choruses, the aisles separating the scene house from the orchestra were covered, causing the buildings to form a single architectural unit, rather than two (as in Greek theatres). The facades were decorated with such details as statuary, niches, and columns. A roof extended over part of the stage, both protecting the elaborate facades and improving acoustics. Audience comfort remained a high priority, with awnings sometimes protecting audiences from sun and rain and, in at least one theatre, a primitive air conditioning system consisting of large fans blowing over ice brought down from mountaintops.

Theatrical Entertainments

Into these theatres came new theatrical entertainments that replaced comedy and tragedy. An indigenous rural Italian farce, called Atellan farce after the region in which it originated and featuring four grotesquely masked characters, was popular for a while. Pantomime, a solo dance performed by a nonspeaking performer (wearing a mask with a closed mouth), could be comic but was more often serious. It filled the void left by tragedy.

Most popular of all, however, was mime, which may have come from Greece because Greek mime (the word refers both to the form and the performers) had a long history, although it was never performed at Greek festivals. In Greece, mime seemed unimportant, but Roman mime became so popular during the empire that it drove all other forms of theatre from the stage.

Several traits of mime make it important:

- Mime included women as performers, the only theatrical entertainment in Greece or Rome to do so.
- Performers in the mime did not usually wear masks, so their faces were both noticeable and important. Indeed, mime performers were often successful because of their looks: the handsome or beautiful and the extraordinarily grotesque or ugly.

Mimes could be either comic or serious, simple or spectacular, but whatever their form, they usually dealt with contemporary life. They became both Rome's most popular and most notorious theatrical entertainment during the empire (in both east and west). Some female mime actors set fashions in clothes and behavior; one (Theodora) married an emperor; and some became the equivalent of movie stars. Despite this popularity, few complete mime scripts have been passed down to us; the assumption is that they, perhaps like sitcom scripts, were thought (by those who kept libraries) to have no lasting value.

FIGURE 12.5

Verona Arena

This Roman amphitheatre in Verona, Italy, could seat about thirty thousand spectators when it was build in about 30 CE. Now a popular venue for rock concerts and opera performances, here it is configured in a proscenium actor-audience arrangement.

Christian Opposition to Theatre

Christianity's opposition to theatre was not to Roman comedies or tragedies, which it had not seen and did not know. The opposition was to mime. Because some mimes included sex and violence as part of the performance and because many of them mocked Christianity, Christian writers and believers demanded—unsuccessfully—the outlawing of theatre. Mime was not alone in its excesses; equally popular were chariot racing, gladiatorial contests, animal fights, and sea battles in which violence and death were also expected and applauded. Although these entertainments took place in special buildings such as amphitheatres (e.g., Rome's Colosseum) and circuses (the Circus Maximus), theatres were occasionally appropriated for such events, reinforcing the arguments of those who wanted to ban theatre. That mime had to compete directly with these other kinds of performance probably explains its occasional rawness. That mime replaced comedy and tragedy in Rome's public theatres surely offers hints about Romans and their culture. The antipathy between theatre and the church, which dates from the early Roman Empire, echoes still today.

THE BREAKUP OF THE EMPIRE

By the early 300s CE, the Roman Empire had become too large and unwieldy to rule effectively. It was therefore broken into two administrative units, with the western unit claiming Rome as its capital and the eastern unit being ruled from Constantinople, a new city built by the Emperor Constantine. Constantine moved to this new capital, taking much of the population of Rome with him, thus tilting the empire's center of gravity far to the east. The result was a shift in power and cultural influence. Constantinople grew more powerful and turned eastward. Rome, now a much smaller city, once again found itself on the western fringe of the civilized world.

FIGURE 12.6

Roman Entertainments

During the Roman Empire, elaborate entertainments with animal fights, chariot races, and even naval battles became popular and drove traditional theatre from the center of cultural life.

By the middle of the sixth century (500s), the western empire was disintegrating, its system of roads and waterways crumbling, its trade sporadic, and its security destroyed. Whatever unity remained in Western Europe came mostly from the Christian church through a network of churches and religious houses bound through the pope in Rome, but the center of the western empire had fallen.

THE EASTERN (BYZANTINE) EMPIRE AND THEATRE

Constantinople and the eastern empire, on the other hand, flourished. Considering themselves Romans, the citizens for a time continued to speak Latin, to enjoy chariot races and theatre, and to trade with such Italian satellites as Ravenna, but increasingly trade was with countries to the east. Later the eastern Romans adopted Greek for official documents, however; established a Christianity (now called Orthodox) that was tied more closely to the government than to the pope; and gradually easternized, some say "orientalized," their culture. Later called *Byzantine* (after the early town of Byzantium, which Constantinople had replaced), this empire had a thriving trade, a successful military, and a highly developed culture that included theatre.

Weakened by one of the Western crusades in the thirteenth century (1200s), the eastern Roman Empire was finally overwhelmed by Muslim Turks in the fifteenth century (1400s), just as the former Western empire was beginning to recuperate and enter its great Renaissance.

Byzantine theatre is not well known in today's Western world, for a couple of reasons. The languages in which its records appear are not those in which most Western scholars are competent, and many of the records were, until the late 1980s, inaccessible because they were held behind the so-called Iron

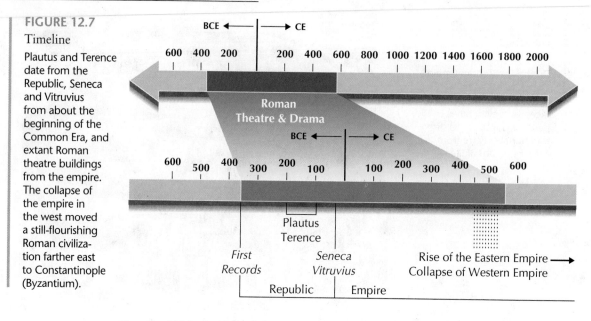

FIGURE 12.7

Timeline

Plautus and Terence date from the Republic, Seneca and Vitruvius from about the beginning of the Common Era, and extant Roman theatre buildings from the empire. The collapse of the empire in the west moved a still-flourishing Roman civilization farther east to Constantinople (Byzantium).

Curtain. With the fall of the Soviet Union and the political realignment of Russia and the United States, however, more information is now becoming available. The scholarship suggests that Byzantine theatre included:

- The continuation of mime.
- An interest in Greek tragedy (which may have been literary only).
- The exportation of performances and an idea of performance to Asia Minor and what is now Ukraine.

Just as Roman theatre of the West left a legacy for the Renaissance in Western Europe, so, too, may have Byzantine theatre. There are tantalizing hints that Byzantine theatre may have influenced both Italian popular theatre and the medieval theatre of Europe.

The Roman Empire—east and west—was thus unparalleled among great civilizations because it remained intact so long, although its final iterations would scarcely have been recognized by the Italians who first created it.

KEY TERMS

Check your understanding against this list. Brief definitions are included in the Glossary; persons are page-referenced in the Index.

amphitheatres   194
ludi [LOO-dee]   186
mime   193

pantomime   193
periaktoi
   [peh-ree-AKH-toy]   188

IIIB

EMBLEM, ENVIRONMENT, AND SIMULTANEITY
(c. 950–c. 1650)

The second phase of theatrical and dramatic history began in the tenth century and ended about 1650 (approximately two hundred years earlier in Italy). Theatres during these six hundred years shared several important theatrical conventions and so can be usefully studied together. Their major shared traits are:

- The communication of meaning through emblems, shorthand embodiments of richer content (e.g., a flag standing for a country, a crown for a king).
- The use of existing environments for performance.
- A staging convention of simultaneous settings in which several locations are presented at the same time to the audience.
- Complicated plays with numerous characters, many lines of action, and elastic time and place.
- A mostly male theatre, in which women participated only as audience.

Over the last two centuries of this period, rapid change led to overlap between this period and a new one then coming into being. This overlap was possible because of social and economic stratification into a court theatre, a popular theatre, and an embryonic professional theatre.

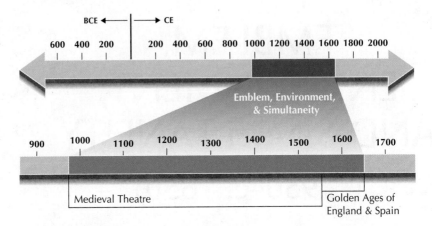

FIGURE IIIB.1

After the fall of the western Roman Empire (c. 550 CE), organized theatre disappeared from Europe until the end of the tenth century, when it reappeared using different conventions. These conventions were, in turn, replaced after about 1650.

14

The Golden Ages of England and Spain

An Italianate angled wing perspective by the seventeenth-century Englishman, Inigo Jones.

OBJECTIVES

When you have completed this chapter, you should be able to:

- Discuss major traits associated with the Renaissance.

- List the principal kinds of drama, important playwrights, and plays from the age of Shakespeare and the Spanish Golden Age.

- Distinguish between public and private theatres.

- Describe the major staging conventions of Shakespeare's theatre and compare them (that is, note similarities and differences) with medieval conventions.

- Compare the physical theatres of Shakespeare and the Spanish Golden Age.

- Compare the role of women in the theatres of Shakespeare and Spain.

- Explain the importance of masques in English theatre history.

CONTEXT

Italy, perhaps because it was still weakly tied to Constantinople by tradition and trade or perhaps because it was once the heart of an empire, made the transition from a feudal society to a modern, commercial one earlier than the rest of Western Europe. Indeed, by 1300 in Italy, new ideas, social organizations, attitudes, and discoveries had begun to peek through the medieval order. For the next two hundred years, these new ideas gradually took hold and spread throughout Western Europe, heralding the arrival of the Renaissance ("rebirth"). (The Renaissance in Italy is covered in the next chapter.)

Once under way, the Renaissance unfolded throughout Western Europe, but it did so at different rates and with different effects:

- Italy and southern Europe embraced Renaissance ideas earlier and developed somewhat differently from England, Spain, and northern Europe, at least for a while. But even within the Renaissance of northern Europe, stark differences were visible.
- Spain and England, both strong naval powers and vigorous traders, were early rivals. Spain, importing gold from its Central and South American colonies, pulled money to its profligate central government and clung to Roman Catholicism and absolute monarchy. England, on the other hand, developed a strong merchant class, broke with Rome, and moved toward constitutional monarchy.

By c. 1550 (when medieval religious drama ended), the Renaissance had already revolutionized many former attitudes and practices throughout Western Europe, though it had done so on different timetables and with different effects. Regardless of date or location, however, several traits distinguish this new Renaissance culture from the medieval culture preceding it.

Humanism

People of the early Middle Ages had supposed that the temporal world would be destroyed, that the unrighteous would be purged, and that the righteous would be transported to a world of bliss. In the Renaissance, however, new secular and temporal interests joined earlier divine and eternal ones. A love of God, long the basis of human behavior, was joined by a newfound admiration for humankind, whose worth, intelligence, and beauty began to be celebrated. This new concern for people and their earthly lives was called humanism.

Secularism

At about the same time, the older theology, a complete system based on divine revelation, gave way to competing philosophical systems that stressed secularism (that is, they advocated ethical conduct as an end in itself rather than as a prerequisite to heaven, and they argued for logical systems of thought independent of divine revelation). In science, an earth-centered astronomy was challenged by a sun-centered universe in which human beings were relegated to life on a relatively minor planet, no longer at the center of creation.

Reformation

Within the church, demands for reform led to breaks with Rome: Some Christians (such as Martin Luther) protested against the church at Rome and launched what came to be called the *Reformation.*

In sum, although God, church, and theology remained a central fact of human life in the Renaissance, they were no longer absolute and unquestioned. Humanism and secularism were competing with them for acceptance. But the emergence of new ideas and attitudes was only part of the phenomenon. Vital, too, were factors that encouraged the widespread dissemination of the new spirit, factors such as the growth of trade and the arrival of the printing press.

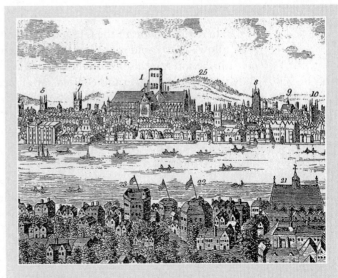

FIGURE 14.1

London before the Great Fire of 1666

This engraving is of London sometime before the Great Fire of 1666. On the north side of the Thames, the original St. Paul's Cathedral dominates the city. On the south side are several tall buildings with flags, probably theatres or bear-baiting arenas.

The World Widens

By the Renaissance, exploration and discovery had increased commercial areas far beyond the Mediterranean and close-in Atlantic. Marco Polo had opened Asia, Columbus had opened the Americas, and a series of West African ports hopscotching to the Cape of Good Hope opened a feasible sea route to India. Improved navigation aids and some road improvements joined with new postal systems to improve both transportation and communication (e.g., a trip of seventy-five miles that took eight days in 1500 took only six by 1600.) New organizations arose for raising capital (e.g., joint stock companies) and insuring against catastrophic loss (e.g., associations among merchants). Wholesalers and middlemen transformed the nature of trade and took their share of the growing profits.

The Fall of Constantinople

Along with goods, trade led to the exchange of ideas. At the center of most of the various trade routes of the fourteenth century were the city-states of Italy, which soon became centers of commerce in ideas, skills, and products. When Constantinople fell to the Turks in 1453, many scholars and artists came to Italy and with them came plays and treatises from ancient Greece and Rome, rescued from endangered libraries. Their study and interpretation began almost at once.

The Printing Press

The introduction of the Gutenberg printing press to Italy at about the same time allowed the rapid reproduction of documents arriving from the East as well as of the interpretations and imitations of these documents. Certainly, the printing press allowed a veritable explosion of accessible information, so much so that, by 1500, numerous academies in the city-states of Italy were devoted to the study and production of Roman plays. Shortly thereafter, Italians began writing their own plays in imitation of the Roman models.

The Arts

Patronage of the arts during the Renaissance was a major and acknowledged source of prestige, and, because the nobles' courts engaged in rivalries over which was to become the cultural center, painters, musicians, sculptors, architects, and writers flourished.

Such changes in viewpoint and technology predictably brought changes in theatre and drama. Theatres in both England and Spain, although influenced by Renaissance ideas, also built on secular staging conventions of the late Middle Ages. Both produced glorious dramas and robust public theatres soon after the end of medieval religious drama (c. 1550). By 1600, both were enjoying their Golden Ages of theatre and drama, with new freestanding theatres, professional players, paying audiences, and expansive plays of great complexity.

THE RENAISSANCE IN ENGLAND: THE AGE OF SHAKESPEARE

The reign of Elizabeth I (1558–1603) brought greatness to England. With her ascent to the throne, the nation achieved the political and religious stability that permitted its arts and literature to thrive. When, in an attempt to mute religious controversies, the government outlawed religious drama, it opened the way for the rapid development of a secular tradition of plays and playgoing. When the queen finally agreed to the execution of Mary Stuart, her chief rival for the throne and the center of Catholic assaults on the church and throne, Elizabeth's political situation was secured, and the domination of Anglican Protestants within the Church of England was affirmed. The English navy defeated the Spanish Armada in 1588 and established itself as ruler of the seas and leader among the trading nations. England, for the first time in generations, was at peace at home and abroad and was filled with a national confidence and a lust for life seldom paralleled in history.

Physical Theatre

In 1576, two commercial theatres opened in London, one an outdoor (or "public") theatre and the other an indoor (or "private") theatre. Therefore, when Shakespeare arrived in London about fifteen years later, these two sorts of theatre were well established, and he wrote for and acted in both. Although

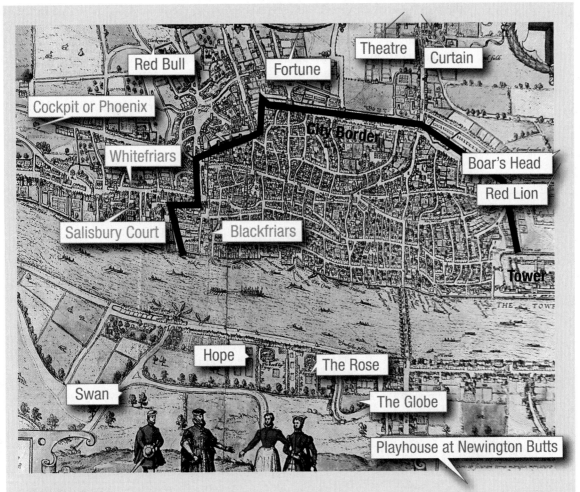

FIGURE 14.2

Theatres in London

Superimposed on this map from about 1572 are the theatres of Elizabethan London. Public theaters are in blue; private theatres are in orange. Note that all the public theatres and all the private theatres but the Blackfriars are outside the city borders.

their precise appearance cannot be known, their general features are well established.

PUBLIC THEATRES   Outdoor, public theatres (a number of which were built between 1576 and 1642) consisted of a round or polygonal, roofed, multileveled auditorium that surrounded an open yard, into which jutted a platform raised to a height of four to six feet. The entire yard (or pit) and part of the stage platform were unroofed. The audience, probably numbering as many as 2,500, surrounded the playing area on three sides, some standing in the pit and others seated in the galleries or the still more exclusive lords' rooms.

The actors worked on a raised stage and apparently awaited cues and changed costumes in a tiring house, located at the rear of the platform. Covering part of the stage was a roof (the heavens) supported by columns resting on the stage and apparently decorated on its underside with pictures of stars, planets, and signs of the zodiac. Gods and properties flew in from the heavens.

The stage floor was pierced with traps, through which characters could appear and disappear. Connecting the tiring house with the stage were at least two doors, which often represented widely divergent locations (as, for example, when one led to the fields of France and the other to the shores of England). Atop the tiring house, a flag flew on days of performance, and at a level just below, in an area called the hut, were probably housed the various pieces of equipment and machinery needed for special effects. A musicians' gallery was apparently located just below the hut, at the third level above the stage.

Other points are less certain. The plays clearly required two playing levels, an upper and a lower, and some sort of discovery space, a place where objects and characters could be hidden from view and discovered at the appropriate time. Because the available evidence will not permit the issues to be resolved, ideas about the appearance of Shakespeare's playhouse must remain tentative.

PRIVATE THEATRES   About the indoor private theatres even less is known. They were roofed, smaller, and therefore more expensive to attend than the public playhouses. Despite their name, they were open to anyone caring to pay. Initially, the private theatres attracted the most fashionable audiences of London, who came to see erudite plays performed by troupes of boy actors. As the popularity of children's troupes waned, the adult troupes that performed in the public theatres in the summer took over the private houses for their winter performances. The fact is significant because it indicates that the arrangement of the stage spaces in the theatres was probably similar.

Audience

Audiences for the public theatres were like medieval audiences, but more urbanized and probably more sophisticated. They did not include the poor or the very rich. Audiences were sometimes rowdy,

FIGURE 14.3

Public Theatre

The Swan drawing is a rare piece of visual evidence for an Elizabethan public theatre: It shows a theatre open to the sky, with a roofed structure pierced by doors, and an audience on three sides of a raised stage that is thrust out from the structure.

easily distracted, and they were probably heavily male. A good portion of the audience was educated enough to get jokes and learned allusions; most of them were fascinated by language, and so sat rapt through long soliloquies and much lyric poetry.

Private theatres supposedly attracted a more discerning and probably a more affluent audience. They sat indoors, were warmer in winter, less bothered by rain and slush. Probably mostly male, they were self-aware as embodiments of the "new."

Production Practices

Both the physical arrangement of Elizabethan theatres and the medieval features of the plays argue against the use of elaborate scenery. In the theatre, there were few places to hide scenery and no way of moving it on and off stage readily, and the action moved from place to place quickly, with little or no break. Small properties were therefore important, and we find stage directions for the use of ladders, chairs and tables, tapestries, a freestanding arbor, and so on. The underlying conventions were clearly medieval, with a chair representing a throne room, for example, and an arbor for a garden. The onstage columns and the two doors also sometimes represented specific locations, thus resembling medieval mansions. On the other hand, such things as "a view of Rome" appeared on lists of properties, and so perhaps some locations were illustrated in paintings. Most of the stage platform worked like a medieval *platea*, serving alternately as a bedroom, a throne room, and a rampart in quick succession.

Costuming was probably more important than scenery to spectacle. Contemporary accounts mention rich fabrics in many colors. Again, the basic convention was medieval, undoubtedly emblematic, with real Elizabethan dress the basic look. Nonetheless, other periods, countries, and races were signified by individual costume pieces—a turban, a Roman breastplate—but historical accuracy was unknown.

Most actors wore contemporary dress, some of it the castoffs of patrons or wealthy friends. Actors mostly supplied their own costumes, and building up a stock would have been important to an actor; however, unusual characters—devils, angels, allegorical figures, Turks, savages—would have called for help from the theatre company. This was a society emerging from medieval ignorance of the great world, and the theatre was one place where sophisticated London saw its new knowledge in three living dimensions.

Masks were used rarely, and then only for specific reasons; they were no longer a major convention of theatre.

Actors and Acting

A royal official, the Master of the Revels, licensed acting companies. The license protected actors from harsh medieval laws against players ("rogues and vagabonds" as they were called in England's Vagrancy Act of 1714). Actors in the London troupes were further protected by nominal servant status in noble households: Servants "belonged" to a household and found a medieval (feudal) shelter

Tommy Thompson

FIGURE 14.4

Private Elizabethan and Jacobean Theatre

Here, the Blackfriars Playhouse at the American Shakespeare Center in Staunton, Virginia. This modern and speculative reconstruction of the Blackfriars indoor theatre is based on documents from the period, none of them visual. Note the two audience galleries that go around three sides of the theatre (the original structure had three galleries). The modern audience area is not darkened during these performances, and the audience sits on benches, as probably did the original audiences. Note the audience seated on stage.

there. Despite this status, a few actors became wealthy. Shakespeare, for one example, was able to retire as a gentleman.

The troupes themselves were organized as self-governing units—sharing companies—whose members shared expenses, profits, and responsibilities for production. Few members owned a part of the theatre building itself; these were called householders. The most valuable members of the company held a whole share in the costumes, properties, and other company possessions; lesser members owned only half or quarter shares, with their influence and income reduced accordingly. In addition, each company hired some actors and stagehands (hirelings), who worked for a salary rather than for a share of the profits.

The precise style of acting is unclear, but vocal power and flexibility were prized. Plays of the period offered ample opportunity to display breath control and verbal dexterity in the monologues, soliloquies, complicated figures of speech, and symmetrical and extended phrases. On the other hand, oratorical and rhetorical techniques did not seem to overpower the actors' search for naturalness. Contemporary accounts, including lines from Shakespeare's *Hamlet*, speak of an acting style capable of moving actors and audiences alike. The goal was apparently a convincing representation of a character in action performed by an actor with a well-tuned vocal instrument.

Because all actors were male, the roles of women were taken by men or young boys, many of whom were apprenticed to leading actors in the troupe. Among the actors, most specialized in certain kinds of roles (e.g., clowns, women, or heroes), and some were widely admired in Shakespeare's day: Richard Tarleton as a clown, Richard Burbage as a tragedian.

By the time Shakespeare arrived in London about 1590, then, his was a proud and growing nation whose power wanted to be celebrated. In place in the capital was an English secular theatre with permanent buildings, professional actors, and a legitimacy based on its own identification with capital and court.

FIGURE 14.5

Shakespeare's Reach

Twelfth Night is one of Shakespeare's most often staged comedies. Actors, directors, and designers have been attracted to the scope and challenges of the play. Here, a production at Kutztown University in Pennsylvania surrounded by mirrors, perhaps to reflect the many disguises in the play.

Plays and Playwrights

Adding to the general well-being of the nation was the vigor of the court, the schools, and the universities, where scholars were remaking Italian humanism and classical documents with an eye to English needs and preferences. In particular, some university students (the University Wits) were applying classical scholarship to the English public stage and laying the foundations for the vigorous theatre to come. These University Wits brought the erudition of humanistic scholarship to the English stage.

Thomas Kyd and Christopher Marlowe, in particular, broke new ground in tragedy. Both adapted techniques from Seneca. Marlowe created a "mighty line" of sonorous blank verse, the tragedy *Doctor Faustus*, and the history play *Edward the Second*. Kyd is remembered for his revenge play *The Spanish Tragedy*.

SHAKESPEARE (1564–1616)   Born in 1564 in provincial Stratford-upon-Avon, a day's journey from London, Shakespeare was a middle-class boy who grew up as the nation moved from medieval to Renaissance culture. Not university educated,

Shakespeare nonetheless received the solid basics of village schools: Latin, the classics, and the foundation of writing style. His early life appears to have included acquaintance with powerful local families; his father, although a tradesman, was a man of position in the town.

Shakespeare married a local woman but did not stay long in his hometown. By his midtwenties, he had gone to London to take up the perilous profession of acting, putting his father's trade behind him. He took with him, however, the rural England and the English characters of his youth, which would inform his plays and his poetry for his entire life.

Between 1590 and 1613, a period now acknowledged as the greatest age of English drama, Shakespeare wrote thirty-eight plays, which for convenience are customarily divided into three types:

- History plays (those treating English history): *Richard II*, *Henry IV* (Parts 1 and 2), *Henry V*, *Henry VI* (Parts 1, 2, and 3), *Richard III*, and *Henry VIII*.
- Tragedies: *Romeo and Juliet*, *Julius Caesar*, *Hamlet*, *King Lear*, *Othello*, *Macbeth*, and *Antony and Cleopatra*.
- Comedies: Ranging from popular romantic works, like *Love's Labor's Lost*, *As You Like It*, *Twelfth Night*, *Much Ado about Nothing*, and *A Midsummer Night's Dream*, to the darker tragicomedies, like *All's Well That Ends Well* and *Measure for Measure*.

Shakespeare's plays and those of his contemporaries in England (and Spain) shared more ideas and techniques of playwriting with the Middle Ages than with Greece and Rome. Six important traits of Golden Age plays (including those of Shakespeare) are:

- *An Early Point of Attack:* Plays begin near the beginning of the story, with the result that the audience sees the story develop onstage rather than learning about it secondhand through messengers or reporters.
- *Several Lines of Action ("Subplots"):* Early in the plays, the various lines appear to be separate and independent, but as the play moves toward its resolution, the several lines gradually merge so that, by the play's end, the unity of the various lines is evident.
- *A Large Number and Variety of Incidents:* The mixing of tears and laughter is not uncommon, nor is the close juxtaposition of tender scenes of love with brawling scenes of confrontation.
- *Free Use of Time and Place:* Action unfolds across several months or years and in several locales.
- *A Large Number and Variety of Characters:* Casts of thirty are common, and among the characters can be found kings and gravediggers, pedants and clowns, old people and youths, city dwellers and rustics, rich people and poor ones.
- *A Varied Language:* Within the same play are found lyric passages, elegant figures of speech, ribald slang, witty aphorisms, and pedestrian prose, all carefully chosen to enhance the play's dramatic action.

The art of Shakespeare and his contemporaries was an expansive one that filled a large dramatic canvas with portraits of a wide cross section of humanity

FIGURE 14.6

The New Globe Theatre in London

Completed in the late 1990s, the structure seeks to replicate the original Globe, the outdoor theatre where many of Shakespeare's plays were first staged. The New Globe is located on the south bank of the Thames close to the site of the original. The modern theatre holds 1,880, five hundred of whom stand in the pit. The wide-lens used for this photo makes the building look bigger than it really is.

engaged in acts ranging from the heroic to the mundane. The texture of the plays is rich, detailed, and allusive. With Shakespeare's death in 1616 came a decline in the quality, if not the quantity, of drama. Although many playwrights were esteemed in their own day, none has achieved the modern admiration accorded Shakespeare. The Golden Age of English theatre was already in decline after 1616.

Court Masques and New Conventions: Inigo Jones

Not all theatre was done in public and private playhouses. By invitation only, some individuals formed a courtly audience for plays and spectacles staged in royal and noble houses. Although both Henry VIII (Elizabeth's father) and Elizabeth had supported theatrical entertainments, it was the Stuart kings who followed them, James I and Charles I, who perfected splendid court masques.

Stuart masques were allegorical stories designed to compliment a particular individual or occasion. Their texts were little more than pretexts for elaborate scenic displays and lavish costumes. Although the major roles and all of the comic or villainous characters were played by professionals, the courtiers themselves performed the heart of the masques, three spectacular dances. Great sums of money ensured the splendor of the entertainments; one such masque cost a staggering twenty-one thousand pounds at a time when the average *annual* wage for a skilled worker was about twenty-five pounds.

Although many leading dramatists wrote masques, Ben Jonson was the most significant. Annoyed that the text assumed such a clearly secondary position to the scenery, Jonson stopped writing masques in 1631.

The star of the masques was not the playwright but the scenic designer, Inigo Jones. An Englishman by birth, Jones studied in Italy, where he learned the newest techniques of stage painting, rigging, and design. He introduced many of these into the English court when, in 1605, he staged his first masque for James I. By the end of his career, Jones had introduced into the English courts (but not into the theatres) all the major elements of Italianate staging then developed. (For more about Italianate staging, see Chapter 15.)

Stuart masques, then, have a significance greater than one might surmise based on the number of persons who saw them:

■ First, they were using Italianate systems of staging during the first half of the seventeenth century, at a time when the English public and private theatres still relied on scenic practices that were essentially medieval.

FIGURE 14.7

Inigo Jones Characters in Court Masques

These two sketches for masque characters are among the few colored drawings that Jones produced. He usually drew a quick monochrome sketch, made a few notes about color and fabric, and then passed it on to the costume construction crew. The first character is a torchbearer used to lead the dancers to the main floor for their featured appearance; the second is a winged dancer.

■ Second, the close association of the masques with the monarchy, added to their expense, were major factors in the closing of theatres when a shift in power occurred.

THE CLOSING OF ENGLISH THEATRES

In 1642, a civil war broke out. It pitted those in favor of monarchy, courtiers, and an Anglican Church that echoed Roman Catholicism against (to oversimplify the many contentious issues to the point of caricature) those who favored Parliament, merchants, and a much simplified Anglicanism. The parliamentarians under Oliver Cromwell won, deposed the king, seized power, and closed the theatres (in part because they had been so closely associated with the monarchy). Music, however, was not banned, and so a writer of masques named William Davenant produced operas, staging them using the Italianate system. Thus were Italianate conventions of staging introduced to the English public, having by then been used at court for almost forty years.

With the closing of the theatres in 1642, an English secular theatre based loosely on medieval conventions closed as well. When English theatres reopened in 1660, England adopted the Italianate conventions already in use on the Continent.

THE SPANISH GOLDEN AGE

During the Middle Ages, Spain's theatre had paralleled England's in important ways. Its medieval dramas had included Latin music drama, religious plays, comedies and farces, school and university plays, and even court interludes. Their staging conventions were similar; both used movable more often than fixed staging. During the transitional period from the Middle Ages to the Golden Age, small troupes of professional players toured until permanent theatres were built in Madrid in the early 1580s.

The public theatres of Spain, like the English theatres, remained essentially medieval. The earliest permanent public theatres, the Corral del Cruz and the Corral del Principe, were both outdoor theatres with thrust stages. Audiences stood in a central yard or sat in galleries and boxes on three sides of the stage. The stages, whose backgrounds were pierced with entrances, were partially roofed (held up by two columns), were served by traps and flying machines, and featured both a discovery space and a secondary acting area above the stage. Conventions of scenery, costume, and playwriting also resembled those of England. As in England, only the Spanish court theatres used the newer, Italian conventions.

The location of Spanish theatres, each of which was typically set up in the yard at the center of a block of houses, was a telling difference between English and Spanish theatres. An awning stretched over a part of the yard as protection against the elements. Audiences not only stood or sat in covered benches along the side of this yard or in galleries or boxes opposite the stage, but they also could rent spaces in the windows of adjoining houses.

Spotlight

A conjectural drawing of the Corral del Principe, thought to be typical of Spanish Theatres of the Golden Age.
The reconstruction by John J. Allen, reprinted with permission of the University Press of Florida.

Spanish Theatre: The Corral del Principe

In the early 1580s, two new theatres were built in Madrid to replace those that had existed since the 1560s. One, the Corral del Principe, became the city's dominant theatre for more than a century. Both were owned by a religious confraternity to raise money for its hospitals; the theatres also got some needed legitimacy.

Corral—the word for the open space among several houses—became the synonym for a permanent theatre. It was the Spanish solution to the problem of creating an enclosed space in which audiences could be controlled and made to pay a fee to enter. Inside the rectangle enclosed by the houses, builders put up at one end a stage only twenty-eight feet wide and twenty-five feet deep. It was raised above the *patio* (pit), the cheapest area (standing room behind, benches in front), which was only the width of the stage and about fifty feet long. Along its sides ran a raised level of boxes or loges, preferred and more expensive seating. Opposite the stage at the end of the patio were more boxes and, above them, a separate seating area for women with its own entrance from the street. From the back of the women's gallery to the back wall of the stage and from side to side, this was an intimate theater—the size of the in-bounds area of a modern basketball court.

Like other *corrales*, the Principe also used windows in the houses on each side, behind which were high-end boxes—rooms, really—owned and controlled by the house owner. Their privacy apparently attracted upper-class women, and the women's gallery above the patio may have become a middle- and lower-class area like the patio itself and as rambunctious.

The stage was roofed. Part of the patio could be covered with an awning, although this seems to have been for sun, not rain.

At the back of the stage was a two-level area that could be curtained; there seem also to have been doors there and on the sides. The stage floor was trapped, and overhead was fairly sophisticated flying machinery. Music was common, but it is unlikely that either musicians or audience members sat on the small stage.

Scenery in the Corral del Principe was selective but sometimes complex: fountains, trees, a ship's mast and rigging (presumably for the actors to climb), and the castles (superstructures) of a Moorish and a Christian ship. By the first third of the seventeenth century, costumes were often expensive and showy, although with only emblematic historical accuracy (turbans for Moors, togas for Romans) and mostly contemporary clothes.

The Corral del Principe may be taken as typical of Spanish theatres of the Golden Age. It was small, rather medieval in its arrangements, and often rowdy, but some of the greatest of the world's plays were first performed there.

Women as Audience and as Actors

The Spanish theatre's acceptance of women was significantly different from the English, at the same time more permissive and more restrictive. It allowed women to act after the mid-1580s but put women audience members in a separate gallery with its own entrance—guarded—from the street. Many women went there masked, perhaps to avoid being recognized.

Legal permission for women to act was also shaky. Attempts were made to rescind the permission to act as early as 1587; in 1589, churchmen made a determined push to remove them and replace them with boys—so long as the boys wore no makeup. The governing council thought that the risk of boys in makeup was greater than the risk of women and so said the women could stay. Spanish actresses, however, like actresses in many countries, were long considered immoral and a threat to men.

Plays and Playwrights

Spain's Golden Age, however, was noted not for its theatrical practices but for its plays. During these one hundred years, Spanish playwrights wrote thousands of plays. Like medieval and contemporaneous English plays, they featured a welter of characters and events, spanned many times and places, and mixed laughter and tears. Secular tragicomedies, plays on religious subjects, cloak-and-sword plays, and farces were all popular.

The earliest important playwright, Lope de Rueda, specialized in farces and religious plays. Another, Lope de Vega, may have originated the cape-and-sword plays, swashbucklers that subsequently influenced both English and French dramatists. The author of more than five hundred works, Lope de Vega is now best known for his play *Fuenteovejuna*. The most respected Spanish playwright of the Golden Age, however, was Pedro Calderón de la Barca, whose *Life Is a Dream* (see Figure 14.8) epitomized the poetry and intellect of his best works. Calderón stopped writing for the stage about 1640; the theatres were closed shortly thereafter for royal mourning (1644–1649). When they reopened, the Golden Age had passed, although the public theatres remained in use into the eighteenth century.

In summary, the Golden Age theatres of England and Spain mixed medieval conventions with new practices. Both cultures maintained essentially medieval conventions of drama and theatre (except at their courts, where Italian conventions prevailed), but with one important difference: Both could now boast a

FIGURE 14.8

Spanish Classic in Modern Production

Here, a modern interpretation at Old Dominion University of Calderon de la Barca's *La vida es sueno* (*Life Is a Dream*), written before 1636.

Anita Tripathi Easterling

sophisticated secular drama performed by professional actors in theatres built specifically to house them. In a major departure from medieval theatrical practice, theatre had become professional rather than communal.

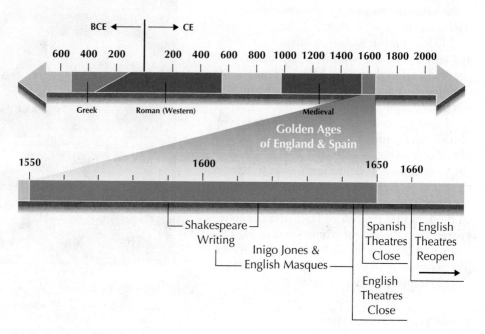

FIGURE 14.9

Timeline

The Golden Ages of England and Spain overlapped the final years of medieval theatre, beginning roughly in 1550 (when religious drama ended) and ending about 1650, when both theatres were closed for political reasons. When English theatres reopened in 1660, they were physically different and almost immediately used female actors.

KEY TERMS

Check your understanding against this list. Brief definitions are included in the Glossary; persons are page-referenced in the Index.

IIIC

ILLUSIONISM

(c. 1550–c. 1950)

The third phase of theatre's history dates from about 1550 through about 1950. Theatres during these four hundred years shared several important theatrical conventions and so can be grouped for study. Their major shared traits are:

■ Theatre buildings with a proscenium arch, which frames the action on stage.
■ Scenery and costumes that seek to create the illusion of fidelity to life outside the theatre.
■ A mostly commercial environment.
■ A mix of men and women.
■ A stratification of theatre.

These new conventions took hold first in Italy and then spread throughout Western Europe and its colonies, where they dominated theatre practice through much of the twentieth century.

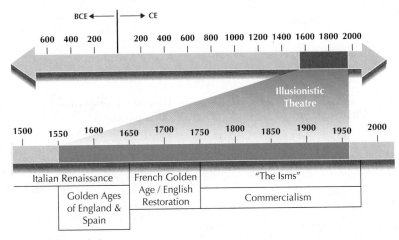

FIGURE IIIC.1

A new set of dramatic and theatrical conventions arose during Italy's Renaissance and soon spread throughout most of Western Europe.

15

The Italian Renaissance

A modern model of the first purpose-built theatre in Italy, which was erected in Sabbionetta shortly after the Teatro Olimpico was completed.

OBJECTIVES

When you have completed this chapter, you should be able to:

- Define and discuss neoclassicism, Italianate staging, and commedia dell'arte.

- Explain how neoclassicism departed so radically from medieval theatre.

- Trace Italianate staging from Vitruvius through Serlio to Torelli.

- Discuss the importance of Roman ideas and their interpretation to Renaissance theatres.

CONTEXT

The Renaissance in Italy, unlike the same years in England and Spain, revolutionized theatre and drama. In their efforts to recapture the practices of Greece and Rome, Italian artists set theatres in Europe on a new path—a path toward illusionism. Theatre was thereafter to seek an illusion of real life.

Three contributions of the Italians were to have far-reaching effects:

- The neoclassical ideal in playwriting and criticism.
- The Italianate system of staging and architecture.
- A popular theatre known as commedia dell'arte.

MAINSTREAM THEATRE

Theory: Neoclassicism

Neoclassicism literally means "new classicism," but in fact it was based far more heavily on Rome than on Greece. Neoclassicism, as first developed by the Italians and later adopted throughout most of Western Europe, rested on five major points:

- Verisimilitude and decorum.
- Purity of genres.
- The three unities.
- The five-act form.
- A twofold purpose—to teach and to please.

VERISIMILITUDE   Central to neoclassical doctrine was a complex concept called verisimilitude—literally, "truth seeming." But the meaning of *verisimilitude* is more involved than its facile definition might suggest because artists have always aimed to tell the "truth." Thus, the critical problem for a student of neoclassicism is to understand what *truth* meant to the neoclassicist.

Truth for the neoclassicist resided in the essential, the general, the typical, and the class rather than in the particular, the individual, and the unique. To get at truth, a neoclassical artist had to cut away all that was temporary or accidental in favor of those qualities that were fundamental and unchanging. To be "True" meant to be usually true, generally accurate, or typically the case. Such a view of truth placed a premium on classification and categorization, and in verisimilitude, truth had a meaning different from that ascribed to it by our own age's view of the importance of individuality and uniqueness.

Neoclassical truth implied other matters as well. Verisimilitude in drama required the elimination of events that could not reasonably be expected to happen in real life. Although an exception was made when ancient stories or myths incorporating supernatural events were dramatized, even then the dramatist was expected to minimize the importance of such events, perhaps by putting them offstage. Because in real life people generally talk to one another rather than to themselves, monologues and soliloquies were customarily abandoned in favor of dialogue between major characters and their confidants.

FIGURE 15.1

Torquato Tasso's *Aminta*

This adaptation of Tasso's 1573 pastoral drama at Butler University Theatre emphasizes the lighthearted nature of the original. Italian plays of the early Renaissance are not often revived.

Characters in neoclassical drama were expected to embody the traits normally held by members of their group in manners and conduct; that is, they were to behave as was appropriate for their sex, age, social class, and so on. Such characters were said to display decorum. Indecorous characters drove the plots of neoclassical plays because they were the ones who suffered either tragic consequences or comic ridicule.

Finally, because it was believed that God ruled the world in accord with a divine plan and that he was a good God, verisimilitude required that dramatic actions be organized according to moral principles—so that good was rewarded and evil punished. Although in daily life good occasionally went unrewarded and evil unpunished, such observable events were believed to be aberrational and therefore unsuitable subjects for drama.

PURITY OF GENRES Verisimilitude also inspired purity of genres, meaning that the two major forms, tragedy and comedy, must not be mixed. The injunction against mixing did not mean merely that funny scenes were improper for tragedy or that unhappy endings were inappropriate for comedy. Both tragedy and comedy were far more rigidly defined than today, and the rule against mixing the forms meant that no element belonging to the one should appear in the other. For example, tragedy was supposed to depict people of high station involved in affairs of state; its language was to be elevated and poetic; its endings were to be unhappy. Comedy, on the other hand, was supposed to display persons of the lower and middle classes embroiled in domestic difficulties and intrigues. Its language was always to be less elevated, often prosaic, and its endings were to be happy. Purity of genres meant, then, that a prose tragedy or a domestic tragedy could not exist—both were a contradiction in terms. It also meant that kings and queens could not appear in comedies, nor were affairs of state suitable subjects for comedy.

THE THREE UNITIES Verisimilitude and interpretations of classical examples created the neoclassical notion of the three unities—time, place, and action. Although Aristotle had argued cogently for plays with a unified action, neoclassical theorists were more concerned that their plays unfold within a reasonable time and a limited place so that verisimilitude would not be strained. No audience would believe, the neoclassical argument went, that months had passed or oceans had been crossed while the audience sat in the same place for a few hours. Theorists varied in the strictness of their requirements for unity: some argued for a single room, others for a single town; some required that the playing time of the drama equal the actual time elapsed; and others that no more than twenty-four hours elapse. Most Italian theorists accepted some version of the three unities after about 1570.

THE FIVE-ACT FORM   By then, as well, neoclassicists had adopted the five-act play as standard for drama, a norm probably derived from the theories of Horace and the practices of Seneca (five sections separated by choruses), although neither had used the "act" as a dramatic unit.

A TWOFOLD PURPOSE—TO TEACH AND TO PLEASE   The neoclassicists found a justification for drama and theatre in the ability of these to teach morality while entertaining an audience. To teach and to please were defined as the dual purposes of drama, and playwrights took care that their plays did both. The idea of a drama existing only for its own sake or as an expression of an individual artist was not accepted.

By 1600, neoclassical ideals were being accepted in other parts of Europe. They remained dominant for the next two hundred years among educated and courtly audiences. Neoclassicism's propriety and concentration may account for its lack of appeal to many people, who sought more spectacle than the three unities permitted. Thus, despite the acceptance of neoclassicism as an ideal, its tenets were undercut in a variety of ways—by spectacle, for example.

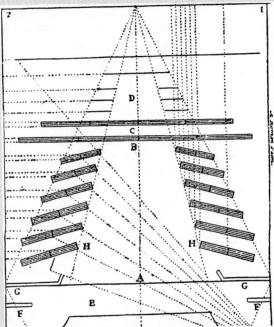

FIGURE 15.2

One-Point Perspective Stage Layout

Behind the Renaissance forestage, a single vanishing point was the apparent meeting place of lines that created an illusion of depth greater than the actual theatre could offer.

Physical Theatre: Illusionism

The Italianate theatre and its system of staging, like neoclassicism itself, developed as a mixture of ideas and techniques from ancient Greece, Rome, and contemporary Italy. Most important from the ancients was the work of Vitruvius. (Vitruvius is discussed in more detail in Chapter 12.)

VITRUVIUS IN THE RENAISSANCE Early in Italy's Renaissance, Vitruvius's Roman work on architecture, which had existed only in manuscripts, was printed. By 1500 it was the acknowledged authority in the field, and interpretations and commentaries in Italian followed. Although he had written about architecture and scenery, Vitruvius had provided no illustrations. As a result, the Italians translated him and provided illustrations in terms of their practices, most notably a fascination with *linear perspective*—a means of representing spatial depth (three dimensions) on a two-dimensional surface. On the stage, perspective became a means of representing greater depth than in fact existed.

PERSPECTIVE Although known to the Romans, perspective, when rediscovered by Italian painters, caused an artistic revolution. Artists worked to master the "new" technique, and spectators hailed its ability to trick the senses. The "vanishing point," to which objects receded away from the viewer, became, in stage design, the key to false, or forced, perspective, through which a stage depth of thirty feet could be made to seem three hundred. On the stage, achieving this sense of depth often meant actually constructing three-dimensional objects (usually buildings) in false perspective. An actor—whose real size could not be changed—would dwarf the upstage buildings if he appeared up there, and so acting took place in front of the scenery.

In 1545, an Italian, Sebastiano Serlio, published *Dell'Architectura*, an interpretation of Vitruvius that dominated theatre architecture and design for the next century. Vitruvius, of course, had described the circular, outdoor Roman theatre. But wealthy Italians wanted plays done indoors in wealthy homes. Therefore, when the first indoor theatres were designed, the task was to adapt Vitruvius to rectangular spaces and to accommodate the new spaces to linear perspective.

An early solution was the Teatro Olimpico, which had five onstage doorways (corresponding to Vitruvius's five stage openings), but with a separate vista in perspective constructed behind each doorway, each with its own vanishing point.

Although the uniqueness of the Teatro Olimpico fascinates scholars, the facade stage with perspective alleys became an anomaly. Instead, the plan of another wooden theatre, the Teatro Farnese built in 1618–1619 in Parma, became the model for theatre architects for hundreds of years.

Production Practices: Illusionism

Vitruvius's scanty descriptions of tragic, comic, and satyric scenes became, in Serlio's books, detailed illustrations in false perspective. In the remainder of *Dell' Architectura*, Serlio provided tips on the use of colored lights, fire effects, fanciful

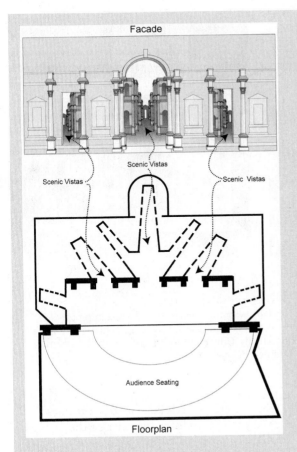

Facade

Scenic Vistas

Scenic Vistas

Scenic Vistas

Audience Seating

Floorplan

FIGURE 15.3

Teatro Olimpico

The Teatro Olimpico was an early compromise between a Roman facade stage and the Renaissance passion for perspective. Five stage doors framed seven three-dimensional vistas in false perspective, giving each member of the audience a view down at least one. Actors played on the forestage. They probably used the doorways but did not walk into the false-perspective structures because the scenery seemed to shrink but the actor would not have done so. Compare the diagram with the picture of the actual space (*right*). Note the slightly widened semi-circle of the orchestra.

costumes, and pasteboard figures in a perspective setting. Serlio's scenography was thus the basis for what we now call Italianate staging.

ITALIANATE STAGING   With certain modifications related to place and date, Italianate settings throughout Europe shared the following features during the sixteenth, seventeenth, and early eighteenth centuries:

- Scenery painted in **single-point perspective** (all objects recede to the same vanishing point), as calculated from one seat toward the back of the orchestra (usually the seat of the most important noble or patron).

FIGURE 15.4

Serlio

Combining Vitruvius's writings on the Roman theatre with the Renaissance interest in perspective, Serlio created his own ideal scenery for tragedy, comedy (*above left*), and pastoral plays. The Centre for Advanced Studies in Architecture, University of Bath, United Kingdom, created the color rendering of Serlio's comedy scene using computer-assisted design.

- Scenery consisting of wings, which were paired flats (wooden frames covered with fabric and painted), each pair closer together as they were farther from the audience, so that the lines of the inner edges of the flats receded toward the vanishing point. The setting culminated upstage in a backdrop (painted two-dimensional hanging) or a shutter, a pair of wings pushed together. Shutters could be opened to reveal even deeper perspective space or pierced to make a *relieve* through which greater depth was glimpsed.
- Scenery placed behind both a proscenium arch and the actors, forming a background rather than an environment to surround them.
- A raked stage, slanted upward from front to back to increase the sense of depth. Sometimes only the stage behind the proscenium arch was raked, sometimes it was the entire stage, causing the actors to climb or descend (hence our terms *upstage* and *downstage*).
- Machinery and rigging hidden overhead by borders, framed or unframed fabric painted like sky, clouds, leaves, and so on.

MOVABLE SCENERY: TORELLI   Having developed this system, Italian artists set about almost at once to give it movement, to shift scenery, and to allow rapid changes of place. The most effective system was shown in 1645 when Giacomo Torelli astonished audiences with fluid, fast, apparently magical changes. The secret was

Spotlight

Teatro Farnese

The Teatro Farnese offered a different compromise between a Roman theatre and emerging Italianate architectural conventions. A Roman-style semicircular seating area was shoehorned inside a rectangular building, and the elaborate facade of Roman theatres appeared to the sides of a new proscenium arch.

Teatro Farnese, Parma, Italy

The Farnese theatre shares some of the architectural attributes of the Teatro Olimpico. Both are wooden structures (set inside of a stone building) in which theatres inspired by Roman models were fitted into a large, rectangular room. Much of the architectural detail in both theatres reflects the ornate facades of many Roman theatres.

But there the likenesses diverge radically. The Olimpico, built between 1580 and 1584, housed a facade stage with perspective alleys, whereas the Farnese, built about thirty-five years later, made a bold leap in theatre architecture by installing a permanent proscenium stage, complete with a mechanism under the stage to change scenery.

The Farnese is the first permanent indoor proscenium-arch theatre. Designed by Giovanni Battista Aleotti and built between 1618 and

A Horse Act during a Performance of *Neptune*

1619, the theatre was never much used. It was largely destroyed by an Allied bombing raid during the Second World War. Reconstruction based on drawings and engravings began in 1952 and was completed about a decade later.

Shown here is a model of the horseshoe-shaped seating used in the reconstruction of the theatre; it can seat about three thousand. The flat floor in front of the seats was used for balls or was sometimes flooded for mock naval battles. The etching of a proscenium view (*top left*) shows the intricate facade that echoes its Roman antecedent.

Model of Seating Area

FIGURE 15.5

Special Effects Machines

Renaissance stage designers devised more and more elaborate systems, using ropes and winches, to create visual effects. These inventions were used for centuries. Here, a ship is made to sway to simulate the effect of waves.

his chariot-and-pole system. Small wheeled wagons ran on tracks under the stage, each with a pole that extended through a slit in the stage high enough to support a flat. The idea was elegant and simple: As the chariots moved, so the flats moved; pulling a chariot toward the center brought a flat into view; pulling the chariot away from the center caused a flat to disappear. With the chariots harnessed by ropes and pulleys to the same winch, stage mechanics could turn one wheel to change an entire setting. Torelli, no stranger to self-promotion, earned the title The Great Wizard by coordinating these changes with special effects, such as flying, lightning, and explosions.

Contradiction in Mainstream Theatre

A contradiction clearly existed between the ideals of theory—the unities of time, place, and action and an avoidance of the supernatural—and the ideals of scenic design, whose artists increasingly emphasized rapid change of place and spectacle. This tension was resolved by keeping an austere style for neoclassical plays while expending creativity and money on operas, ballets, and lavish *intermezzi* (entertainments given between the acts of a neoclassical play)—a way of having cake and eating it at the same time.

By the mid–seventeenth century, Italian opera had become the most popular (and spectacular) form of entertainment in Italy. As it was exported to the rest of Europe, so were its scenic techniques. (In London, Davenant had staged operas after the theatres were closed in 1642; even in English, the word *opera* probably signified as much about scenery as it did about music.)

AN ALTERNATIVE THEATRE: COMMEDIA DELL'ARTE

Neoclassical dramas and elaborately staged operas were primarily the entertainment of the noble, the wealthy, and the educated. Among other classes, another, different kind of entertainment flourished in Italy: the commedia dell'arte ("professional playing"). Although neither the origins nor the sources of commedia are well understood, its major characteristics were well established by 1550, and Italian troupes were touring Western Europe by 1600.

Commedia players—both male and female—worked from a basic story outline (scenario), within which they improvised much of their dialogue and action. Each actor in the troupe played the same stock character in almost

FIGURE 15.6

Commedia dell'Arte

Commedia troupes had both male and female performers, as well as masked and unmasked stock characters. Starting with a basic scenario or storyline, the performers would improvise much of the entertainment. Here, five French interpretations of commedia dell'arte characters thought to reflect the tradition as they evolved from the 1550s to the 1750s. From left, Tartaglia, Pantalone, Doctore, Brigella, and Coviello.

every scenario and therefore wore the same costume and mask, reused the same bits of comic business (*lazzi*), and even repeated some of the same dialogue from scenario to scenario. Most troupes had ten or twelve members; each troupe had one or two sets of young lovers (*innamorati*) and a number of comic "masks" (characters)—Capitano (the captain), Pantalone (the merchant), Dottore (the doctor), and several *zanni* (servants) such as Arlecchino (Harlequin), Brighella, Scaramuccio, and Pulcinello. Male actors outnumbered female. Both mask and costume became traditional for each character except the lovers, who wore no masks.

Organized as sharing companies, such troupes toured constantly as they tried to scratch out a living without the protection or the financial support of noble houses. Although the influence of commedia extended throughout Europe, its ephemeral nature militated against its leaving a lasting record (especially scripts), although this popular Italian comedy has been revived and imitated in many more recent cultures.

ITALY: ECLIPSE

Despite Italy's unquestioned leadership in dramatic theory and scenic display and despite its unique popular comedy, by 1750, except for opera, Italy was no longer a world leader in theatre. Both England and France had outstripped their teacher and attained an international reputation by the end of the seventeenth century, and both achieved a lasting acclaim never given the Italians from whom they drew.

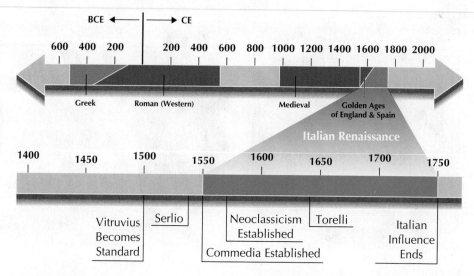

FIGURE 15.7

Timeline

The Italian Renaissance began about a hundred years before the Golden Ages of Spain and England. By c. 1550 (when religious drama was ending in England), neoclassicism, Italianate staging, and commedia dell'arte were known in Italy. Italianate staging long continued to be important.

KEY TERMS

Check your understanding against this list. Brief definitions are included in the Glossary; persons are page-referenced in the Index.

16

The Triumph and Decline of Neoclassicism

Louis XIII seated in the first French theatre with a fixed proscenium, later called the Palais Royal.

OBJECTIVES

When you have completed this chapter, you should be able to:

- Explain the significance of the production of *Le Cid*.

- Discuss the different performances likely to have been seen in the public and the court theatres of France.

- Sketch events leading to the formation of the Comédie Française.

- Explain how sentimentalism affected French drama and theatre.

- Discuss the relationship between French theatre and English Restoration theatre.

- Describe the major conventions of English Restoration theatre.

- Name major kinds of drama existing during the English Restoration.

- Suggest how changes in English law facilitated the beginnings of English-speaking theatre in the American colonies.

FRENCH THEATRE

Its Beginnings

The ideas and practices of the Italian Renaissance reached France early, but France, which was politically unstable, had little energy for developing a strong secular theatre. The early steps of French theatre were therefore tentative. Through the early 1600s, its practices remained essentially medieval. Farces performed by traveling actors were the mainstay of a scattered French theatre, and its audiences were famous for their unruliness. At about the time of Shakespeare, the first notable (and extremely prolific) French playwright appeared, Aléxandre Hardy, whose plays resembled those of England's and Spain's Golden Ages (e.g., many characters and sprawling actions). Like those of his contemporaries, Hardy's plays used simultaneous settings and emblematic costumes. Although his audiences were more genteel than those for the previous farces and included women as well as some people from the court, his theatre was still a pretty rough place.

With increasing political stability, Paris became France's theatrical center. The first professional acting troupe established itself there permanently in 1625. Its theatre was the Hotel de Bourgogne, a space built seventy-five years previously for the production of religious plays—just as they were being banned. (*Hotel* in this period referred to a substantial building that saw many visitors, not the commercial room accommodations of today.) When rival professionals began to settle in Paris, however, they chose indoor tennis courts for their theatres. A theatre converted from a tennis court had a long, narrow auditorium with a small stage at one end, probably with an upper level (as in both London and Madrid) and some sort of "inner stage" below. The resulting theatres were small and intimate, holding six or seven hundred people. Staging conventions remained basically medieval.

Thus, at a time when the English and Spanish theatres were well into their Golden Ages and Italian theatre was revolutionizing theory and scenery, the French theatre was just establishing itself.

By the 1630s, however, French theatre and its audience were sufficiently important to make them a focus of government

FIGURE 16.1

French Theatre in the Early 1600s

French theatre remained mostly emblematic and simultaneous, with scenery still scattered rather than gathered in one place.

FIGURE 16.2

Italian Influence on French Theatre

By the 1630s, Italian conventions were encroaching on French practice. Note the backdrop in single-point perspective and the medieval influence still visible, as shown in the simultaneous representation of different places stage right and stage left.

interest. Because the French court of the time was closely linked by marriage and policy to Italy, Italian practices became the model for France, in theatre as elsewhere. In theatre, Italian practice meant promoting Neoclassicism and Italianate staging.

NEOCLASSICISM: CORNEILLE AND *LE CID*   A number of well-educated men began to write for the theatre. Chief among them was Pierre Corneille, whose play *Le Cid* (1636) marked a turning point in French theatre. Based on a Spanish play of the Golden Age, *Le Cid* was reshaped by Corneille to bring it closer to neoclassical ideas but not into strict conformity with them: The original six acts were reduced to five; its several years were compressed into a single day; the many locales were squeezed into a single town. Still, the play had a happy ending, and its numerous incidents strained neoclassical verisimilitude. The recently formed French Academy—itself an example of aggressive neoclassicism, a literary society supported by those in power—praised the elements of *Le Cid* that conformed to the rules but condemned those that strayed. French playwrights, including Corneille, got the message: Critical acclaim (and approval from those in political, financial, and social power) would come from lining up with Neoclassicism. After 1636, neoclassicism would dominate French drama for more than a hundred years. In 1641, the first Italianate theatre was built in Paris. Giacomo Torelli (see Chapter 15) was brought to Paris in 1645 to install a chariot-and-pole system. His productions marked the acceptance of all Italianate scenic practices in Paris: Almost immediately, the tennis court (public) theatres had to adapt or die; they installed some form of Italianate scenery. Thereafter, simple Neoclassical settings competed with lavish operas, ballets, and machine plays (plays written specifically to exploit the new scenery).

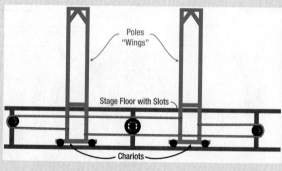

FIGURE 16.3

Torelli brought to France the chariot-and-pole system. *Left*, an etching of idealized design that obscures the wings, background, and overhead boarders that would have been seen by the audience. *Right*, a schematic of the mechanics that changed the scenery.

ITALIANATE STAGING: PUBLIC VERSUS COURT THEATRES   Italian theory and staging played out differently in France, however. The triumph of Neoclassicism was manifest primarily in the French *public* theatres, where a distinct French style of drama developed, one both austere and terse. The triumph of Italianate staging, on the other hand, found its fullest expression in the *court* theatres, where plays from the public theatres were restaged with ballet interludes, movable scenery, and gorgeous costumes and where king and courtiers played heroes of romance and mythology in purpose-written entertainments that moved out into parks and gardens, sometimes with mock tournaments and battles. Italianate scenery in the public theatres was more modest but shared the basic visual conventions of the court.

The Sun King and the Golden Age

Both the court and the public theatres reached their peak during the reign of Louis XIV, a king who drew power to himself as the sun attracts the planets. Calling himself "The Sun King," Louis XIV declared, "I am the state," and he believed it. Absolute power, ego, and show were summed up in the word *gloire* ("glory"), which carried over from war into theatre; it also extended to the building of great follies, such as Louis's palace at Versailles, where he surrounded himself with France's nobility. When Versailles opened, the court withdrew from Paris. Louis pursued an aggressive campaign of national self-display, not only through military adventures but also through the arts, including theatre.

Theatres benefited. They got both royal subsidy and royal patronage but not enough to survive without public support, and so they were sometimes in the position of serving two masters at once. At its best, this theatre offered great variety and superb quality, satisfying an audience that became the most demanding and sophisticated in Europe—and which replaced Italy's as the model for Europe.

In addition to the continuing dominance of Neoclassicism and enthusiasm for Italianate staging, the pinnacle of French theatre meant:

- The emergence of two great playwrights to join Corneille
- The expansion to five permanent professional theatres in Paris—later reduced to three—with strict government control through monopolies

PLAYWRIGHTS

Racine.   Although Pierre Corneille continued writing, his fame was eclipsed by that of Jean Racine. Born three years after the first production of *Le Cid*, Racine was educated by Jansenists, a Catholic sect with an overriding preoccupation with sin and guilt, which were concerns that permeated Racine's major plays. Trained in the classics, Racine based his only comedy, *The Litigants*, on Aristophanes's comedy *The Wasps*, and his most esteemed tragedy, *Phèdre*, on Euripides's *Hippolytus*.

Phèdre is a model of Neoclassicism. Because the play's major conflicts occur within the character Phèdre, the neoclassical requirements for unity are easily accommodated, and because Phèdre's passion leads to her downfall, neoclassical commitment to the punishment of evil is satisfied. *Phèdre*, unlike *Le Cid*, is neoclassical through and through, and its achievement in plot, character, and diction placed it among the masterpieces of dramatic literature. France had accomplished what England would not: lasting and popular drama based on neoclassical theory.

Molière.   French comedy found its genius in the actor-dramatist Molière. At about the time that theatres were closing in England, Molière was leaving home to join a traveling theatrical troupe in France. By 1660, he was head of the troupe, wrote most of its plays, and had firmly established it as a favorite of Louis XIV. Perhaps the greatest comic writer of all times, Molière used his own experiences as an actor as well as his knowledge of Roman comedy, Italian commedia, and French farce to create comedies that ridiculed social and moral pretentiousness.

Molière's comedy typically depicts characters made ludicrous by their deviations from decorum. Although his dialogue is often clever, verbal elegance and wit for their own sake do not form the core of his plays; instead, the comedies depend heavily on farcical business (such as commedia's lazzi) and visual gags. Of his more than twenty plays, the best known are probably *Tartuffe*, *The Miser*,

FIGURE 16.4

The Sun King

Lavish court entertainments including theatre flourished under Louis XIV's patronage. Pictured here is a ballet costume worn by Louis XIV as Apollo, The Sun.

and *The Imaginary Invalid*, whose leading role Molière was playing when he was became ill and died. Denied last rites by the church because he was an actor, he was granted Christian burial only through the direct intervention of Louis XIV. Neoclassical tragedies are only rarely revived today. Molière's comedies are performed often, translated into many languages.

Spotlight

Rachel, a great French actress, performed Phaedra throughout much of Europe in the 1840s.

Jean Racine's *Phèdre*, 1677

Racine (1639–1699), Corneille, and Molière were the greatest French playwrights of the latter half of the seventeenth century. In Racine's *Phèdre*—based on Euripides's *Hippolytus*—the title character lusts after Hippolytus, her stepson. *Phèdre* is the quintessential neoclassical tragedy, embracing all of the elements of Neoclassicism, including a five-act structure written in verse. The play also observes the three unities of time, place, and action. Phèdre is, in keeping with neoclassic doctrine, punished for her evil desires by death.

The Story of the Play

In Troezen, Hippolytus, son of Theseus, the king of Athens, is about to set out to look for his long-absent father; he confesses he is doing so partly to avoid Aricia, whom he loves despite "glorying in his chastity."

Phaedra, Theseus's wife and Hippolytus's stepmother, is said to be "dying in her nurse's arms." She appears—weak, distraught—but the mention of Hippolytus rouses her, clearly causing pain. She confesses to her nurse, Oenone, that she loves him and is dying of that love.

Word comes that Theseus is dead. Phaedra can now confess her love to Hippolytus; however, his thoughts are of Aricia, whom he tells he will support as a claimant to the Athenian throne. Phaedra tells Hippolytus she loves him and begs him to kill her.

However, Theseus suddenly returns; the rumor of his death was wrong. Phaedra is guilt-stricken, horrified, frightened, but her nurse advises her to protect herself by accusing Hippolytus of having tried to seduce her. Given permission by the frantic Phaedra, the nurse then does so; Theseus confronts his son, who refuses, as a matter of honor, to tell his father the truth about Phaedra. Theseus asks Neptune to avenge him on Hippolytus.

Phaedra learns that Hippolytus loves Aricia and rages. Hippolytus and Aricia vow to marry and to flee.

Hippolytus rides off alone in his chariot. A messenger brings the news that Neptune has sent a monster from the ocean that so terrified Hippolytus's horses that they have dragged him to his death.

The nurse drowns herself. Phaedra commits suicide.

THEATRE COMPANIES By 1660, there were five permanent, professional troupes in Paris, including Molière's, a commedia troupe from Italy, and the opera, music, and dance troupe headed by Jean-Baptiste Lully. All were sharing companies and all included women. Only the most talented actors settled in Paris as members of

Spotlight

Molière was an active member of his troupe and acted many key comedic roles. Here, a 19th century illustration of the title character in *Tartuffe*.

Molière's *Tartuffe*, 1669

Born Jean-Baptist Poquelin (1622–1673), the actor, dramatist, and company manager, took Molière as his stage name. Molière's first great success in Paris was his performance before the young King Louis XIV of *The Doctor in Love*, which he wrote and played the title role. His strength as a comic actor was quickly recognized. He wrote more than thirty-six plays, many of which, including *Tartuffe*, are regularly staged today.

The Story of the Play

Orgon, a well-to-do bourgeois, has made a religious zealot, Tartuffe, a pampered guest in his house. Orgon is obsessed by Tartuffe—will hear no wrong of him and cannot do enough for him—despite Tartuffe's being despised as a hypocrite by Orgon's brother, Cléante; his wife, Elmire; his son, Damis; and the witty servant, Dorine. Cléante pleads that Orgon use moderation and restraint, but Orgon is unmovable. Orgon tells his daughter, Mariane, that he wants her to marry Tartuffe, but Mariane loves Valère and is disgusted by Tartuffe.

Tartuffe tries to make love to Elmire; he is overheard by Damis, who tries to expose him to Orgon. Tartuffe turns the accusation upside down by saying he is too humble and too pious to defend himself. Orgon turns against his son and throws him out of the house, swearing he will strike him out of his will and make Tartuffe his sole heir. He urges Tartuffe to be with Elmire constantly to show Orgon's faith in him.

Elmire, disgusted, tells Orgon that until then she had passed off men's advances as something a wife dealt with herself, but his actions toward Damis are too much: She will show him the truth about Tartuffe. She hides Orgon under a table and then calls Tartuffe into the room and pretends to welcome his advances. Tartuffe is eager, lustful; he wants "tangible proof" of her feelings. Elmire coughs to get Orgon's attention, but he doesn't come out from under the table. She asks about Tartuffe's piety; he tells her that he can "remove Heaven's scruples" about adultery. She keeps coughing. Finally, unable to get Orgon to come out, she sends Tartuffe to make sure nobody is nearby and then all but pulls Orgon out. He is stunned. Elmire is sarcastic: "What, coming out so soon? Why don't you wait until the climax?"

Orgon, his obsession ended, confronts Tartuffe and tells him to leave the house, but Tartuffe instead orders Orgon and the family out: Tartuffe owns the house through Orgon's deed of gift. Worse, Tartuffe has private papers that Orgon entrusted to him that can ruin Orgon with the government.

A process server arrives, threatening Orgon's arrest. The police follow, but they arrest Tartuffe instead—the king knows the truth of Tartuffe's hypocrisy and is just.

these troupes; the rest still toured. (France had no householders—actors who, in England, owned parts of the theatre building.)

Within fifteen years, however, government control and a tendency toward centralization affected the acting companies. With Molière's death, his troupe joined with two others to form the Comédie Française, and it became France's national theatre. Membership in this sharing company was fixed; therefore, new members could not be elected until others had retired or died. Because of its financial rewards, including a substantial pension for retired members, the list of applicants was long.

The Comédie Française was granted a monopoly on the (legal) performance of tragedies and comedies in Paris. Lully's company held a monopoly on musical entertainments and spectacles. The Italian troupe—after a short banishment for a political indiscretion—got exclusive rights to what came to be called comic operas. Thus, less than a century after the freewheeling days of the first professionals, French theatre was rigidly structured, with three legal troupes that were expected to continue their traditions, not to initiate the new. The result was a highly polished but conservative theatre—and the suppression of competition.

Sentimentalism

As Louis XIV became both more conservative and more religious with advancing age, French culture in general shifted toward conservativism, adopting a set of values now called Sentimentalism. According to this view of the world, each individual is basically good. This doctrine contrasted with the previous (neoclassical) view that human existence was a continuing struggle between good and evil. According to the sentimentalist, evil came about through corruption; it was not part of human nature at birth. Sentimentalism thus implied that, although people might not be perfect, they were perfectible. Literature should therefore show virtuous people acting virtuously in their daily lives. Sentimentalism affected both serious dramas and comedies.

FIGURE 16.5

Multipoint Perspective

Adding second and third vanishing points and shifting the main vanishing point off center extends the vista behind the actors—and sometimes dwarfed them. As this etching demonstrates, multipoint perspective made the scenic background more interesting.

CHANGES IN PRODUCTION PRACTICES   Design likewise began to change. Although the basic conventions of costume remained unchanged (contemporary rather than historical), the costumes themselves were prettified and sentimentalized, even in commedia. In scenery, the introduction of angle perspective (moving the vanishing point away from the center and toward the side) and of multiple vanishing points not only allowed actors to work closer to the scenery but also increased the number of "perfect" seats in the audience, suggesting the acceptance of more than one perception or "truth."

CHANGES IN PERFORMANCE PRACTICES   Acting, too, grew ever more conservative. The previous tendency of actors to specialize in certain kinds of roles became gradually more rigid until, by 1750, clearly defined lines of business emerged. New actors, both male and female, were hired as utility players and gained their experience by playing a great number of small and varied roles. They then declared a specialty in a specific kind of role: a "walking" lady or gentleman (third line); a specialist in low comedy, or "stage eccentric" (second line); a hero or heroine (first line). Once committed to a particular line of business, actors did not stray far from it, regardless of age.

Along with lines of business came a practice known as possession of parts, an agreement that an actor who played a role in the company possessed that role for as long as he or she remained in the company. Both practices placed a premium on tradition—and, often, on age—and inhibited innovation.

Acting style depended heavily on vocal power and versatility and on formality and elegance rather than "truth to life." For example, some actors apparently intoned or chanted the poetic and lyrical passages of tragedies, much as the recitative of opera is delivered today, and many actors played for *points*, expecting to receive applause for passages particularly well delivered (in which case, the actor might repeat the passage).

With no outlet for the talents of the many actors and writers who did not get into the Comédie Française, and with dwindling enthusiasm for Neoclassicism, French men and women began to work in illegal theatres—that is, theatres other than the monopolies. Joining jugglers, dancers, and others who had worked at fairs for centuries, theatrical troupes began to play outside the law, practicing all kinds of tricks to avoid open conflict with the monopolies. From the experiments of these "illegitimate" theatres came a robust alternative to the government theatres—a theatre that was strictly commercial, supported by a paying audience. Housed in the fairs (it would move to the boulevard theatres of central Paris in the next century), this theatre aimed to be entertaining and to attract the largest number of spectators possible, their money paying the actors and providing the spectacle.

ENGLISH RESTORATION THEATRE AND BEYOND (1660–C. 1750)

We left the English theatre in Chapter 14 at the moment when another Stuart king was being restored to the throne (1660), hence the name of the period, the Restoration. During the years the English theatre had been closed, William Davenant had produced his few "operas," introducing Italianate staging to the English public for the first time. (It had long been in court masques.)

With the return of the English king and court from France, English theatres reopened in 1660. Their model, however, was not the theatre of Shakespeare's London; it was the theatre of Paris. The English theatre now included at least four French traits:

- Women actors, who quickly assumed all female roles except witches and comic old women, which continued to be played by men (as in Molière's company). The presence of women on stage encouraged, fairly or not, the risqué reputation of Restoration theatre.
- Conventions of Italianate staging.
- Newly designed theatre buildings that met the needs of Italianate staging.
- New, French-inspired producing arrangements. The king granted two monopoly patents, one to Davenant and another to Thomas Killigrew, thus limiting London to only two "legitimate" theatres. Although often challenged, these patents were reaffirmed through most of the 1700s.

When theatres first reopened in 1660, they used either old theatre buildings that still stood, or they adapted tennis courts, as in France. As new theatres were built, however, they blended Shakespearean and French features. The auditorium was divided into box, pit (now with benches), and gallery. Favored audience members now sat on the stage itself, as in France. The stage comprised both a proscenium arch with a raked stage behind it and a forestage that thrust into the pit. Most scenery was located behind the proscenium arch, where grooves were installed to facilitate scene changes, but most acting took place on the forestage, which was roughly the size of the area behind the proscenium. Early Restoration playhouses were intimate, with as little as thirty feet from forestage to rear boxes.

Staging conventions were Italian by way of France. Wings, borders, and shutters formed stock sets appropriate for comedies, tragedies, and pastorals. For costumes, most actors wore a sumptuous version of contemporary fashion. Acting depended heavily on vocal power and versatility and on formality and elegance rather than "truth to life." Lines of business and possession of parts determined which actors played which roles, contributing in England, as in France, to an increasingly conservative style of acting. Lighting was still by candle, and so audience and actors were equally visible.

Restoration Drama

Dramas of the Restoration likewise showed French influence. Plays written during the age of Shakespeare continued to be produced, but they were often adapted to bring them into closer accord with neoclassical theory. Newly written plays differed in both content and form from the Elizabethan. The worlds they embodied were those of a highly artificial, aristocratic society, probably influenced by life at Louis XIV's court, and their dramaturgy more closely reflected continental Neoclassicism than Shakespeare. Most famous today are the Restoration comedies of manners, plays whose witty dialogue and sophisticated sexual behavior reflect the highly artificial, mannered, and aristocratic society of the day. The heroes and heroines are "virtuous" if they succeed in capturing a lover or tricking a husband. "Honor" depends not on integrity but on reputation and "wit" (the ability to express ideas in a clever and apt way) is prized above

Jason Ayer

FIGURE 16.6

English Restoration Theatre

This contemporary production of William Wycherley's *The Country Wife* at Theatre South Carolina incorporates the conventions of the English Restoration stage into its design. There is a deep forestage (reached here by four steps), a proscenium arch (with proscenium doors and stage boxes above them), and scenery in single-point perspective.

all. The admirable characters in the plays are those who can operate successfully within an intricate social sphere; the foolish and laughable are those whose lack of wit or upbringing denies them access to social elegance. In short, the comedies depict the mores and conventions of a courtly society in which elegance of phrase and the appearance of propriety were more highly prized than morals and sincere feelings. Among the most famous authors of Restoration comedies were William Congreve, whose *The Way of the World* is still produced, and William Wycherley, whose *The Country Wife* can still titillate and amuse.

"Heroic" tragedies presented a conflict between love and duty. In a world far removed from that of the Restoration comedies, tragic heroes were flawless and heroines chaste. The dialogue was based on heroic couplets, two-line units of rhymed iambic pentameter. The idealization and formality of this kind of tragedy made it unusually susceptible to parody, and so burlesques of it soon appeared.

Succumbing to both the onslaught of burlesque and the changing tastes of audiences, heroic tragedies declined in public favor, their place being filled by neoclassical tragedies such as John Dryden's *All for Love*, a rewriting of Shakespeare's *Antony and Cleopatra* that brought it closer to the principles of Neoclassicism.

Audiences

Restoration audiences were small (theatres seated about 650) and fairly cohesive—young, courtly, and self-confident. Regularly in attendance were royalty and the upper aristocracy, many of them veterans of exile in France with the king. Some women in the audience wore masks, as much to increase their attractions as to hide them. This theatre was a place to be seen as well as to enjoy the plays. Within fifteen years, however, noncourtiers began to take up theatre as a leisure-time activity in ever-larger numbers, causing a shift in audience taste.

Sentimentalism

In England as in France, the eighteenth century brought with it a change of values. Between about 1700 and 1750, society steadily grew more conservative, middle class, moralistic, and sentimental.

The amoral tone of the Restoration comedy of manners became offensive to many, and in its place developed the view that drama should teach morality. At first, the change was merely in the plays' endings: Young lovers philandered and cuckolded throughout four acts of the play but, in the fifth, repented and declared their intention to lead a moral and upright life henceforth.

SENTIMENTAL COMEDY   By the 1730s, however, heroes and heroines were becoming embodiments of middle-class values, struggling cheerfully against adversity until, at the end, their courage and persistence were rewarded. Prized especially were characters able to express their insights into human goodness in pithy statements (sentiments). Thus, the label "sentimental hero" implied not only one who embodied virtue but also one whose speech was rich in sentiments. The audiences of the day experienced "a pleasure too exquisite for laughter," and so sentimental comedy dominated English comic drama by the middle of the eighteenth century—a clear break with Neoclassicism.

SERIOUS PLAYS   Heroic and neoclassical tragedy were increasingly replaced by a kind of serious drama, alternately called domestic tragedy and *middle-class tragedy*. George Lillo's *The London Merchant* (1731), for example, was a major break with the neoclassical ideal: A middle-class hero is led astray by love and is ultimately punished. Although the play aimed to teach morality by showing the punishment of evil, it was nonetheless a far cry from strict Neoclassicism because it was written in prose, featured a middle-class hero, and dealt with affairs of

FIGURE 16.7
An etching, originally by the artist William Hogarth in 1733, and later colored, depicts a laughing London audience with "orange girls" plying their wares.

the heart and the marketplace rather than affairs of state. None of these more serious plays, however, satisfied the English taste for scenic splendor and spectacular effects.

MINOR FORMS   Opera and a number of so-called minor forms developed to provide outlets for visual display. Native English opera was gradually replaced by spectacular Italian opera, whose popularity soared in the eighteenth century. As well, English pantomimes combined elements of commedia dell'arte, farce, mythology, and contemporary satire with elaborate scenes of spectacle in short afterpieces (short entertainments to be performed after the evening's main play). Often, the dialogue was merely an excuse for major scenes of transformation, in which Harlequin, by a wave of his magic wand, changed places and people into new and dazzling locales and characters. Because new scenery was often commissioned for pantomimes, many innovations in the design and execution of settings in England can be credited to pantomime. (Pantomime or "panto" for short continues in England today as a Christmas holiday tradition for children and family entertainment.)

CHANGES IN PRODUCTION AND PERFORMANCE PRACTICES   Such changes in drama were accompanied by changes in production and performance practices. As more middle-class people came into the audience, existing theatres were enlarged, and new theatres built larger; within a hundred years, the intimate theatre of the Restoration had been superceded by those seating 1,500 or more. Theatres began to commission painters to provide new settings for some plays (especially those featuring familiar locations), and these painters, adopting new techniques for suggesting depth, made it possible for actors to work closer to scenery than before. Increased emphasis on scenery led to a gradual decrease in the size of the forestage and a need for more space behind the proscenium arch. As a result of these shifts, there was little difference in appearance between English and continental theatres by 1750.

By the middle of the 1700s, then, English theatres, like French theatres, had adopted the conventions of Italianate staging, neoclassical drama, and formal acting. In both, women were now on stage and in the audience. Both cultures had developed theatrical centers in their capital cities, where their kings maintained monopolies over a strictly limited number of theatres. Actors talented and experienced enough to perform in the monopoly theatres lived good lives; others, however, lived precariously, working in small cities and towns and touring outlying areas.

By the early 1700s, European audiences (including those of a just-developing German theatre) had already begun to tire of the austerity of neoclassical dramas. As audiences became increasingly middle class, sentimentalism and spectacle began to be prized; both found expression in opera, ballet, and new dramatic forms. When monopoly theatres disdained the innovations, commercial theatres sprang up to house them, first at the fairs of London and Paris (hence, fair theatres) and later in London's West End and Paris's boulevards. Actors who found themselves squeezed out of the monopoly theatres played there or toured the provinces.

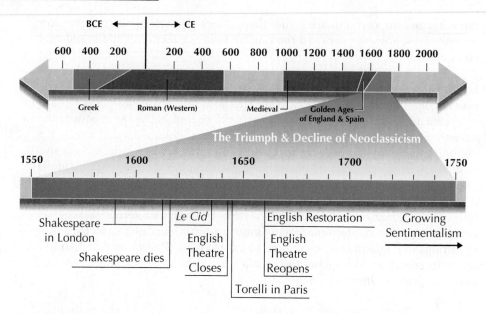

FIGURE 16.8

Timeline

The golden age of French theatre did not begin until those of England, Spain, and Italy were nearing their ends. French theatre, like France itself, came to dominate Europe, influencing English theatrical conventions and bringing them closer to continental practice after 1660.

ENGLISH THEATRE IN AMERICA

From among the many English actors who found themselves squeezed out of the London theatre came the beginnings of theatre in the American colonies. Rather than touring rural England, William and Lewis Hallam chose to assemble a company (mostly families) and sail to a distant English province, an outpost of the New World. In 1752 the troupe arrived in Virginia and, after building a theatre, opened with Shakespeare's *The Merchant of Venice*. This group, reorganized and enlarged after the death of Lewis Hallam and renamed the American Company in recognition of America's break with England, toured the towns of the East Coast with almost no competition until the 1790s. Its repertory, acting styles, and production conventions were English, with appropriate adjustments made for the needs of almost constant touring.

KEY TERMS

Check your understanding against this list. Brief definitions are included in the Glossary; persons are page-referenced in the Index.

17

Successful Failure
Theatre and Reform,
c. 1750 to the 1950s

An abstract, period illustration of some exercises for biomechanic actor training.

OBJECTIVES

When you have completed this chapter, you should be able to:

- Describe the split in the Western theatre in the late 1700s.

- List several major traits of Romanticism.

- Sketch the arrangement of audience areas in the theatre before and after Wagner.

- Compare Romanticism and Realism, Realism and Naturalism.

- Describe changes in acting in the shift from Romanticism to Realism.

- List and briefly define the major avant-garde theories from c. 1890s–c. 1950s.

CONTEXT

History is filled with contradictions, none, perhaps, greater than those of the theater from the mid-eighteenth century until the mid-twentieth century. On the one hand, theatre in Europe and the United States achieved a popularity never before equaled; on the other, people in those same places tried with increasing energy to reform, restore, improve, or save it. These attempts split both theatre and drama into a commercial strand and a something else that was later called the avant-garde ("advance guard"—the term was, significantly, a military one). Because the two strands developed along different, although connected, paths, we are treating them in two chapters; this chapter deals with the avant-garde from the mid-eighteenth to the mid-twentieth centuries. The next chapter deals with the commercial theatre and the ways in which it used avant-garde experiments.

THREE COUNTRIES, TWO EXPERIENCES

Germany

Germany's experience was different from England and France's. "Germany" was still a hodgepodge of small states, duchies, and principalities linked by little except language. Despite a glorious tradition of music, it had no permanent theatres at the beginning of the 1700s. Such traveling players as there were played idiotic low comedy or blood-and-thunder bombast for (powerless) low-class audiences. In 1725, however, Johann Gottsched (a Neoclassicist and playwright) and Carolina Neuber (head of an acting troupe) introduced the first "serious" German drama and theatre; other permanent theatres quickly sprang up, sixty-five of them by 1800. But they were not located in a central capital that was also a nexus of absolute power; they were spread all over the German cultural area. German theorists and artists were not so much reformers, then, as innovators: They were trying to assert a cultural centrality that German theatre had never known, and they used the language of art and seriousness. They tilted toward English models. (They knew Shakespeare from touring seventeenth-century English companies; some critics promoted French ideas, but failed.)

FIGURE 17.1

English Comedy

Richard Brinsley Sheridan's *The School for Scandal,* a comedy of manners like many of the comedies of the Restoration but with sentimentalism instead of cynicism, opened at the Theatre Royal in Drury Lane in 1777. Here, a production by the University of Missouri.

England and France

How did the separation of theatre into commercial and avant-garde start in England and France? As we have seen, by the early 1700s the theatre had begun to lose its ties to the old monarchies. At the same time, the audience base started growing, first into the middle and then into the working class, with the result that the theatre's potential audience grew, but not necessarily for the old kind of theatre. England had its Glorious Revolution in 1688, ending the Restoration period, and thereafter Parliament shared power with a king who ruled less by divine right than by the negotiated consent of the governed. In France, Louis XIV died in 1715 after seventy-two years of first nominal, then actual absolute power, and he was replaced by a corrupt regime that was wiped out by the revolution of 1789. The monopolies that had tied the theatres to power weakened, and in their place came large audiences who had not power but money, which they used to buy entrance to new, "illegitimate," commercial theatres (e.g., of the fairs and boulevards).

By the mid-1700s, theatrical energy was shifting to these commercial theatres, which offered new kinds of plays in spectacular settings, leaving the monopoly theatres to traditional practices and traditional audiences. As a result, theatre flourished, but the more popular it became in its new venues, the farther it got from the old center of power. A series of reformers began to try to steer it back—the subject of this chapter. They usually couched their pleas in terms of art, not of literal connections to central power, often asking for a return to "serious" drama and theatre—a language that now looks like an unconscious recognition of what was really happening.

FIGURE 17.2

Frankenstein

Mary Shelley's *Frankenstein; or, The Modern Prometheus* was published in 1818 when she was twenty-one. The novel is romantic through its concern with a strange version of the natural man (the "Creature"), and being critical of science. *Frankenstein* has been repeatedly staged and filmed. Here, a scene from the Royal National Theatre's recent production in which the Creature attacks Dr. Frankenstein.

Reforms

Thus, the accelerating movement that tried to reconnect theatrical art with power and with the elite that wielded it started in all three countries. Major waves of would-be reform came at the turn of the nineteenth century (Romanticism), in the last quarter of the nineteenth century (Realism), and throughout the first half of the twentieth century (all kinds of *-isms*). All had impact on the popular, commercial theatre. All failed. Theatre never recovered its ability to "validate the center of power."

Theatrical innovators—reformers—were often a generation behind these changes. They saw their own declining centrality, but they tried to aim their demands for seriousness and art at a world that was going or already gone.

The commercial theatre, however, was happy to sweep up such innovations as pleased its audience.

FIRST WAVE: ROMANTICISM, 1750–1850

Context

What do these things have in common?

- The Declaration of Independence, 1776
- *Frankenstein,* the novel by Mary Shelley published in 1818
- "'Beauty is truth, truth beauty,'–that is all / Ye know on earth, and all ye need to know." A line from John Keats' poem "Ode on a Grecian Urn," published in 1820
- *The Rights of Man,* a book by Thomas Paine, published in 1791, arguing that revolution is justified when the government does not protect the people's rights or interests

There are two answers: First, they fall into the same hundred years, and second, they are expressions of Romanticism. What was Romanticism? To start, it is helpful to realize that Romanticism and the word *romance*—referring to love and sexual attraction—come from the same etymological roots but are not related in meaning. In fact, the meaning of Romanticism is not simple to detail.

The period from about 1750 to about 1850 was "the world turn'd upside-down," as the title of a popular English sermon published in 1791 had it. Major political revolutions happened in the Americas and France; the industrial revolution began; and demographics changed as population migrated from country to city and across oceans and borders to North America, Australia, and South America. Steam power, mass communications (high-volume printing, cheap newspapers), railroads, and photography came into being. For the first time, nations supported compulsory education. The international slave trade was outlawed by Britain, the ban enforced by its navy. Out of this turmoil, the cultural and intellectual cluster we call Romanticism came into being.

The Nature of Romanticism: The Beginning of Our World

We now tend to think of Romanticism as a set of theoretical ideas.

It is better to think of it as a set of effects, which were then articulated as theoretical ideas by several people in several countries at more or less the same time, those ideas then becoming causes in their turn. This is an early example of a cultural feedback loop, where a result becomes a cause leading to more results. And it is wise to remember that these were political ideas as well as ideas about society, psychology, art, and the nature of the world; that they were only secondarily about the theatre; and that the ideas were not necessarily consistent. One critic much later suggested that we should speak of romanticism*s* (plural), not one Romanticism. Nonetheless, long after the fact we can see five certain common interests:

- *Rebellion:* Romanticisms were revolutionary. In art, Romanticism wanted to overturn Neoclassicism. In politics, equality and the idea of a social contract binding government and governed were Romantic.

Socially, early feminism, personal religion, and opposition to slavery were Romantic. Romanticisms hated a status quo that inhibited equality and individualism.

■ *Art with a capital* A: Creative and intellectual Romantics all but invented the idea of Art as a special activity. The Artist was a special being—a creative genius able to see truths hidden from others. Before Romanticism, artists were seen as craftsmen, some better than others. After Romanticism began, people saw the preromantic artists as creative geniuses as well.

■ *Nature:* Natural feelings were more reliable than reason or authority. Civilization and education corrupted nature. Children, savages, and peasants were uncorrupted, therefore nearer innocence. Nature was a window through which the child and the Artist could see Truth.

■ *Anti-industrialism:* Art and beauty were "sublime"; factories were "dark Satanic mills." Cities were unnatural and corrupting. Romantics saw early industrialists as greedy bean counters without souls—the opposite of the Artist. Industry was ugly (noise, smoke, buildings) and therefore the opposite of Beauty (another way to Truth).

■ *Uniqueness:* Truth was also found in the particular, not the general. To establish uniqueness was to establish identity. Note that this is nearly the opposite of Neoclassicism's verisimilitude, which sought truth in the general and typical.

People at the time did not necessarily see these five ideas clearly. Political activists saw mostly their own impatience with top-down government; artists saw their own disgust with top-down "rules"; and middle-class people saw their own distaste for slavery or slums or dreadful working conditions. Many literate people picked up the jargon of Romantic art—*sublime, picturesque,* and *grotesque*—and, insofar as they used it, they were Romantic, but the spread of the jargon probably had more to do with mass communications than with commitment. But the romanticisms have a contemporary feel to them. If you could step back right now into the world of 1740, you would find its culture and its behavior alien, but if you could step back into the world of 1820, you would find some of it familiar—ideas about individualism, freedom of choice, human rights, and the environment. To be sure, you'd have to land among the right people—mostly upper middle class and educated— but if you did, you would see why Romanticism is still important: It was the beginning of our world.

Romanticism in the Theatre

The effects on the theatre were significant, if erratic. Romantic theatre artists disdained Neoclassicism *and* frivolous theatre and tried to reform both. They began slowly and unevenly, and they were rejected by conservative theatres, above all the Comédie Française; yet contradictorily, perhaps, it was in the monopoly theatres where the Romantics wanted to see their ideas applied—that, after all, was where the connection with power had been and where the connection to the

FIGURE 17.3

Romantic Theatres

Theatre buildings got larger after 1750, with the audience in box-pit-and-gallery seating. Here, a rendering of Covent Garden Theatre in the early 1800s; the play appears to be Shakespeare's *Henry IV, Part I.*

upper class still was. Romantics didn't see the contradiction in their striving: If their art was performed in the mainstream theatres, it would be accepted and popular and no longer revolutionary.

Yet where ideas crept in partly unnoticed were the popular commercial theatres called "boulevard theatres" from their locations in Paris, fair (big public fairs were outside the old laws), and nonmonopoly theatres. The ideas were "in the air"—they had come, after all, from the same causes that let ordinary people see and think in new ways, including in the theatres as audiences. International trade and imperialism, for example, created a knowledge of exotic places, and so they began to show up in plays and settings. The new interest in childhood and primitivism brought children, common people, American Indians, peasants, and Africans to the stage, both as hot topics for hack playwrights and as real concerns of intellectuals. Plays were set in newly detailed scenery of forests, dungeons, jungles, and caves, both because new plays required them and because visual artists were themselves now more interested in nature and detail. (This trend in scenic design was supported by the development of new technology, too.) The new faith in feelings brought plays that appealed to emotions rather than intellect to audiences already attuned to Sentimentalism, to emotional religious sects, and to new novels about the emotions.

In England, most of all, then in Germany and the United States, Shakespeare was elevated to a cultural icon. His plays were performed from London to the

California gold fields; they were read aloud in Hamburg drawing rooms and around the fires of the fur-trapping "mountain men." With the King James Bible, Shakespeare became a binding force of English-language culture that gave it a frame of reference, a common elevated language, and a common rhythm that lasted well into the twentieth century. (In France, however, where Neoclassicism persisted longer, Shakespeare was not seen on the stage until an English company brought the plays in the 1830s.)

Perhaps the most important outside force acting on the theatre, however, was demographic. Migration and urban growth meant that for the first time a mass audience existed. Industrial employment meant that large parts of the working class could afford the theatre. These changes affected the size of theatres, which got bigger; the nature of the drama, which got more sensational; and the business organization of the companies, which got more commercial as the old monopolies withered or ossified.

ROMANTIC ATTEMPTS AT REFORM   The most conscious efforts to put Romantic ideas into effect in the theatre came in dramatic theory and drama. Especially in Germany, a distinct body of "serious" Romantic plays was written and is still in the German repertory. A recognizable gap appeared, however, between "important" (serious, literary) plays and popular ones in France and England. Partly, this was the gap between the old monopolies and the new, mostly commercial theatres; partly it was the gap between self-aware Art and what was called hackwork. Over the long haul, Art lost, in good part because it would not see the theatre itself as art; rather, the theatre was a corrupted thing that had to be reformed.

FIGURE 17.4
Edwin Booth's Playhouse
This watercolor of the interior of Booth's theatre in New York reveals that by 1869 some theatres had eliminated the proscenium doors. Instead there are three boxes close to the stage. Note the orchestra, pit, and three balconies.

Germany.   Romantic drama found its home in Germany. Germany produced a seminal theoretical work, Gotthold Lessing's *Hamburg Dramaturgy* (1770), which rejected French Neoclassicism as a model and recommended instead Shakespeare. Lessing wrote specifically of art and genius, recommended natural language, praised sentimental comedy and domestic tragedy, and argued for heroes who were human beings, not aristocratic or royal titles. He also wrote several plays, including so-called philosophical dramas, the most lasting—as a literary, not a theatrical, work—*Nathan the Wise*.

Hamburg Dramaturgy, and especially its urging of Shakespeare as a model, in turn influenced young German radicals calling themselves the ***Sturm und Drang*** (**storm and stress**)—an in-your-face term of the day. Two were to become German classics:

- Johann Wolfgang von Goethe, whose *Faust* is an acknowledged literary, but not theatrical, masterpiece, and whose novel *The Sorrows of Werther* ("spleen, morbid sentimentality, romantic melancholy, and disgust of life," according to one critic) gave Romantics a mythic hero and even a costume.

- Friedrich von Schiller, whose commitment to liberty showed in *The Robbers* and *William Tell*, both successes that led to many imitations.

The subjects of these plays tell us much about self-aware Romanticism—love and loss, liberty, the fight against despotism, free will, and wisdom. So do the kinds of characters—robbers, rebels, lovers, and questioners. Perhaps most significant is the form of the plays, whose authors demanded the right to roam freely in time and space (like Shakespeare) and not be limited by "the unities," and their poetry, which was intense, usually unrhymed, and rhythmic—neither everyday speech nor neoclassical artifice.

England.   In England, however, attempts to create a serious body of Romantic drama labored too closely in the shadow of Shakespeare, and a false Shakespearism ruined many plays. Too, serious English Romantics refused to meet the needs of the theatre, including pleasing the audience, which they thought was the problem, not the solution. Even when England's great poets tried seriousness in the theatre, they usually failed; Byron did write a tragedy that worked, *Werner*, a lurid tale of revenge and despair, but it barely escaped the trap into which most serious Romantic drama fell—that of mistaking the most extreme moments of Shakespearean tragedy for the tragedy itself. English Romantics who wanted to bring a new seriousness to the theatre were not alone in failing to find a dramaturgy to match the emotional expression in which they believed; thus, the resulting plays often lacked internal probability and had long passages of great dullness separating moments of incredible bombast. Romantic language pushed the envelope and sometimes became wild, torrential, and overblown—a verbal diarrhea to match the emotional diarrhea of its heroes. Few of these plays have lasted, and no wonder; rather, what has lasted have been Italian operas made from them, in which music supplied the quality that the spoken dramas couldn't.

France.   In Paris, Romantic dramas made it to the boulevard theatres in 1790 but were shut out of the then-hidebound Comédie Française until 1830, when Victor Hugo's self-aware *Hernani* was staged and caused a riot. Hugo won and dragged Romanticism into the Comédie, but it was just too late. The Comédie was belatedly revived by the energy of Romanticism, but only briefly because the Romantic movement itself ran out of steam a few years later, so watered down in the popular theatres by that time that storm, stress, and riot fizzled.

Drama had been caught in a contradiction: Serious literary Romantics wanted to create art for a sensitive, therefore limited, audience; the theatres wanted to bring in the largest possible audience. The extreme artistic position was closet drama, plays written to be read, not staged. Neither closet dramas nor bad poetic tragedies could restore the theatre to its neoclassical importance.

Romanticism was pretty well over as a movement by the 1840s. It had succeeded in destroying Neoclassicism; it had planted its flag at the Comédie Française; the English monopoly "patents" had died of old age; and German theatre had had what one source calls its Golden Age. Romantic drama had not reformed the theatre, however.

What persisted was Sentimentalism, which had adapted itself to trivialized Romanticism and that matched Victorian taste, which was middle class, fussy, and "moral." What the Romantics left most conspicuously to the future, however, was the image of the Artist—special, gifted, emotional, inspired—and of Art, which entered Victorian culture as a kind of secular religion (so long as it was moral and approved by experts).

An Aftershock: Richard Wagner

Richard Wagner is now known as an opera composer. His influence on modern theatre, however, has been enormous for two innovations: (1) the idea of unity and a unifying artist and (2) a separate, classless audience space.

THE MASTER ARTWORK   Wagner had a huge ego and knew he was a genius in the Romantic mold. His concept of a unified theatrical production meant a *gesamtkunstwerk* (master artwork), a "unified art work," conceived and executed by a "master artist" who would run the whole show (ideally, Wagner himself). The idea would go far to establish the director in the modern theatre.

THE SEPARATED AUDIENCE   In 1876, Wagner got his own theatre at Bayreuth. It epitomized his ideas: several "nesting" proscenium arches between audience and actors, not just one; a hidden orchestra pit; and steam jets between audience and playing area to emphasize a "mystic chasm"—the separation of the master artwork from the audience.

Perhaps more important, Wagner put his audience in the dark and got rid of box, pit, and gallery. Now, the audience sat in a fan-shaped orchestra that was "classless," and every seat had an equally good view of the stage. Called continental seating, the arrangement became standard in the twentieth century.

The effect was in one sense a democratic one, but it had the paradoxical effect of putting the entire audience in the same passive surrender to the stage—no catcalls from upper galleries, no bored aristocrats whispering in boxes. It was a top-down theatre space for an art in which the master artist gave and the audience received.

FIGURE 17.5

Wagner the Theoretician

The interior of Wagner's theatre at Bayreuth was an important influence on the future of theatre architecture and audience seating. Wagner eliminated box, pit, and gallery (creating the most common modern audience arrangement) and put the emphasis on the proscenium arches and what went on within them.

SECOND WAVE: REALISM, 1850–1950

The phenomenal popularity of commercial theatres in the nineteenth century did little to satisfy reformers. What they saw was a theatre with a huge audience, doing productions that used the best technology of the day, all of which seemed to them wasted; some saw it as wasted in sheer overproduction; others saw it as wasted on triviality. Again, a call for "seriousness" came; this time, however, the buzzword was not Romanticism, but **Realism**.

The idea that art should show real life was hardly new. It was implicit in Renaissance theory, explicit in every portrait or still life. It was explicit in *Hamburg Dramaturgy*. And a literal rendering of life became concrete with the invention about 1840 of photography. In the theatre, local color and scenic detail dated to the eighteenth century, as did the prototype of the **box set**, an imitation of a room with side walls rather than wings; the box set was common by the end of the Romantic period. In drama, commercial playwrights were writing "problem plays" that seemed to examine real-life issues. Why, then, a new theatrical radicalism that called itself Realism? Because the prerealisms mentioned earlier were inconsistent; because the plays, including "problem plays," were more trendy than serious; because acting was obviously acting, not being; because box sets, with their painted canvas walls, were obviously sets; because the theatre, the radicals said, was all about laying on *stuff* and not getting serious.

The Realists got serious.

By the 1850s, problems of inequality, industrialization, and urbanization were well known and widely discussed. Urban poverty was on the rise, and with it, urban crime. Fear of political instability (a legacy of Romanticism) led toward repression, which fanned dissatisfaction. For some, it was the best of worlds, but for many, it was the worst; the tension is part of what we mean by the word *Victorian*—the middle- and upper-class ability to maintain awareness of problems while using apparent ignorance as a coping mechanism ("Nice people don't mention such things").

Science was offering new theories that threatened old ideas: Charles Darwin proposed evolution, which left humanity without uniqueness and apparently at the mercy of environment. At century's end, Sigmund Freud proposed the unconscious, which jerked the feet from under good intentions and double standards. One effect of both was to dislodge humankind from the philosophical pedestal on which it had rested since the Middle Ages; another was to displace romantic ideas, especially their optimism and their faith in nature as a window on the ideal. Instead, it became, in poet Alfred Lord Tennyson's phrase, "Nature red in tooth and claw." At the same time, "social Darwinism" gave oppressors a response to do-gooders: Social inequity was merely a survival of the fittest. The impact on serious art, including theatre, was to turn it toward question and challenge of the status quo.

FIGURE 17.6

Realism and Naturalism

Here, Anton Chekhov's *The Three Sisters* at the Moscow Art Theatre in a realistic setting. Compare this image with that of the same play in Figure 17.11.

REALISM AND NATURALISM: THREE IMPORTANT LEADERS

Realists—and their more extreme relatives, advocates of Naturalism—believed that truth resided in the material objects observable in the physical, external world. They were also objectivists: They believed that truth could be discovered through the application of scientific observation and could be replicated by a series of objective observers, not by Romantic art.

According to the Realists and the Naturalists, the function of art, like that of science, was the betterment of humankind, and the method of the artist should be that of the scientist. Plays should be set in contemporary times and places because only they could be observed firsthand by the playwright. Because the highest purpose of art was the betterment of humanity, the subject of plays should be contemporary life and its problems.

Although sharing with Realists a belief in science as a solver of problems, the Naturalists differed in their definition of what problems most needed attention and in their hope for the future. The Naturalists stressed the problems of the poor and tended to be pessimistic about their solution. According to the Naturalists, people were victims, not actors in life. Their destiny was controlled by factors such as heredity and environment, over which they had little influence. Because the Naturalists attempted to give the impression that their plays were an actual record of life, the dramas often appeared formless and unstructured, traits that gave rise to the phrase "a slice of life" to describe some Naturalist plays.

Despite the period's interest in the mass of people, and despite democratizing forces, this was an era of self-defined great men (and a few women). Forceful people—remember Wagner—tried to change the world. The master artist appeared in several guises.

Georg II, Duke of Saxe-Meiningen

One of the earliest creators of realistic staging was Georg II, Duke of Saxe-Meiningen (fl. 1870s–1880s). In some ways, the duke was merely perfecting and popularizing ideals of staging promulgated much earlier; nonetheless, it was he who influenced later Realists.

Saxe-Meiningen objected to many practices of the commercial mainstream because they resulted in productions that lacked unity (internal consistency) and seemed artificial. For the duke and his court theatre, the art of the theatre was the art of providing the illusion of reality; he therefore sought methods of production that would lead to an intensified reality that would give events on stage the feeling of being lived for the first time. To this end, the duke stressed accurate scenery, costumes, and properties; lifelike acting; and unity.

PRODUCTION PRACTICES   The duke believed that all elements of a production required coordination. The setting must be an integral part of the play, and so he encouraged his actors to move *within* the setting rather than merely playing in front of it as was fashionable at the time. If actors were to move within an environment, the scenic details had to be three-dimensional rather than painted, and so actual objects were used in the settings. Simultaneously, the duke strove to provide several levels (e.g., rocks, steps, and platforms) so that the scenic design would not stop abruptly at the stage floor. In these ways, he did much to popularize the use of three-dimensional staging.

Historical accuracy in both scenery and costumes was important. To increase accuracy, he divided each century into thirds and differentiated among various national groups within each period. He used authentic fabrics instead of the cheaper substitutes often seen in commercial theatres of the day.

ACTING   There were no stars in Saxe-Meiningen's group. Each member of the company was eligible to play any role; and each member, if not cast as a major character, was required to play in crowd scenes, something commercial stars never did. Each actor in a crowd scene was given lines and actions and put into a group led by an experienced actor. Actors were to avoid parallel lines on stage, to make crosses diagonally rather than parallel with the curtain line, to keep one foot off the ground whenever possible (by placing it on a step or by kneeling

FIGURE 17.7

Saxe-Meiningen as Director

The new stage Realism—individualized crowd members, varying levels, and varied postures and arm positions—is shown in an engraving of the funeral-oration scene in *Julius Caesar*. The Duke of Saxe-Meiningen is said to be the first director, although he had predecessors.

on one knee), and not to copy his or her neighbor's stance. Actors were told to look at one another rather than the audience, to react to what was said and done onstage, and to behave naturally, even if it meant delivering a line while not facing the audience. Makeup was based on historical portraits. These practices now seem obvious, but in the 1870s they were startling.

INFLUENCE   Beginning in 1874 (eight years after the duke took over the theatre), the Meiningen company began touring Western Europe and Russia. The troupe gave more than 2,800 performances in thirty-six cities. From these performances came its international reputation and its influence.

André Antoine and the Théâtre-Libre

André Antoine, an amateur actor, abhorred the commercial theatres of Paris, disapproved of the way actors were trained at the Paris Conservatoire (France's leading school for actors), objected to the scenic practices of the major theatres, and decried the flimsiness of contemporary popular drama. What was needed, Antoine concluded, was a theatre in which new and controversial plays could get realistic productions. Therefore, when an amateur group to which he belonged balked at producing a new play, Antoine undertook the production himself and, spurred by early success, became the full-time director of his own new theatre in 1887. He named it the Théâtre-Libre (Free Theatre) and described it as nothing less than "a machine of war, poised for the conquest of Paris." It was, among other things, an alternative, or avant-garde, theatre. It is worth noting the differences between Antoine and Saxe-Meiningen at this point:

- Antoine was far more interested in new plays.
- Antoine faced tough government censorship.
- Antoine had to make a theatre from scratch.

PLAYS   Although Antoine produced a wide range of plays at the Théâtre-Libre, he seemed most comfortable with plays in the Realistic and Naturalistic styles. Because Antoine organized his theatre as a members-only subscription house, he was able to bypass threats of censorship. Consequently, he was able to introduce to Parisians a wide range of French and foreign authors whose works were considered too scandalous for production in major theatres.

PRODUCTION PRACTICES: THE "FOURTH WALL"   Antoine believed like the Naturalists that environment influenced human behavior, so he made his settings as believable and lifelike as possible. He designed a room and then decided which "wall" of the room was to be removed so that the audience could see in. Antoine also used actual three-dimensional objects rather than their painted substitutes. For one play, he brought real sides of beef on his stage; for another, real trees and birds' nests; and for another, a student's actual room furnishings. The attention he paid to realistic detail and his reliance on actual objects led to his being called by many the father of Naturalistic staging. The front of the stage was the "fourth wall," transparent for the public but opaque for the actors.

FIGURE 17.8

The Fourth Wall

The "box set," three walls filling the proscenium arch, developed in the 1840s. The "fourth wall" was not built so the audience could view the production. Here, a box set from the 1860s complete with ceiling.

ACTING Antoine believed that actors should appear to be people, not actors. He wanted his actors to say their lines naturally, just as one might engage in a conversation with friends and, at the same time, to move about the furniture and accessories as in real life. Sincerity and conviction were the qualities he sought, and so he advised his actors to ignore the audience and to speak to one another in conversational tones—in short, to try to *be*, rather than to *act*, the characters in the play. Perhaps for these reasons, Antoine often used amateurs who had not received conventional training for the commercial theatre and who were therefore more receptive to the experimental style of Naturalistic acting.

INFLUENCE The major contributions of Antoine and the Théâtre-Libre were

- To popularize acting techniques leading toward naturalness on stage.
- To gain acceptance for scenic practices now known as fourth-wall Realism, with all that implies about scenic detail and literal objects.
- To introduce a new generation of playwrights (both French and foreign) to the theatregoing public of Paris.
- To establish a model for a censor-free theatre.

The most significant experimental theatre of its day, the Théâtre-Libre gave rise to a number of similar noncommercial theatres throughout the world. Called the independent theatre movement, this blossoming of small theatres in several countries almost simultaneously gave the impetus to, first, an international, albeit fringe, theatre movement that was reform minded and socially engaged and then an ultimate acceptance of Realism as the mainstream of the commercial theatre, an acceptance complete by early in the twentieth century.

Konstantin Stanislavski and the Moscow Art Theatre

When the Meiningen company toured Russia in 1885 and 1890, Konstantin Stanislavski and Vladimir Nemirovich-Danchenko saw it. They decided to establish a new kind of theatre in Moscow whose goals were to remain free of the demands of commercialism, to avoid overemphasis on the scenic elements of production, and to reflect the inner truth of the play. For this theatre, the Moscow Art Theatre established in 1898, Nemirovich-Danchenko was to select the plays and handle the administration, and Stanislavski was to serve as the production director.

ACTING AND DIRECTING   By 1917, Stanislavski had developed, from personal experience and observation of others, his major ideas for training actors, ideas that he codified in a series of books that have since been translated into more than twenty languages (the dates are for the US editions): *My Life in Art* (1924), *An Actor Prepares* (1936), *Building a Character* (1949), and *Creating a Role* (1961). Together, these books represent what has come to be called the Stanislavski system of actor training, although Stanislavski himself insisted neither that his was the only way to train actors nor that his methods should be studied and mastered by everyone.

FIGURE 17.9
Stanislavski and the Moscow Art Theatre
Here, Maxim Gorky's *The Lower Depths*, a Naturalistic play set in a flophouse. Stanislavski is center on the table.

As a director during the early years of the Moscow Art Theatre, Stanislavski worked in a rather autocratic fashion, planning each detail of his actors' vocal inflections, gestures, and movements. But as his interest in the problems of the actor grew, and as his actors became more skillful, he abandoned his dogmatic approach and became an interpreter and helper to the actors. His ideal became for the director and the actors to grow together in their understanding of the play. Only after the group had grasped the psychology of the roles and the complex interrelationships (often a three-month process) did the actors begin to work on the stage.

INFLUENCE   What began in 1898 as an experiment in external Realism was by 1906 an experiment in psychological Realism. When the Moscow Art Theatre toured Britain and the United States early in the twentieth century, the word *ensemble* was used again and again to describe the company, which seemed natural and unified, without stars. The Stanislavski ideal had become an established tradition in Russia by the time of the revolution (1917). Because a number of Russians trained in "the system" then left their country and became acting teachers, the ideas of Stanislavski came to London, New York, and then Hollywood.

Plays and Playwrights

Although other writers had presaged Realism, it was the Norwegian Henrik Ibsen who launched Realism as a major artistic movement.

IBSEN   With plays such as *A Doll's House* (1879) and *Hedda Gabler* (1891), Ibsen assumed his controversial role as an attacker of society's values. Structurally, his plays were fairly traditional: They told a story and moved logically from event to event, just as well-made plays had done for years. But their content was shocking: When individuals came into

Lenny Cohen

FIGURE 17.10

Henrik Ibsen

Ibsen's *Hedda Gabler* continues to be one of the most revived plays from this period. Here, *Hedda Gabler* in a contemporary production at North Carolina's Triad Stage.

conflict with society, they were no longer assumed to be guilty and society blameless. Indeed, social customs and traditional morality were exposed by Ibsen as a tangle of inconsistencies and irrelevancies. Questions such as the proper role of women, the ethics of euthanasia, the morality of business and war, and the economics of religion formed the basis of serious probings into social behavior. Theatrical producers throughout the world who believed that drama should be involved in the social issues of the day applauded the Norwegian dramatist, and soon other artists began to translate, produce, and later, emulate his plays.

SHAW   In England, George Bernard Shaw became one of Ibsen's most vocal and influential supporters. Unlike many realists, Shaw always retained his sense of humor; he almost always wrote comedies (e.g., *Major Barbara* [1905] and *Misalliance* [1910]), and their popularity did much to ensure the final acceptance of Realistic drama in England before the close of World War I.

CHEKHOV   Anton Chekhov scored his first success in 1898 when *The Seagull* was produced at the Moscow Art Theatre. Chekhov's plays differed from those of Ibsen and Shaw in their tendency toward poetic expression and symbolism. His manipulation of language, with measured pauses and artful repetitions, produced a sense of reality as well as music and allusion. In some ways, he foretold the Russian Revolution by depicting the isolation of the aristocracy and its inevitable extinction.

FIGURE 17.11

Anton Chekhov's *The Three Sisters*

In Chekhov's lifetime, the Moscow Art Theatre produced his plays realistically (see Figure 17.6). In this production by Virginia Commonwealth University, the setting is simplified with selected realistic properties.

NATURALISTIC PLAYWRIGHTS   In 1893, French novelist Émile Zola called for a theatre of "living characters taken from real life," who spoke everyday language and offered "a material reproduction of life"; he called for playwrights who scientifically analyzed and faithfully reported the social problems of the world with a view to their correction. In essence, Zola advocated Naturalism.

Among the most successful playwrights in the Naturalistic style were Gerhart Hauptmann and Maxim Gorky. Hauptmann's *The Weavers* (1892) uses a group protagonist to show the devastation that comes to already impoverished workers when industrialization threatens their way of life. Gorky's *The Lower Depths* (1902), by depicting the seemingly hopeless lives of people living in a flophouse, explores whether religion or political reform offers the best chance for change.

THIRD WAVE: AVANT-GARDISM, 1890–1950

Although the Realists were themselves innovators, another group reacted against them almost immediately. The split deepened as a trivialized Realism was taken over by the commercial theatre, and Art again dictated that serious people would revolt against both Realism and its commercial adaptation.

But what was wrong with Realism? In essence, the objections to it boiled down to three:

- Realism wasn't *theatrical*. The audience was shut out; a separate world existed beyond the fourth wall, with actors behaving as though the audience wasn't there. It was *too much* like life.
- Realism was dull: The language was mundane, the characters flat, and the action—if truly lifelike—boring.
- Realism had to struggle to be significant; if no more was at stake than the fate of one ordinary individual, what was the larger meaning?

These objections to Realism coalesced around a view that Realism was inimical to Art, a view that is one of the bases of the avant-garde ideas called "Modernism" in all the arts. (Significantly, major Realists didn't talk much about Art.) We know Modernism best in painting (Picasso, Cubism) and in literature (James Joyce), but it was also a force in the theatre, where it was believed that the theatre had to be "retheatricalized," that innovation itself was valuable, and that form or style was as important as content so long as both were *artistic*.

Many modernist attempts followed to retheatricalize the theatre. In one direction, they redefined theatrical space by throwing out the proscenium arch and the picture-frame stage; in another, they threw out the box set and detailed settings, replacing them with varying kinds of stylized or abstract scenery, including settings of ramps, stairs, and levels. Others tried to retheatricalize acting by throwing out "ensemble" and "inner truth" and going for a style that was bigger, more external, more physical and symbolic. None replaced Realism but several modified it.

Scenic Pioneers against Realism

Two major figures were influential in moving stage design away from realism: Adolphe Appia and Gordon Craig. Appia believed that artistic unity was the fundamental goal of theatrical production and that lighting was the element best able to fuse all others into an artistic whole. Like music, light was capable of continual change to reflect shifting moods and emotions within the play, and light could be orchestrated by variations in its direction, intensity, and color to produce a rhythm to match the dramatic action. Because he found an aesthetic contradiction between the three-dimensional actor and a two-dimensional floor set at right angles to two-dimensional painted scenes, Appia gave the stage floor and scenery mass. He solved the problem in part by devising three-dimensional settings composed of steps, ramps, and platforms, among which the living actor could comfortably move.

Like Appia, Craig opposed scenic illusion and favored instead a simple visual statement that eliminated inessential details and avoided photographic reproduction. His emphasis was on the manipulation of line and mass to achieve, first, a

Spotlight

Henrik Ibsen

Henrik Ibsen's *A Doll's House*, 1879

Ibsen (1808–1906) is often called the father of modern drama. He wrote more than two dozen plays in every major style of the nineteenth century—from romanticism to symbolism—but his realistic plays like *A Doll's House* are those most often produced today. When he turned exclusively to writing plays in his early forties, he was already an experienced company manager, stage manager, and director.

The Story of the Play

Nora Helmer is a married woman and a mother, but some of her behavior is childlike, and her husband Torvald, a priggish bank manager, treats her as a charming toy (and, implicitly, a sexual toy). When an old friend of Nora's, Mrs. Linde, comes to ask if Torvald can give her a job at the bank, Nora confesses that she is not so childish as she appears: She has "saved Torvald's life" by borrowing money when he was ill to send him to recuperate in Italy. Torvald does not know of the debt, which she has been repaying from her household money, so Torvald thinks she is a spendthrift, as well.

Her creditor is Krogstad, who works at Torvald's bank and is going to be fired; he demands that Nora intercede for him or he will reveal to Torvald not only her borrowing but also the fact that she forged her now-dead father's signature to the note.

Krogstad is fired; his job is to go to Mrs. Linde. He demands again that Nora help him get a better job at the bank; when she cannot, he leaves a letter for Torvald in the letterbox. Nora, recognizing that the truth must come out, believes that Torvald will stand by her, even share the blame; she tells Mrs. Linde that there will be a "miracle." Still, waiting for her husband to find the letter, she becomes more and more frantic and talks of suicide; she dances for her husband a tarentella that becomes wild, manic.

Krogstad and Mrs. Linde meet at Nora's and recognize each other—they are former lovers who now decide to reconcile. Krogstad says he will retrieve the letter, but Mrs. Linde tells him that "this unhappy secret must come out."

After a party, Nora tries to keep Torvald from the letter. Torvald is sexually aroused; he calls her his "most precious possession." He reads the letter and his mood changes: She has "ruined his happiness, threatened his future." They will have to go on living together "for public appearances," but she will not be allowed to raise his children. Nora's "miracle" does not happen.

The maid brings another letter. Torvald reads it and cries, "I am saved!" Krogstad has sent him the forged note to destroy and said he will keep silent.

Nora has become quieter and quieter. Now she sits her husband down at the table and, in a lengthy scene, explains how wronged she has been. "I have been your doll wife, Torvald." Finally, she leaves him and the children—coolly, calmly—telling him that her first duty is to herself. She goes out; Torvald cries out her name, then says that there is still hope—and there is the sound of the house's outer door slamming.

unity of design and, ultimately, a unity for the total production. Although Craig placed less emphasis on the importance of the actor and the text than Appia, they agreed on the importance of the visual elements of the production. Perhaps it would not be an injustice to designate Appia as the formulator of the theories that Craig later popularized. Appia and Craig influenced the new stagecraft and then commercial theatrical design.

Reactions against Realism: Four Important "-isms"

Impressionism (fl. 1890s) was a style that sought to capture fleeting moments of awareness that were believed to constitute the essence of existence. By reproducing these glimpses, art could provide insights into the truth that lay underneath the external world—the opposite of Realism. Probably the playwright who wrote most successfully in the style was Maurice Maeterlinck. In short plays like *The Intruder* (1890), Maeterlinck presented a world far removed from reality. Subjectivity permeates the plays, which are typically moody and mysterious, hinting at a life controlled by unseen and inexplicable forces. The actions seem hazy, distant, out of focus; indeed, in the theatre, the plays were often played behind gauzes (scrims) or clouds of fog, and they moved between patches of light, dark, and shadow.

Symbolism (fl. 1890s) was a style that believed that the truths of life could not be expressed directly but only in metaphorical and allusive manner. Symbolists endowed particular images or objects with figurative, not literal meaning. It can be difficult to clearly differentiate Symbolism from Impressionism. For example, Maeterlinck, identified as an Impressionist playwright, is also often called a Symbolist playwright. Nevertheless, some of Symbolism's techniques were adopted by Realists like Ibsen in his later plays, Chekhov, and Tennessee Williams.

Expressionism (fl. 1910–1930s) usually focused on political and social questions in a stage world close to nightmare. Plays unfolded in a world of bizarre and garish colors, jagged angles, and oddly proportioned objects. Actors moved in mechanical or puppetlike ways and often spoke in disconnected or telegraphic conversations. They bore names of types rather than people: The Mother, The Son, The Cipher. Conventional ideas of time and space collapsed. Expressionism in theatre and film shows a world as seen through the distorted perceptions of the main character, affected by anxiety or psychosis.

Expressionism has been influential for three reasons:

- Many of the techniques were adapted and used in film (*The Cabinet of Doctor Caligari*).
- Techniques were adapted by Realistic playwrights, notably Eugene O'Neill and Arthur Miller.
- It was an influence on "epic theatre."

Constructivism (fl. 1920–1935), the practice of Vsevolod Meyerhold, paralleled that of the German Expressionists. Although early in his career Meyerhold directed experimental works for Stanislavski, during the 1920s he

FIGURE 17.12

The Metamorphosis

If Symbolism resembled a dream, Expressionism resembled a nightmare. Here, an adaptation of Franz Kafka's short story *The Metamorphosis*, staged by Butler University Theatre. The distortion of a nightmare is clearly expressed though lighting and set. The set seems both constructivist and expressionist.

devoted himself to developing a theatrical art suitable for a machine age. He relied on two major techniques: biomechanics and constructivism. Biomechanics was a training system and performance style for actors based on an industrial theory of work: They were to be well-trained "machines" for carrying out the assignments given them, and so they needed rigorous physical training in ballet, gymnastics, and circus techniques. Constructivism was a theory of visual art in which scenery did not attempt to represent any particular place but provided a "machine" on which actors could perform. In practice, sets designed for Meyerhold were combinations of platforms, steps, ramps, wheels, and trapezes. A goal of both biomechanics and Constructivism was to retheatricalize the theatre.

Brecht and Artaud

Although these styles (-*isms*) have influenced today's theatre, the theories and practices of Bertolt Brecht and Antonin Artaud have probably been more influential. These two theorists operated from quite different sets of assumptions about the nature of theatre and the purpose of art, but they shared a disdain for Realism. Together, their theories can help account for much theatrical experimentation of the 1960s and 1970s.

BRECHT AND EPIC THEATRE   Bertolt Brecht believed that theatre should educate *citizens* (participants in a political system) in how to bring about socially responsible change. He saw theatre as a way of making a controversial topic easier to consider.

Traditional German theatres, whether those of Wagner or Saxe-Meiningen, had sought an illusion that allowed the members of the audience to believe in and identify with the onstage actions. Because Brecht was a Marxist and viewed theatre as an instrument for change, he objected to a theatre that mesmerized its audiences and made them passive. He therefore tried to redefine the relationship between the theatre, its audience, and society. He proposed that if he jarred audiences out of their identification with the action, he would succeed in forcing them to think about what they saw onstage. Brecht sought, therefore, alternately to engage and estrange his audiences, a technique he called *Verfremdungseffekt* (usually translated as the alienation effect (or A-effect).

The complex of staging and playwriting used by Brecht came to be called epic theatre. *Epic* captured many of the qualities that Brecht prized: the mixing of narrative and dramatic episodes, the telescoping of time and place, and the spanning of years and countries (similar to epic poetry).

Although Brecht was not the first to use either these techniques or the term *epic*, Brecht popularized the term and the practices through his own plays, his theoretical writings (particularly the "Little Organon for the Theatre," 1948), and his productions at the Berliner Ensemble, after 1954 East Germany's most prestigious theatre.

ARTAUD AND THE THEATRE OF CRUELTY   Although Antonin Artaud was an actor, director, playwright, poet, and screenwriter, it was as a theorist that he made his greatest impact. *The Theatre and Its Double*, a compilation of Artaud's major essays, was published in France in 1938 but was not translated into English until the late 1950s. Because Artaud believed that important ideas came not from logical reasoning or rational thinking but from intuition, experience, and feelings, he developed his ideas through images and visual metaphors rather than language.

Artaud rejected the primacy of language. He wanted to remove the script from the center of his theatre because he believed that words and grammar were insufficient carriers of meaning. Truth came instead from spiritual signs whose meaning emerged intuitively and "with enough violence to make useless any translation into logical discursive language." Artaud wished to substitute gestures, signs, symbols, rhythms, and sounds. For Artaud, theatre was intuitive, primitive, magical, and potentially powerful.

FIGURE 17.13

Constructivism

In 1930, Vsevolod Meyerhold staged *The Bathhouse*, a play that ridiculed Soviet bureaucracy, at his theatre in Moscow. This constructivist setting is clearly antirealistic and nonrepresentational. One critic described Meyerhold's settings as "machines for acting."

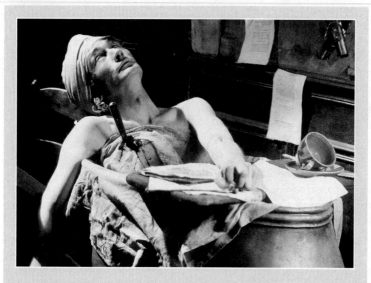

FIGURE 17.14

Antonin Artaud

Artaud was a stage and film actor, theatre director, and a theorist. He can be seen today in two silent films: *Napoleon,* 1927 and *The Passion of Joan of Arc,* 1928. Here, from the former film, Artaud depicts Jean-Paul Marat after he has been stabbed in a bathtub.

Artaud called for a theatre of cruelty. To achieve it, he developed a number of techniques seldom used in commercial productions. He wanted to bombard the senses and so experimented with ways of manipulating light and sound. In both, he adopted the abrupt, the discordant, the sudden, the shrill, and the garish. Lights changed colors quickly and alternated intensity violently; sound was sudden and often amplified. Scenery was subservient to the other elements of production, with the audience placed in an environment created by actors, lights, sound, and space (Artaud preferred barns and factories to conventional theatres). The actors were encouraged to use their bodies and their voices to provide scenery, sounds, and visual effects and not to be bound by notions of psychological realism and character analysis. Actors were to address the senses of the spectators, not merely their minds.

Artaud's theories, in many forms and with many distortions, were appropriated and applied after 1960 by theatre artists, moviemakers, and especially rock musicians. Whatever one may think of his pronouncements, it is clear that, although long in coming, their exploitation has been widespread.

AVANT-GARDE THEATRES AND MOVEMENTS

The Art Theatre Movement

Reactions to realism and to commercial theatre came in the form of new kinds of theatres as well as the new kinds of theories and plays just discussed. Just as the realists had started the first "independent" theatres, reactions against those theatres brought about a proliferation of "art" theatres, soon followed by other radical or "experimental" or "little" theatres into the 1960s. Taken as a group, they can be called the avant-garde of the early twentieth century.

The art theatre movement was an after-the-fact term for this mixed bag, which included these theatres as well as others as different as the Abbey in Dublin, Ireland. The "art" of the art theatres was still partly romantic but existed against the background of a changed culture, that of turn-of-the-century

Europe—imperialist, stuffy, class-conscious, money-conscious. It foregrounded a somewhat superficial, sometimes glib, sentimentalized belief in the power of beauty to improve life. That belief was mostly elitist, as were the art theatres.

The art theatre came a bit late to the United States. When it did, it was bound up culturally with several other fashions: the civic pageant, which was also genteel and "artistic"; the first programs in "theatre arts" at colleges and universities; and the New Stagecraft.

The New Stagecraft was an avant-garde tendency in stage design that favored simplified, sometimes abstract settings; nonrealism; lighting as a major design component; and alternatives to the proscenium

FIGURE 17.15

Bertolt Brecht

Although the title in English is often rendered as *The Good Woman of Setzuan*, Brecht's German title is less gender specific: *The Good Person of Setzuan*. The play centers around a woman who tries to do good but can't succeed because of the graft and corruption that surrounds her.

stage. European in origin and based heavily on the ideas of Appia and Craig, it surfaced in the United States when Sam Hume (a designer who had been working at the Moscow Art Theatre) organized a New Stagecraft exhibition in Boston and New York in 1914–1915. It was, in fact, the future: Designers such as Norman Bel Geddes, Robert Edmond Jones, and Lee Simonson made the New Stagecraft dominant in US design by 1930.

The first US art theatres arrived more or less with the New Stagecraft; that they soon became known as "little" theatres was significant (i.e., they attracted small audiences). The Abbey Theatre's US tour of 1911 seems to have inspired them: The Chicago Little Theatre began in 1912, the Boston Toy Theatre and the Wisconsin Dramatic Society about the same time, and by 1925 there were little theatres "in barns, barrooms, churches, studios and other odds and ends of civilized building, all the way from Maine to California, from crowded sophisticated Greenwich Village to the open spaces of Vancouver" as an early historian of the art theatre declared. Amateur, artistic, and mostly elitist, their most famous example was the Provincetown Players, which had started in a shack in the art colony at Provincetown, Massachusetts, in the summer and moved to New York's Greenwich Village in 1915. The Provincetown Players staged the early plays of Eugene O'Neill and included people as diverse as journalist John Reed and poet Edna St. Vincent Millay; people from it later helped found the Theatre Guild.

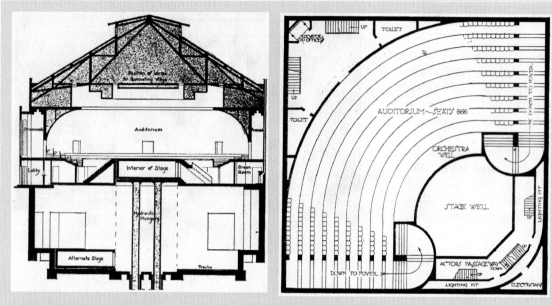

FIGURE 17.16

New Spaces for a New Theatre

Leaders of the new stagecraft were looking to free US theatre from the realistic, picture-frame staging of the proscenium arch. Norman Bel Geddes here proposed an arena space (*left*), shown in side view with a full-stage elevator that allowed the entire set to be lowered to the basement for scene shifts. Thrust stages (*right*), lacking a proscenium arch, placed spectators on three sides of the stage, which jutted out into the audience area.

The little theatre became a movement and an influence because they quickly had a voice: Their organ was *Theatre Arts Magazine*, which gave national distribution to their ideas. It described individual theatres and kept readers up on what was going on in Europe and at home. By 1930, however, *Theatre Arts* was turning toward the New York–based commercial theatre for its copy. The little theatres still existed, but many had used up their enthusiasm for art and had become community theatres. Art and Beauty had not proved potent at either paying the bills or solving social problems, and no wonder: They were ideas from before the Great War—only later called World War I—and the cynicism and striving of the 1920s was not congenial to them. The Great Depression and the rise of fascism in Europe finished Art and Beauty as ideas with power, not least because those ideas were associated with German culture.

The fading of *Theatre Arts Magazine* marked the death of the little theatre movement but not of avant-gardism in the United States. Much of the same energy went into leftist theatre in the 1930s. The avant-garde appeared again in theatre after World War II in new forms.

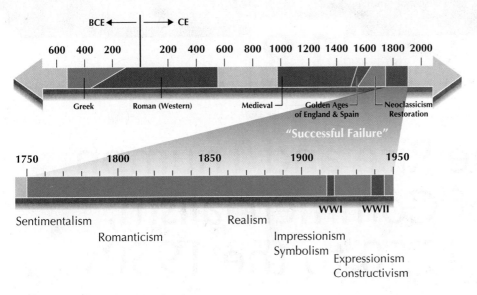

Greek
Roman (Western)
Medieval —
Golden Ages —
of England & Spain
Neoclassicism
Restoration

"Successful Failure"

1750   1800   1850   1900   1950

WWI   WWII

Sentimentalism
Romanticism
Realism
Impressionism
Symbolism
Expressionism
Constructivism

FIGURE 17.17

Timeline—The "*-isms*"

Romanticism flourished in the early 1800s, giving way to realism by the late 1800s.
Thereafter came a flurry of other "-isms," each striving to reposition theatre in its culture.

KEY TERMS

Check your understanding against this list. Brief definitions are included in the Glossary;
persons are page-referenced in the Index.

alienation effect (or
   A-effect)   277
art theatre movement   278
avant-garde   256
biomechanics   276
box set   264
closet drama   263
Constructivism   275
continental seating   263
epic theatre   277

Expressionism   275
fourth wall   269
gesamtkunstwerk (master
   artwork)   275
Impressionism   275
independent theatre
   movement   270
little theatre
   movement   280
Naturalism   266

New Stagecraft   279
Realism   264
Romanticism   258
Sturm und Drang (storm
   and stress)   261
Symbolism   275
theatre of cruelty   278

18

The Rise and Triumph of Commercialism, c. 1750 to the 1950s

The Walnut Street Theatre in Philadelphia opened in 1809.

OBJECTIVES

When you have completed this chapter, you should be able to:

- Describe the ways in which theatre business reflected changing business practices outside theatre.

- List and explain the major traits of melodrama.

- Compare romantic and realistic melodrama.

- Name some major writers of serious and comic drama from the mid-eighteenth to the mid-twentieth centuries.

- Describe the changing theatre buildings and scenic practices during the period.

- Trace the major lighting changes during these years.

20

Eclectic Theatre, c. 1950–c. 2000

Euripides's tragedy, *The Trojan Women*, is given an eclectic production at Theatre South Carolina.

OBJECTIVES

When you have completed this chapter, you should be able to:

- Discuss how modernism and postmodernism differ.

- Discuss the history of commercial and not-for-profit theatre of this period.

- Identify and discuss the principal noncommercial trends of this period.

- Identify and discuss three political theatre movements of this period.

- Define and discuss Absurdism.

- Identify and discuss two avant-garde theatres of this period.

CONTEXT

A false and short-lived sense of stability came to the United States after World War II, bringing with it a brief focus on what at the time was called conformity. That idea of stability, so essential to the nineteenth century, had become the victim of two upheavals—one, World War II itself and its effects; the other, changes in science, technology, and mass communications. These affected even the ideas of art, bringing an end to modernism and initiating so-called postmodernism.

Societal Changes

Thousands of US soldiers, most overseas for the first time, brought back new ideas and expectations from World War II. The GI Bill allowed thousands of (mostly) men to enter college for the first time. Thousands of black soldiers returned to the United States changed by their experience because they had lived and fought in a Europe where Jim Crow laws did not exist. US women who had worked in factories and offices during the war and who had experienced financial and social independence could see for themselves the possibilities of lives beyond the suburban front door.

Technological Changes

Television, computers, and the Internet brought other revolutions. By the late 1950s, television sets were becoming commonplace in US homes and became a binding social force as households watched favorite programs on three major networks.

By the 1970s, the common coin was not Shakespeare and the Bible and the European canon, but television and advertising and rock 'n' roll and then hip-hop. Art, the secular religion that was once going to save humanity, lost all definition and crumbled into pop artist Andy Warhol's 1960s declaration, "Art is whatever you can get away with."

Personal computers appeared in the 1970s and were essential by the late 1990s. The Internet, widely accessible by the early 1990s, changed the ways and the speed with which people got news, music, personal messages, and entertainment, making it possible for everybody to be in touch from home, from a car, from the street. The results have been, first,

FIGURE 20.1

Theatre Spaces

The Arena Stage in Washington, D.C., founded in 1950, became one of the most respected regional theatres in the United States. In 2010, its two existing theatres and well as a new stage were enclosed in a large eclectically-shaped glass cover providing much needed lobby and administrative space.

self-definition by ethnic, political, religious, sexual, and social groups whose members had before not been able to find one another; and, second, a shift from "engagement" or direct individual experience to observation—virtual experience.

Changes in Worldview

Postmodernism is an ill-defined term for another set of changes that accelerated beginning in the 1950s. The assumptions underlying postmodernism include:

- doubt of the concepts of objectivity and truth.
- doubt of the concept of absolute meaning.
- belief in bottom-up participation rather than top-down dictation.
- belief in differences and shades of meaning rather than black/white opposites.
- suspicion of ideas of progress, objectivity, reason, certainty, and personal identity.
- belief in a "truth" shaped by cultural bias, myth, metaphor, and political content.

Some postmodern art came to be characterized by parody, satire, self-reference, irony, and wit. Other postmodern works emphasized the impossibility of communication or political or social improvement—a general nihilism.

Postmodern plays, as they evolved after the 1960s, were often not unified in tone, time, or style. Instead of linear actions organized by psychology and causality, postmodern theatre created unity through image, allusion, and metaphor; it appropriated the images and stories of popular culture and used them in subversive ways.

FIGURE 20.2

Plays Develop over Time

The two parts of *Angels in America: A Gay Fantasia on National Themes* won the Pulitzer Prize in 1993. Tony Kushner developed *Angels* in productions at four not-for-profit theatres including the Royal National Theatre in London. During those early productions Kushner sharpened and shortened the play. Here, a production at Ball State University. Kushner is very much a postmodernist.

Theatrical Changes

Given the stunning changes following World War II in society and worldview, science, and technology, it was inevitable that changes in art and in theatre would emerge. And, in fact, the older practices that had held theatre practice together grew weaker because theater was under assault by many new alternatives. Thus, if anything can be said to characterize the theatre (both commercial and noncommercial) from about 1950 to about 2000, it has been its eclecticism—its exploitation of the trappings of many styles and practices. The theatre buildings of the period were variously shaped and located. Theatrical productions were variously conceived, with wildly different styles. Plays were of mixed forms, mixed media, and mixed theories.

Several of the theatrical venues that we take for granted today became widespread during the years after World War II.

- Dinner theatres, established in the early 1950s, had their heyday in the 1970s and were in decline by the mid-1980s.
- Community theatres continued to increase in number and importance.
- Off-Off Broadway emerged in New York in the late 1950s as a "complete rejection of commercial theatre" and was housed in small spaces like coffee houses, church basements, and warehouses.
- Educational theatres developed and multiplied as veterans returning from World War II flooded to college campuses, multiplying their enrollments. It was during these boom years that most colleges established their own theatre departments, with graduate and undergraduate degrees in theatre.
- With theatre departments and degrees came active producing programs on campus, a trend that quickly trickled down to high schools and primary grades and established educational theatre as a major production venue in the United States.

Most important of all was Off-Broadway, usually dated from 1952, when Tennessee Williams's *Summer and Smoke* appeared there—the first major hit in thirty years in a theatre below Forty-second Street in Manhattan. From then through the 1960s, Off-Broadway served as a showcase for new talent and "experimental" plays. By century's end, however, Off-Broadway had moved toward commercialism and eclipsed Broadway in the number and quality of nonmusical plays.

Although much of US and European theatre after 1950 continued to be commercial (the "mainstream"), there was also a strong avant-garde movement through the early years of the period, and growing numbers of not-for-profit professional theatres appeared across the United States and Canada. The avant-garde groups remained vital for a while, many getting new life from resistance to the Vietnam War. However, they did not become the mainstream any more than the avant-garde of 1890–1900 had done, although they influenced the mainstream importantly.

After the 1950s, the center of US culture moved away from the theatre and toward pop culture, especially music and television. Much of theatre persisted as a moderately successful kind of commerce. It had offshoots in other activities, but, by the new millennium, it had little that was truly avant-garde.

AVANT-GARDE THEATRE

The 1950s introduced the most recent *-ism* to the theatre: absurdism. Plays called "absurdist" by critics (not by their authors) appeared just after World War II in Europe, when several new playwrights were so grouped together by critics. *Absurd* meant not "ridiculous" but "without meaning." Absurdists abandoned story and dramatic unity based on causality. The plays were often constructed as a circle (ending just where they had begun, after displaying a series of unrelated incidents) or as the intensification of a single event, sometimes ending just where they had begun. Usually, the puzzling quality of the plays came from the devaluation of language as a carrier of meaning: In the plays, what *happened* on stage often transcended and contradicted what was *said* there. Absurdists included Samuel Beckett (*Waiting for Godot*), Eugene Ionesco, Edward Albee, and Arthur Kopit; they influenced later playwrights like Harold Pinter.

The 1950s and 1960s also saw a powerful counterculture that persisted into the 1980s. Partly the product of the Vietnam War, partly the product of political leftism, it challenged established values. This counterculture expressed itself in theatre through a new wave of avant-gardism that began Off-Off-Broadway and in other tiny New York theatres but quickly decentralized.

Early during this period, street theatre and guerilla theatre were names given to political performances that went to the audience, the first into the streets, the second in hit-and-run "guerilla" raids on nontheatrical spaces wherever people could be found (e.g., elevators, department stores). Big in the 1960s, these two were soon replaced by other sorts of political theatre, each tied to a major social

Joan Marcus

FIGURE 20.3

Postmodern Theatre

Waiting for Godot, by Samuel Beckett, here in a production by the not-for profit Roundabout Theatre Company in New York, was first called an "absurdist play" by many critics in the 1960s. On stage for this revival are, from left, John Glover, Bill Irwin, Nathan Lane, and John Goodman.

movement: black theatre, tied to the Black Power movement; women's theatre, tied to the feminist movement; and gay and lesbian theatre, tied to the gay rights movement. Although these shared many basic assumptions, they differed in several ways.

The trajectory of this avant-garde movement can be suggested by briefly tracking the history of one of its most important organizations, the Living Theatre.

The Movement in Miniature: The Living Theatre

The Living Theatre, founded in 1947 by Julian Beck and Judith Malina, started as an art theatre in New York. The last of the modernist theatres, it looked back toward the previous avant-garde in Europe and did plays by such Europeans as Luigi Pirandello and Bertolt Brecht. In the late 1950s, however, the group shifted toward new US works such as *The Connection*, a realistic look at the (then) little-known drug culture, and *The Brig*, a harsh treatment of military prison. By the late 1960s, following a European tour, it became a political theatre, reorganizing into a commune to promote a revolution through "benevolent anarchy." With a change in goals came a change in its approach to theatre. It quickly became famous for the direct participation of the audience, for performances that turned into protest marches, and for such shock tactics as nudity and obscenity. It had moved from modernism to postmodernism.

Probably its most famous production during this period was *Paradise Now*, which began with actors milling about the audience. Throughout the four or more hours of performance, actors verbally abused any spectators who seemed apathetic or hostile, shouting slogans and obscenities at them. Such confrontations, sometimes in the nude, were common in performance, and often, at the play's end, the group urged spectators to join it in taking the revolution out of the theatre and into the streets. When the performers did so, they were occasionally arrested and charged with things like disturbing the peace, indecent exposure, and interfering with law enforcement.

Following another overseas tour, the group returned to the United States in the 1970s. With radicalism on the decline (from the drawdown of the Vietnam War and the muting of civil rights agitation), the Living Theatre entered a new phase, splitting itself into four "cells," each in a different city and each with a different emphasis: politics, the environment, the culture, and the spirit. Although the group remained active, by the 1980s its influence on US theatre and culture had abated, the victim of waning interest in revolution, to be replaced by other groups whose concerns were more fashionable.

The Living Theatre, then, tracked the major shifts of the US avant-garde, from its early roots in European practice, through a period of revolutionary politics, into expanding interests and locations, and finally into self-induced disappearance. It continued into the new millennium but almost invisibly. Its importance lies in its aftereffects and in the energy and innovativeness of its two founders. The Living Theatre embodied both major strands of twentieth-century US avant-gardism—politics and art.

Spotlight

Ella Bromblin

Here, *Gem of the Ocean* at Tisch Graduate School of the Arts in New York City.

August Wilson: A Century of African American Life

August Wilson set out to write a ten-play series devoted to the black experience, with one play set in each decade of the twentieth century. Collectively known as the *Pittsburgh Cycle*, named for the city where nine of the plays are set, the plays were produced in New York after development in not-for-profit theatres. The pattern of three or more regional productions allowed Wilson to hone the dramas for Broadway and Off-Broadway.

The first, *Ma Rainey's Black Bottom*, appeared in 1985, the last, *Radio Golf*, in 2005. Within those twenty years, Wilson became one of the most important playwrights of his generation. His plays stand as a landmark in the history of black culture, US literature, and Broadway theatre. Perhaps the

most honored playwright in the past quarter century, Wilson was awarded two Tony Awards, seven New York Drama Critics Circle Awards, a Pulitzer Prize, and the Olivier Award (the British equivalent of the Tony), among many other prestigious awards.

The plays, and the decade which they characterize are: *Gem of the Ocean* (1900s), *Joe Turner's Come and Gone* (1910s), *Ma Rainey's Black Bottom* (1920s), *The Piano Lesson* (1930s), *Seven Guitars* (1940s), *Fences* (1950s), *Two Trains Running* (1960s), *Jitney* (1970s), *King Hedley II* (1980s), and *Radio Golf* (1990s). They were not written or produced in this order, however.

These plays are connected by several shared traits. All but one play is set in the black neighborhood of Pittsburgh's Hill District; characters from one play occasionally appear in others; the characters usually speak in the street dialect of the Hill, but Wilson manages to make the dialogue sound poetic and even musical; most are focused more on character than plot; and supernatural elements abound. The guiding spirit of the cycle seems to be Aunt Esther, a woman said to have lived for more than three centuries.

Quite soon after his death in 2005, a Broadway theatre was renamed in his honor—the August Wilson Theatre.

Theatre of Underrepresented Peoples

The innovators in the United States after World War II were partly like the older ones—that is, they were committed to reforming the art of theatre—but different in that some were overtly political. Political here, however, must be taken in a large sense because it included not only the politics of the anti-Vietnam War movement but also the emergence of groups that had until then been unidentified or invisible—African Americans, Asian Americans, Latinos, women, and homosexuals.

Black Theatre.   Although African American performers in the United States date from well before the Civil War, and African American theatre companies were firmly established within African American communities well before World War II; they were mostly unknown in mainstream theatre where African Americans were often played by whites in blackface.

Two important plays seen by both white and black audiences shortly after World War II, however, heralded a change. In 1959, Lorraine Hansberry's *A Raisin in the Sun* was produced on Broadway. This study of African American family life, in which the tensions between women and men were sympathetically and sensitively dramatized, won the Drama Critics Circle Award. The same year, French playwright Jean Genet's *The Blacks* was produced Off-Broadway; it reversed the traditions of the minstrel show and used African American actors in whiteface to reveal abuses of white power. Although many African Americans rejected the play's thesis—that blacks will come to power only by adopting the tactics of their white oppressors—few failed to realize that the play represented a turning point in the theatrical portrayal of black people. Note that Hansberry was American, black, female, and wrote a realistic play. Gide was white, French, and wrote a play many would now consider postmodern.

Revolutionary black theatre grew out of the racial turmoil of the 1950s and 1960s, when blacks turned in large numbers to the arts as a way of demanding change and repairing their ruptured society: The black theatre movement dates from 1964 and the Off-Broadway production of LeRoi Jones's *The Toilet* and *Dutchman*, both of which presented chilling pictures of racial barriers, human hatred, and the suffering that results from racism. Thereafter, the stereotypical stage negro was increasingly replaced by more honest, if sometimes less loveable, black characters. Throughout the 1960s and early 1970s, Jones (now self-renamed Imamu Amiri Baraka) remained the most militant and best-known black playwright.

By the mid-1970s, African American authors could criticize their own community. Ntozake Shange's *For Colored Girls Who Have Considered Suicide/When the Rainbow is Enuf* (1976) explored the double oppression of being black and female. It was an unflattering portrait of some black men as brutalizing black women

FIGURE 20.4

Black, Feminist Theatre.

Playwright Ntozake Shange's *For Colored Girls* began as a choreopoem—Shange's name for a series of monologues with movement—in California. It moved to Broadway but remained controversial within the black community because of its negative portrayal of black men. Here, *For Colored Girls* at the University of Missouri at Columbia.

as they themselves had been brutalized by whites. Originally staged in an African American theatre, this powerful "choreopoem" (a postmodern form) eventually moved to Broadway, where it earned a Tony Award.

With the gradual improvement in the position of black people and the increasing conservativism sweeping the United States by the mid-1980s, the energy of the black revolutionary theatre subsided. Although some African American theatres and revolutionary playwrights and criticism persisted, black playwrights increasingly moved into mainstream theatres. One important example of this assimilation is the late playwright August Wilson.

Women's Theatre.   Whereas black theatre and drama arose from the social upheavals of the late 1950s and 1960s, women's theatre was a phenomenon of the 1970s. Increasing numbers of people, mostly female, banded together into theatrical units that aimed to promote the goals of feminism, the careers of women artists, or both. By the mid-1970s, more than forty such groups were flourishing; by 1980, more than a hundred had formed. Unlike black theatres, which were usually found in high concentrations of blacks in cities, women's theatres sprang up in places as diverse as New York City; Missoula, Montana; and Greenville, South Carolina.

The theatres ranged in size from those depending on one or two unpaid and inexperienced volunteers to organizations of professionals numbering in the hundreds. Budgets, too, varied widely, with some groups existing on a shoestring and the good wishes of friends, and others displaying a financial statement in the hundreds of thousands of dollars. Organization, repertory, working methods, and artistic excellence were highly diversified, but the groups all shared the conviction that women had been subjected to unfair discrimination based on their gender and that theatre could serve in some way to correct the resulting inequities.

FIGURE 20.5
Commercial Women's Theatre

Uncommon Women and Others (1977) by Wendy Wasserstein in a production at the University of Michigan. The play, Wasserstein's thesis production at the Yale School of Drama, drew on her undergraduate experiences at Mount Holyoke College. Her career spanned four decades. She died in 2006.

Pete Smith

Two techniques in particular came to be associated with revolutionary women's theatres: a preference for collective or communal organization and the use of improvised performance material, much of it uncommonly personal.

By 1990, however, leading feminist playwrights had moved to other matters, and women's theatres were in flux. Although hundreds of feminist plays were written, none became widely known. Their influence, however, is visible in commercial works such as Wendy Wasserstein's *Uncommon Women and Others*; Marsha Norman's *Getting Out*, and Beth Henley's *Crimes of the Heart*.

Gay and Lesbian Theatre. Many US cities had had self-aware gay and lesbian communities long before the 1960s, but these were largely covert or "in the closet." Homosexual acts were illegal in most of the United States; public homosexual conduct, even language, was sometimes punishable under laws against indecency and obscenity. Therefore, plays about homosexuality usually fell under the heading of prohibited speech. This situation changed in the 1960s, however, because court rulings extended free speech and concepts of privacy.

In 1968, Mart Crowley's *The Boys in the Band* was produced Off-Broadway and became the first homosexual hit comedy in a mainstream venue. Sympathetic to the lives and problems of gay men, Crowley's play made a place in commercial theatre for plays in which homosexuality was acceptable and nonthreatening—and funny. Self-deprecating and sometimes self-destructive wit positioned homosexuals as victims, however, and thus ran the risk of sentimentality.

Gay and lesbian theatre is usually dated from 1976, when John Glines opened his theatre in New York City. The Glines theatre was dedicated to producing plays by and about gay people, including lesbians. Specifically lesbian theatres surfaced in the 1980s (e.g., Split Britches in New York City). Also by the 1980s, sympathetic gay plays grew common in mainstream theatre, the more so when the AIDS epidemic became national news, and "AIDS plays" became a subgenre (e.g., *As Is*, 1984).

In gay and lesbian theatre, coherent theoretical bases were elusive because of real problems of definition. What is a gay play—a play about gay men? By a gay man? Does a play by a gay or lesbian author but with a different subject fit? Is a negative play about gay men a gay play? What of those plays of the past by homosexual authors (e.g., Oscar Wilde, Tennessee Williams) that have no ostensibly homosexual content? Partly to deal with such theoretical problems, the idea of queer theatre and queer studies evolved, where *queer* is both an umbrella and a political term, a weapon

FIGURE 20.6

Gay Theatre

Martin Sherman's *Bent* (1976) focuses on the purge of gays in Nazi Germany in 1934. The slang word *bent*, used in some European countries, refers to homosexuals; gays are not "straight," so they're "bent." Here, a production at Frostburg University, Maryland.

seized from "the enemy" and turned around. Queer theatre announces itself (i.e., it does not speak in code) and has pride in itself (i.e., it is not apologetic).

ARTISTIC AVANT-GARDE THEATRE   Unlike political theatres, which sought to change society, some avant-garde theatres strove to change the art of the theatre. Such groups wanted to explore—either alone or in some combination—the nature of theatre, its relation to other kinds of performance and media, its arrangements for production, and the role of both script and audience in a performance. Probably closer to the previous European avant-garde than to the political theatres in their goals, these artistic theatres nonetheless differed profoundly from both the previous art theatres and the political theatres contemporary with them. (The Living Theatre began as artistic, but quickly moved to become political.)

Joseph Chaikin and the Open Theatre.   Among the most influential of such theatres was that of Joseph Chaikin, who proposed an "open" theatre to distinguish it from the "closed" (rigid, text-bound, uncreative) theatres of Broadway. Believing that most theatres were overwhelmed by nonessentials, Chaikin sought a performance in which the primary focus was on the actor and groups of artists working together.

Thus, ensemble became the cornerstone of the Open Theatre, and actors were trained to work as a group rather than as individuals. To accomplish such an ensemble, Chaikin used a variety of theatre games and improvisations designed to develop sensitivity to group rhythms and dynamics, to increase mutual trust, and to replace competition for the audience's attention with cooperation among the group. The playwright, too, was considered a member of the ensemble and was encouraged to develop texts for the group out of the ideas of the group. Typically the writer would provide a scenario, an outline of the situation, and the group would improvise dialogue and action. The improvisations would be repeated several times, and the writer would select the best of them, add new materials as needed, rearrange sections, and finally develop "the text."

Although the plays varied enormously, they tended to share some combination of these characteristics:

- A unity achieved through exploring a central idea or theme (rather than a story).
- A rather free and often disconnected treatment of time and place.
- The use of *transformations*, a technique in which actors played first one character and then another without corresponding changes in costumes or makeup and without clear transitions provided by dialogue.
- A reliance on actors to provide their own environment by "becoming" the setting and sounds. (For example, an actor plays a sheep in a field, another a snake on a tree; several become ambulance sirens.)

Although the Open Theatre existed for only ten years (1963–1973), its influence was lasting and profound. It focused attention on the centrality of the actor in performance; it demonstrated the willingness of audiences to substitute their imaginations for the usual setting, lights, and costumes; it popularized theatre games and improvisation as tools for training actors and as a source for group-inspired plays; and it showed that the usual theatrical hierarchy (a director leading a team of theatre specialists) was not the only way to organize theatrical production. Its techniques and theories are now part of the theatrical mainstream.

The Influence of the Avant-Garde

The political avant-garde remained vital only as long as political and social uneasiness were high. In the 1980s, however, the United States got over the most extreme divisions of Vietnam and became an apparently more optimistic and less-questioning place: Quick wars in Grenada and Panama and the first Iraq invasion were generally popular; society seemed not to want to probe or protest anymore. Material comfort became supremely important. Political avant-gardism became like kicking a pillow. By the late 1980s, theorists were proclaiming avant-gardism dead.

Avant-gardism may have dwindled not only because a historical shift undercut its political strength, but also because postmodernism's redefinitions of art undercut its aesthetic strengths. Avant-gardism, as well, was primarily reactive, and by the mid-1980s there was little to react against. By the 1990s, the decade of e-commerce and big money, only local vestiges remained.

Nevertheless, several practices pioneered by the avant-garde of the 1960s and 1970s appeared, if modified, in the commercial theatre, which

- displayed greater freedom of language, dress, and subject; nudity and profanity were readily accepted, and previously taboo subjects were now freely treated—for example, *Torch Song Trilogy* (1983, homosexuality), *'Night, Mother* (1983, suicide), *As Is* (1985, AIDS), and *Love! Valour! Compassion!* (1994, gay life in the age of AIDS).
- awarded prizes to plays by African American authors—*A Soldier's Play* by Charles Fuller (Pulitzer, 1982); *The Piano Lesson* (Pulitzer, 1990) and *Fences* (Tony Award for Best Play, 1987), both by August Wilson.
- awarded prizes to plays by female and Hispanic playwrights in larger numbers than before—*Crimes of the Heart* by Beth Henley (Pulitzer Prize for drama, 1981), *Baltimore Waltz* (1992) and *How I Learned to Drive* (Pulitzer, 1997) by Paula Vogel; Margaret Edson, *Wit* (Pulitzer, 1999); and Edwardo Ivan Lopez, *Spanish Eyes* (1990).
- produced plays by authors who openly acknowledged their homosexuality including the outstanding serious drama of the 1990s, *Angels in America*, by Tony Kushner, which won prestigious prizes in both 1993 and 1994. The play's principal subjects were homosexual life, only recently real to most Americans; AIDS, an epidemic little more than a decade old when the play was written; love and personal loyalty; and, through the real historical figure Roy Cohn, political and moral corruption. The play also established Kushner, long well known in gay theatre, firmly in the mainstream commercial theatre.

PROFESSIONAL THEATRE

Whereas most avant-garde theatres operated on modest budgets, the professional theatre was marked by its relatively large budgets and by artists who made their living in the theatre. Professional theatres comprised not only the commercial theatres, which existed to make a profit, but also a growing number of not-for-profit theatres.

New York City remained the center of US professional theatre by virtue of the sheer number and scale of productions staged there each year. Between 1950 and 2000, New York was the home of Broadway's about forty theatres, Off-Broadway's approximately seventy-eight spaces, and the myriad small "studio" venues. What these spaces shared was their "professional" status—that is, they were covered by union contracts that guaranteed that the performers and other theatre workers were paid contracted-for amounts and thus were professional.

By 2000, professional productions included those in most Broadway and off-Broadway theatres; touring productions ("the road"); and productions staged in Las Vegas, Los Angeles, Chicago, Atlanta, and other large cities.

There were many more not-for-profit professional theatres than commercial ones. The distinction between the two types of organizations was one of tax status. Each commercial production was a fully taxed, one-time venture, whereas not-for-profits were ongoing ventures that received tax incentives to encourage supporters to give them charitable contributions.

Early on, it was typical for plays established on Broadway to be produced later in regional not-for-profit theatres. After the late 1960s, there emerged a different synergy between the commercial theatre and the not-for-profit theatre, with entire productions transferred from a not-for-profit to a commercial Broadway run. This trend of transferring not-for-profit productions to Broadway began with Washington, D.C.'s Arena Stage, when its production of *The Great White Hope* moved to Broadway in 1967. It won a Tony Award, the New York Drama Critics Award, and the Pulitzer Prize for drama. By 2000, a connection between not-for-profit productions from around the country and the Broadway stage was commonplace, a relationship where new material often originated in the not-for-profit theatre and, if deemed potentially commercial, moved to the Broadway stage.

Commercial Theatre

BROADWAY   Except for a slump in attendance in the late 1980s, attendance at Broadway trended upward throughout the period, but the number of new productions was significantly lower: about 55 openings in 1950 and 1960, but only 31 in 1998 (compared with 88 in 1900 and 235 in 1930). Throughout the period, too, costs of production continued to rise: In 1964, the original production of the musical *Fiddler on the Roof* cost $380,000, but its revival in 1976 cost almost double that. The musical *Rent* opened in 1994 at an estimated cost of $10 million.

As production costs rose, long runs and higher ticket prices became more important. One theatre businessman estimated that a play that took ten weeks to break even in 1956 would have taken twenty weeks by the mid-1970s, and that a musical that took fifteen to twenty weeks to break even in 1956 would have taken a year or more by the mid-1970s. The average Broadway theatre ticket cost about ten dollars in 1975, about thirty dollars by 1985, more than forty-five by 1995, and about fifty-five by decade's end. The average ticket cost in the 2011–2012 season was a little more than eighty-six dollars.

As costs and prices rose, audiences and repertories got more conservative. By the late 1990s, revivals made up an increasing percentage of productions, more and more musicals were produced, and nonmusical plays grew rarer and appeared mostly Off-Broadway or in not-for-profit theatres.

COMEDY   Commercial theatre also relied on comedy to ensure box-office revenues. Through most of the period, Neil Simon was the playwright most successful—phenomenally successful—with audiences. Such major plays from the 1960s and 1970s as *The Odd Couple* established his reputation as the master gag writer of the theatre and were transferred to movies and television. And in 1991, he won the Pulitzer Prize for *Lost in Yonkers*. No other comic US writer showed either Simon's ability or his staying power.

Two of Wendy Wasserstein's feminist plays cemented her reputation as a writer of successfully commercial comedies. *The Heidi Chronicles* transferred from a not-for-profit Off-Broadway run to Broadway in 1989, winning several major prizes. Wasserstein wrote five more successful plays before her death in 2006 at age fifty-five.

FIGURE 20.7

Broadway Sells

Peter and the Starcatcher explores the back-story for the character Peter Pan and serves as a prequel to J. M. Barrie's stage play *Peter Pan, or The Boy Who Wouldn't Grow Up*. After a premiere in California, *Starcatcher* transferred to Off-Broadway and opened on Broadway in April 2012. A national tour is set to begin in 2013.

SERIOUS DRAMA   Some playwrights from the 1940s continued writing: Lillian Hellman, Tennessee Williams, Arthur Miller. Edward Albee was a new voice Off-Broadway in the 1950s who became a commercial success on Broadway in the 1960s with works like *Who's Afraid of Virginia Woolf?* and *A Delicate Balance*. His later plays were less commercially successful but were often critically praised and closer to the avant-garde. He remained a major force in US drama well past the end of the century, still winning top artistic awards. In 1994 he earned a Pulitzer Prize for *Three Tall Women*. In the 1970s and 1980s, David Mamet (*Glengarry Glen Ross*) and Sam Shepard (*Buried Child*) both won major prizes, and each wrote other important works. Several other important playwrights were the heirs of the advances made by the political avant-gardes.

Despite these playwrights, the US commercial theatre would have been impoverished had it not been for imports. From the 1950s through the 1990s, some of Broadway's best productions had already succeeded abroad. England's Harold Pinter intrigued—and sometimes baffled—US audiences with his absurdist-influenced plays. The feminist British playwright Caryl Churchill (*Cloud Nine* and *Top Girls*) became a major presence, as did Tom Stoppard with such plays as *Rosencrantz and Guildenstern Are Dead* and *Jumpers*. South African Athol Fugard's antiapartheid plays (*Master Harold and the Boys*) also came to New York by way of London.

Not-for-Profit Theatre

After a slow start in the late 1940s, professional not-for-profit theatres surged in the 1960s, with new not-for profits in places like Minneapolis, Los Angeles, Baltimore, New Haven, and Louisville. In a departure from current New York practices, some of these theatres built spaces without prosceniums, preferring theatres in the round (e.g., Dallas and Washington, D.C.) or thrust stages (e.g., Minneapolis). More than sixty such companies existed across the country by the mid-1970s and several hundred by the late 1990s.

An example of the strength and endurance of the not-for-profit theatre is the Guthrie Theater in Minneapolis. Inspired by the Shakespeare Festival in Ontario, Canada, the Guthrie began in 1963 with a production of Shakespeare's *Hamlet* as part of a four-play season. In June 2006, it opened a new three-stage building on the Mississippi river. In now employs more than nine hundred people and has a budget of more than $33 million a year. The theatre has an extensive education program for schools during the academic year.

FIGURE 20.8

Sam Shepard

Sam Shepard was one of the most important playwrights of the 1970s and 1980s. Shepard won the 1979 Pulitzer Prize for his macabre exploration of the disintegrating US dream, *Buried Child,* shown here at Theatre South Carolina.

Jason Ayer

Not-for-profit theatres also opened in New York City, offering an alternative to the commercial theatres there. Of these, one of the most successful was the Roundabout Theatre Company. Opened in 1965, it went bankrupt in the 1970s but recovered and prospered in the 1980s, earning its first of many Tony awards. By the late 1980s, it had New York's largest subscription audience and regularly sent shows to Broadway. During the 1990s, it moved to a permanent theatre on Broadway, added a second and a third theatre, and earned many, many awards. And like the Guthrie, the Roundabout sponsored a strong educational outreach program. Other not-for-profits with Broadway theatres are the Manhattan Theatre Club and Lincoln Center Theatre.

THE DECLINE AND CULTURAL DISPLACEMENT OF THEATRE

Despite its many successes, US theatre in the last half of the twentieth century was giving out warning signals. The robust avant-garde of the 1960s through 1980s was all but dead by the 1990s. Dinner theatre was in steep decline. On the bright side, not-for-profit theatres, educational theatres, and community theatres remained healthy. But the Broadway theatre—the theatre most people think of when they think of theatre—was struggling against rising costs, rising ticket prices, and stagnant audiences.

Some of theatre's problems came simply from increasing competition for the entertainment dollar. Just as radio and moving pictures had begun to compete with theatre for audiences before World War II, television, DVDs, computers, and cell phones all competed for attention after it—and mostly, they won. Television had a set in nine of ten US households by the late 1960s. Computers, which required a room to house their vacuum tubes in the 1960s, sat on desks by the 1980s. They allowed e-mails and Internet communication by the 1990s, when DVDs and cell phones also became widespread. Such technologies could bring movies, sports, and spectacles into a living room—some could bring them into a car or up to the top of a mountain by 2000—and for less money than a theatre ticket.

But the changing technologies also seemed to lead (or maybe simply to reflect) a change in the needs and desires of people. The desire to participate with a group brought together for a single event—a theatre audience—seemed to give way before individual enjoyment in front of a machine or even interacting with that machine. Theatre, a product of an oral culture, seemed increasingly out of place in a world dominated by an electronic one.

KEY TERMS

Check your understanding against this list. Brief definitions are included in the Glossary; persons are page-referenced in the index.

21

US Theatre from 2000

A staging from Fairmont State University of the musical *Rent* in its "high school" edition.

OBJECTIVES

When you have completed this chapter, you should be able to:

- Explain some ways in which theatre has reacted to terrorist attacks and new wars.

- Describe the nature and advantages of limited-run commercial productions.

- Explain how some formerly underrepresented groups have moved into the theatrical mainstream.

- Describe Broadway since 2000.

- Understand the importance of not-for-profit theatres in the development of new plays.

- Characterize Las Vegas theatre and theatre on the road in the past decade.

CONTEXT

Cultural and historic eras do not respect the calendar. With hindsight, we know a new era started, at least for many, on September 11, 2001, when terrorists flew two passenger planes loaded with jet fuel into the matching towers of the World Trade Center in lower Manhattan. The world watched on television as the towers, for some time the tallest buildings in the world, first burned and then collapsed. Later the rest of the story surfaced—a third plane crashed into the Pentagon and a fourth ditched in a Pennsylvania field, probably because of heroic action by the passengers against the hijackers.

The United States received the sympathy of much of the world. Soon, other countries—England and Spain foremost—suffered bombings on public transport, lesser in scope but nearly as terrifying. Many Europeans and some US citizens, once united in sympathy and shared defense, recoiled when the US government took precipitous action: invading Iraq (which the US public later discovered had no discernible involvement in terrorist acts or weapons of mass destruction); enforcing broad government secrecy; restricting international travel; torturing presumed enemies and jailing them without trial; and secretly eavesdropping on domestic communications. Governmental rashness was not the only problem in the United States: Americans were overweight and used a disproportionate amount of the world's energy and raw materials, but millions were dying of starvation in the southern hemisphere. The United States was rich but was also crime-ridden and violent. US capitalism "triumphed," but huge businesses went bankrupt overnight, the stock market yo-yoed and then crashed, economies around the world suffered, and states from South America to central Europe questioned the free market. Contradictions, complexities, and uncertainties thus marked the first years of the new millennium. The most historic change of this period was the election in 2008 of Barack Obama, an African American, as president of the United States.

THEATRICAL CHANGES

No new theatrical style or movement started in 2000—at least so far as one can see at this time. Several general theatre trends noted in the previous chapter continued:

- the importance of the not-for-profit theatre in new play development.
- the continued profit potential of long-running musicals in the commercial theatre.
- the absorption of avant-garde techniques and styles into mainstream performance, evidence of continued eclecticism in theatre.
- an incremental growth of new voices in the commercial and not-for-profit theatres, namely the voices of women, African Americans, Hispanics, and gays and lesbians.
- the continuation of the most visible venues of mainstream US theatre in New York and other large cities.
- the inexorable rise of Broadway ticket prices.
- the perseverance of community theatres, exhibiting varying degrees of skill, staging successful musicals and comedies from past seasons.

FIGURE 21.1

Metamorphoses

The play, first staged at Northwestern University, moved to the not-for-profit Lookingglass Theatre in Chicago under the title *Six Myths*. When it moved to New York, it was renamed *Metamorphoses*. Here, a scene from a later production at Virginia Commonwealth University.

Educational theatre, however, was seriously undermined by significant cuts in funding as a result of the world recession that began in 2008. Many public school districts, under the stresses of lowered budgets and federally mandated testing, eliminated arts training, including theatre. Colleges and universities also suffered: some programs were reduced or eliminated.

Theatrical Responses to 9/11

Theatre *did* react to a new millennium characterized by audacious terrorist acts and the reactions of Western governments. The response of theatre to millennial changes in politics and offense to public values was sometimes tentative, sometimes coincidental, and sometimes international. Five productions may stand for the theatre's responses to 9/11 and US actions thereafter.

METAMORPHOSES Mary Zimmerman had worked for some years in Chicago on a stage adaptation of tales by the Roman writer Ovid. She called the play

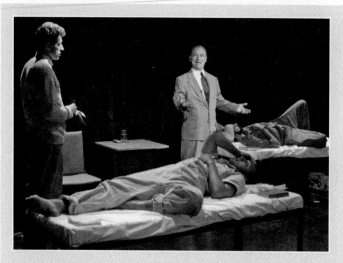

FIGURE 21.2

Political Theatre

This British play, *Guantánamo: Honor Bound to Defend Freedom*, based on the lives of actual detainees, portrays a military interrogator at Guantánamo Bay that explores what fresh horrors to unleash on her subjects to get them to talk. The five stories told on stage are from Muslims who were innocent of knowing anything about terrorist acts against the United States. The play was fashioned "from spoken evidence" by Victoria Brittain and Gillian Slovo.

Metamorphoses and it was a gentle, humorous, often moving short evening of tales, many about love that lasts past death. The production came to New York City's Second Stage Theatre, a not-for-profit, in October 2001, less than a month after the 9/11 destruction and seemed to soothe the stunned city. It was reported that every night men and women in the audience openly cried. *Metamorphoses* later had a successful commercial run on Broadway, opening in February 2002.

GUANTÁNAMO   *Guantánamo: Honor Bound to Defend Freedom* was a documentary play, originating in Britain, which was produced in New York by the Culture Project in August 2004. The play is made of crisscrossing monologues, sometimes surprisingly witty, from the actual words of five British detainees released from the US military prison at Guantánamo, Cuba, along with letters of other captives and testimony from family members, lawyers, and public officials. Since the New York production, the play has been staged across the United States and Europe

THE LYSISTRATA PROJECT   As a peace action, Kathryn Blume and Sharon Bower organized "The Lysistrata Project: The First-Ever Worldwide Theatrical Act of Dissent." Thus, March 3, 2003, saw 1,029 performances of the ancient Greek satirical play *Lysistrata* staged in fifty-nine countries and all fifty US states. In Aristophanes's comedy, Lysistrata convinces the women of Greece to withhold sex to force the men to negotiate a peace. In the play, unlike real life, the blackmail works and the war is ended. "The Lysistrata Project" saw readings and stagings of varied accomplishment, some with amateur performers and some with a few of the best-known actors in the world.

BLACK WATCH   Out of the National Theatre of Scotland in 2006 came *Black Watch*, a view of the Iraq War by soldiers in a Scottish regiment. The play moves between postwar interviews in pubs and reenacted deployment scenes depicting the crushing boredom of war spiked by moments of terror, all spiced by the music of regimental folk songs and bagpipes. The production toured Scotland, the United States, Australia, Scotland, and the United States again, and then played London, where it won four 2009 Olivier Awards, the London equivalent of the Tony Awards.

ALL MY SONS   In 2008, a commercial revival of Arthur Miller's 1947 play *All My Sons* opened on Broadway. The story is straightforward. Shortly after World War II, a midwestern family comes apart as a long-held secret is revealed: The father, who became wealthy as a supplier to the military, had knowingly shipped defective airplane engine parts, causing the deaths of twenty pilots. One of the pilots may have been the family's eldest son, a pilot who is missing and presumed dead. The shame of one man's profiting by death in war was not lost on an audience in the era of the Iraq War and the government's granting no-bid contracts for rebuilding.

Commercial theatre, not-for-profit theatre, and grassroots political theatre attempted to help their audiences come to terms with important issues of the times. The response, then, of the theatre to the terrorists' attacks and the Iraq occupation was in many ways sympathetic, antiwar, and suspicious of government.

FIGURE 21.3

"The Lysistrata Project"

A global "act of dissent," *Lysistrata* was performed more than one thousand times on a single day. Here, in an undergraduate production at the University of South Carolina, Lysistrata leads the women of Athens to withhold sex to persuade their men to end the war.

The Assimilation of Identity Theatres

Political theatres identified by race or gender, which we refer to as identity theatres, were further assimilated into the mainstream. African American, women's, Latino, and gay and lesbian theatre remained sometimes political but more often they were devoted to personal expression.

IDENTITY THEATRE: WOMEN   Women were more widely accepted as important playwrights and directors, including such playwriting talents as Claudia Shear *(Dirty Blonde)*, Suzan-Lori Parks *(TopDog/Underdog)*, Lynn Nottage *(Ruined)*, Marsha Norman *(The Color Purple)*, and Sarah Ruhl *(Eurydice, The Clean House, In the Next Room)*. These plays and others by women playwrights were mostly developed in the not-for-profit theatre and then staged on Broadway or Off-Broadway and throughout the United States.

Three women playwrights, Suzan-Lori Parks, Lynn Nottage, and Quiara Alegria Hudes won Pulitzer Prizes, in 2002, 2009, and 2012, respectively. Nottage's *Ruined* was inspired by Bertolt Brecht's *Mother Courage and Her Children* although placed in the African nation of Congo during the civil war of 1998–2003. Hudes's play *Water by the Spoonful*, not staged in New York at the time of receiving the prize, centers on a US soldier wrestling with his demons following his return from the Iraq War. Parks and Nottage are African Americans; Hudes is Hispanic.

Ella Bromblin (The Clean House)

FIGURE 21.4

A New Voice

Sarah Ruhl gained widespread recognition for her comedy, *The Clean House*, inspired by a remark over-heard at a cocktail party about a domestic worker who aspires to be a comedian in New York yet tells her jokes in her native Portuguese. Here, a production at Tisch Graduate School of the Arts. Ruhl's play *Eurydice*, in a staging at Butler University that pictures Orpheus and Eurydice, retells the myth of Orpheus from the perspective of Eurydice.

Female directors also guided major productions: Julie Taymor *(Spider-Man)*, Susan Stroman *(Young Frankenstein)*, Phyllida Lloyd *(Mamma Mia!* and *Mary Stuart)*, Emily Mann *(Anna in the Tropics, Translations)*, Anna D. Shapiro *(August: Osage County)*, and Diane Paulus *(Hair* and *The Gershwins' Porgy and Bess)*.

IDENTITY THEATRE: AFRICAN AMERICANS   Plays by and about African Americans grew even more common in mainstream theatres. These scripts included nearly all of the works of the late August Wilson and plays by Suzan-Lori Parks, Stew, and Anna Devere Smith.

Black plays and productions featuring African Americans also appeared on Broadway in greater number, including the musical *Passing Strange*, and the historical plays *Thurgood* and *The Mountaintop*. Sarah Jones's one-woman show *Bridge & Tunnel* had a successful Broadway run.

A musical adaptation of Alice Walker's novel *The Color Purple* played Broadway from 2005 through 2008 and toured the United States. Lorraine Hansberry's classic 1959 African American drama, *A Raisin in the Sun*, was a successful revival on Broadway with a cast that included Sean "Diddy" Combs. Broadway saw not only a revival of Tennessee Williams's *Cat on a Hot Tin Roof* with an all–African American cast but also a race-blind pro-duction of William Inge's *Come Back, Little Sheba* starring African American television actress S. Epatha Merkerson as the lead in an otherwise white cast. Opening to mixed reviews in 2012 was a mixed-cast revival of Tennessee Williams' *A Streetcar Named Desire*. African American audiences, however, have not generally grown much, except for the gospel plays of the chitlin' circuit.

IDENTITY THEATRE: LATINOS/
LATINAS Lionized Latino(a) playwrights including Nilo Cruz, Eduardo Machado, Sylvia Bofill, Quiara Alegria Hudes, Ricardo Bracho, María Irene Fornés, Ed Cardona, Jr., and others gradually moved toward the mainstream.

Cruz won the Pulitzer Prize for *Anna in the Tropics*. The play takes place in a cigar factory in Tampa's Spanish-Cuban area at the start of the Great Depression of the 1930s. During work, a reader or *lector* reads Tolstoy's *Anna Karenina* aloud to the employees. First staged in a not-for-profit theatre in Miami, the play was publicized by a local reviewer whose notice led to the Pulitzer and a Broadway production in 2001. Cruz's plays are produced at many leading not-for-profits.

Latino(a) artists are now produced in the commercial theatres. The energetic musical *In the Heights*, by Lin-Manuel Miranda and Quiara Alegría Hudes, about a mixed Hispanic New York City neighborhood graduated from Off-Broadway to a commercial Broadway production and quickly turned a profit.

Elle Bromblin

FIGURE 21.5
Wilson's Last Play
A dream-like moment from *Gem of the Ocean*, one play in the ten-play cycle by August Wilson that chronicles the decade-by-decade experiences of African Americans in the last century.

IDENTITY THEATRE: GAYS AND LESBIANS Plays with stories of special interest to gay people continued to cross over from not-for-profit theatres to commercial Broadway houses. Doug Wright's *I Am My Own Wife*, for example, is a biographical one-person play about the German transvestite Charlotte von Mahlsdorf. She survived life under both the Nazi and East German socialist regimes. The question: Was she a gay hero for living an open life as a cross-dresser in these repressive regimes or a gay villain because of unsavory acts she undertook to survive? Another Broadway critical and financial success, Richard Greenburg's comedy *Take Me Out*, concerned a star baseball

Spotlight

The Chitlin' Circuit and Tyler Perry

The noted African American Harvard professor, Henry Louis Gates, Jr., borrowed the term *chitlin' circuit* to describe a contemporary touring theatre of plays made by, for, and about African Americans. The chitlin' circuit flourishes away from Broadway, Off-Broadway, and the not-for-profit theatre. It's professional in that everyone involved gets paid, but it's entirely nonunion. It's made loads of money for many involved.

The characters in chitlin' circuit plays are as standardized as those of commedia dell'arte. Typical roles include an outspoken fat woman, a beautiful woman of questionable morals, an over-the-top swishy gay man, and a handsome stud. The comedy is crude, full of insults and trash talk. At some point a gospel song is belted out. At stake in the plot is the loss of a family member or friend to drugs, gangs, prison, or prostitution. The happy ending often comes about from prayer and sometimes even from divine intervention in the form of angels or ghosts.

The audiences, as Gates noted in his *New Yorker* essay, "are basically blue-collar and pink-collar, and not the type to attend traditional theatre." Gates continues, "However crude the script and the production, they're generating the kind of audience response that most playwrights can only dream of."

Some chitlin' circuit participants prefer to call their endeavors *urban theatre*, perhaps adapting the term from music promoters to describe music with particular appeal to African Americans as *urban music*.

The cross-over financial star of the chitlin' circuit is clearly Tyler Perry. In 1998, he staged his first play, *I Know I've Been Changed*, at Atlanta's House of Blues. He sold out eight nights at the House of Blues and two more nights at the 4,500-seat Fox Theatre. Soon Perry was doing two to three hundred performances a year, playing to thirty thousand people a week. Perry wrote, directed, produced, composed, did makeup and set design, all to keep the budget tight.

Perry's innovation on the chitlin' circuit formula was to play the mother character himself, all six-foot-five of him, in drag. This character, Madea, takes the idea of the strong black mother's holding the family together a gigantic step further. Madea carries two guns in her handbag and will whip them out if necessary. She smokes grass and is blunt-spoken.

In 2005 and 2006, Perry made his first two Madea films for a total budget of $11 million; each opened at number one, and together they grossed more than $110 million. His eleven stage plays have grossed more than $150 million, and DVDs of his movies and plays have sold more than eleven million copies. He wrote a best-selling book in 2006, *Don't Make a Black Woman Take Off Her Earrings: Madea's Uninhibited Commentaries on Love and Life*. In 2011, Forbes magazine called him the highest paid man in entertainment, earning $130 million during the 2010–2011 season. In 2012, Perry had four plays touring the country that he wrote, directed, and produced, including, *Aunt Bam's Place, I Don't Want To Do Wrong!, The Haves and the Have Nots*, and *Madea Gets a Job*. He appeared in the last title as Madea. He also released three movies in 2012, titled *Good Deeds; I, Alex Cross*; and *Madea's Witness Protection*.

player—handsome, well spoken, well paid, and masculine—who announces he is gay. Banter among the players in the locker and shower rooms is never the same. Larry Kramer's 1985 off-Broadway play about the early responses of the New York City gay community to AIDS, *The Normal Heart*, was revived on Broadway for a successful limited run in 2011.

Meanwhile, plays with gay themes, including *Rent* and *The Laramie Project*, were being produced at churches and regional, community, and college theatres. The Tectonic Theatre Project conducted interviews with inhabitants of Laramie, Wyoming, in the aftermath of the brutal killing of Matthew Shepard. An openly gay college student, Shepard was enticed from a bar by two men and then robbed and beaten to death, his body left by the side of a rural road. In the resulting documentary play, *The Laramie Project*, eight actors portrayed more than sixty characters in a series of short scenes.

INTO THE MAINSTREAM   Perhaps two productions will serve to highlight the transition of identity theatres into the broader theatrical culture. Tony Kushner, working with Jeanine Tesori, wrote the musical *Caroline, or Change*. Caroline, an African American maid working for a middle-class Jewish family in Louisiana in 1963, is instructed to keep any loose change she finds in the son's pockets during laundry as a way of teaching the boy to be more careful. The bits of money mean little to the family but become significant for Caroline's household. A crisis develops when a twenty-dollar bill is found in the laundry. Kushner, author of *Angels in America*, is a gay man; both he and Tesori are Jewish. The musical was directed by George C. Wolfe, a gay African American. Significantly, almost no commentator noted any conflict in a white man and woman telling an African American story.

Assimilation of African American playwrights into the mainstream was not always without controversy. In 2009, a revival of August Wilson's *Joe Turner's Come and Gone* was staged on Broadway. The play's setting is a Pittsburgh

FIGURE 21.6

In the Hispanic Neighborhood

Lin-Manuel Miranda conceived, wrote the music and lyrics, and starred in this invigorating look at Latino life *In the Heights*. The book writer was Quiara Alegria Hudes, later to win the 2012 Pulitzer Prize for her nonmusical play, *Water by the Spoonful*.

Joan Marcus

boardinghouse that serves as a makeshift home for a changing mix of African Americans during the "great migration" (the first decade of the twentieth century), when descendants of former slaves moved toward the industrial cities of the North seeking jobs and new starts in life. Some people active in African American theatre, however, bemoaned that the $1.7 million production was directed by a white man, Bartlett Sher. In his lifetime, August Wilson would not approve a white director for any of his plays; this insistence is, in part, why no films have been made of his stories. The reason for demanding African American directors was to get them work. But the playwright's widow, Constanza Romero, personally approved the production with Sher as director, saying, "My work is to get these stories out there and to help ensure that audiences walk out of the plays with a deeper understanding for these American stories and for the ways our cultures intertwine."

Romero's work—getting the stories out there—has been at the heart of identity theatre's goals. Both the commercial and not-for-profit theatres increasingly acknowledge and showcase the unity of the human experience in people of many races and both genders.

A Faded Avant-garde

As theatre by and for women, African Americans, Latinos, and gays moved to the theatrical center, the avant-garde continued to fade from US stages. Still, a limited avant-garde continued in a small number of troupes. Mabou Mines toured a postmodern production of Henrik Ibsen's *A Doll's House* (1879) with a much altered script, mock period music, an interpolated puppet opera, and most stunningly, all the male roles played by midgets and dwarfs. The tall female actors could barely sit on the tiny furniture made to accommodate the men. The casting and staging exaggerated outrageously the themes of the original play. In the script, the men are small-minded; here they were literally small. The setting became almost literally a doll house in which adult women do not fit.

Elements of much of the late twentieth-century avant-garde kept cropping up in otherwise mainstream productions, accepted by audiences with little note. A revival of Stephen Sondheim's opera-like musical *Sweeney Todd* was staged without a traditional orchestra; instead, the performers played the accompaniment on a variety of instruments when not actually singing. The female lead played the triangle and the tuba. Frank Wedekind's 1891 play about teenage sexual tumult, *Spring's Awakening*, was adapted into a musical of almost the same name, with the dialogue scenes set in the original late-Victorian period but the songs styled as twenty-first-century rock. Both shows played on Broadway after initial productions at not-for-profit theatres.

The biography of US President Andrew Jackson was put through the postmodern wringer becoming the book of a new rock musical, *Bloody, Bloody, Andrew Jackson*. The show played in several not-for-profit theatres, opening on Broadway in October 2010. Despite positive reviews it closed after 120 performances.

Not-for-profit Lincoln Center Theatre brought to Broadway *War Horse*, staged originally by the National Theatre in London. Based on a 1982 young-person's novel about the survival of a boy and his horse during the First World

War, the play is staged with puppets as the horses and other animals. Many in the audience find themselves stifling tears as the horse's fate is revealed.

In big ways and small, unity of tone and progression continued to be breached in twenty-first-century theatre—that is, eclecticism continued to mark much of theatre in the new millennium.

COMMERCIAL AND NOT-FOR-PROFIT THEATRE

Broadway

Long-running musicals continued to dominate Broadway and populate the road. Three musicals running on Broadway in January 2000 were still playing as of the winter of 2012: *The Phantom of the Opera* (1988), *Chicago* (1996), and *The Lion King* (1997). Other financially successful musicals opened during this period. Still playing in the summer of 2012 were *Mamma Mia!* (2001), *Wicked* (2003), *Jersey Boys* (2005), and *Mary Poppins* (2006). None of these musicals had anything much in the way of stylistic breakthroughs, timely themes, or songs that anyone wanted to sing outside the theatre. Broadway's successful musicals since at least 2000 have been characterized by some commentators as expensive carnival rides, colorful and fast-paced diversions that are quickly forgotten.

REVIVALS   In 2009, a commercial Broadway revival of the 1950s musical *West Side Story* was notable. The musical reworks Shakespeare's *Romeo and Juliet*, placing it in 1950s New York City. The feud between the Capulets and the Montagues is replaced by gang wars between Irish and newly arrived Puerto Rican youths. At the age of ninety-one, the author of the original book, Arthur Laurents, directed the production. His springboard for this revival was to translate some dialogue and two songs into Spanish. Actors from Spanish-speaking countries of the Americas were recruited for the production.

LIMITED RUNS   A growing number of star-studded, limited runs of comedies and serious plays had impressive Broadway success. They were characterized by short playing periods and were loaded with familiar names from television, movies, and theatre including *Macbeth* with Patrick Stewart, *A Moon for the Misbegotten* with Kevin Spacey, *God of Carnage* with James Gandolfini, *The Country Girl* with Morgan Freeman, *The Odd Couple* with Nathan Lane and Matthew Broderick, *Death of a Salesman* with Phillip Seymour Hoffman and Andrew Garfield, *Driving Miss Daisy* with James Earl Jones and Vanessa Redgrave, *The Merchant of Venice* and *Glengarry Glen Ross* with Al Pacino, *How to Succeed in Business without Really Trying* with Daniel Radcliffe and John Larroquette, *Evita* with Ricky Martin, and others. For producers, salaries for their stars were expensive, but name recognition made sizable audiences more likely.

CONCERTS AND ONE-PERSON SHOWS   Concerts and one-person shows played in Broadway theatres for limited runs, including in the 2010–2011 and 2011–2012 seasons performances by Harry Connick, Jr.; Patti LuPone and Mandy Patinkin; Hugh Jackman; Kathy Griffin; Donnie and Marie Osmond; John Lequizamo; Colin Quinn; and William Shatner.

FIGURE 21.7

A New Disney Musical

Newsies is the latest effort by the Disney Corporation to capitalize on its films. Here, a moment from the 2012 Broadway production, based on the 1992 movie.

A DEARTH OF NEW US PLAYS   Successful new US plays, however, were rare for commercial Broadway runs. David Auburn's *Proof* (2000) revolved about a mentally damaged but intellectually brilliant daughter of a recently deceased mathematics genius and tried to answer the question: Did he leave important findings behind in his unpublished papers? *Doubt: A Parable* (2004) by John Patrick Shanley dramatized the standoff between a nun and a priest over whether a male student at their Catholic school had been or was being molested. Cross-dressing Off-Broadway playwright and performer, Charles Busch had a Broadway success as the author of a conventional comedy, *The Tale of the Allergist's Wife* (2000), about an upper-middle-class woman's midlife crisis. All had long runs.

In his seventy-fourth year, the prize-winning playwright Edward Albee saw the premiere in 2002 of *The Goat, or Who is Sylvia?*, an unlikely comedy about a man who falls in love with and has sex with a goat. The play ends when the main character's wife drags the dead goat through the front door of their swank apartment. Successful on Broadway, *The Goat* is being staged across the United States. Albee, then, continued his ability to shock audiences, a quality evident in his first plays, staged in the late 1950s. Albee's first Broadway shocker *Who's Afraid of Virginia Woolf?* from 1962 was revived on Broadway in 2005 and 2012, to mostly rave reviews.

Other noteworthy new plays include *Other Desert Cities* by Jon Robin Baitz and *Clybourne Park* by Bruce Norris. *Other Desert Cities* is a realistic family drama. *Clybourne Park* is a postmodern riff on Lorraine Hansberry's groundbreaking play of 1959, *A Raisin in the Sun*.

British imports continued to enliven the Broadway theatre, including openings in the 2010–2011 and 2011–2012 seasons of eight new plays and musicals and five revivals transferred from London.

Not-for-Profits

In the new millennium, the nation's not-for-profit theatres continued to develop new plays and theatre artists. This trend, clear in the late twentieth century, became even more pronounced: Almost all new plays are now developed in workshops, readings, and initial productions in regional theatres throughout the United States. Since 2000, more than one-half of productions opening on Broadway originated in the not-for-profit theatre.

The recession that began in 2007 had a drastic effect on many not-for-profit arts groups, including theatres. A number closed and a few went into bankruptcy. Seasons have been truncated and less adventurous plays with smaller casts chosen.

Las Vegas

The millennium saw Broadway and Off-Broadway musicals open in Las Vegas hotel-casinos, often with excellent results, at least financially. Perhaps the best example of the synergy that has developed between Broadway and Las Vegas is *The Phantom of the Opera*, performed in the Venetian hotel-casino in a new theatre space specially designed to mirror the Paris opera house in which the musical is set. The Las Vegas production, retitled *Phantom—The Las Vegas Spectacular*, was shortened from the two-hour-plus playing time in New York to ninety-five minutes,

FIGURE 21.8

Las Vegas

Flashy signs are everywhere in Las Vegas. Here, the Venetian hotel advertises *Phantom* while a passing cab promotes a magician appearing at another hotel-casino.

with ten performances a week instead of Broadway's eight. *Phantom*'s physical production was overhauled and highly computerized to take advantage of Las Vegas's superior technical facilities. The Las Vegas *Phantom* closed in September 2012, having played 2,691 performances.

Mamma Mia! was performed more than two thousand times in Las Vegas. *Hairspray* also played there, as did *The Producers*, *Avenue Q*, and *Spamalot*. The original Broadway creative team for each musical—director and all designers— was involved in recreating these Broadway hits. The shows are usually shortened because the casino owners, who house and bankroll the shows, want theatergoers to get up from their seats and get back to gambling.

Las Vegas is also home to a handful of Cirque du Soleil productions, each a hybrid of crowd-pleasing high-tech scenery, costumes, lights, clowning, a modest suggestion of a storyline, and traditional circus acts. Their look and feel is often otherworldly and dream like. Although not what is usually meant by drama, such productions are highly theatrical.

Las Vegas theatre, then, is a millennial reflection of a trend noted in commercial Broadway productions and road shows. It epitomizes the shift from theatre art to theatre entertainment: shortened productions, a reliance on spectacle, and the downplaying of the spoken word.

The Road

Although recent grosses were slightly lower as a result of the recession, the road continued to prosper financially and continued to present to the US Broadway's proven material. The revenues from touring shows produced by members of the Broadway League were $804 million in 2010–2011 and $947 million in 2009–2010. These dollar amounts are only slightly less than the gross revenues of Broadway theatre. Ticket sales declined a little in this time: fewer people were spending for Broadway theatre.

THEATRICAL TRENDS IN THE NEW MILLENNIUM

Time is needed for historians and critics to sift through the apparent successes and failures of an era, highlighting some as significant and letting others retreat to the shadows as fads.

The business of theatre is another matter. Figures can be tallied to provide a year-by-year financial picture of Broadway productions. The good news is that during the severe recession that began in 2007 Broadway survived, even prospered. Each season from 2008–2009 through 2010–2012 saw gains in gross revenues.

In many countries of Europe today, theatre is supported by the government. In the United States, not-for-profit theatres receive little federal government support, on average less than 1 percent of a theatre's budget. Instead, aesthetically and socially ambitious US theatres rely on donations from wealthy individuals and grants from charitable foundations. Even then, ticket prices for live theatre are often too high for the average citizen to afford. Affordability is one reason that both commercial and art theatres are not as central to US culture as are film and television.

THE LONG VIEW

In many past eras, theatre was at the heart of the culture—performances were civic, religious events that engaged much of the populace. In some eras, royal patronage protected and encouraged plays and the companies that produced them. In the age of Elizabeth I, a penny admitted a spectator to the plays of Shakespeare and his contemporaries. Until the 1700s, there was no division between "commercial" and "artistic" theatre; rather, the division was social and cultural, between court and popular theatre. Since about 1800, however, a rift has developed between a commercial theatre and an art theatre. The commercial theatre has been characterized by sensationalism and thrills, the art theatre by attempts at artistic and social significance. In the United States now, a division between the commercial and the not-for-profit theatre has become particularly distinct. Today, most commercial Broadway theatres and the musicals they send on the road are entertainments, business ventures. Like rides at amusement parks, they have little artistic ambition and scarce relevancy to our times and culture. Developing new plays and producing historical, classic plays are now the province of not-for-profit theatres. Educational theatres, especially at the college and university level, echo the not-for-profits, whereas community theatres tilt toward Broadway.

Theatre itself may now be a sidebar to Western culture, loved by some but ignored by many. Theatre is expensive because it is hand-made and maybe that theatre is artisinal will be its saving feature. When all of culture is mediated by technology, theatre will remain immediate, ephemeral, and in person.

KEY TERMS

Check your understanding against this list. Brief definitions are included in the Glossary; persons are page-referenced in the Index.

identity theatres   339   limited run   345

Global Theatre

This woodblock print pictures the interior of a Kabuki theatre in about 1765.

OBJECTIVES

When you have completed this chapter, you should be able to:

- Explain how traits of ritual differ from similar practices in Western theatre.
- List traits shared by most African dramas.

- Differentiate among ritual, paratheatricals, and theatre.
- Describe kinds of theatre and drama from Japan, India, and China.

- Differentiate between Kabuki, Kyogen, and Noh.

India. One example is theatre for development—that is, a use of theatre to define and help solve local problems. Originally conceived as a top-down educational form in which a government, a charitable nongovernmental organization (NGO), or university would develop a script, rehearse actors, and send them out to perform, it is now conceived cooperatively. The top-down model is now seen as paternalistic, Western, and colonial.

Instead, a few actors now go into a village to live. With local people, they develop and rehearse a script in the local language about a local problem (AIDS, marriage laws, pollution). Everybody is encouraged to participate, which includes watching rehearsals. Everybody is invited to contribute. Discussion follows public performance, but the process itself is seen as more important than the performance. Theatre thus becomes a way of studying a problem, devising a solution, and showing how to effect it—a way of "performing" real life to understand it. This bottom-up model assumes that people who have problems will be able to identify them and suggest ways of solving them.

Theatre for development is not without its critics. Perhaps because it has been most often practiced by activists of the political left, theatre for development is often opposed by those on the right. Others argue that expecting uneducated villagers to analyze their problems and suggest feasible solutions is naive and unrealistic, and thus unproductive. Still others maintain that, although theatre for development may be socially useful, it is neither artistic nor aesthetically pleasing and so is not really theatre at all.

KEY TERMS

Check your understanding against this list. Brief definitions are included in the Glossary; persons are page-referenced in the Index.

Beijing opera 359
hanamichi [ha-nyah-MEE-chee] 358
hashigakari [HA-shee-ga-kar-ee] 357
hikinuki [HI-kee-no-kee] 359
Kabuki 358

Kathakali [KA-the-ka-lee] 355
Kutiyatam [kuh-yee-AHT-um] 350
Kyogen [kee-OH-gehn] 358
Natyasastra [naht-ya-SAS-trah] 354

Noh [no] 350
paratheatrical 352
rasa [RAH-sah] 355
ritual 352
sanskrit drama 350
shite 357
theatre for development 365

GLOSSARY

What follows is a compilation of Key Terms found at the end of each chapter as well as a few additional terms used in the text. Numbers at the end of each entry refer to the page(s) where a fuller discussion can be found.

abstraction An artistic depiction that is different from a literal, photographic representation of the thing depicted, usually by being more generalized, less particular. (55)

absurdism A style of drama popularized in France after World War II that viewed human existence as meaningless and treated language as an inadequate means of communication. (332)

action According to Aristotle, a causally linked sequence of events, with beginning, middle, and end; the proper and best way to unify a play. More popularly, the single and unified human process of which a drama is the imitation. To some modern critics, an interaction (between dramatic protagonist and others). (33)

actor-manager A starring actor who is head and nominal artistic director of a company. (284)

advertising Paid-for material, such as posters, billboards, tv and radio spots, to promote something. (66)

aesthetic response Audience reaction to art object as art, not as idea, meaning, and so on; implies some idea of "beauty." (7)

afterpiece A short play that followed the main attraction. (253)

agent Professional who represents theatre artists for a percentage of their income. (67)

alienation effect (A-effect) Customary, but perhaps misleading, translation of the German *Verfremdungseffekt*, "to make strange." Term now almost always associated with Bertolt Brecht's epic theatre, which aims to distance the spectator from the play's action to force conscious consideration of the political and social issues raised by the play. Shortened often to *A-effect*. (277)

alley stage Performance area shape that puts audience on each side, with the performance area, usually a long rectangle, between. (73)

amateur theatre A producing organization in which most participants are not paid or are paid only token amounts well below professional levels. Usually community and educational theatres are amateur theatres. (81)

American Musical A type of theatre combining story, song, and dance that originated in the U S around 1900. (204)

amphitheatre In Roman theatre, a large public space for paratheatrical entertainments, like animal fights. (194)

angle perspective Multipoint perspective; results when several vanishing points are located away from the center of the stage so that vistas appear toward the wings. (294)

antagonist The opponent in an agon, or contest; in drama, either of two opponents in conflict, or the character who opposes the protagonist. (36)

antiquarianism The study of the details of past civilizations, often with a view to reproducing historically accurate settings onstage. (296)

applause Positive response to performance by clapping hands. (17)

apron That part of a stage that extends in front of the proscenium arch. (71)

arena stage A stage in which the audience completely surrounds the playing area. Also called *theatre in the round*. (72)

art Activity done for its own ends, separable from both life and practicality, although it may be applied to practical as well as aesthetic purposes. (6)

art theatre movement A theatrical movement of the late nineteenth and early twentieth centuries that tried to separate itself from commercial theatre and the reliance on box office. (278)

audition A session at which a theatre artist, usually an actor, displays his or her craft to secure a job. (112)

auditorium "Hearing place"; audience section of theatre. (53)

automated fixtures Flexible focusing and special effect lighting fixtures. By a remote signal these instruments can move from area to area on the stage and change color. They are standard equipment in rock concerts and light shows and increasingly in musical theatre.

avant-garde "Advance guard"; art thought ahead of the mainstream, experimental. (256)

backdrop Painted two-dimensional hanging, usually as part of a scenic background. (236)

balance On the proscenium stage, the visual equalizing of the two halves of the stage picture as seen from the audience. In any stage moment, the attempt to achieve a sense of equal weight between the people and objects on stage. (131)

balcony Elevated audience area. (71)

beat A small unit in a play; defined variously by different actors and directors. (134)

Beijing opera Traditional Chinese theatrical form, spectacular, nonrealistic. (359)

biomechanics The concept and the complex of techniques devised by Vsevolod Meyerhold to train actors so that their bodies could be as responsive as machines. (276)

black theatre A theatre movement of the 1960s and after, primarily for black audiences, actors, and playwrights, originally connected with the black power movement, a political ideology. (326)

blocking Stage movement for actors, given in rehearsal (usually) by the director. (128)

book (1) The spoken text of a play or musical. (2) Several flats hinged together and folded together form a book of flats. (3) To book a production is to schedule a performance of it. (305)

book musical See *American Musical*. The term "book musical" is sometimes juxtaposed to the term "integrated musical." (307)

booth stage A temporary stage structure where actors erect a curtain and perform in front of it, either on a raised platform or in a cleared area. (73)

border Curtain, or less often flats or cutouts, suspended at intervals behind the proscenium arch to mask the overhead rigging. Particularly important in Italianate settings. (236)

box Historically the favored, and most expensive, seats in a theatre. Made by sectioning off parts of a gallery, boxes were spacious and outfitted with armchairs, in contrast to the crowded galleries, whose seats consisted of backless benches, and to the pit, where originally no seats were provided. (72)

box set Interior setting represented by flats forming three sides of a room (the fourth wall being the proscenium line); first used around 1830 and common after 1850. (264)

Broadway In popular parlance, the area of New York City on and adjacent to the street named Broadway, where the commercial theatre of the United States is concentrated. There are forty Broadway theatres as of 2013. By union contracts, Broadway theatres have five hundred or more seats and only productions in Broadway theatres are eligible for Tony Awards. (74)

burlesque In eighteenth- and nineteenth-century theatre, a form of "minor" drama popular in England and featuring satire and parody. In the United States of the late nineteenth century and the twentieth century, a kind of entertainment originally dependent on a series of variety acts but later including elements of female display (including striptease) in its major offerings. After moving to the fringes of respectability by the 1940s, burlesque disappeared in the United States by the late 1950s. (303)

casting The process of selecting a specific actor to play a specific role. (127)

casting director Mediates between actors and producer(s), for whom he or she works; makes initial sifting of acting pool. (67)

causal plot Plot of linked, internally consistent cause and effect. (34)

character One of Aristotle's six parts of a play, the material of plot and the formal cause of thought; an agent (participant, doer) in the play whose qualities and traits arise from ethical deliberation. In popular parlance, the agents or "people" in the play. (35)

chariot-and-pole system An elaborate system for changing elements of the scenery simultaneously: the system involving scenery attached to poles that rose through slits in the stage floor from chariots (wheeled carts) that ran on tracks in the basement and depended on an intricate system of interlocking ropes, pulleys, wheels, and windlasses for their simultaneous movement. (238)

chorus In Greek drama of the fifth century BCE, a group of men who sang, chanted, spoke, and moved, usually in unison, and who, with the actors, performed the plays. In the Renaissance, a single character named Chorus who provided information and commentary about the action in some tragedies. In modern times, the groups that sing or dance in musical comedies, operettas, ballets, and operas. (170)

climax   The highest point of plot excitement for the audience. (35)

closet drama   Plays written to be read, not performed. (263)

comedy   A form (genre) of drama variously discussed in terms of its having a happy ending; dealing with the material, mundane world; dealing with the low and middle classes; dealing with myths of rebirth and social regeneration; and so on. (232)

comedy, middle   See *middle comedy*.

comedy, new   See *new comedy*.

comedy, old   See *old comedy*.

comedy of manners   Refers most often to seventeenth- and eighteenth-century comedies whose focus is the proper social behavior of a single class. (250)

commedia dell'arte   Italian popular comedy of the fifteenth through seventeenth centuries. Featured performances improvised from scenarios by a set of stock characters and repeated from play to play and troupe to troupe. See also *lazzi*. (238)

commercial theatre   After about 1860 financing of theatre moved from the state, a wealthy individual, or the church to companies or individuals that wished to make a profit through the sale of tickets, making a fully profit-making or commercial theatre. (283)

community theatre   Theatre performed by and for members of a given community, especially a city or town. Usually amateur, sometimes with professional directors, designers, and business staff. (82)

complication   Ascending or tying action. That part of the plot in which the action is growing tenser and more intricate up to the point of crisis (turning point), after which the action unties and resolves in a section called the denouement. (34)

composition   Arrangement of visual elements for aesthetic effect. (128)

computer-assisted design (CAD)   Use of computer programs to draft, elevate, rotate, color, etc., designs. (152)

concept musical   A version of the American musical that emerged in the 1960s whose story is organized around an idea rather than a central character. (312)

confidant(e)   In drama, a character to whom another leading character gives private information. (36, 231)

conflict   Clash of characters, seen either as objectives that create obstacles for one another, or as actions, neither of which can succeed unless the other fails. (34)

confraternity   In France, a religious brotherhood, many of which sponsored or produced plays during the Middle Ages. (207)

constructivism   A nonrealistic style of scenic design associated with Vsevolod Meyerhold and marked by the view that a good set is a machine for doing plays, not a representation of familiar locales. Incorporated simple machines on stage and often revealed the method of its own construction. (275)

continental seating   First devised by Richard Wagner in the late nineteenth century for his theatre at Bayreuth; eschews a central aisle in favor of entrances and exits at the end of each aisle. Continental seating has neither boxes nor galleries. (236)

convention (dramatic, theatrical)   A way of doing things agreed on by a (usually unstated) contract between audience and artists; for example, characters' singing their most important feelings and emotions is a convention of musical comedy. (54)

copyright   Legal concept of intellectual property rights that the creator of an original work can control the financial exploitation of the work for a set number of years. (96)

Corpus Christi plays   Medieval cycle plays and cosmic dramas (see entries) often performed during a spring festival established in the fourteenth century in honor of the Christian Eucharist. (204)

cosmic drama   Long dramatic presentations popular in the Middle Ages that depicted religious events from the creation to the Last Judgment. Short plays were combined until the total presentation could last several days or weeks and occasionally a month or more. See also *cycle play*. (205)

costume design   The discipline of designing costumes for a theatrical production. (142)

cothurnus   High boot with platform sole for tragic actor, Hellenistic Greece. (182)

court theatre   A theatre located at the court of a nobleman. After the Renaissance, Italianate theatre, whose perspective was drawn with the vanishing points established from the chair of the theatre where the ruler sat, making his the best seat in the house. (225)

crisis   Decisive moment at the high point of a rising action; turning point. (34)

criticism   The careful, systematic, and imaginative study and evaluation of works of drama and theatre (or any other form of art); dramatic criticism, of plays; performance criticism, of live performances. (63)

culture   The set of beliefs, values, and lifestyle of a group. (18)

cycle play   Medieval (especially English) dramas covering the "cycle" of history from the creation of the world to doomsday. See also *cosmic drama*. (205)

decorum   In neoclassical theory, the behavior of a dramatic character in keeping with his or her social status, age, sex, and occupation; based on the requirements of verisimilitude (see *verisimilitude*). (232)

denouement   That part of the plot that follows the crisis (turning point) and that includes the untangling or resolving of the play's complications. (34)

dialogue   Character interaction through language. (93)

dimming   Controlling the intensity of light by manipulating the amount of electricity that reaches individual lamps. (145)

discovery   According to Aristotle, any passage from ignorance to knowledge within a play, by means of, for example, sign, emotion, reasoning, action. Good discoveries grow out of suffering (awareness) and lead to reversal (change of direction). (33)

discovery space   Permanent or temporary space in the Elizabethan playhouse that permitted actors and locales to be hidden from view and then "discovered" (or revealed) when needed. (218)

domestic tragedy   A serious play dealing with domestic problems of the middle or lower classes. In the eighteenth century, a reaction against "regular" or neoclassical tragedy. (252)

dramaturg   Dramatic advisor and researcher for theatre or production. (64)

dress rehearsal   A final rehearsal in which all visual elements of production, including costumes, are used. Typically a rehearsal that strives to duplicate, insofar as possible, an actual performance. (135)

eccyclema   In classical Greece, a machine used to thrust objects or people (often dead) from inside the *skene* into view of the audience. Probably some sort of wheeled platform that rolled or rotated through the skene's central door. (177)

eclectic(ism)   Gathering of materials from many sources; popularly, a mixture of styles and methods. In twentieth-century theatre, the idea that each play calls forth its own production style. (321)

educational theatre   Theatre by and (in part) for students in an elementary, secondary, or collegiate setting. (81)

elements of design   The abstract components that make up a design, such as, line, color, texture, etc. (140)

emblem   A device (usually an object or picture of an object) used as an identifying mark; something that stands for something else. In the Middle Ages, a key stood for St. Peter, a crooked staff for a bishop. (197)

encore   Part of performance repeated in response to audience applause. (17)

environment   The visual and spatial surrounding of the play, influenced by such matters as mood and visual meaning. (123)

ephemeral art   Art that cannot be repeated exactly. (10)

epic theatre   Term originated by Erwin Piscator and popularized by Bertolt Brecht to describe a theatre in which the audience response is objective, not subjective, and in which such narrative devices as film projections, titles, and storytelling are used. See also *alienation effect*. (277)

episodic plot   Plot whose incidents are connected by idea or metaphor or character, not by cause and effect. (35)

exposition   Necessary information about prior events, or a part of a play given over to communicating such information; because it is a "telling" and not an enacting of narrative, it is usually nondramatic. (32)

expressionism   A style of theatre in Europe after World War I and typified by symbolic presentation of meaning, often as viewed from the standpoint of the main character; distortions of time, space, and proportion are common. (275)

facade stage   One that puts the actors in front of a neutral (nonrepresentational) surface. (176)

fair theatre   Non-monopoly ("illegitimate") theatres in France and England performed at large, periodic fairs. (253)

feminist theory (of theatre)   An attempt to explain the effects of gender in the workings of theatre and drama and, through them, on society and culture. (62)

flat   A structure on which scenery is painted, consisting of a wooden frame and canvas covering; usually of a size to be carried by one or two persons for shifting. Used in both Italianate staging and box sets (see entries). (177)

floodlight   An unfocused lighting instrument. (145)

focus   The point or object that draws the eye of the audience to the stage picture. (131)

foil   A minor character intended to set off another character through contrast. (36)

follow spot   Powerful, hard-edged lighting instrument mounted so that an operator can "follow" action with the light. (146)

footlights   Light sources arranged along the front of a stage (between actors and audience) to throw light upward from stage level to eliminate shadows from harsh overhead lighting, standard equipment c. 1650–1920. (145)

forestage   That level part of the stage in front of the scenery, especially in Renaissance stages. See also *apron*. (71)

for-profit   Professional theatre that is fully taxed and gets its income from ticket sales and related sources. Also called "commercial theatre." (26)

fourth wall (realism)   Nineteenth-century concept of a completely Realistic performance space that the audience looked into through a removed or invisible "wall" (the proscenium plane). (269)

French scene   Scene division between entrance or exit of major character(s). (134)

gallery   The highest audience areas in nineteenth-century theatres, hence, the cheapest seats; the balconies. (218)

gay and lesbian theatre   Theatre of, by, and often for a gay and lesbian community. (328)

gel   In stage lighting, a medium for coloring the beam of light. (145)

generic criticism   Criticism by identification of genre (comedy, tragedy, etc.) (41)

genre   In dramatic criticism, a category of plays: comedy, tragedy, melodrama, farce. Popularly, any category. (41)

gentlemanly melodrama   Later melodrama for middle-class audiences with upper-middle-class subjects and settings. (289)

Gesamtkunstwerk   (total art work). Both term and concept popularized by Richard Wagner, who argued that such a work would be the artistic fusion of all major artistic elements, including music, into a single work under the artistic supervision of a single master artist. (275)

given circumstances   Basic facts that define the world of the play; conditions of place, period, social level, and so on. (53)

given circumstances (of characters)   In Stanislavskian vocabulary, those aspects of character that are beyond the character's or actor's control: age, sex, state of health, and so on. (109)

glory   In medieval and Renaissance art, a cloud or sunburst in which divinities appeared. In the theatre of those periods, a flown platform made to look like a cloud or sunburst. (208)

Golden Age   The great age of any culture. For theatre, in Spain, the period c. 1550–1650, the greatest age of Spanish drama; in France, the age of Louis XIV; in England, the age of Elizabeth and Shakespeare. (216)

Graeco-Roman period   That period in Greece and Greek lands when Roman domination had arrived, usually dated from c. 100 BCE to the fall of the Western Roman Empire, c. 550 CE. In theatre architecture, those Greek theatres that were remodeled to bring them in closer accord with the Roman ideals. (183)

Great American Songbook   Term for a not fully-defined subset of enduringly popular songs from about 1920 through about 1960, much of which originated in the Broadway musical or in musical films. The emergence of rock and roll, folk music, etc.—the beginning of the era of the singer-songwriter—essentially ended the Great American Songbook although the music is still performed. (307)

Great Dionysia   One of the festivals in ancient Athens that included contests of playwrights and performers playing the protagonists. (171)

ground plan   The "map" of the playing area for a scene, with doors, furniture, walls, and so on indicated to scale. (126)

guerilla theatre   Didactic political theatre done in nontheatrical spaces—streets, factories, subways—without previous announcement; hit-and-run performances like guerrilla attacks. (323)

guild   Religious and, sometimes, trade or professional organization in the Middle Ages that became the producer of civic medieval theatre. (207)

hanamichi   In the Japanese Kabuki theatre, a walkway through the audience used by actors to get to and from the stage. (358)

hashigakari   In the Japanese Noh theatre, a walkway at the side of the stage for the actors' entrances and exits. (357)

heavens   (1) Area above the stage: in the Elizabethan theatre, the underside of the roof that extended over the stage. (2) In the nineteenth century, the highest gallery. (218)

Hellenistic period   (1) That period of Greek history dating from the coming of Alexander the Great (c. 336 BCE) to the Greco-Roman period starting c. 100 CE. (2) In theatre architecture, those Greek theatres built during the Hellenistic period. (179)

hikinuki   In Japanese Kabuki performance, the sudden transformation of a costume into a completely different one. (359)

hireling   In professional companies of the Renaissance and after, an actor or technician hired by the shareholders to work for a set wage at a set task. (220)

householder   Member of an acting company who owned a share of the theatre building itself. (220)

humanism   A philosophy that believes that people should be at the center of their own deepest concerns. (214)

hut   In Elizabethan public theatre, small space below roof, probably for machinery. (218)

idea   In Aristotelian criticism, the moral expression of character through language; more generally, the intellectual statement of the meaning of a play or a performance. (37)

identity theatre   Political theatre associated with race, nationality, sexual preference, or gender. (339)

illusionism   Scenic practices (with analogs in acting, directing, and other theatre arts) that rely on a belief in the theatrical imitation of the real world. (231)

impersonation   Pretending to be another. (10)

impressionism   A style of art that sought truth in fleeting moments of consciousness. In the drama and theatre of the 1890s, Impressionism was noted for its moody and mysterious quality. (275)

improvisation   Acting technique or exercise emphasizing immediacy of response and invention rather than rehearsed behavior. (108)

independent theatre movement   In nineteenth-century Europe, the appearance of noncommercial theatres in several countries more or less simultaneously, most of them amateur or nontraditional and able to operate outside the usual censorship, "independent" of commercial demands. (270)

instrument   For actors, their bodies in relation to developable physical qualities, such as, strength, agility, vocal range, etc. (105)

integrated musical   Musical with songs and dances that are organic parts of story and character. (309)

Italianate staging   A kind of staging developed during the Renaissance in Italy and marked by a proscenium arch and perspective scenery arranged in wing and shutter. (235)

jukebox musical   A musical using existing music by a single composer or music identified with a single performer or performing group. (316)

Kabuki   Traditional Japanese theatre of great spectacle and powerful stories, often heroic and chivalric or military. (358)

Kathakali   Traditional Indian dance-drama form. (355)

Kuttiyatam   Indian theatrical form, probably derived from Sanskrit drama. (350)

Kyogen   Japanese theatre form: comic interludes between parts of a Noh performance. (358)

Latin music drama   Medieval dramas performed inside churches by clergy. The dramas unfolded in Latin rather than the vernacular and were sung rather than spoken, thus the name. Also called *liturgical drama.* (203)

lazzi   Stock bits of business designed to provoke a particular response, usually laughter, from the audience. Associated particularly with the commedia dell'arte and the French farce of the seventeenth century. (239)

light plot   The lighting designer's graphic rendering of the arrangement of lights and their connections. (145)

librettist   Author of the book of a musical or opera. (305)

lighting designer   Creator of the lighting plan for a production. (144)

limited run   A production scheduled for a certain number of performances, as opposed to an open run. (345)

lines of business   A range of roles in which an actor would specialize for the major part of his or her acting career (e.g., young lover, walking gentlewoman, comic servant). Particularly important during the seventeenth and eighteenth centuries. (249)

little theatre movement   In the early twentieth-century United States, the appearance of noncommercial theatres throughout the country dedicated to art; many became community theatres. (280)

liturgy   The rites of worship of the church. (202)

liturgical drama   The kinds of plays that were done inside churches as part of the religious services and thus were performed in Latin, by the clergy, and were usually chanted or sung rather than spoken. Liturgical drama is also called *Latin music drama.* (202)

Living Theatre   Important US avant-garde theatre, second half of twentieth century. (332)

lords' room   Expansive space close to the tiring house in Elizabethan theatre. (218)

ludi   (1) In Rome, festivals given for public worship of a variety of gods and on various public occasions like military victories and the funerals of government officials. As drama was often included as a part of ludi, they are important in a history of Roman theatre. (2) Early medieval term for plays. (186)

lyricist   The writer of the words for songs. (305)

machine play   Any play written especially to show off the special effects and movable scenery in a theatre. Especially popular during the neoclassical period, when regular plays obeyed "unity of place" and so had few opportunities for elaborate scenic changes. (243)

mansion   The particularized setting in the medieval theatre that, together with the platea, or generalized playing space, constituted the major staging elements of the theatre. Several mansions were placed around or adjacent to the platea at once—thus "simultaneous staging." See also *platea*. (203)

marketing   That part of an organization that focuses outward on consumers; oversees public relations and advertising. (65)

Marxist theory   Theory of theatre or drama based on Karl Marx's economic and political ideas. (62)

masque   Spectacular theatrical form, especially of the Renaissance and the neoclassical periods, usually associated with *court theatres* (see entry) or special events. Emphasis was put on costumes and effects, with much music and dancing; amateur actors frequently performed. (223)

master artwork   see *Gesamtkunstwerk*.

master of secrets   That craftsman/artist of the medieval theatre charged with the execution of special effects in the dramas. (208)

mechane   Literally, machine. In classical Greece, a crane by means of which actors and objects could be flown into the playing area. (177)

mediator   One who comes between—in theatre, somebody who stands between audience and performance, affecting audience perception or artist access to work. (60)

medieval   That period of world history dating roughly from the fall of the Western Roman Empire (c. 550 CE) to the fall of Constantinople and the beginning of the Renaissance (c. 1450). In drama, the period between 975, the first record of drama after the fall of Rome, and c. 1550, when religious drama was outlawed in many countries throughout Europe. (201)

melodrama   Literally "music drama." A kind of drama associated with a simplified moral universe, a set of stock characters (hero, heroine, villain, comic relief), rapid turns in the dramatic action. Leading form of drama throughout the nineteenth century. (286)

Middle Ages   An early name for the period dating roughly from the fall of Rome to the Renaissance. In the mid-twentieth century, this period was often erroneously labled the "dark ages." (201)

middle comedy   That transitional kind of Greek comedy dating from c. 404 BCE, the defeat of Athens by Sparta, to 336 BCE, the beginning of the Hellenistic period. Less topical than Greek old comedy, middle comedy dealt more with domestic issues and everyday life of the Athenian middle class. (179)

milk an audience   When a performer tries to evoke a response from an audience beyond that it seems inclined to give. (17)

mime   (1) A kind of drama in which unmasked actors of both sexes portrayed often bawdy and obscene stories. In Rome, it became the most popular kind of drama after the first century CE. (2) Form of silent modern theatre. (182, 193)

miracle play   Medieval play treating the lives of saints. (205)

modernism   Name for art of a period (roughly 1890–1950) identified by radical experimentation with form and nonrealism. (62)

mood   Overall feeling or emotion. (149)

morality play   Allegorical medieval play, like *Everyman*, that depicts the eternal struggle between good and evil that transpires in this world, using characters like Vice, Virtue, Wisdom, and so on. (205)

motivation   In Stanislavskian vocabulary, the internal springboard for an action or a set of behaviors onstage. (109)

music hall   A British term for variety entertainment, roughly equivalent to vaudeville in the US. (303)

musicians' gallery   A space for musicians. In the Elizabethan theatre, it is above the stage. (218)

mystery plays   Usually drawn from biblical stories, these medieval plays were often staged in cycles, treating events from the creation to the Last Judgment. Often staged in connection with Christian festivals, some mysteries were quite elaborate and took days or even weeks to perform. (205)

naturalism   A style of theatre and drama most popular from c. 1880 to 1900 that dealt with the sordid problems of the middle and lower classes in settings remarkable for the number and accuracy of details. Practitioners included Émile Zola, André Antoine, and Maxim Gorky. (266)

Natyasastra Ancient Indian (Sanskrit) work on theatre aesthetics. (354)

neoclassicism A style of drama and theatre from the Italian Renaissance based loosely on interpretations of Aristotle and Horace. Major tenets were verisimilitude, decorum, purity of genres (see these three terms), the five-act form, and the twofold purpose of drama: to teach and to please. (231)

new comedy That form of Greek comedy dating from the Hellenistic and Graeco-Roman periods and treating the domestic complications of the Athenian middle class. A major source for Roman comedy. (180)

new stagecraft A movement in stage design in the United States that favored simplified, often abstract, settings. It was, in effect, a reaction to overly realistic settings. Lighting played an important part in the design. Designers of the new stagecraft often sought alternatives to the proscenium stage like the arena or thrust configurations. (279)

Noh Austere, poetic drama of medieval Japan, based in Zen Buddhism. (350)

not-for-profit Professional theatre whose income comes only partly from ticket sales, the rest from donations and grants; given federal tax breaks. (26)

objective In Stanislavskian vocabulary, a character's goal within a beat or scene; the goal of a motivation. (109)

Off-Broadway Popularly, those small, originally experimental but now often quite commercial theatres that are located mostly outside the Times Square/Broadway area of New York City. Theatres with a seating capacity of fewer than five hundred that pay lower wages and fees than the larger Broadway houses. (77)

Off-Off-Broadway Popularly, the small nontraditional theatres located in churches, coffeehouses, and so on of New York City that fall considerably out of the commercial mainstream. Theatres with fewer than one hundred seats that may be granted exemptions from a wide variety of union regulations and scales. (77)

old comedy That form of Greek comedy written during the classical period and featuring topical political and social commentary set in highly predictable structural and metrical patterns. (175)

onkos The high headdress of the Roman, and perhaps Hellenistic Greek, actor. (182)

Open Theatre Important US avant-garde theatre, 1960s and 1970s; major influence on acting and production. (329)

operetta A form of music theatre originating in France and Germany that was usually comic and romantic, using both song and dialogue, with upperclass characters and voices that were not as trained as those of opera, popular from the mid-nineteenth century but dwindling in popularlity through the first half of the twentieth century. Also refers to the works of the English writers Gilbert and Sullivan, whose musical theater creations were wholly comic and mildly satirical. (303)

orchestra (1) That area of the Greek and Roman theatre that lay between the audience area and the scene house. (2) Originally the circular space where actors and chorus danced and performed plays; later a half circle that was used as a seating space for important people and only occasionally as a performance area. (3) In modern times, the prized seating area on the ground level of a theatre and adjacent to the stage. (71, 176)

pace Apparent rate of performance; partly a matter of speed with which the performance goes forward, but also related to intensity of action and complication and the artistic ways (e.g., actor's intensity) that the action is realized. (132)

pageant In the medieval period, a movable stage, a wagon on which plays were mounted and performed in parts of England, Spain, and occasionally continental Europe. By extension, the plays performed on such wagons. (208)

pageant wagon See *pageant*.

pantomime In the Roman theatre, a dance/story performed by a single actor with the accompaniment of a small group of musicians, particularly during the Christian era. In the eighteenth and nineteenth centuries, a "minor" form of entertainment marked by elaborate spectacle and often featuring commedia-like characters and a scene of magical transformation. (193, 253)

paratheatrical Related to or parallel to the theatrical; sharing some characteristics of theatre but not all characteristics of theatre. Used to refer to activities tangential to theatre: circus, parades, and so on. (352)

performance In life, the execution of an action (or the action executed) or a behavior taken in response to a stimulus. In art, the action of representing a character in a play, or, more generally, any public presentation. (3)

performing art   Any art that depends on a live performer in the presence of a live audience, for example, theatre, dance, opera, musical concerts. (4)

periaktoi   Stage machines in use by the Hellenistic period in Greece. An early method of scene changing that consisted of a triangle extended in space and mounted on a central pivot so that when the pivot was rotated, one of three different scenes could be shown to an audience. (188)

perspective   Simulation of visual distance by the manipulation of size of objects. (235)

picturization   Directorial creation of stage groupings that show or symbolize relationships or meanings; storytelling through stage pictures. (128)

pit   (1) Area of the audience on the ground floor and adjacent to the stage. Historically an inexpensive area because originally no seats were provided there and later only backless benches were used. (2) Now refers often to the area reserved for members of the orchestra playing for opera, ballet, and musical comedy. (217)

platea   The unlocalized playing area in the medieval theatre. See also *mansion*. (203)

play reader   Mediates between playwright and producer(s) by reading and judging submitted scripts; employee of producers(s). (68)

plot   (1) In Aristotle, one of the six parts of a play and the most important of the six; the formal cause of character; the soul of tragedy; the architectonic part of a play. (2) Popularly the story of a play, a novel, and so on. (32)

point of attack   The place in the story where a dramatic plot begins. Typically, Greek plays have a late point of attack, and medieval and Shakespearean plays have an early point of attack. (33)

possession of parts   During the seventeenth and especially the eighteenth centuries, the practice of leaving a role with an actor throughout a career. (249)

postmodernism   A critical approach that doubts the possibility of objectivity and that favors, consequently, the open acknowledgement of socially constructed meanings and investigates the implications of those meanings. (62, 312)

presence   Being there—the actuality of the live actor; also, loosely, the onstage magnetism of the actor. (10)

private theatre   In Elizabethan and Stuart England, indoor theatres that were open to the public but

were expensive because of their relatively limited seating capacity. Located on monastic lands, these theatres were outside the jurisdiction of the city of London. (218)

producer   Executive who arranges financing and who oversees a commercial production. (24)

professional theatre   As used in this book, the term means that the participants—director, choreographer, actors, designers, and stagehands—work and are paid. In many venues, the participants are employed under the aegis of a union. Here, the term does not refer to the quality of a particular production. (74, 331)

projection designer   A relatively new design role, responsible for projections and light emitting diode (led) displays used as part of scenery. (146)

properties   Objects used on stage—furniture, cigarettes, dishware. (142)

proscenium (theatre, arch)   Theatre building in which the audience area is set off from the acting area by a proscenium arch that frames the stage, protects the perspective, masks the backstage area, etc. The audience views the onstage action from one side only. (71)

protagonist   In Greek theatre, the first (or major) actor, the one who competed for the prize in acting. Later, the leading character in any play (the "hero"). (36, 177)

public relations   The business of causing the public to understand and esteem an event, institution, or cause. In theatre, it usually includes activities like press releases, press interviews, distribution of production photos, etc. Public relations is one part of promotion, the other being *advertising*. (65)

public theatre   In Elizabethan and Stuart England, outdoor theatres like the Globe. Because larger than the indoor theatres, public theatres tended to be relatively inexpensive and so attracted a general audience. (217)

purity of genres   Neoclassical tenet that elements of tragedy and those of comedy could not be mixed. The injunction was not merely against including funny scenes in tragedy but also against treating domestic issues or writing in prose, these elements being of the nature of comedy. (232)

Quem Quaeritis   A liturgical trope that opens, "Whom do you seek?" and that has early connection to drama, most especially in Ethelwold's *Regularis*

Concordia, in which the trope is accompanied by directions for staging. (203)

raisonneur   In drama, a character who speaks for the author. (36)

raked stage   Stage slanted up from front to back to enhance the perspective. Stages began their rakes either at the front of the apron or at the proscenium line. (236)

rasa   Important element of Sanskrit aesthetic theory—the inducing of an appropriate emotion in the audience. (355)

realism   The style of drama and theatre dating from the late nineteenth and early twentieth centuries that strove to reproduce on stage the details of everyday life with a view to improving the human and social condition. (264)

recitative   Dialogue given in a rhythmic way, often underscored, but not sung. This text is usually not rhymed and does not use the formal repetitions of song lyrics. (314)

Renaissance   Literally, "rebirth"; refers to a renewed interest in the learning and culture of ancient Greece and Rome. Beginning in Italy, the Renaissance spread throughout Western Europe from c. 1450 to c. 1650. (214)

rendering   Theatrical designers' finished drawings or paintings intended to show how the item(s) will look when built and placed on the stage. (148)

reversal   According to Aristotle, a change in the direction of action or in the expectation of character. Reversals result in complex plots, preferred over simple plots for tragedies. (33)

reviewer   A person who views an artistic event and then writes his or her descriptive evaluation of it for immediate publication. (64)

revival   A new production of a play after its initial run. (332)

revue   A mixed-form production, including singing, dancing, comedy, and often spectacular costumes. (304)

rhythm   Regular and measurable repetition. (132)

rising action   Action of increasing complication. (34)

ritual   Actions performed for symbolic value, often connected to religious or supernatural beliefs. (6, 352)

ritual theory   A theory that asserts that drama derived from religious rituals (e.g., in Greece religious rituals devoted to the worship of the god Dionysus). (169)

road   or **the road.** A complex of theatrical circuits for travelling and performing plays outside of New York City. (78)

road show   Production for the road. (76)

romanticism   A style of theatre and drama dating from c. 1790 to c. 1850 and marked by an interest in the exotic, the subjective, the emotional, and the individual. Began in part as a reaction against the strictures of neoclassicism; grew out of the eighteenth century's *sentimentalism* (see entry). (258)

royalties   Payments made to authors for permission to reproduce their artistic products. (96, 291)

run-through   A kind of rehearsal in which the actors perform long sections of the play (or the whole play) without interruption, usually for the purpose of improving the sense of continuity, shaping the whole, and so on. (135)

Sanskrit drama   Drama of ancient India, from about 200 BCE to 900 BCE. (350)

satyr play   A short, rustic, and often obscene play included in the Dionysian festivals of Greece at the conclusion of the tragedies. (171)

scaffold   In medieval staging in England, the localizing structure in or near the *platea*. See also *mansion*. (208)

scenario   In general, the prose description of a play's story. In the commedia dell'arte, the written outline of plot and characters from which the actors improvised the particular actions of performance. (238)

scene designer   Person responsible for creating the scenery. (141)

scrolling color changer   A device placed in front of a standard lighting instrument that can, through a remote signal, change the light from one color to another. (145)

secularism   Belief in the validity and importance of life and things on earth. Often contrasted with spiritualism, otherworldliness, or religiosity. (214)

semiotics   The study of signs, things that stand for other things. When applied to language, art, and criticism, semiotics focuses attention on the meanings that audiences create from the words or images of a playscript or a performance. (62)

sense memory   Recall of a sensory response—smell, taste, sound—with both its cause and the actor's reaction; important to the creation of a character's behavior in some theories of acting. (107)

sentimental comedy   A kind of comedy particularly popular during the eighteenth century in which people's virtues rather than their foibles were stressed. The audience was expected to experience something "too exquisite for laughter." Virtuous characters expressed themselves in pious "sentiments." (252)

sentimentalism   Prevalent during the eighteenth century, sentimentalism assumed the innate goodness of humanity and attributed evil to faulty instruction or bad example. A precursor of the romanticism of the nineteenth century. (248)

sentimentality   The arousing of feelings out of proportion to their cause. (286)

sharing company   A theatre group where some participants, termed "shareholders," split the group's earnings. (23, 220)

shite   In Noh theatre, the protagonist. (357)

shutter   Large flat, paired with another of the same kind, to close off the back of the scene in Italianate staging; an alternative to a backdrop; sometimes used for units at the sides. When pierced with a cutout, it became a "relieve" and showed a diorama. (236)

sight lines   Extreme limits of the audience's vision, drawn from the farthest or highest seat on each side through the proscenium arch or scenery obtruding farthest onstage. Anything beyond the sight lines cannot be seen by some members of the audience. (72)

signature music   Music associated with certain characters or certain types of characters, particularly in the melodramas of the nineteenth century. (288)

silhouette   The outline of a body or costume—its apparent mass. (143)

simultaneous staging   The practice, particularly during the Middle Ages, of representing several locations on the stage at one time. In medieval staging, several *mansions* (see entry), representing particular places, were arranged around a *platea*, or generalized playing space. (202)

single-point perspective   A technique for achieving a sense of depth by establishing a single vanishing point and painting or building all objects to diminish to it. (235)

skene   The scene house in the Greek theatre. (176)

spectacle   One of Aristotle's six parts of a play, the part of least interest to the poet but of most importance in differentiating the dramatic form from the narrative and the epic. In everyday parlance, all visual elements of production and, by extension, particular plays, scenes, or events in which visual elements predominate. (40)

spotlight   Stage light with hard-edged focus intended to highlight a person or object in its beams. (145)

springboard   A director's initial reaction to a play, a "taking off place"—perhaps visual, perhaps rational—that leads to an interpretation for play production. (124)

staging   The director's shaping of movement and timing in rehearsal; see also *blocking*. (128)

standing ovation   An audience showing supreme approval of a performance by standing while applauding. (17)

star system   Company organization in which minor characters are played by actors for the season, whereas central roles are taken by stars (see entry) brought in for one production; still common in opera, sometimes seen in summer theatres. (284)

storm and stress   see *Sturm und Drang*. (261)

story   Narrative; coherent sequence of incidents; "what happens." A general, nontechnical term that should not be confused with *plot*. (50)

street theatre   Theatre, often political, that takes place outside traditional theatre spaces and without traditional theatrical trappings. (323)

striplights   Series of connected lights located overhead or in the wings; usually used to bathe the stage in light; also light border. (146)

Sturm und Drang   A theatrical movement in Germany during the 1770s and 1780s that was marked by its militant experimentation with dramatic form, theatrical style, and social statement. (261)

style   (1) Distinctive combination of elements. (2) In Aristotelian terms, the way in which the manner is joined to the means. (3) Particulars of surface, as distinguished from substance. (4) "The way a thing is done" in a time and place. (55)

sung-through musical   A musical with no or nearly no spoken dialogue, sometimes using recitative to bridge songs, also called "pop opera." (314)

superobjective   In Stanislavskian vocabulary, the "life goal" of the character. (109)

surprise   An unexpected discovery or event. In dramatic surprise, the surprise, although unanticipated, must be seen in retrospect to be quite probable. (51)

surrealism   A style arising immediately following World War I that rejected everyday logic in favor of a free expression of the subconscious (or dream) state.

suspense   An increasing sense of expectation or dread, provoked by establishing strong anticipations and then delaying outcomes. (51)

symbolism   A style of theatre and drama arising during the 1890s and the early twentieth century that stressed the importance of subjectivity and spirituality and sought its effects through the use of symbol, legend, myth, and mood. (275)

table work   Reading aloud of the script by cast and director before staging begins. (134)

technical director   The person charged with coordinating backstage activities preparatory to production, including the coordination required to transform the scenic designer's vision into finished settings. (155)

technical rehearsal   Rehearsal devoted to the practice and perfection of the various technical elements of the show (lighting, sound, flying, trapping, and so on). (135)

theatre for development   Use of theatrical techniques for both community involvement and community instruction. (365)

theatre of cruelty   Phrase of Antonin Artaud's to describe a kind of theatre that touched the basic precivilized elements of people through disrupting normal "civilized" expectations about appearance, practice, sound, and so forth. (278)

theory   Any systematic attempt to explain a phenomenon; dramatic theory, of play texts; performance theory, of live performances. (1, 60)

three unities   In neoclassical dramatic theory, the unities of time, place, and action. (232)

through line   In Stanislavskian vocabulary, a consistent element of character running through a scene or a play. (109)

thrust stage   Dominant kind of staging during Shakespeare's time in England that is being revived in many contemporary theatres. Also called three-quarter round because the audience surrounds the action on three sides as the stage thrusts into the audience area. (72)

timing   Actor's sense of tempo and rhythm. (132)

tiring house   The building from which the Elizabethan platform, or thrust, stage extended. A place where the actors attired themselves. (218)

tone   The attitude of a work towards its subject. Some examples of tone might include solemn, playful, serious, light-hearted, satirical or parodistic, etc. (149)

tragedy   In popular parlance, any serious play, usually including an unhappy ending. According to Aristotle, "an imitation of a worthy or illustrious and perfect action, possessing magnitude, in pleasing language, using separately the several species of imitation in its parts, by men acting, and not through narration, through pity and fear effecting a catharsis of such passion." (232)

transformation   (1) Technique popularized in the 1960s whereby an actor portrayed several characters without any changes in costume, makeup, or mask, relying instead on changing voice and body attitudes in full view of the audience. (2) In medieval and Renaissance theatre, seemingly magical changes of men into beasts, women into salt, and so on. (3) In English pantomime, magical changes made by Harlequin's wand. (111)

trap   Unit in stage floor for appearances and disappearances; varies from a simple door to complex machines for raising and lowering while moving forward, backward, and sideways. (218)

trope   An interpolation in a liturgical text. (202)

utility player   Actor hired to play a variety of small roles as needed. (249)

vaudeville   (1) In the United States in the nineteenth and twentieth centuries, vaudeville was popular family entertainment featuring a collection of variety acts, skits, short plays, and song-and-dance routines. (2) In France in the eighteenth and nineteenth centuries, vaudeville referred to comédie-en-vaudeville, short satiric pieces, often topical, that were interspersed with new lyrics set to familiar tunes and sprinkled with rhyming couplets (vaudevilles). (303)

verisimilitude   Central concept in neoclassical theory and criticism. Literal meaning is "truth-seemingness," but used historically, at a time when truth referred to the general, typical, categorical truth. Not to be confused with realism. (231)

vomitory   Audience entrance for many ancient Roman performance spaces into middle of auditorium through passage under part of audience area. (72)

well-made play   A play written by or in the manner of Eugène Scribe and marked by careful preparation, seeming cause-and-effect organization of action, announced entrances and exits, and heavy reliance on external objects or characters to provide apparent connections between diverse lines of action. Now often used as a term of derision. (293)

wing-and-drop scenery   An illusionistic arrangement, common from the Renaissance through the nineteenth century in Europe and the United States, of paired wings along the sides and a drop along the back of the stage. (295)

wings   (1) Scenic pieces (flats) placed parallel to the stage front, or nearly so, on each side of the stage. (2) The offstage area beyond the side units of scenery—"in the wings." (71, 236)

women's theatre   A theatre whose repertories and practices are devoted to the advancement of women. Such theatres offer some combination of theatre by women, for women, and about women. (327)

wright   "Maker," as in playwright. (85)

yard   Another name for the pit in the Shakespearean theatre; where patrons stood on the ground in front of the stage. (217)

p. 7, Scapen, Photo: Matt Orton, courtesy of the University of Montevallo; p. 10, Bat Boy, Southern Illinois University Theatre; p. 11, Big Love, Virginia Commonwealth University Theatre; p. 12, Vanderveen Photographers; p. 16, Courtesy of the University of South Carolina Theatre; p. 18, Kevin Berne Images; p. 20, The Full Monty, Ball State University Theatre; p. 21, Colored Museum, Ball State University Theatre; p. 22, SARA KRULWICH/The New York Times/Redux Pictures; p. 24, Joan Marcus; p. 28, Courtesy of the University of South Carolina Theatre; p. 30, Twelfth Night, Barry University. Directed by Hugh M. Murphy. Scene Design, Sean McLelland. Lighting, Ronald Burns; p. 37, The House of Artrerus, Guthrie Theater; p. 37, The House of Artrerus, Guthrie Theater; p. 37, The House of Artrerus, Guthrie Theater; p. 37, The House of Artrerus, Guthrie Theater; p. 39, A Street Car Named Desire, Triad Stage, North Carolina; p. 40, Palestine, Center Theater Group, Photo: Craig Schwartz; p. 43, Pride and Prejudice, University of Michigan Theater. Photo: Pete Smith; p. 45, Hedda Gabler, Triad Stage, North Carolina; p. 52, (left) The Shape of Things, Purdue University Theater; p. 52, (right) Macbeth, University of Michigan Theater; p. 55, Brother Wolf, Triad Stage, North Carolina; p. 56, Angels in America, Wake Forest University Theater; p. 59, Joan Marcus; p. 61, (top) Triad Stage, North Carolina; p. 61, (bottom) Triad Stage, North Carolina; p. 70, The Civil War, Virginia Commonwealth University Theater; p. 71, The Civil War, Virginia Commonwealth Theater; p. 71, University of Montevallo; p. 71, Southern Illinois University Theater; p. 71, The Miracle Worker, Barry University. Directed by Hugh M. Murphy. Scene Design, Sean McLelland. Lighting, Ronald Burns; p. 71, Angels in America, Ball State University Theatre; p. 72, photo by Karl Hugh, Copyright Utah Shakespeare Festival 2008; p. 73, Courtesy of Arena Stage at the Mead Centre for American Theatre; p. 79, Guthrie Theater; p. 82, The Underpants, Purdue University Theater; p. 83, directed by Hugh M. Murphy, scene design Michael P. Amico, lighting, John Hall; p. 84, Richard Anderson Photography; p. 85, Putnam County Spelling Bee, Kutztown University Theater, Photo by Robert Reinecke; p. 88, Angels in America, Ball State University Theatre; p. 89, (left) At Home at the Zoo, Philadelphia Theatre Company, Mark Garvin; p. 89, (right) At Home at the Zoo, Philadelphia Theatre Company, Mark Garvin; p. 91, The Civil War, Virginia Commonwealth University Theater; p. 92, Ma Rainey's Black Bottom, Center Stage, Baltimore, Photo by Richard Anderson; p. 94, Ruined by Lynne Nottage, La Jolla Playhouse. Photo: Kevin Berne Images; p. 98, Richard III, Virginia Commonwealth University Theatre; p. 99, © Lynn Goldsmith/Corbis; p. 101, The Miracle Worker, Barry University. Directed by Hugh M. Murphy. Scene Design, Sean McLelland. Lighting, Ronald Burns; p. 102, Southern Illinois University Theater; p. 104, © Everett Collection Inc/Alamy; p. 107, Next To Normal, Center Theater Group, Photo: Craig Schwartz; p. 108, The Civil War, Virginia Commonwealth Theater; p. 110, M. Butterfly, Philadelphia Theater Company, Photo: Mark Garvin; p. 111, University of Michigan Theater; p. 113, Parade, Center Stage, Baltimore, Photo: Craig Schwartz; p. 115, Frostburg State University; p. 117, Center Theater Group; p. 121, University of Montevallo; p. 123, Southern Illinois University; p. 125, Joan Marcus; p. 126, (left) VCU and University of Michigan; p. 126, (right) VCU and University of Michigan; p. 129, (top) University of South Carolina; p. 129, (bottom) University of South Carolina; p. 131, Howard Community College; p. 133, Center Theatre Group; p. 137, Ball State University; p. 139, Clemson University; p. 141, directed by Jayce Tromsniss, scene design by Shannon Robers, lighting design by Tony Penna, costume design by Kendra Johnson; p. 143, Ball State University; p. 145, photo and lighting design by Anita Tripathi Easterling; p. 146, Clemson University; p. 147, Center Theatre Group; p. 148, University of Michigan; p. 149, Mark Garvin; p. 152, University of Michigan; p. 153, The Lost Colony; p. 155, (top) Backstage at Northeastern Illinois University. David Ropinski, photographer; p. 155, (middle) Backstage at Northeastern Illinois University. David Ropinski, photographer; p. 155, (bottom) Backstage at Northeastern Illinois University. David Ropinski, photographer; p. 157, Ball State University; p. 161, (left) Biancoloto/Shutterstock; p. 162, (left) University of South Carolina; p. 162, (right) University of South Carolina; p. 163, (left) photo by Karl Hugh, Copyright Utah Shakespeare Festival 2008; p. 163, Emi Cristea/Shutterstock; p. 170, Guthrie Theatre; p. 171, University of South Carolina; p. 173, Naples Museum; p. 174, University of Montevallo; p. 178, Copyright 2009 by Roanoke Island Historical Association, Inc; p. 181, Naples Museum; p. 185, badajoz/shutterstock; p. 189, Virginia Commonwealth

University; p. 190, Fairmont State University; p. 192, Courtesy: Marjorie F. Hill; p. 197, Milonk/Shutterstock; p. 199, York Mystery Plays Archive, the National Centre for Early Music, St Margaret's, Off Walmgate, York, Yo1 9TK, UK; p. 207, York Mystery Plays Archive, the National Centre for Early Music, St Margaret's, Off Walmgate, York, Yo1 9TK, UK; p. 220, John Hurrell in Shakespeare's *Henry V*, 2011; p. 221, Courtesy Robert Reinecke; p. 224, from the archives of the Duke of Devonshire ; p. 226, *The Reconstruction of a Spanish Global Playhouse*, 1983; p. 227, UNC Charlotte; p. 229, Virginia Commonwealth University; p. 229, Arena Stage; p. 229, University of Missouri-Columbia; p. 232, Butler University; p. 251, University of South Carolina; p. 256, Virginia Commonwealth University; p. 257, © Geraint Lewis/Alamy; p. 271, Triad Stage; p. 272, Virginia Commonwealth University; p. 276, Butler University; p. 279, Virginia Commonwealth University; p. 290, Intiman Theatre; p. 302, Joan Marcus; p. 307, Arena Stage; p. 307, Arena Stage; p. 308, Joan Marcus; p. 310, University of Nevada, Las Vegas; p. 310, University of Nevada, Las Vegas; p. 312, Joan Marcus; p. 313, Ball State University; p. 315, Southern Illiinois University; p. 317, Joan Marcus; p. 318, SARA KRULWICH/The New York Times/Redux Pictures; p. 319, Jason Ayer; p. 320, Arena Stage; p. 321, Ball State University; p. 323, Joan Marcus; p. 325, Fifth Floor Theatre, directed by Benny Sato Ambush, scenery by Sara Walsh, costumes by Jennifer Nweke, lighting by Zack Brown; p. 328, University of Michigan; p. 328, Frostburg State University; p. 333, University of South Carolina; p. 335, Ball State University; p. 337, Metamorphoses, Virginia Commonwealth University Theatre; p. 338, © Robert Termine/The New York Times/Redux Pictures; p. 339, University of South Carolina; p. 340, (left) Tisch School of Arts; p. 340, (right) *The Clean House*, Atlas Theatre, directed Giovanna Sardelli, scenery by Jason Simms, costumes by Malgosia Turzanska, lighting by Greg Goff; p. 341, Tisch Graduate School of the Arts , Fifth Floor Theatre, directed by Benny Sato Ambush, scenery by Sara Walsh, costumes by Jennifer Nweke, lighting by Zack Brown; p. 343, Joan Marcus; p. 346, SARA KRULWICH/The New York Times/Redux Pictures; p. 360, (left) Butler University; p. 360, (right) Butler University; p. 362, Southern Illinois University; p. 363, University of Michigan p. 364, Triad Stage.